NARRATING VICTIMHOOD

Space and Place

Bodily, geographic, and architectural sites are embedded with cultural knowledge and social value. This series provides ethnographically rich analyses of the cultural organization and meanings of these sites of space, architecture, landscape, and places of the body. Contributions examine the symbolic meanings of space and place, the cultural and historical processes involved in their construction and contestation, and how they communicate with wider political, religious, social, and economic institutions.

For a full series listing, please see end matter.

NARRATING VICTIMHOOD

Gender, Religion and the Making of Place in
Post-War Croatia

᳕• •᳕

Michaela Schäuble

berghahn
NEW YORK · OXFORD
www.berghahnbooks.com

First published in 2014 by
Berghahn Books
www.berghahnbooks.com

Library of Congress Cataloging-in-Publication Data
Schäuble, Michaela.
   Narrating victimhood: gender, religion and the making of place in post-war
Croatia / Michaela Schäuble.
      pages cm. -- (Space and place; Volume 11)
   Includes bibliographical references and index.
   ISBN 978-1-78238-260-7 (hardback: alk. paper) -- ISBN 978-1-78533-740-6
(paperback) -- ISBN 978-1-78238-261-4 (ebook)
1. Group identity--Croatia--Sinj. 2. Collective memory--Croatia--Sinj.
3.Croats--Croatia--Sinj--Ethnic identity. 4. Sinj (Croatia)--Social conditions. I.
Title.
   HN638.S56S45 2014
   305.8918'3--dc23

                                                                    2013042955

British Library Cataloguing in Publication Data
A catalogue record for this book is available from the British Library

ISBN 978-1-78238-260-7 (hardback)
ISBN 978-1-78533-740-6 (paperback)
ISBN 978-1-78238-261-4 (ebook)

To

Heinz & Veronika
and
Ivan & Mara

Contents

Figures

Map

Preface

Ways of Looking and Knowing

A few months into my fieldwork Marko took me up a hill called Kriz [cross]. Standing under a huge marble cross we had a spectacular 360-degree view overlooking vast parts of the Central Dalmatian hinterland: the barren rocks of the Dinaric mountain range separating Croatia from nearby Bosnia-Herzegovina to the north-east, the large fertile Sinjsko polje plateau that stretches beside the small town of Sinj, and the mountains to the south that cut off the area from the Adriatic sea. Small hamlets, part enveloped with smoke, lay speckled across the immediate vicinity.

Marko regularly set up his telescope on this hill and would immerse himself in observing the surrounding landscape for hours. Bringing me along to this spot, he said, he wanted me to see where he belonged and to understand why he could never live anywhere else. Standing up against the strong, chilly north wind, the *bura*, Marko directed the viewfinder to the curve of the River Cetina, the half-abandoned aerodrome of Sinj, his parents' *vikendica* [weekend house] in the mountains, and the steep rugged hill where the medieval fortress of Sinj had once stood. He also pointed to the unmarked course of the border with Herzegovina and showed me where his army squad was stationed during the Domovinski rat, the Croatian Homeland War, in the 1990s.

Marko's telescopic view enabled him to perceive the surrounding landscape as a framed and separate object that, according to Eric Hirsch's definition of place, can best be viewed when gazed upon from a distance (Hirsch and O'Hanlon 1995; see also Green 2005: 89).

Looking at the landscape through his telescope, Marko had precise points of reference and knew exactly where to look for them. When he passed the telescope to me, however, I not only failed to see or recognise any of the places he mentioned but also found myself unable to ascribe meaning or emotional sense to anything I was looking at.

In his analysis of the social formation of symbolic landscape Denis Cosgrove notes that one of the prevailing notions of landscape is attributable to the visualist paradigm and has been continually fostered by technical innovations. Over the past few centuries, he writes,

Figure 0.1. The hill Kriz [cross] from which Marko and I were looking at the surrounding landscape. Photo: M. Schäuble

> the idea of landscape came to denote the artistic and literary representation of the visible world, the scenery (literally that which is seen) which is viewed by a spectator. It implied a particular sensibility ... closely connected to a growing dependency on the faculty of sight as the medium through which truth was to be attained: 'seeing is believing'. Significant technical innovations for representing this truth include single-point perspective and the invention of aids to sight like the microscope, telescope and camera. (Cosgrove 1984: 9)

Although I could relate to the aesthetic dimension of the surroundings and enjoy the scenery of the Dalmatian hinterland, the detached and disembodied vision of the 'single-point perspective' did not, I thought, offer me much of an overview over my field site or help me to approach it better. 'Zooming in' seemed to me a rather unsettling way of looking – more irritating and disorienting than anything else.

It was only much later, after I left Croatia, that it occurred to me that the significance of Marko's telescopic view and my view as an anthropologist amounted to something much more than simply two different or opposing ways of looking. His view and mine, I realised, became metaphors of situated and embodied knowledges (Haraway 1988: 583) that enable understandings of practices and politics of positioning in the course of 'making sense' of the world and relating to surroundings. As an instrument of vision Marko's telescope mediates standpoints and draws attention to the partiality not only of sight but also of knowledge production in general. Anna Grimshaw in her analysis of ways of seeing in modern anthropology stresses that vision 'functions as a methodological strategy, a technique, within modern ethnographic practice' and simultaneously constitutes 'a metaphor for knowledge, for particular ways of knowing the world' (Grimshaw 2001: 7). Through imagery of vision, observers position themselves both spatially and socially. It became clear to me that Marko uses the telescope as an optical instrument of disengagement from the world surrounding him and thus avoids visual reciprocity. His deliberate spatial detachment from his physical surroundings and withdrawal from the social environment are closely related to his experiences as a volunteer in the Homeland War. At the age of nineteen and without any prior training, Marko had been stationed at a missile defence unit in the nearby mountains, monitoring air traffic. Today, almost twenty years after the ceasefire, he still suffers severely from symptoms such as flashbacks, hyperreflexia, insomnia and acute anxiety attacks. He is very restless at times and has difficulties handling complex social situations that involve many people. He told me that he feels best when he does not have to interact with other people and can wander around in the mountains by himself. Climbing up a hill with the telescope was his way of distancing himself from the world while still being able to take a close look at it and, as he put it, feel in control. The clearly framed images and the disembodied gaze seemed to provide him protection from the presence of things, and possibly helped him to refocus by physically narrowing his visual field.

'Vision is *always* a question of the power to see', writes Donna Haraway (1988: 585). Clearly this is true too of anthropology. The privileged status of anthropological ways of looking facilitates specific ways of knowing. When 'looking at' or 'seeing' the landscape, Marko and I not only situated ourselves differently in our surroundings but also embraced different meanings and connotations.

To Marko the barren mountain slopes and the vast plain of Sinjsko polje meant rootedness and offered a source of calm, whereas to me they aroused no such feeling. Marko's way of looking, infused as it was with historical, biographical, commemorative, emotional and imaginative knowledge(s), rested on a sense of belonging that materialised in the very landscape around him and his viewfinder. The cultural and experiential lenses that I was looking through, by contrast, disabled me from sharing Marko's view in any comprehensive way.[1] He, along with other interlocutors and friends in 'the field', tried to educate my perception of the world. Yet it was only little by little that I improved my understanding and managed to make sense of local people's relations to their surroundings – whilst struggling to keep an 'overview' and to position myself.

Different ways of looking thus not only enhance different ways of knowing but also enable different ways of experiencing and engaging with one's surroundings. Whilst Marko was seeking regular disengagement and intentionally withdrew from the social world, I had no choice but to endeavour an understanding by way of involvement. As an anthropologist, I comprehend vision as an ethnographic technique of enquiry that requires active and immediate engagement. This ethnographic approach – commonly known as 'participant observation' yet probably more accurately describable as experiencing and engaging through shifting ways of looking – was assisted and simultaneously constricted by various audio-visual appliances. My technical equipment – consisting of a DV-camera, a digital photo camera, a reflex camera and a mini-disc player to tape interviews – proved to be useful pictorial and acoustic recording devices. As essential aids to my memory as well as important modes of illustration and (re-)presentation, however, they were all apparatuses of static single-pointed perception. During my fieldwork they served mainly as tools of detachment – in a negative as well as positive sense. Acknowledged as a, if not the, principal trope in modern anthropology, vision and/or observation have still been increasingly criticised for their 'objectifying and dehumanising' stance on reality (cf. Grimshaw 2001: 6). This seeming contradiction corresponds to my own experiences during fieldwork, suggesting that while immediacy and unmediated presence – engaging all our senses, not just vision – are indispensable modes of understanding, constant physical (as well as emotional) proximity can also prove rather counterproductive, and tends to blur one's view. I would thus plead for an ethnographic practice that entails shifting ways of perception, following Christopher Tilley's description of the phenomenological perspective in terms of oscillation between states of being and 'a process of objectivation in which people objectify the world by setting themselves apart from it' (Tilley 1994: 12).

This methodological epistemology of versatile perception is also mirrored in Haraway's notion of a partial perspective whose aim is not to seek closure but to open up (to) the world.

> Subjectivity is multidimensional, so, therefore, is vision. The knowing self is partial in all its guises, never finished, whole, simply there and original; it is always constructed and stitched together imperfectly and *therefore* able to join with another to see together without claiming to be the other. Here is the promise of objectivity: a scientific knower seeks the subject position, not of identity, but of objectivity, that is, partial connection. (Haraway 1988: 586)

It is this multidimensional – and, as I would add, multi-sensorial – subjective stance in the shape of objective partiality and situated, embodied knowledge(s) that I have been actively seeking to take on during my fieldwork, as well as in the subsequent process of transforming personal experience into anthropologically relevant information, and finally text.

Drawing on the framework of social phenomenology, visual anthropologists increasingly invert earlier ideas about the all-too-close contact with the object of study and claim that 'it is through our distance from things that we, as seeing persons, can become close to them. In vision, therefore, distance and proximity are not mutually exclusive, but rather imply one another' (Willerslev 2007: 26). Taking this analytical position into account and linking it to the perpetual correlation between personal experience and the production of meaning and scientific knowledge about the world, it becomes apparent 'that it is in the movement between proximity and distance, that empirical data is transformed into anthropological analysis' (Øien 2007).

Moving between proximity and distance is thus a crucial part of the anthropological endeavour that is necessitated by the transition between being-in and *describing* the world we all inhabit. 'Perception does not give me truth like geometry but presences', writes Merleau-Ponty ([1942] 1962: 14), and it is a sequence of these presences in terms of embodied perceptions that have considerably shaped my physical as well as social interactions with my surroundings during fieldwork. It has been my personal experience of changing vision, however, that has facilitated my analytical capacity and eventually enabled me to develop a narrative voice of my own.

Note

1. Haraway points at the dangers inherent in alternatively 'romanticizing and/ or appropriating the vision of the less powerful while claiming to see from their position', yet failing to critically acknowledge that such 'subjugated knowledges' are not intrinsically 'innocent' positions but facilitate rather relativist 'ways of being nowhere while claiming to see comprehensively' (Haraway 1988: 584).

Acknowledgements

Over the ten years of conducting ethnographic fieldwork from 2003 to the completion of this book, Croatia has changed enormously. I would like to thank wholeheartedly all the people who shared their lives and thoughts with me and who offered help, advice, patience and kindness during the many stages of researching and writing.

First and foremost I am indebted to Thomas Hauschild, who has supported and inspired me ever since I started to study anthropology at the University of Tübingen. Over the years, he has regularly given me valuable comments, criticisms and suggestions on which my work grew. And, most importantly, he still keeps encouraging my fascination with anthropology. I am also very grateful to Dorle Dracklé for her stimulating and pragmatic advice and her sincere encouragement.

A Doctoral Award from the Heinrich-Böll Foundation supported my research, including fifteen months of ethnographic fieldwork in Croatia, and enabled me to realise the idea for this book. Being part of the Promovierendenkolleg 'Gender Dynamics in Violent Conflict' at Bremen University was a highly rewarding experience. I am particularly grateful to Christine Eifler for her warm and generous support, her insightful comments and ongoing interest in my work. Ruth Seifert has also followed my research for long periods and contributed valuable comments. My colleagues at the Promovierendenkolleg, namely Andrea Hapke, Anne Jenichen, Natalie Mutlak and Miriam Schroer-Hippel, have been very supportive.

I am also very grateful to Wendy Bracewell who acted as my supervisor during a six-month Marie Curie Research Fellowship at UCL. Her enthusiasm has been very contagious and I profited immensely from her vast knowledge of the history of the former Yugoslavia. I also wish to express my wholehearted gratitude to Stef Jansen for his straightforward and honest comments on my work and his invaluable help in structuring my material. Many people have read and commented on earlier chapters of this book and I am particularly grateful to Pamela Ballinger, Birgit Bock-Luna, Ana Carden-Coyne, Gerald Creed, Annemarie Gronover, Elissa Helms, Frances Pine and Monique Scheer for their insightful comments on draft chapters of this book.

Being a member of EastBordNet ('Remaking Eastern Borders in Europe: A Network Exploring Social, Moral and Material Relocations of Europe's Eastern Peripheries') from 2007 to 2013 enabled me to continuously rethink and discuss my ethnographic material in the context of borders – concrete geographical borders as well as ethno-national and gendered imaginations – and to meet a lot of inspirational colleagues from all over Europe. Above all, Sarah Green's work has immensely influenced my way of thinking about the Balkans and I am very grateful for her encouragement.

My colleagues at the Institute for Social and Cultural Anthropology at the University of Halle have also been hugely supportive. I particularly want to thank Katharina Schramm, Conny Heimann and Daniel Münster for their ongoing friendship and many animated discussions.

The time I spent as a fellow at the Mahindra Humanities Center at Harvard University in 2012/13 allowed me to update and finally complete this book.

Conducting such an emotionally affecting fieldwork, I have depended more than usual on my friends and family. Daniel Šuber was the perfect mediator between two worlds, and although we usually strongly disagree on 'all things Balkan' it is mainly due to him that I did not lose my sanity during fieldwork. Annemarie Gronover, Angela Dressler, Cecilie Øien and Larissa Vetters are all longstanding friends and our conversations have been a constant source of inspiration. Their ways of seeing the world and practising anthropology have never ceased to motivate and encourage me; I thank them too for all the laughs we shared together. I would also like to thank Michael Ebmeyer and Martina Lüdicke, along with many other friends in Berlin, for giving me such a joyful counterbalance to academic life and for providing me with a home whenever I returned from one of my many journeys. In addition, I would like to thank Chris Schaal who visited me during fieldwork with his then four-year-old daughter and who opened up hearts and doors for me that would otherwise have remained closed.

I am most grateful to Austin Harrington for his support and patience over the years – his sharp analysis, indulgent critique of my work and tireless reassurance were invaluable to me. Our daughter Marta is my greatest happiness. My mother, my sister, her husband and their children provide me with all the love, support and strength one could ever hope for. I want to dedicate this book to my mother Veronika, as well as to the memory of my father Heinz who sadly did not live to see the completion of the volume.

In Croatia, I recognise my everlasting debt to all the people who agreed to be interviewed and quizzed by me and who have been generously hospitable and supportive in every imaginable way. They are too many to be mentioned individually, but I want to name specifically Tamara and Renata Omerčić, Vesna Teršelić, Danijela Mažar, Gabriele Müller and the Meyer family in Vukovar. Conducting fieldwork in Sinj has not been an easy task, but the completion of this research relied significantly on the help and cooperation of the friars of the Franjevački Samostan, the Franciscan Monastery in Sinj, who entrusted me with their vast knowledge and insights. I am specifically indebted to Fra Karlo, Fra Zvonko, gvardijan Petar Klapež and above all to Fra Joško Kodžoman, whom I sincerely hope not to have disappointed in this study.

More than to anyone else, however, I owe my thanks and gratitude to two families. The Vranješ's not only gave me many lifts to and throughout Croatia, let me stay in their apartment in Zagreb and their *vikendica* at the seaside but also introduced me to many wonderful people. They sensitively, honestly and unsentimentally told me all the things about the painful break-up of Yugoslavia that one could never learn from history books. I immensely enjoyed the company of these big-hearted people. Duška Vranješ has been *moja duškica*, literally the 'good soul', of this dissertation. She helped me with countless translations and unfailingly explained undertones, details and allusions to me that I did not get. She has been a dear and indispensable companion over the years, and our travels throughout the Balkans are continual eye-openers for me. Thanks to her sensitivity, understanding, patience and humour I managed to despair less often than I would have done without her constant support.

Last but not least, my deepest and heartfelt thanks go to Ivan and Mara Modrić and their whole extended family in Glavice and Sinj. Without them this work would not have been possible. I owe much more to them than I will ever be able to express, and so it is to them also that this book is dedicated.

Hvala!

Notes on the Text

Transliteration

The Croatian language (*hrvatski jezik*) is classified as belonging to the Central South Slavic diasystem, also commonly referred to as 'Serbo-Croatian' or 'Croato-Serbian'.

With the break-up of Yugoslavia in the 1990s its languages formally followed suit, and Croatian, Serbian and Bosnian became separate standards. Today, use of the term 'Serbo-Croatian' is highly controversial and the alternative name that has emerged in official usage is Bosnian/Croatian/Serbian (BHS). BHS spelling is equally phonetic, that is each letter of the alphabet represents the same sound. The following brief guide to pronunciation includes only those letters whose pronunciation is significantly different from English.

C,c	ts as in cats
Č,č	ch as in church
Ć,ć	a soft 'tch'
Đ,đ	g as in gentle
DŽ,dž	j as in Jack (roughly Đ,đ but harder)
G,g	g as in gate
H,h	ch as in loch (pronounced with a Scottish accent)
J,j	y as in yellow
LJ,lj	ll as in million
NJ,nj	n as in news
R,r	r as in rolled
Š,š	sh as in she
Ž,ž	zh as in treasure

Pseudonyms

I have used pseudonyms for the majority of the people discussed in the text to protect their privacy. Some public officials, politicians, church dignitaries and certain military officers constitute an exception whenever the disclosure of their identity is crucial for the understanding of the context in which they are being discussed.

Introduction

Rethinking the B-Word[1]

W hether labelled as *bure baruta*, or the 'powder keg' of Europe, whether evoked as Europe's unconscious (Žižek 1999) or as a geological fracture zone (Winchester 1999), whether depicted as a toxin threatening the health of Europe (Glenny 1999: xxiv) or as Europe's cesspool (Bjelić 2006), whether unmasked as a site of nested Orientalism (Bakić-Hayden 1995), or whether located between globalisation and fragmentation (Bjelić and Savić 2005a) or treated simply as metaphor (ibid.), the Balkans have a long tradition of being maintained as the constitutive opposite and outside of 'Western modernity'. It has become increasingly clear, however, that the region threatens the very logic of this modernist dichotomy (Žižek 1997; Todorova 1997; Iveković 2001; Bjelić and Savić 2005a; Green 2005). In the case of the former Yugoslavia, an association of Balkan history with recurrent conflict, instability and fragmentation has often led to its portrayal as something almost constant, as a more or less independent variable. Indeed, 'the violent break-up of Yugoslavia in the 1990s … came to appear as a case of Balkan history repeating itself' (Brown 2003: 23). It is this perception of the region's alleged timelessness that reproduces hegemonic concepts of a mythical Balkans as 'dishevelled' Europe (Todorova 1997: 14) and consequently confirms the 'atomistic fractiousness and insubordination of the Oriental within' (Herzfeld 2005: ix).

Slavoj Žižek, intellectual *enfant terrible* of Balkans philosophy, has termed this cultural hegemony exerted by the West over the Balkans as '"reflexive", politically correct racism'. Žižek denounces 'the liberal, multiculturalist perception of the Balkans as a site of ethnic horrors and intolerance, of primitive, tribal, irrational passions, opposed to the reasonableness of post-nation-state conflict resolution by negotiation and compromise' (Žižek 1999). He reveals the mechanisms by which the self-proclaimed civilised, democratic West instrumentalises the Balkan Other in an attempt to illustrate and legitimate its own emancipatory project whilst simultaneously celebrating the very same Balkan Other's exotic authenticity. In other words, nationalist fundamentalism and fervent ethnic and/or religious identification are constructed as

irrational, divisive forces that threaten post-war reconstruction, democratisation and peaceful multiethnic coexistence in the region – and beyond. Further, Žižek also argues that on another equally meta-theoretical
level, the same fundamentalisms are often treated by Western commen-
tators as strategies of subversion and insubordination that resourcefully
resist discourses of late-capitalist rationality (Žižek 1995, 1999). By then
appropriating this dangerous and potentially subversive Balkan otherness to its symbolic universe, definitional hegemonic discourse on the
Balkans – either in the guise of political correctness or by way of an
assumed impenetrable complexity – generates a hypocritical form of
'Balkanism' that is not just deployed by outsiders but by the very people
who it is meant to describe. It is in this context that Žižek advocates that
'[o]ne should resist the temptation to "understand" [i.e. the Yugoslav
wars], and accomplish a gesture analogous to turning off the sound of a
TV: all of a sudden, the movement of the people on the screen, deprived
of their vocal support, look like meaningless, ridiculous, gesticulations'
(Žižek 1997: 62). But however thought-provoking and auspicious this
radical device of non-compliance with prevailing Balkanist discourse
might appear at first glance, just as disputable is its applicability in view
of any attempt to provide a pertinent account of the proliferation of
power relations between liberal Western democracies and their peripheries. In contrast to Žižek's suggestion I have sought not to 'switch off
the sound' but instead to listen closely to what local actors have to say
about their role in the construction of Croatian 'nationness' and how
they engage in competing claims over history and truth.

The narrative (re-)construction and interconnection of historical
memory and national (as well as regional) consciousness counteracts the
imputed 'in-betweenness', ambivalence and 'transitoriness' that define
the Balkans in hegemonic discourse and interventionist rhetoric. Within
the context of an ideology of globalisation, the politics of self-depiction
as victims or 'self-victimisation' and 'blaming the other' that are so often associated with the Balkans have thus to be considered in the light
of a conflicting and often contradictory self-positioning that oscillates
between, on the one hand, a desire to overcome systematic exclusion
and achieve alignment with larger geopolitical schemes of power (i.e. the
EU) and, on the other hand, radical dismissal of supra-national powers
and international organisations. In the following, I attempt to provide
an in-depth description of local responses to present processes of the
European Union's 'integration' policy and analyse how and where people in post-war rural Dalmatia position themselves within the imaginary
cartography of the 'new Europe' – and/or its immediate outside. I do
so without claiming to fully grasp or explain the preceding outbreak of

violent conflict in the 1990s and/or to capture all aspects of the ongoing strengthening of post-Yugoslav nationalism(s). I am also aware of the danger of over-rationalising or celebrating local strategies of empowerment, insubordination and resistance to a global modernity that tend to subsist in and around marginal places, and I am thus careful not to overrate the political scope of marginality in destabilising central authority. That said, I am convinced that political conceptions of conflicts in the south-eastern peripheries of Europe as struggles against centres (and as triggered by centres), have to be taken seriously. The political involvement of – as well as battles between – 'Great Powers' (the Ottomans, the Habsburgs, France, Russia, Britain, the United States, etc.) in the region causes a continual dismemberment that fosters a capacity of the Balkans to appear as a site of both 'cultural exoticism and cultural exorcism' in relation to civilised Europe (Bjelić 2005: 10; Blažević 2007: 92). In this sense, Western self-absolution or self-beautification is not only problematised by Balkan fragmentation, self-marginalisation and self-abjection, but also blatantly dependent on images of the latter phenomenon (Herzfeld 2005).

This study can be read in a number of different ways. It is, first of all, an ethnography of a marginal place. Croatia is located at the frontier of the 'new Europe' and it is this marginality that, in contrast with conventional understandings, displaces and calls into question oppositions between 'West' and 'East', 'Orient' and 'Occident'. For centuries the country has been the subject of other powers' longing for colonisation and domination – by actual or symbolic violence – and the instability so closely associated with the region can therefore be understood as part of continual attempts to resolve ambiguities by asserting fixed partitions and borders (Green 2005). The Republic of Croatia in its present shape is in turn divided into several provinces and regions, the southernmost of which is Dalmatia.

This area is one of the poorest regions of Croatia and is characterised by a stony, infertile soil and heavily fragmented landholdings. I conducted fifteen months of stationary anthropological field research (from April 2004 to September 2005, together with several infrequent visits between 2006 and summer 2012), first in the capital Zagreb and later in a rural community in the Dalmatinska Zagora, the Dalmatian hinterland. My major field site, the small town of Sinj, is located on a plateau between the Dinaric mountain range that separates Croatia from Bosnia-Herzegovina and the coastal town of Split. Sinj consists of fourteen rural settlements, encompasses an area of 181 square kilometres, and according to the last population census in 2011 has 24,832 inhabitants (Croatian Bureau of Statistics). The barren landscape, with traditionally

weak infrastructure and a subsequently high degree of subsistence farming, not only shapes and influences people's livelihoods and modes of
existence but also bears a significant resemblance to other 'catastrophic'
regions in the Mediterranean (Horden and Purcell 2000: 298ff.). As part
of the typical small-scale niche structure in the Mediterranean, contemporary Dalmatia holds a strong local footing, yet also has to face constant
states of crisis, induced by recurring militant conflict and subsequent
poverty. I argue that in such unstable regions, large-scale revitalisations
and local inventions of religious and folkloristic tradition are used as

Map of Croatia. © United Nations Department of Peacekeeping
Operations Cartographic Section

strategies of survival and resistance to supra-regional influences. The region is known both as a Catholic stronghold as well as the heartland of Croatian nationalism. Sinj is acclaimed nationwide as a pilgrimage site that not only hosts a renowned Marian shrine but is also home to one of the country's largest and most influential Franciscan monasteries. The area surrounding Sinj witnessed some of the most extreme violence both in the Second World War and in the post-Yugoslav wars (cf. Glenny 1992; Bowman 1994; Denich 1994; Hayden 1994; Silber and Little 1995). During Titoism, the region remained a stronghold of Croatian separatism, even while being subjected to severe retaliations by the Socialist government. Many neighbouring villages were deliberately deprived of plumbing and electricity until the 1970s with the intention of breaking the local population's resistance to state politics. This, among other factors, has fuelled a depiction of Yugoslav history that rewrites forty years of multicultural coexistence in terms of a litany of national suffering and Croat victimisation (cf. Jansen 2002: 77). In labelling official history writing as 'a bunch of lies' or as a 'distorted history of the winners', my interlocutors create a 'subaltern memory' in which they assign themselves the role of the 'eternally cheated'.

My focus is on continual contestations over truth, history and memory and on how these generate narratives of victimhood and shape local identities in the current postsocialist, post-war, and 'pre-EU-accession' scenario. In analysing how the residual affliction of militant conflict (1991–1995) is dealt with at the individual, regional and national level, I am particularly interested in moments of historical transformation as seen and narrated from the perspective of the nation's margin. I attempt to understand ways in which people in the Dalmatinska Zagora engage their marginality by protesting, but also by actively pursuing and reconstructing, their exceptional position. The concept of marginality is tricky in so far as it implies an 'ambivalent relevance to the heart of things' (Green 2005: 1) and is always relational: the marginality of marginal regions and people is prone to increase with growing globalisation and international competition for trade and development (Gurung and Kollmair 2005). In the following, however, I use the term to refer to distinctive and unequal subject positions within common fields of power and knowledge, and to structural disadvantages in the struggle for access to certain resources (Lowenhaupt Tsing 1993: xi; Gurung and Kollmair 2005). For the case of Croatia – as for 'the Balkans' in general – this implies localisation at the margins of Europe. Within the relatively young Republic of Croatia, Dalmatia – particularly rural Dalmatia – is additionally marginalised in its spatial as well as societal (socio-cultural, political and economic) seclusion from the capital Zagreb. Rural Dalmatians speak from a perspective that is clearly distinct from those of urban Croatians, by whom they are commonly ridiculed as backward, ultra-traditionalist and anachronistically pious and paternalistic. Understood in this sense, my interlocutors in the Dalmatian hinterland have to come to terms with 'multiple marginalities' (Allcock 2000: 226) as they are considered 'marginal within the marginal' (Green 2005: 6) and yet are simultaneously ascribed a key role in potentially proliferating insecurity and spreading conflicts elsewhere.

Anthropological research is often criticised for resting too heavily on 'the examination of obscure, peripheral communities', as Michael Herzfeld has pointed out with particular reference to his own research in Greece (Herzfeld 1985: xvi). This criticism is nowhere more appropriate than in the context of my specific fieldwork in a small town community in the Dalmatian hinterland. Nevertheless, I also draw on Herzfeld's own overruling of this criticism, for it is just as true that marginal communities 'have played a vital role in the formation of national self-stereotypes' (ibid.). 'To understand [a country's] relationship to the world at large', Herzfeld notes,

> it is necessary to understand the relationship of such 'eccentric' communities to the administrative centre ... In that sense, the villager's view of the matter, rather than that of the critics of anthropological research, offers a better prospect of understanding. And this, in turn, strengthens the case for an ethnographic focus on the rhetoric or discourse of local identity. (ibid.)

My research is based on the observation that people at the margins – the margins of the nation-state [*država*] as well as those of Europe – paradoxically oscillate between rootlessness and simultaneous regional rootedness, and increasingly oppose themselves to a transnational and secular modernity. The local accounts I analyse are characterised by strong scepticism towards centralised and/or international economic and political intervention in the region and are accompanied by a recent redefinition of identities that clearly contradicts any proclaimed notion of multiculturalism.

Based on extensive ethnographic research, my aim is to explore the impact that processes of globalisation and global change have on local people's efforts to create a sense of certainty, stability and belonging in what is perceived as an insecure and transitory world. My questions are: how do people hold their worlds together in terms of religious beliefs, social cohesion, family relations, gender norms, livelihood practices, and 'idioms of roots, relatedness and place' (Lien and Melhuus 2007: ix)?

How are seemingly abstract categories like 'history', 'locality', 'economic globalisation' or 'transnational political integration' incorporated into everyday discourses? And how are these categories used by and made meaningful to local actors in rural Dalmatia?

The accelerating process of globalisation threatens to undermine the relevance of area-based knowledge (Driessen 2001: 20). I argue, however, that the significance of globalising processes is best understood as an experiential, imaginary and epistemological dimension in people's lives, which may not necessarily be linked to transnational movements, mobility or flows (Lowenhaupt Tsing 2004; Lien and Melhuus 2007). I am therefore convinced that the pitfalls of national transition and global integration can best be studied in marginal and seemingly stagnant places like Sinj.

From Balkanism to Postsocialism to Euroscepticism

The -*isms* that ever more densely preoccupy contemporary (critical) theory refer to paradigms, systems of representations or temporal phases that seem awkwardly inadequate when it comes to capturing the current living conditions, or 'lifeworld', of my interlocutors in the Dalmatian hinterland – whether these -*isms* be Balkanism, postsocialism, neo- or late capitalism, nationalism, or, of late, Euroscepticism, anti-Europeanism or anti-globalism (see Gilbert et al. 2008a: 10). This shortcoming reflects the complexity and multiplicity of social and historical circumstances in the former Yugoslavia and points towards the need for alternative imaginaries, rooted in social practice and forms of communication, that also take material possibilities into consideration.

Recent analysis of Yugoslavia and its successor states has often been centred on the study of nationalism, ethnic conflict and 'cultural trauma', rather than on socialist and postsocialist processes (Gilbert et al. 2008a: 10). The recent history of war and violence continues to encourage political and scholarly narratives that foreground ethnic conflict and democratic failure at the expense sometimes of conceptualisations that focus on, for instance, socialism and postsocialist transformation. Despite this fact, the study of postsocialism has provided a number of valuable starting points, particularly with regard to phenomena such as privatisation, marketisation, civil society and the rise of nationalism(s) – all of these being themes of what is now commonly referred to as 'transition literature' (Verdery 1996: 11) – and with regard to the significance of emotional dynamics in political processes (Verdery 1991, 1996, 1999; Bridger and Pine 1998; Creed 1995, 1999; Hann 2002; Humphrey 2002; Pine et al. 2004; Svašek 2006). In my study, however, I am particularly interested in the observation that the postsocialist experience is often accompanied by a radical re-evaluation of the socialist past and a concomitant rewriting of historical events and personal narratives in that period. In the course of my fieldwork I noticed that the aim of my interlocutors' recollections was to dramatise the past. For in constantly remembering, re-enacting and emotionally revisiting the past, the people I worked with were not simply reproducing past events but actively performing and reinterpreting them, both in light of certain important subsequent events and experiences, and in anticipation of consequences they imagined might follow in the future. In this sense, their altered views of history informed retrospective accounts of the past just as much as images of the future – the past and the future here being mutually constituted.

I do not claim to be able to develop new discursive frameworks for theorising about the Balkans, but in this work I emphasise creative practices through which people imagine and engage with possible futures and formulate their aspirations. These practices, however, also include expressions of scepticism and occasionally generate pessimistic narratives – mainly in relation to the accession routes of the newly founded nation-states into Europe and their role within international power politics.

> Such projected post-millennial futures may include religious salvation, teleologies of market and democracy as well as narratives of chaos, conspiracy and degeneration. Few contexts bring these issues more to the fore than the post-Yugoslav states, with their history of socialist developmentalism (a modernist imaginary par excellence) and its violent disintegration, producing new and reconfigured utopic and dystopic visions. (Gilbert et al. 2008b)[2]

In my view, this assessment throws light on the context in which growing Eurosceptic, anti-Europeanist and anti-globalist sentiment are embedded and currently acted out in underprivileged regions of the former Yugoslavia, such as the Dalmatian hinterland.

I proceed from the assumption that drastic transformation processes since the 1990s have precipitated certain kinds of disambiguation of the past. In the case of the former Yugoslavia, the memory politics involved in contesting the meanings of the past are not only related to negotiations of fixed national and/or regional identities but also considerably shape the meaning of the region's future. The sentiment of continuity with an unambiguous past – which is expected to create stability at times when lifeworlds are fragmented and people are uprooted – potentially creates a shared sense of a collective out-look. In the following, I will illustrate how the way in which people remember (and envision) their own individual life stories is intimately entwined with how they remember (and envision) the regional and na-tional story (cf. Hodgkin and Radstone 2003b: 170). In this sense, local experience is integrated into a temporal continuum, stretching from the distant past into an anticipated future, and linked to global posi-tioning. I often encountered a sense of hopelessness and powerlessness in everyday conversations of my interlocutors. I attribute this to a way in which 'initial feelings of hope for a better future have, in many cases, been replaced by disillusionment … Widespread unemployment, new class differences, poverty, corruption scandals, disagreements about the restitution and appropriation of state property, and the economic advantages taken by the old nomenklatura have generated increasing distrust in the new "democratic" states' – as Maruška Svašek discerns for the postsocialist scenario in general (Svašek 2006: 11; see also Kalb et al. 1999). A feeling of extreme powerlessness is transferred to poli-tics – to state politics and to international political developments – and dominates a situation in which 'resignation functions as a coping pattern' (Jansen 2006: 437).

However, in this study I resist a framework of analysis that places too great an emphasis on despair. Instead my concern is to search for alternative spaces that people create in order to actively participate in imagining and shaping their future. Many Croatians do not consider in-tegration into 'political Europe' as promising an option as the pattern that Katherine Verdery has described in terms of a form of postsocial-ist 'feudalism' in which personalism and patronage play an increasingly important role (cf. Verdery 1996: 204–28). The alternative ideals I en-countered in my fieldwork in rural Dalmatia included a strengthening of the private sphere (i.e. family, patriarchal gender regimes), a striving for economic independence (i.e. subsistence farming and small-scale ani-mal husbandry), anti-liberalism, an emphasis on regional footing, mili-tarism and an explicit reversion to religion. All of these developments are interconnected and have highly elaborate narratives of victimhood as their common denominator.

Memory, Victimhood and the Claim to Truth

The title of this book, *Narrating Victimhood*, draws on pervasive my-thologies of (self-)victimisation in contemporary Croatia. Central to this (self-)victimisation trope are narratives indicating that one's own *nacija* (lit. people, nation) has been systematically persecuted, has suffered more than any other, and is consequently innocent of any injustice or war crime. This trope is, however, far from limited to nationalist Croatians. Marko Živković, for instance, persuasively revealed the resemblance to Serbian, Slovenian and Bosnian Muslim narratives and characterised the competing accounts for the all-embracing victim status as a 'Jewish trope' (Živković 2000). The assumption that (self-)victimisation provides an important vehicle for nationalist sentiment echoes Ivaylo Ditchev's laconic remark that victimisation and horror constitute enormous 'natural' resources in the Balkans (Ditchev 2005).[3]

The concept of 'resource', or rather 'reserve' as Thomas Hauschild terms it, turns out to be a very feasible category with which to describe elementary structures of politicisation and (ritualistic) anchorage – often with recourse to 'old', rejected or long-lost habits, practices and beliefs (Hauschild 2011: xv, 5–7; see also Gronover 2007). Derived from the Latin verb *reservare*, to keep back, the term reserve or reservation can be understood in terms of the gathering of provisions, as well as in the more familiar sense of 'guardedness'. 'Cultural reserves' thus denote the reserves that people draw on or mobilise for regeneration when facing deprivation, insecurity and powerlessness. Such reserves do not exclusively assume the shape of narratives but equally comprise material as well as ideational goods. In Croatia, and particularly in under-privileged regions such as rural Dalmatia, recourse to such reserves can take manifold forms. Alongside the revitalisation of certain aspects of what is commonly referred to as 'traditional rural lifestyle', narratives of (self-)victimisation and suffering are commonly employed as forms of moral assets. This victimary capital is in turn strongly associated with the emergence of 'new localisms' of an ethnic, religious and/or regional nature that stress demands over centres (Eriksen 1993: 150) – practices and discourses that Don Kalb calls 'counter-narratives of nationalism, localism, religion and tradition' (Kalb 2005: 187).

A number of globalisation theorists have recently acknowledged these phenomena. In the early 1990s Jonathan Friedman tellingly stated that '[m]odernity moves east, leaving postmodernity in its wake; religious revival, ethnic renaissance, roots and nationalism are resurgent as modernist identity becomes increasingly futile in the West' (Friedman 1992: 360). I find Friedman's seemingly clear-cut distinction between East and West rather disputable, and would, quite to the contrary, argue in the case of the Balkans that it is the region's ambiguity – and intrinsic postmodern character – that renders clear modernist distinctions inoperative (cf. Green 2005). The ethno-nationalist and religious revivals he describes, however, nonetheless correspond to my empirical findings, and I therefore argue that the various (and often violent) local strategies of dissociation of 'multiculturalism' should rather be seen as 'part of continual attempts to resolve the ambiguities by imposing fixed separations' (Green 2005: back cover). In my view, the rhetoric and workings of such attempts can best be explored by closely analysing how, under what circumstances, and with what effect the local (re-)emerges in different niches of the global system.

The narrative element in my work provides the theoretical and analytical framework for interpreting and writing about people's imaginaries and their representations of memory, experience and vision. The ambivalences and ambiguities entailed in personal as well as collective narratives highlight their constructive character and elucidate their role as 'vehicles of memory' through which imagined communities and imagined selves are created (Lambek 1996: 242, 244). Analysing the relationship between narratives of past experiences and imaginative processes that are at work in these narratives seems a feasible way of coming to a closer understanding of how people in a postwar community in Dalmatia ascribe meaning to their lifeworlds. Local narratives of (self-)victimisation are strategies of empowerment and expressions of the attempt to have a say in the determination of official historiography.

In the case of Croatia, the 'grand narrative' is one of perceived lack of historical control, subordination and foreign exploitation. The perspective that the country has disproportionally suffered is also contained in the famous saying '*mali narod, velika nepravda*', or 'small nation, great injustice' – which evidently refers only to endured injustices and not to committed injustice. Tomislav Z. Longinović interprets this self-assessment as follows:

> The destiny of small peoples is thus a symptom of the imaginary hypertrophy of their collective identity, which results from the memory of historical victimization. This unhealed injury is then covered with stories of one's greatness, which perpetuate the historical imagination and reverberate in the literary and cultural narratives of oppressed peoples. (Longinović 2005: 41f.)

This mechanism constitutes the descriptive centrepiece of the present study. By means of analysing diverse stories of greatness, bravery, the heroic battle against foreign intruders, and divine protection that I encountered during my fieldwork in the Dalmatian hinterland – and that underlie the omnipresent narratives of victimhood – I illustrate the effect such mythical stories have on ethno-nationalist ideas. Furthermore,

I seek to find out what role such narratives play in local explanations and justifications of (war) violence so closely related to the region.

In doing so, I explicitly distance myself from approaches which exclusively draw on concepts of 'cultural trauma' to explain the resurgence and manipulability of post-Yugoslav nationalisms (i.e. Meštrović 1993, 1996; Meštrović et al. 1993; Šuber 2004, 2006). References to Second World War traumas are highly problematic as they constitute 'the Balkans' as an irrevocable site of trauma (Jansen 2006). Recourse to past atrocities, however, is a very widespread strategy for local actors to make their voices heard in terms of their particular memories of historical victimisation. And as described by Longinović above, a number of my Dalmatian interlocutors did indeed seem to imagine themselves under a constant state of threat and victimisation. In order to understand this scepticism from a historical perspective, one must bear in mind that a serious deficit of sovereignty has been a general feature in the region: for centuries Dalmatia has been controlled by transnational economic, political and military interests. Venetian administrative rule and Ottoman intrusion were followed by Habsburg dominance and later replaced by centralised Yugoslav administration. The current monetary and economic constraints of European integration and globalisation are perceived by many as directly continuing longstanding foreign domination and victimisation of Croatia and, even more so, of rural Dalmatia. Local actors' distressing experiences and their exposure to severe injustices, however, should not obscure the fact that narratives of (self-)victimisation are frequently misused as a vehicle for nationalist propaganda and as rhetorical devices for pointing fingers of blame at the crimes of others in order to elude accountability for wrongs of one's own doing.

Significant numbers of Croats, and Dalmatians in particular, understand themselves as guardians of Europe and award Croatia the title of *Antemurale Christianitatis* [Bulwark of Christianity], a phrase that dates from the medieval crusades at the beginning of the Ottoman invasion. Indicating that they and their ancestors have successfully protected, and still protect, the borders of Europe against intruding forces 'from the East', this theme increasingly expresses a complaint that their historic role is not adequately acknowledged in Europe today. Such discourses – alongside alleged inequities during the past decades – stimulate the gradual formation of a self-image that can be called a collective victim identity (Jalušić 2004: 40–67). However, forms of systematic self-victimisation are not only used to reinterpret past events but are simultaneously deployed both in the articulation and rhetorical renegotiation of current political issues and in setting the terrain for future debates and contestations of power. Recent discussions, be they in relation to the imminent EU membership or assessment of the war crimes tribunal in The Hague, are perceived as a continuation of previous 'wrongs', whereby the meanings of past, present and future overlap with narratives of historical injustice and strategies of blaming the other.

Reflections on the Fieldwork Setting

The site of my fieldwork in Dalmatia is relatively cut off from the rest of the country in the sense that the rural–urban divide in present-day Croatia creates a large gap between people's lifeworlds. Despite being a classic 'out-of the-way place', Sinj is the quasi-urban centre of an area known as Cetinska krajina, a group of settlements situated on the karstic field of Sinjsko polje, through which the River Cetina passes. Most of the mountainous region is stony and marked by a scarcity of productive arable land suitable for cultivation. The majority of the population are employees in the service sector or work as animal breeders, pastoralists or small farmers who produce little beyond their personal needs. The region is still off the beaten tourist track and Sinj is mainly visited as a pilgrimage site. The largest institution of the site is a Franciscan monastery that hosts a famous Marian shrine and an allegedly miraculous painting named *Gospa Sinjska* [Our Lady of Sinj] – a sight for which Sinj is renowned throughout the whole country and beyond.

During my fieldwork I lived partly with a host family from Glavice, an adjunct village, and partly in a one-room apartment in a housing scheme set up for war veterans [*branitelji*] in Sinj. A number of war veterans were given a flat in newly built residential complexes as compensation for their war service. My renter, however, suffered from trauma-related symptoms to such an extent that he could not live by himself and therefore let the apartment to me. To my knowledge, I was the only foreigner living in Sinj at the time and was therefore well known throughout the town, and critically eyed at every turn. The exceedingly cordial reception and support of my host family in Glavice, however, facilitated my access to hard-to-reach people and aided my ability to broach difficult topics. Living with this family as a quasi-permanent guest also considerably influenced the thematic focus of my research in as much as all four sons had voluntarily joined the army during the Homeland War at a very young age and were still suffering from the grisly after-effects. Listening to the narratives (or the portentous silences) of traumatised and/or heavily injured ex-combatants on a daily basis directed my attention to the concerns of these young men and made me conscious of their struggles to come to terms with the past, their attempts to make a living and establish future perspectives for themselves, as well as their efforts to win public acknowledgement of their veteran status and appreciation of their 'service for the homeland'. Their accounts, concerns and worries further highlighted my interest in issues such as the role of gender, hero worship, narratives of victimisation and continued militarisation in the post-war era.

Doing fieldwork as a woman in a predominantly male environment has clearly shaped my access to the field and influenced my 'body of information'. This factor, however, will hereafter not be specifically emphasised in my text, unless it essentially contributes to my findings in form and content. The same goes for my religious positioning in the field. I shared the same denomination but not the same convictions and beliefs as the people of the congregation I studied. This enabled me to easily 'blend in' in terms of following the Catholic liturgy and emulating the bodily practices involved. Simultaneously, however, I obtained the position of an outsider and could thus keep a critical distance to the miraculous tales of Marian apparitions in the region (Skrbiš 2005: 445).

The language barrier turned out to be another obstacle during my fieldwork in certain respects. Some of the political speeches and sermons that I attended were hard to follow, partly because they were given in a heavy Dalmatian dialect, and partly because in the beginning I did not pick up on all the various allusions. I therefore recorded a number of orations and announcements at public assemblies or at church ceremonies and later transcribed them with the help of native speakers, usually friends of mine from Zagreb. As a general rule, my 'interpreters' were simultaneously amused and upset about the tone and content of my recorded material. They usually started a lengthy discussion on the data I had gathered, which gave me a chance to discuss the material with people who had had quite a different upbringing from that of my interlocutors and who shared different political opinions. I could then take those comments back to 'the field' and contrast them to the lifeworlds of the people in Sinj and adjacencies.

This leads me to my major ethical dilemma. Living and working with people whose political views I do not share posed and continues to pose a number of political, social and ethical predicaments. It has proved to be a highly difficult task to contextualise local narratives – at times entailing radical nationalist, racist, sexist or homophobic positions – without compromising the accounts of the people I had come to like and esteem. Such disagreements caused numerous conflicts during fieldwork and frequent quandaries in the process of writing-up; more than once I found myself troubled in my attempts to record convictions and beliefs diametrically opposed to my own. Representing my interlocutors' 'lifeworlds' intelligibly without always having to distance myself from their political viewpoints and thereby potentially betraying their trust proved to be quite a tightrope act. In the end, I decided to follow Michael Jackson's assessment entailing that 'compassion and conflict are ... complementary poles of intersubjectivity, the first affirming identity, the second confirming difference' (Jackson 1998: 4). In the case of my fieldwork this means that I took an intersubjective stance in highly respecting and empathising with my interlocutors, while at the same time critically challenging their trope of victimisation and strongly disagreeing with their nationalist and at times openly fascist stance.

Throughout this study I make use of multiple methodological devices, such as participant observation, informal conversations, interviews, 'thick descriptions' and analyses of various forms of written as well as spoken (sometimes even recited or sung) texts, images and events.[4] My conception of anthropological work, however, is grounded in the belief that semiotics (discourse and text) should not be prioritised over phenomenology, and that issues of 'lived experience' and immediacy do not rank behind problems of representation. In this sense, the data I collected are informed by the sensory, imaginary, emotional, moral and intellectual dimensions of my actual experiences during fieldwork. Documenting this process I kept a field diary and wrote extensive field notes, containing everything from detailed conversation and observation minutes – via topographies, personal descriptions, situation analyses, notes on conversations and comments I overheard – through to the copy of inscriptions and random impressions. The excerpts from my field notes that I quote throughout the text acknowledge this synthesis.

Outline of the Book

Drawing on my reflections on ways of looking and the production of knowledge as described in my Preface, I decided to arrange the ensuing text according to a camera or telescope movement of zooming out. I start with a close-up description of my fieldwork setting, and then broaden my perspective by gradually including more aspects of my interlocutors' lifeworlds. After situating my field site within its temporal or historical and spatial context on local and regional levels, I open the lens and attempt to examine people's everyday practices, narratives and explanatory models with regard to national as well as international political processes – including an analysis of local actors' strategies of situating themselves within a globalising world.

Chapter 1 provides a brief outline of Dalmatian history and introduces the region as an important economic, cultural and religious intersection in the Mediterranean. It further establishes Dalmatia as a metaphorical space that traditionally marks the transition from 'Occident' to 'Orient' and that has inspired a number of travel accounts that simultaneously romanticise the inhabitants of Dalmatia as 'noble savages' of the Adriatic Empire and turn them into a spectacle of anthropological entertainment for the age of Enlightenment. Assessing these discourses together with a rendition and close analysis of local legends and myths, I seek to give a comprehensive picture of both Western Balkanist ascriptions and current modes of local self-perception and self-representation. In this I draw on ethnographic data and mainly focus on a crucial marker of local identity in the small town of Sinj in the Dalmatian hinterland, the Sinjska Alka, a local knight's tournament that dates back to the year 1715 when local defence forces successfully defended the ancient fortress of Sinj against the Ottoman troops. I demonstrate how the mythology surrounding this historic battle has recurrently been revitalised and used to explain and justify recent violence in the region, particularly during the Homeland War (1991–1995).

Closely linked to the Alka tournament is the commemoration of the alleged Marian apparition in 1715 that has turned the Marian shrine in Sinj into a national pilgrimage site. In Chapter 2 I give a detailed account of the annual pilgrimage to this shrine and analyse practices of Marian devotion in the light of its (changing) political role and utility – during and immediately after the Second World War, at the time of Yugoslav state socialism, in connection with Croatia's independence and the years of the Homeland War, and finally in the current postsocialist, post-war times. I place my analysis in the context of the politics of Marian veneration in general, and of the role of Mother Mary as Kraljica Hrvata (Queen of the Croats) and patron saint of Croat soldiers in particular. Finally, the portrayal of a visit to a Marian apparition site in Gala, a small village near Sinj that did not develop into an internationally acclaimed pilgrimage site provides a general idea of the mechanisms regarding the politicisation and (prevented) institutionalisation of narratives about Marian apparitions. In analysing the religious imaginary and devout practices of local people, I argue that in the case of the apparition in Gala the repression of religion in the former Yugoslavia has triggered the (re-)appearance of the Virgin Mary as phantasmagoric figure that has the capacity to question the legitimacy of political order, irrespective of the prevalent state power, and functions as a tool of social criticism down to the present day.

Chapter 3 discusses various aspects of space and place, and conceptualises an alternative topography of Sinj and the Dalmatian–Herzegovinian border region as a memorial landscape. I analyse how people in the Dalmatinska Zagora perceive their surroundings in terms of genealogies and territory, and how they constitute their identity in relation to the environment in which they live. Attempting to illustrate how history 'takes place', I trace the construction of geographic and sacralised landscapes in a context of ritual commemoration of massacre victims and argue that people's memory is literally entailed and inscribed in the landscape. The area is full of massacre sites and mass graves – dating from different epochs and conflicts – that had previously been concealed under Tito's regime. With the unearthing of mass graves in the early 1990s, notions of ancestry and territory were drastically re-evaluated, public resentment about suppressed memories of past atrocities was fuelled, and previously suppressed ethno-national tensions increasingly started to escalate. In this sense, 'dead body politics' (Verdery 1999), as Verdery calls the phenomenon of turning the dead into political messengers, are key to understanding how past atrocities were revived and fuelled the (ethno-)political consciousness of the late 1980s and early 1990s. The unearthing of previously unacknowledged massacre sites occurs in the region even now, and the commemoration of 'victims of communist atrocities' at a natural pit [*jama*] in the limestone karst mountains that surround Sinj continues to stir strong emotions and connects narratives of 'historical injustice and concealment' to specific places and landscapes of victimisation. Focusing on long-neglected spatial aspects of the political in the region, I contend that landscapes constitute mnemonic agents and sites of historic revisions.

In Chapter 4 I focus on discourses on the role of Croatian soldiers during the Homeland War and its aftermath. Exploring the relationship between nationalism, masculinity and militarisation, my aim is to delineate the current challenges that this correlation poses to stability and democratisation in the region. Many nationalist Croatians perceive the Croatian ex-generals who stood accused of war crimes as heroes who fought for the country's independence. They equate the indictments of the International Criminal Tribunal for the former Yugoslavia (ICTY) in The Hague with an attack on the legitimacy of the Homeland War, and until recently feared that guilty verdicts might excite doubts regarding the legitimacy of Croatia as a nation. Thus they continue to understand the extradition or conviction of Croatian former military officers as submission to blackmail and as sacrifices that Croatia was forced to make in order to join the European Union. A fundamental premise of this chapter is that one cannot understand the debates about the role of combatants during the Homeland War without examining the history and current resurgence of ethno-nationalist sentiment in relation to militarised notions of masculinity. I interpret the continually proclaimed need for (militarised) self-defence as part of a regional refusal to cooperate with political, economic and ideological incorporation into the global arena. Finally, I suggest that masculinity continues to be a central mobilising source for nationalist forces that influences discourses on European integration and attitudes towards globalisation.

Chapter 5 is entitled 'Mobilising Local Reserves' and covers various modes of survival in postsocialist post-war rural Dalmatia, ranging from a revival of traditional family, kinship and gender arrangements over the proliferation of alternative rural economies such as subsistence and backyard farming, to a recent fortification of regionalism, Euroscepticism and anti-globalism. The term 'reserves', as I use it here, describes local perceptions of the exploitation of natural, technological and human resources as well as reactive behaviour towards damaged or lost access to these resources. Furthermore, the (re-)appropriation of local traditions and culture can also be understood as a 'great reserve against a world of purchasability, mercenary goods and services' and 'stocks of knowledge' that can thus be stored for an uncertain future or in case of crisis and collapse (Hauschild 2002: 11, 14, my translation; see Mühlfried 2007: 10). In this chapter I also discuss a possible return to the Mediterranean as an alternative affiliation or 'zone of belonging' by which local actors attempt to link the region directly to classical antiquity – in order to define Dalmatia as the cradle of European civilisation and to avoid any connection with the unpredictability and bloodshed commonly associated with the Balkans. All in all, this study attempts to explore the ways in which rural Dalmatians narrate and dignify their lives in a time and a place where resources are scarce and their status is low.

Notes

1. This pun was stolen from Bracewell and Alex Drace-Francis's essay (1999), p. 58.
2. These ideas emerged in collective discussion among the participants in the workshops of 'Towards an Anthropology of Hope? Comparative Post-Yugoslav Ethnographies' held in Manchester (UK) in November 2007, as well as at the workshop 'Critical Spaces of Hope: Locating Postsocialism and the Future in Post-Yugoslav Anthropology', held at the University of Chicago Center for East European and Russian/Eurasian Studies in October 2008, at both of which I participated.

3. According to Ditchev, this victimary capital constitutes the reverse side of their *joissance* – leisure, cuisine, and exoticism (Ditchev 2005; see also Bjelić 2005: 17).
4. My data are mainly based on continual informal conversations, one-to-one dialogue, attendance of innumerable church services and religious celebrations, and daily participation in family and small-town life. Additionally, I conducted twenty-two in-depth semi-structured interviews with male and (one) female ex-combatants (*branitelji*), Franciscan priests, therapists working with traumatised ex-combatants, Zagreb peace activists and several members of the local community in Sinj. The interviews lasted between half an hour and five hours. In addition, I studied numerous pamphlets and booklets published by the local monastery in Sinj, as well as publications by the local branch of the cultural institution Matica Hrvatska. Alongside my analysis of graffiti, posters, placards and advertisement campaigns, I also found valuable sources of information in national and regional newspapers and magazines.

Chapter 1

(In-)Subordination at the Margins of Europe

Dalmatia is the land of the past and the land of the future!
The land of past history, the land of future travel!

— Maude M. Holbach, *Dalmatia:*
The Land where East Meets West

Dalmatia – 'The Land where East Meets West'

On 5 August 2007, then Croatian president Stjepan Mesić visited the small town of Sinj in the Dalmatian hinterland to attend the local folkloristic knights' tournament 'Sinjska Alka'. A game of skill performed in historical costumes, the Sinjska Alka is held annually in commemoration of a victorious battle against the Ottoman Turks of 1715. The tournament, in which each contestant rides his horse down the racetrack at full gallop and tries to hit the Alka ring with his spear, is widely perceived as a celebration of 'local resistance to intruders' and a re-enactment of courageous opposition to foreign domination.

On this occasion President Mesić delivered a speech in which he stressed the importance of the festival for the whole Croatian nation. He addressed the citizens of Sinj and declared that the 'Alka symbolises the freedom-loving spirit of Sinj, the Cetina region as well as of all Croatia, a spirit that we reaffirmed in the anti-fascist struggle and in the Homeland War, and that we are reaffirming today by building a free and democratic Croatia. That is why [the] Sinjska Alka has significance not only for locals, but for all of us, for the Croatian people and for all Croatian citizens'. The Alka tournament is commonly known as a hotbed of extremist Croatian nationalism and has in the past been criticised and ridiculed by liberal urban Croats for its 'rural backwardness' and for its folkloristic display of a coarse combative spirit. The Alka habitually ensures a charged and politically tense atmosphere. In 2001, for example, the Alka tournament hit the headlines, because it was used as a nationalist platform to support Croatian ex-generals who stood accused of having committed war crimes during the Homeland War (1991–1995).[1] Delegates of President Mesić had been regularly hissed down at this event and publicly insulted as part of a protest against the government's liberal approach to opening the Croatian economy to foreign investment and Mesić's promotion of Croatia's anticipated membership of the EU and NATO.

Mesić and the politics he represented in 2007 stand in stark contrast to the nationalist symbolism of the Alka event, which makes his address and the message it conveys quite surprising at first glance. Despite paying lip service to the Croatian nation, the president was actually using an event highly encoded with nationalist sentiments to launch his pro-European political course. By reaffirming that 'Croatia's future is the united Europe founded on anti-fascism, democracy, tolerance, respect for and exercise of human and minority rights', Mesić inverted the values that the Alka traditionally stands for. His declaration that 'Croatia's future is Europe, where borders will connect and not separate, a community of equal states and peoples' can thus be understood as a major attempt to re-signify the previous meaning of the festival as a celebration of bulkheading and essentialist notions of local, regional and national identity. By using the symbolic power of the Alka as a performance of traditionalism and local pride, and by trying to mobilise the tournament's fervent political potential for his leftist pro-European course, he publicly promoted pluralism and the increasing permeability of national borders – the very developments abhorred by radical nationalists.

This incident in August 2007 left me utterly astonished, because the same people who previously raged against the government and official authorities now seemed honoured by the attention and the importance that was ascribed to 'their' tournament. When I mentioned the deprecatory and rancorous remarks about Mesić that I had earlier come across in Sinj, my host Joško simply replied, 'this is all about politics and I am not interested in politics any more, as you know'. This seeming contradiction between people's asserted disenchantment with politics and their highly politicised demeanour was seized upon in Mesić's plea that the tournament should overcome its localised political significance. He stated: 'My sponsorship is a sign that [the] Sinjska Alka is moving away from politics. When I say that, I mean daily politics which used [the] Alka for narrow political interests'. With this tightrope-walk, Mesić pretended to uncouple the Alka from its previous political manipulation and thus to restore the breakdown of ties between the state centre and periphery – whilst at the same time using this rhetoric on his own political account and under the pretext of broadening people's political awareness. I therefore interpret Mesić's endeavour to make the Alka part of 'building a free and democratic Croatia' as an attempt to create a feasible political vision directed towards a European future that specifically addresses and includes those who hitherto feel most opposed to it.

Drawing on the ethnographic example of the Sinjska Alka, I will, in what follows, analyse the dynamics of local transformation processes particularly with regard to Europeanisation and globalisation. But to fully understand the symbolic significance of this festival for the self-image of the inhabitants of Sinj and the Dalmatian hinterland, as well as for the role that the ritualised commemoration of Croatia's past is to play in the new Europe, it is necessary first to provide a brief outline of the history of the region and to underline the exceptional geopolitical and imaginary position of Dalmatia.

Described as 'the land where East and West meet' by Maude Holbach in her 1908 travelogue, Dalmatia has habitually been constructed as a metaphorical space that marks the transition from Occident to Orient. Not quite associated with the roughness of 'the Balkans' but considered too exotic to belong to Europe proper, a number of Western travellers and writers have been fascinated with this narrow, elongated region on the eastern coast of the Adriatic Sea. The visible traces of the Ottoman legacy, along with traces of various Western colonial cultures, constitute the region as a prototypical 'liminal zone between the situated ethics of exotic peoples and the ordered morality of European culture', as Herzfeld has tellingly characterised prevalent conceptions of the Mediterranean (Herzfeld 1987: 130). Like most Mediterranean regions, Dalmatia has been an important route for merchants and travellers since ancient times and continues to be a popular tourist destination. Encompassing the scenic coastline with its numerous islands as well as the sparsely populated inhospitable hinterland, the region's environmental qualities in conjunction with its multicultural history make Dalmatia not only a long-standing location of the Western imaginary but also an important economic, cultural and religious intersection that is characterised by its highly localised sense of connectedness.

The following synopsis of the complex history of the region is relevant for my analysis in as much as it provides the grounds upon which I attempt to understand the dynamics of regional belonging and the politics of place-making in Dalmatia today. Thus in the following section I present a brief outline of the settlement history of Dalmatia and of Sinj, and demonstrate how the region has been systematically marginalised and exploited by its varying occupying powers. I also discuss how early travel accounts simultaneously romanticised the inhabitants of Dalmatia as 'noble savages' of the Adriatic Empire and turned them into a spectacle of 'anthropological entertainment for the supposedly civilised public of the Enlightenment' (Wolff 2001: 250). I approach these discourses as paradigmatic precursors of modern anthropology and track their influence on 'Balkanist' attributions in subsequent scholarly work as well as on local self-characterisation, and finally link them to the highly politicised history of the Sinjska Alka.

A Brief History of Dalmatia

The medieval fortress 'Castrum regale Zyn' [Royal town of Sinj] was directly located at the border between the Venetian and Ottoman empires.[2] The region had been inhabited from prehistoric times, and due to its strategic location it was particularly heavily fought over.[3] In the mid-fifteenth century, with the Ottoman onset of the wars in Europe, incessant border disputes ensued.[4] The Turks, continuously attacking the Cetina district, eventually conquered the fortress of Sinj in 1524, which henceforth became a part of the Ottoman Empire. The town chronicler of Sinj, Šime Jurić, writes about this period:

> As in other territories occupied by the Turks, the life of the *raja* (Christian subject peoples) was harsh. Living in misery, slaving on the estate of their Turkish masters, they were never safe from passing military units, from raiding parties and reprisals. The Turkish conquest of Klis (1537) and formation of a Turkish *sanjak* (administrative unit) at Klis turned Sinj into an insignificant trading post on what was in other respects an important road leading from Bosnia to the coast. The few travellers that passed though on their way from Split to Bosnia described it as a small, insufficiently manned encampment with a fort, mosque, army granary and a few shingle-roofed houses. (Š. Jurić 1987a: 25)

When in 1683 a Turkish expeditionary force was defeated before the walls of Vienna, this was a signal for revolt in other border regions of the Ottoman Empire. Joining the Holy League against the Turks, Venice resolved to reinforce its troops against Ottoman expansion in Dalmatia, and owing to its importance on the northern border of Christian territory and its strategic position on the main road to the Adriatic coast, the first target selected for liberation was Sinj.

Figure 1.1. Print depicting an attack on Sinj in 1686.
© Croatian National Archive in Zagreb

In 1686 the fortress once again became part of the Venetian Republic and was armoured as a major stronghold in the Turco-Venetian wars. Despite the Treaty of Karlowitz, marking the official end of these wars in 1699 and the handover of previously Turkish-controlled fortresses in Dalmatia, Ottoman troops continued to send forces into the Cetina district. In 1715 the Turkish army led by Mehmed Pasha, the Grand Vizier of the Ottoman Empire, attacked Sinj, after a declaration of war had been delivered to the Venetian governor at Sinj. Yet despite being greatly outnumbered by Turkish forces, the inhabitants of Sinj refused to surrender and defeated the Turks, putting an end to all Turkish attacks from that point onwards.

The fall of the Venetian Republic in 1797, however, terminated Venice's administrative rule in Dalmatia, as Austrian troops henceforth made their appearance in the region. This Austrian occupation only lasted for eight years as Austria was forced to yield all of its Venetian possessions to Napoleon after the battle of Austerlitz in 1805. From early 1806 onwards, Dalmatia fell under French rule, a period that vastly contributed to Croat national awakening. After the fall of Napoleon, the Austrian army annexed Dalmatia for a second time, now subsuming both Croatia and Dalmatia under the Habsburg Empire, with Croatia dependent on Hungary, and Dalmatia on Austria.

After the disintegration of Austria-Hungary in the First World War, Croatia and part of Dalmatia became the first part of an independent state of Slovenes, Croats and Serbs, whereas Istria and the remaining regions of Dalmatia were assigned to Italy. In 1941, during the Second World War, Yugoslavia faced an Italo-German-Hungarian invasion; and while Croatia was incorporated in the fascist Independent State of Croatia (NDH) under Ante Pavelic, Dalmatia remained largely allocated to Italy. After the surrender of Italy in 1943 the Partisan troops led by Tito reconquered the regions occupied by Nazi Germany and dissolved the NDH. Istria and the Dalmatian parts under Italian rule were reassigned to Croatia and integrated into the newly created Federative People's Republic of Yugoslavia. Dalmatia was divided between the three federal republics – Croatia, Montenegro and Bosnia-Herzegovina – and when Yugoslavia fell apart in 1991, the borders of the republic became the borders of the country as they are today.

This radically abridged outline should suffice to reveal something of the marginality as well as connectivity of both Dalmatia and the Sinjska Krajina in the sense that the region has, for centuries, existed at the margins and crossroads of various empires. Poised on the Triplex Confinium, the Ottoman-Habsburg-Venetian frontier, and entangled in the politics and conflicts of 'East' and 'West', Dalmatia lies at what Herzfeld (1987) has termed 'the critical margins of Europe'. This position – at the intersection of several key axes of European symbolic geography and, in recent times, also of fascism, democracy and communism – has been invoked as central to understanding the region as an area of fertile cross-cultural contact as well as a site of violent, tectonic civilisational shifts (cf. Ballinger 2004a).

The concrete historical threat posed by the Ottoman Empire has, according to a number of eminent Balkan scholars, significantly shaped concepts of 'Europeanisation' or 'Westernisation' (Todorova 1997). Rastko Močnik goes as far as to argue that

[t]he 'modern idea' of Europe seems to have been initiated in the fourteenth and fifteenth centuries, precisely in opposition to Islam. It appeared at the historical moment when hopes of a universal Christian Empire had to be abandoned, and the notion of Europe as an 'international' community of sovereign domains began its career ... The European community of 'sovereignties' was then conceived in opposition to the religious entity of Islam. (Močnik 2005: 111, n.39)

In contemporary Dalmatia, this dissociation from 'the religious entity of Islam' still features most prominently in the Croatian–Bosnian border region of the hinterland as well as in the parts of Herzegovina that are mainly inhabited by Catholic Croats, and it finds an evident expression in the fact that Bosnian Muslims are still commonly referred to as 'Turks'. Local identity in Dalmatia is infused with religious symbolism and the region's turbulent history of political domination and foreign rule is intertwined with narratives of the constant defence of Christianity, or, to be more precise, of the Roman Catholic faith. In this context, the most important narrative that accentuates the status of Sinj and the Cetinska krajina as a strenuously fought-over, relentlessly oppressed, yet bravely defended region of the Christian world is the account of the recurrent battles against the Ottoman Turks.

The Historical Defence of Sinj against the Ottoman Troops in 1715

In the popular imagination, no other historical event or encounter is considered more significant for the formation of local identity and self-conception in Sinj than the battle against the forces of the Ottoman Empire in August 1715. This campaign has given rise to a rich repertoire of folk ballads, tales, proverbs and songs, and is widely considered to be the base on which local codes of honour, morals and notions of heroism are built. It is on the grounds of this history that the Dalmatians perceive themselves as a stronghold of regional defence against foreign intruders to the present day.

Although exact numbers are difficult to verify, several sources indicate that a group of around seven hundred poorly armed defenders resisted the attacks of an estimated thirty thousand soldiers of the Ottoman Empire for a full seven days. A journal, kept by one of the soldiers who defended the fortress of Sinj, conveys an idea of how the offensive might have proceeded.[5] This detailed record elucidates the numerical imbalance between attackers and defenders, and gives a rough idea of the damage – in terms of losses, injuries, destruction of basic resources, farmland and buildings – caused by the ferocity of the battle. But we are unlikely to know for certain whether it was the fear of Venetian reinforcements, a general low morale of the troops, the unexpected heavy losses during the siege, a shortage of food supplies or a reported dysentery epidemic, that eventually caused the commander of the Turkish troops to withdraw.

Anyhow, Turkey recognised a new natural boundary with Bosnia along the border marked by the Dinaric mountain ridge, according to the Treaty of Passarowitz, signed by the Ottoman and Habsburg empires and the Venetian Republic three years after this battle, in 1718. The Venetian Republic referred to these regained territories in Dalmatia as *nuovo* or *nuovissimo acquisto* [new or newest acquisitions] and imposed heavy taxations, various monopolies, obligations such as military service as well as various forms of forced labour on the settlers in these new acquisitions. And although the region had been devastated by the many wars fought in defence of the borders of the Venetian empire, the Venetians offered little to help the impoverished peasant population to rebuild the province. The harsh living conditions and struggle for survival of the Dalmatian population were instead often simply romanticised as a primordial way of life that fascinated and inspired scholars throughout eighteenth-century enlightened Europe.

Travels into Dalmatia: Travelogues as Precursors of 'Balkanism' and Modern Anthropology

> I invite you to cross the rocky mountains, which divide from the sea, the beautiful interior parts of Dalmatia, at present inhabited by the Morlacchi.[6]
>
> – Letter to Signor Marsili (Fortis 1778)

From the late seventeenth through to the nineteenth century, Dalmatia was a popular destination not only for travellers but also for 'naturalists'. A number of archaeologists, geologists and geographers published their scientific findings along with detailed descriptions and illustrations of excavation sites, historical monuments, flora, fauna, as well as accounts of their travel adventures and encounters with the local population.[7] The most acclaimed and eminent amongst these scientific travel writers, and the one whose work brought the subject of Dalmatia to the attention of the European Enlightenment, is the Venetian clergyman and polymath Abbé Alberto Fortis. From 1771 to 1774 Fortis undertook an expedition to Dalmatia and penned his famous travel account *Viaggio in Dalmazia* in which he minutely describes regional geographical and geological phenomena as well as archaeological artefacts. Fortis also refers to historical backgrounds and adeptly comments on the customs of the local population. His engravings not only depict minerals and fossils but also landscapes and folkloristic costumes.[8] Initially, his research was intended to advise the Venetian authorities on the development and more effective economic utilisation of the region. However, his accounts were so lively and informative that the publication was instantly translated into German, English and French, and was widely read throughout Europe.[9] Admired as 'a first-rate precursor of modern anthropology' (Masturzo and Colognola 2005: 23; see also Wolff 2001: 127), Fortis's *Viaggio in Dalmazia* is not only a valuable historical document but also contains informative appraisals of the Dalmatian way of life, as well as local beliefs, moral concepts, customs and habits at that time.

In his description of the Cetina district, Fortis refers to the inhabitants as 'the Indians of Venetia'[10] and mentions '[t]he fortress of *Seign*, where the breasts of a few hundred Morlacchi served as bastions against thirty thousand Turks in the last war' (Fortis 1778: 242f.). The 'last war' that Fortis mentions in his account is the legendary battle of 1715 in which the inhabitants of Sinj defended the fortress against the army of Mehmed Pasha. He refers to the locals as 'Morlacchi',[11] a term that derives from the Greek Mavrovlachi or Mauro-Vlachs and simply denotes 'Black Vlachs'. Since the mid-eleventh century, the Morlacchi or Morlachs have populated the mountainous regions of Montenegro, Bosnia, Herzegovina and along the Dalmatian Coast. First mentioned in documents in 1352, the term Morlacchi was used as a toponym for the peasant population of the Dinara and habitually designated Christians, peasants and inhabitants of hinterlands, as opposed to Muslims, urban-dwellers, islanders and the coastal population (cf. Novak 1971: 580; Gulin 1997: 82). In the course of the fourteenth century some Morlachs migrated northwards and later came to serve as guardians at the military frontier that divided the Habsburg and the Ottoman Empires. The Venetians applied the term to the Christian rural population in the Ottoman regions and to those living along the Ottoman–Venetian border.[12]

Fortis's quasi-anthropological study on 'The Customs of the Morlacchi' – Wolff has somewhat sarcastically remarked that '[t]he Slavs of Dalmatia, just across the Adriatic from Venice, offered the Enlightenment its most accessible savage subjects for pioneering the principles of anthropology' (Wolff 2001: 158) – made the mountain dwellers of the Dinara, who had previously been perceived as the most intractable, ferocious and barbarous subjects of Venice's imperial administration, objects of public interest and concern throughout the European world of letters of the time.[13]

But despite its wide and enthusiastic reception, Fortis's account also provoked public debate in Venice and stirred particularly fervent dissent in Dalmatia itself. The first local writer to attack Fortis was Ivan Lovrić (1754–1777), a native of Sinj. His foremost criticism concerns the fact that Fortis had drastically understated the poverty as well as the oppressive social conditions prevailing during the years of Venetian rule in Dalmatia. By romanticising the Morlacchi's archaic customs, Lovrić argued, Fortis had not only praised 'primitivism' and 'ignorance' but also failed to remark on any improvements in the province.

Lovrić's disapproval of the ways in which 'primitive Morlacchi' are made into a spectacle of 'anthropological entertainment for the supposedly civilised public of the Enlightenment' (Wolff 2001: 250) can thus be seen as a critique of the imperial imagination itself. The issue of civilisation and barbarism raised by Fortis in *Viaggio in Dalmazia* triggered the question of national identity and belonging of Dalmatians, and Lovrić's vigorous reaction lastingly altered the notion of the 'silent subaltern of the Adriatic Empire' (Wolff 2001: 330). In this sense, the controversy can be considered one of the first instances in the history of modern anthropology in which the 'subaltern speaks' and publicly challenges the colonial conditions that had rendered ethnographic enquiry possible in the first place.

The Morlacchi were systematically constructed as the 'Other' or the 'Oriental within' and served as a personified epitome of the borderland between the Venetian Republic and the unknown 'barbarian' Ottoman world. This discourse within Venetian Enlightenment concerning the Dalmatians in general and the Morlacchi in particular can be understood as an early predecessor of what Maria Todorova later labelled as 'Balkanism' and described as a discourse that incessantly belabours the 'otherness' of the Balkans vis-à-vis the civility of the Western world (Todorova 1997; see also Wolff 2001: 330). The stereotype of the romanticised Dalmatian 'savage' as well as that of the 'insubordinate Oriental within' (cf. Herzfeld 2005: ix), that this early controversy between Alberto Fortis and Ivan Lovrić instigated, has been sustained in much of the subsequent (travel) literature as well as in scholarly research on Dalmatia and the Cetinska krajina.

Fortis's eighteenth-century account of religious as well as sociocultural and economic practices in rural Dalmatia, however, not only created a romanticised image of the region in Western Europe but also considerably influenced the local self-characterisation to the present day.[14] Discussing Alberto Fortis's *Viaggio in Dalmazia* with Željko, a 32-year-old Franciscan priest at the monastery in Sinj in 2005, I had been wondering who the Morlacchi were and how they are perceived today.[15] Željko answered:

A: They are descendants of the Illyrians – of tribes who settled here before the Croats arrived. Today we are all mixed.

Q: What did they look like? Or what distinguished them? Could you possibly be a Morlach?

A: I couldn't care less. Whether I am called a 'Morlach' or a 'Venetian Indian' – I really don't mind. As long as I am not an Englishman. That is the one thing I really am thankful for.

This brief and somewhat peculiar conversation not only confirms the wide circulation of acquaintance with Fortis's travelogue, but can also be understood as a contemporary variant on 'insubordination' that assumes shape as aversion against the *inglezi*, the English. Such discourses are part of the self-dramatisation of many Dalmatians as unruly people whom the authorities always had difficulty controlling, but who are not what is considered to be the worst insult of all: 'lackeys of the West'.

The rather widespread resentment towards Britain and the British is mainly attributed to the historical role the country played during the Second World War when the Allies – with Churchill leading the way – resolved to side with Tito's Partisan movement, after having previously supported the Serbian royalist Četniks.[16] Since that time Britain has been considered as an ally of Serbia and hence a political archenemy of Croatia, and is also widely held responsible for the Bleiburg massacre of May 1945 in which thousands of Croatian Ustaše, Slovenian Wehrmacht, Domobrans (Home Guards) as well as Četniks were killed in what is perceived as an ambush by British troops. And in relation to the recent Homeland War, the British government and its foreign policy are perceived as mainly responsible for failed peace negotiations prior to the escalation of violence as well as for futile plans for drawing up new borders and rebuilding the infrastructure on the territory of the former Yugoslavia. David Owen, commonly referred to as Lord Owen – the European co-chairman of the International Conference for the Former Yugoslavia, and later joint author of the failed Vance–Owen (VOPP) and Owen–Stoltenberg (OSPP) peace plans – is one of the main targets of Croatian anger regarding the unsuccessful attempts of international mediators to de-escalate. Along with Boutros Boutros Ghali – Secretary-General of the United Nations from January 1992 to December 1996 – Lord Owen is blamed for his pro-Serbian policy by Croats, Bosniaks and Albanians alike, and he is chiefly held responsible for the international community's 'legitimation of ethnic cleansing'. In discussion about the Yugoslav People's Army (JNA) offences, I frequently heard comments like 'Lord Owen is more accountable for the war than the Serbs are', indicating that the EU negotiator 'built an extraordinarily warm relationship with Milošević' (Silber and Little 1995: 262) and deliberately prevented a timely intervention by international troops (cf. Owen 1995: 74ff.). Today, Britain is assumed to be a major driving force behind contemporary imperialist attitudes and globalising tendencies that are, to a certain extent, held responsible for the continuous marginalisation and political as well as economic discrimination of the region.[17] The dialogue just quoted is a representative example of many conversations I conducted or regularly overheard in rural Dalmatia and thus paradigmatically reflects a prevailing sentiment regarding local self-characterisation, and illustrates the rhetorical disassociation from the West's self-essentialisation.

From Legendary Battle to a Mythology of (Self-)Victimisation

At the Crossroads

Almost seventy years after Alberto Fortis's *Viaggio in Dalmazia* was published, Sir John Gardner Wilkinson, more widely known as the 'Father of British Egyptology', also travelled in the Balkan region, and published his observations in two volumes (Wilkinson 1848). Like Fortis, Wilkinson opens his description of the Cetina region by stating the beauty of the landscape: 'The country here is very pretty ... Sign [sic] contains about 2000 inhabitants. It was long the bulwark of the Venetians against the Turks whose frontier is now seven miles off' (Wilkinson 1848: Vol. I, 233ff.). Characterising Sinj as a 'bulwark of the Venetians against the Turks', Wilkinson not only acknowledges the strategic military importance but also the enormous symbolic significance of Sinj as a bastion and outpost of the Western world. His mid-nineteenth-century description touches on aspects of scenic beauty, geographical condition and land cultivation, and provides a brief description of the castle of Sinj and the historic battles for it. In comparison to earlier sources, however, the number of Turkish attackers in the battle of 1715 is rounded up in this account to forty thousand, a figure that is retained and even amplified in ensuing reports, thus facilitating the gradual transformation of the battle into a legendary event. Furthermore, Wilkinson's mention of the 'annual tilting fete (*giostra*)' that is 'celebrated with all the pomp of golden times' in memory of the historic victory over the Turks refers to the Sinjska Alka knight's tournament that is, as mentioned earlier, celebrated to the present day.

However, the two features that are most frequently mentioned in travel accounts and historical documents about Sinj – apart from the 1715 battle and the subsequent Alka tournament – concern the region's attributes as a geographical niche. First of all, foreign as well as local scholars consistently note the distinct sub-Mediterranean climate along with the harsh living conditions on the plateau. However, Sinjsko polje provides a comparatively fertile oasis in the barren karstic soil of the Dalmatinska Zagora, and agriculture as well as animal husbandry in conjunction with semi-transhumant pastoralism constitute the most important branches of economic activity. The second key feature that is commonly noted is the location of the Sinjska krajina at the junction of important transportation routes.[18] However, the situation at the border between the expanding Ottoman-Habsburg-Venetian empires and competition concerning the scarce resources led to recurrent clashes with the neighbouring settlers and resulted in a traditionally high mobility of the population. The pauperist peasants migrated seasonally to the fertile Danube valleys, and large sections of the population migrated overseas at the end of the nineteenth and the beginning of the twentieth centuries in particular.

The construction of roads and railways during the Habsburg Empire (1813–1918) as well as the first Yugoslavia (1918–1941) excluded the Sinjska krajina from its previous transport connexion and contributed to the further impoverishment of the region. In 1911, the Austrian ethnologist Michael Haberlandt wrote on Dalmatia that:

> the land is poor, the people all too much oppressed by harsh necessity. Dalmatia is far richer in folk art, and generally in folkloric respects, for which the causes are to be deduced in the first place from the economic peculiarity and seclusion of the land from large trade. The great primitiveness and antiquity of its inhabitants and their form of life and type of spirit, their economic poverty, which in many ways keep them in a pure natural economy, their seclusion and their particularism are the hitherto strong and undisrupted roots from which folk artistic qualities of the first rank have flowered. (Haberlandt 1911: 194)

Mentioning the rich repertoire of folklore and folk art alongside the region's isolation and the population's harsh living conditions, Haberlandt displays the same fascination with Dalmatia's economic poverty and successful preservation of local customs that had developed in the Venetian Enlightenment with regard to the anticipated dilemma of modernity.

The primordial conduct, nativeness and scarcity romanticised in these celebrations of nature and culture, however, affected the inhabitants of the Dalmatinska Zagora in numerous existential ways. Not only is the area particularly poor, inhospitable and susceptible to earthquakes and other natural disasters but has, until the 1930s, also been characterised by its high levels of child mortality and illiteracy. Since the 1960s many men from the Dalmatian hinterland and the Western Herzegovina went abroad to make money as *Gastarbeiter* (lit. guest workers) and left the agricultural and livestock husbandry to their families and wives. The continual intervention of wars, past and present involvement of various hegemonic regimes, exchange of populations and the process of mass emigration, have considerably shaped people's perception of their environment as well as the prevailing modes of livelihood. However, small-scale agriculture, semi-transhumant pastoralism, and (subsistence) farming continue to be main sources of income in the area; and the spinning mill 'Dalmatinka' that was built in 1951 is still one of the few large industrial employers in Sinj to this day.

Recent Violence in the Region

In the Second World War and the post-Yugoslav wars, Sinj and adjacent hamlets were particularly affected by military violence. In 1941, after Germany had declared war on and invaded Yugoslavia, the fascist Ustaša (from *ustanak*, uprising) were put in charge of the Nezavisna Država Hrvatska (NDH) [Independent State of Croatia], by the Axis Powers, and carried out a cruel genocide amongst Serbs, Jews, Gypsies and a number of Communist Croats. Yet despite these atrocities, many people – particularly in Sinj and in the countryside surrounding the villages – strongly identified with the Ustaša and the Hrvatski Domobran [Croatian Home Guard] whose declared aim was to 'liberate Croatia from alien rule and establish a completely free and independent state over the whole of its national and historic territory' (Horvat 1942: 432, quoted in Tanner 2001: 125). By the end of the war in 1945, however, the Ustaši were utterly defeated by Tito's communist-led Partisan troops. In several Partisan massacres, thousands of presumed Ustaša sympathisers and Croatian civilians had been killed – crimes that were completely silenced and hushed up in Tito's Yugoslavia.

In the years that followed, the Dalmatinska Zagora remained a stronghold of Croatian separatism, even while being subjected to severe retaliations by the Socialist government. According to personal accounts, a number of neighbouring villages were deliberately deprived of plumbing, electricity and telephone connexions until the 1970s with the intention of breaking the local population's resistance towards state politics and thus averting the danger of potential separatist uprisings. Such measures were evidently perceived as deliberate discrimination and in the long run they aggravated rather than alleviated ethno-national tensions between Croatian villagers and residents of the neighbouring, predominantly Serb-populated, *Krajina* [borderland] region. Stef Jansen has noted that 'the existence of privileged Serbian-dominated "partisan" villages next to a black-sheep Croatian-dominated "Ustaša village" reflected a widespread pattern in this part of the Yugoslav Socialist Republic of Croatia. Unlike in larger places in former Yugoslavia, nationality had long been a political issue in these places' (Jansen 2002: 92). It is therefore not entirely surprising that many Croatian men from this region were among the first volunteers to join the army when the conflicts started to escalate in the late 1980s.

In the years directly preceding the war, memories of the previously concealed Partisan violence re-emerged and became a crucial factor in the rise of Croatian nationalism. After the victory of Franjo Tuđman's Croatian Democratic Union, or Hrvatska Demokratska Zajedniza (HDZ), in the 1990 elections and the consequent ratification of a new constitution that changed the status of Serbs in Croatia from a 'constituent nation' to a 'national minority', radical Serbs eventually declared their separation from Croatia. It is a matter of debate as to what extent this move was locally motivated and to what degree the Milošević-led Serb government in Belgrade actually triggered the secession. However, the proclamation of the Republic of Serbian Krajina in April 1991 was the prelude to armed conflict and is frequently viewed as the instigation of the so-called Domovinski rat, the Homeland War.[19]

The Republic of Serbian Krajina remained internationally unrecognised but the local Croat Serb forces – unified under the acronym SVK for 'Srpska Vojska Krajine' [Serbian Army of the Krajina] – were supported by the Serb-dominated Yugoslav People's Army (JNA) in their campaigns against Croatian forces and civilians.[20] Provocations by Serbian hardliners increased and with the 'help' of volunteer militias from Serbia, almost all Croatian inhabitants were violently expelled (cf. Jansen 2006: 434; Leutloff 2000). The Croatian Ministry of the Interior consequently started arming an increasing number of 'special police' forces, which in May 1991 led to the establishment of the Zbor Narodne Garde [Croatian National Guard] from the ranks of police reservists as a quasi-independent army. The troops were poorly equipped and badly organised, as Tuđman did not initially aim to defeat the Serbs militarily but calculated on winning international recognition.[21] Nonetheless, he mobilised scores of volunteers who were willing to go to war and defend Croatia against 'Serb aggression'.[22]

The terrain that the SVK had occupied since 1991 comprised almost one-third of Croatia's territory. In the notorious 1995 military offensive Operacija Oluja [Operation Storm], however, Croatian forces recaptured the majority of the annexed land in a coup that lasted only eighty-four hours.[23] The impact and effects of Operacija Oluja are highly controversial to the present day. On one hand, the military offensive is seen as an act of liberation that denoted *the* turning point of the Wars of Yugoslav Secession and marked a great victory of the Croatian and Bosnian armies. It signified the defeat of Serbia's military power and eventually induced the end of the war. On the Serbian side, however, Operacija Oluja is not only perceived as a major military defeat but is also synonymously associated with devastation and war crimes against Serb civilians. In this 'operation', which was later declared the 'biggest single forcible displacement of people in Europe since the Second World War' (Silber and Little 1995: 358), hundreds of Serbian civilians were killed, thousands of houses destroyed and more than two hundred thousand people evicted.[24]

However, the offensive that commenced on 4 August and ended on 7 August 1995 established the territorial entity of the Republika Hrvatska according to international law, and paved the way for peace talks that resulted in the signing of the Dayton Agreement in November 1995. In Croatia, the date 5 August – the day in 1995 when the Croatian Army took control of Knin, the capital of the self-proclaimed Serbian Republic – is called *Dan pobjede i domovinske zahvalnosti i dan hrvatskih branitelja* [Victory and Homeland Thanksgiving Day and the Day of Croatian Defenders] and is celebrated as a national holiday. In Serbia, on the other hand, it is marked by commemorations for the victims. After the end of the war, Croatian forces were held responsible for widespread actions against Serb civilians as well as for the looting and destruction of Krajina Serb property. At this point the International Criminal Tribunal for the Former Yugoslavia (ICTY) issued indictments against three senior commanders of the Croatian army.[25]

Today, the former 'Krajina' gives the impression of a desolate, scarcely populated zone. The area is economically weak with high unemployment rates (one of the reasons being that Croatian Serbs continue to be disadvantaged in access to employment) and deserted villages featuring heavily damaged and destroyed houses are partly lined with uncleared minefields.[26] By early 2010 approximately 93,000 Croatian Serbs were officially registered as having returned up to that point (most of them elderly citizens); yet according to the UN High Commissioner for Refugees, around 175,000 of the Croatian refugees, mostly Croatian Serbs, have opted for 'naturalisation' in Serbia, while another 61,000 are still displaced.

Some of the Croatian Serbs do not return out of fear of being charged for war crimes committed in the years preceding Operacija Oluja.[27] Marko, a Croatian from Sinj in his forties and one of my core interlocutors, put it as follows: 'Those who know that they are innocent will come back and those who know that they aren't, won't'. But it is obviously not quite as simple as that, and manifold reasons contribute to the reluctance of expelled residents to return. There are still frequent reports about cases of violence, harassment and discrimination against Croatian Serbs and many refugees cannot return to their former homes or claim ownership because they have lost their tenancy rights. Others find that Croats or Bosnian refugees have taken residence in their vacant houses in the meantime (cf. Leutloff-Grandits 2006a, 2006b). The Croatian government has passed a number of laws (including special tax exemptions) and projects aimed at enabling an easier return for refugees and at rebuilding heavily war-torn areas. However, economic hardship and ethno-national tensions prevail alongside a distinct 'pattern of non-communication' (Jansen 2006: 434) and pose a challenge to the peaceful coexistence of Serbs and Croats in the former 'Krajina' and adjacent areas.

Sinj as a 'Town of Courage and Tradition'

Exoticising Dalmatia

> Even now, the people of the Cetina do not aspire to live a
> peaceful life. They only live in peace because they have no
> choice: there is nobody to fight.
> — Dinko Šimunović, *Alkar*

The region referred to as Dalmatia today is about two hundred miles long and occupies the southern portion of the north-east side of the Adriatic Sea. In the north, Dalmatia is about seventy miles across and in the south as little as ten miles wide, the massive mountain range of the Dinaric Alps running parallel to the Adriatic Sea. Sinj is located in the continental part of the Split-Dalmatia county, and the population of the administrative municipality that includes several surrounding villages and scattered *komšiluci* [homesteads] is around twenty-five thousand.

Sinj is widely known as a Catholic stronghold and as the heartland of Croatian nationalism. These are both features from which many liberal urban Croatians seek to distance and dissociate themselves. When I told a young colleague in Zagreb that I had finally decided to do my fieldwork in Sinj, she was rather concerned and said: 'I want you to know that we are not all like the people there. You have to make sure you contextualise the place. In Sinj they are all warriors and eager to defend what they think is Croatia. Even if I personally do not know what that would be'. And although she was instantly aware of and slightly embarrassed by her own worry that Croatia might not be 'properly' portrayed in my writing, her reaction was quite symptomatic. Other comments I heard when indicating my intention to work on Sinj were:

> The people there are as hard as the stone of the mountains in which they live. (Dunja, 28, Zagreb)

> We call the people of that region *kamenista* – stone people. Shepherds. I know it's a prejudice, but we see the people there as very lazy. (Tatjana, 19, Bjelovar)

> The people there are extreme in every respect. They are as hard at the landscape over there. They either praise a thing to heaven or damn it to hell. They simply don't have balanced views. But they are extremely hospitable. You cannot assess these people because they are so incredibly friendly – yet they can also be the worst fascists. Please be careful. (Danko, 55, Zagreb)

> It is a very dark and bleak region – bleak in every respect. (Irina, 50, Otok Brač)

> The people there are as cold as the *bura* [a chilly north wind for which the region is famous]. (Mara, 45, Mostar)

> There is a rather bad climate there, if you know what I mean. (Safa, 60, Mostar)

What is most striking in these comments is the naturalistic quality of the stereotypes attached to this particular region of the Dalmatian hinterland. Comparing the inhabitants of the region to the climate, the cold north wind [*bura*], the stony and barren landscape or the 'bleakness' of the surroundings, the statements illustrate how places are metonymically and metaphorically ascribed and tied to identities. The implied assumption that local characteristics and knowledge are manifest in geographical surroundings is confirmed by the local saying, 'We are the way our surroundings are' (quoted in Bringa 1995: 86). 'But what do you want to do there all winter', Dunja, a young woman friend of mine from Zagreb asked me provocatively, 'sit at home and knit?'

After I had finished my fieldwork, other acquaintances from Zagreb openly wondered how I had managed to last in Sinj without being held at gunpoint. It goes without saying that I was never tempted to take up knitting; nor was I ever threatened or intimidated in the slightest. The remarks – although most likely intended playfully and as somewhat theatrical exaggerations – nevertheless convey a certain belief in the fierce character of the people of the Dinara. They even bear traces of earlier depictions of the Morlacchi as 'fascinating and ferocious primitives' (Wolff 2001: 317), which was already a cliché in the eighteenth century. However, prejudices about these people as coarse, credulous, slothful and prone to violence seem to be persistent. People of the Dalmatinska Zagora are still perceived as fearsome mountain dwellers inclined to reactionary traditionalism, with a steely readiness for warfare. Frequently they are either ridiculed or feared in this light by urban middle-class Croats. Certainly, subsistence in the Dalmatian hinterland seems a rather idiosyncratic way of life by present-day Croatian standards.

The Making and Meaning of a Legend for Local Self-Conception

While urban Croats mainly tend to associate Sinj with a (folkloristic) display of regional belonging and pride, locals rather refer to their hometown as 'the site of fierce combat and great suffering' (Grčić 1987: 15). This phrase alludes to the settlement's long-lasting record of subjugation under imperial rule and its role as a buffer zone attributable to its location in a historical area of conflict. As already mentioned, it is the legendary struggle against the troops of the Ottoman Empire in 1715 that paradigmatically epitomises this position. The townspeople of Sinj held that they owed their victory to divine intervention and a belief in the helping hand of God – or rather the Mother of God in this event is a common notion. Since parts of Dalmatia had been periodically under Turkish rule for almost two centuries, the ultimate defeat of the Ottoman troops who had recurrently tried to capture Sinj and the Cetinska krajina was commonly embraced as miraculous salvation. The battle gave birth to a legendary tale about local heroism and a myth about the people's the divine liberation from the 'Ottoman yoke'.

According to the legend – as it has been propagated and as it is widely related today – a messenger of Mehmed Pasha delivered an ultimatum calling the commander of Sinj to surrender, lest the town be burnt to ashes. Commander Balbo, however, refused to surrender and ordered his outgunned troops to put up resistance. In the meantime, the head of the Franciscan Order, Friar Pavao Vučković, gathered the townspeople to pray in front of a Marian painting that had been erected at the fortification wall for this purpose. The painting had previously been rescued from a monastery in Bosnia and brought to Sinj. On the way it had won the reputation of containing miraculous powers and it was said that the Turks would cease to win their battles wherever the painting emerged. The population of Sinj thus continued to pray for several days while the siege persisted. All of a sudden, however, the Turks were struck with thirst and dysentery, and at daybreak on 15 August a floating lady in a white dress appeared outside the fortification wall. The attackers were terrified at the sight and took immediate flight. Soon thereafter, the news of the Marian apparition in Sinj spread around the country. The townspeople who attributed the defeat of the Turks to the aid of the Marian apparition referred to the painting as *Čudotvorna Slika Blažene Djevice Marije od Milosti* [Miraculous Painting of the Blessed Virgin Mary of Mercy], or simply as *Čudotvorna Gospe Sinjske* [Miraculous Lady of Sinj], and have continued to refer to it in this way ever since. To-day, a small stone chapel, the Zavjetna Crkvica Sv. Gospe [Votive Chapel of Our Lady] stands on the hill on which the ancient fortress was once located. It is referred to as *na gradu* (literally 'up town') and marks an earthly place where the power of the divine was made manifest.[28]

The legend has inspired the popular imagination like no other story and many people in Sinj told me about the historic battle and the Marian apparition in a way that suggested they might have been present themselves. Versions of the legend are also commonly recited in church sermons, during local political rallies and on other public occasions. The drama has also inspired various folk tales,[29] literary works,[30] popular songs and children's stories.

The legend forms an integral part of the folkloristic repertoire in the Cetina region and is mainly passed on by word of mouth. The few printed versions available, however, follow the educational purpose of disseminating local interpretations of history and communicating a heroic code of honour. One particularly evocative example is an illustrated children's book called *Sinjska Alka* that was published in Zagreb in 1994. It recounts the legend from the perspective of a boy called Juriša and has been translated into English, German and Spanish. According to the story, Juriša stole a stirrup from Mehmed Pasha's horse during the attack of the Turks in 1715 in order to help to identify the leader of the Turkish troops. Upon handing the stirrup to the Duke of Sinj, one of the Turkish attackers tried to throw a pointed lance at the leader of the Croats. As Juriša ran between the duke and the lancer, the stirrup in his hands thwarted an intended mortal blow at the duke. But the pointed spearhead pierced the stirrup and bore its way into Juriša's heart. The stirrup in this story later became a symbol of chivalry in the Cetinska krajina and the target in the famous chivalric contest Sinjska Alka.

This lurid tale in which a child is made into a heroic martyr provides a highly dramatised version of the legend. Predicated on epic warrior values, it displays the patriarchal code of honour and self-sacrifice that has traditionally been associated with the people of the Cetina region, and implies that these people have never led a war of conquest but always only defended themselves. As an imaginary historical construction, however, the story involves the risk of promoting militant ideals that are prone to political manipulation and mobilisation. The idea that a victim can become a source of life provides a potential justification for war and/or (self-)sacrifice for 'a just cause' and creates a national consciousness in which the individual has to yield to the collective fate. 'In order to live, the nation asks for victims of its own children', writes Ivan Čolović (1993) in *Bordel Ratnika*. Read in the context of this children's story, this nationalist credo implies that sacrifices are expected – even from the youngest.

Keeping in mind that this is assigned to children, the following excerpt is a particularly alarming depiction of history as a complex of suffering borne by the people:

> Turks never ceased dreaming of recapturing the Croatian south ... History teaches us, ancient and modern alike, that the three worst aggressors (Tartarian, Turkish and Serbian) have always strived to destroy the most precious of Croatian treasures: children and sanctuaries ... Each force from the East first attacked the Church, religion, the Mother of God, the crucified Christ and the Creator himself. Then they attacked the women and children, the weak and the innocent. In the thirteenth century, the Tartars first attacked Croatian cathedrals and then Croatian towns. The Turks followed suit. Now the same pattern was being followed by Turkish vassals. The conquerors knew that the places of worship sheltered those for whose sake the Croatians defended their homeland – children, mothers, elderly people and the wounded. (Pulić 1994: 2, 20)

By constructing Croatia as a fundamental victim and equating an attack on her with an attack on Christianity itself, this text not only glorifies Croatian suffering but also mobilises a substantially racist imagery based on ethno-religious otherness. The cruelty of the 'Turkish attackers' and their violent crimes are described in great detail, thus projecting all evil onto an (exchangeable) enemy while simultaneously disowning all guilt of the defending self. Victimhood and self-defence, however, are expressed and justified in terms of gender relations. It is 'children, mothers, elderly people and the wounded', or, in other words, women, the 'weak and the innocent' who have to be protected by a righteous male defender. In this sense, heroic culture rests on the affirmation of patriarchal, martial and masculine values.

Clearly fascinated with violence, the story of Juriša conveys rab-ble-rousing political propaganda and its authors imbue children not only with fear of an imagined enemy but also with a notion of moral – ethno-national as well as religious – superiority. This assumed superiority culminates in the description of the Marian apparition at the fortification.

> Suddenly before the eyes of the perplexed attackers, the image of Our Lady appeared on the fortress wall ... One minute she disappeared in the smoke of guns, muskets and mortars, the other she appeared on the other side of the wall. She walked along the fortress with a peaceful, curt step, encouraged Croatian heroes and mused upon Sinjsko polje that swarmed with the Turkish troops ... her powers were stronger and bigger than the Turkish munition. They could neither hit nor wound her. Bullets whizzed about her, but they could not destroy her holy image ... The defenders ... thanked the Virgin Mary for her help in an uneven fight for the salvation and the glory of the town of Sinj and their homeland. This happened on 15 August 1715, in the heat of the battle. (Pulić 1994: 34f.)

The moral of this story, revolving around the idea that subjugation, forced migration, suffering and death will eventually pave the way to an ultimate divine liberation, is an essentially Christian discourse (cf. Stojanović 2004: 335). Concrete salvation from enemy attack through a miraculous Marian apparition provides a classic 'founding myth' in the imaginary of a community that sees itself embroiled only in defensive mobilisations against violence recurrently inflicted on it (cf. Bowman 2003: 37).

The children's book *Sinjska Alka* was being circulated by the Franciscan monastery in Sinj during my time in the region and was given to me as a gift by one of the priests to improve my understanding of the importance of the legend. Its tone and message is clearly demagogic and provides an insightful illustration of how nationalist historical consciousness is currently being (re-)constructed with the aid of religious imagery and language. In direct opposition to the previous communist model of collective identity, books like this – and to a lesser extent some of the new history textbooks as well – promote drastic changes of historical awareness and new notions of regional as well as national belonging. The legend of the historic battle of Sinj, narrated and transmitted by religious education and upbringing, intensifies the consciousness that hostility and betrayal describe Croatia's prevailing relationship to her neighbours. As a quasi-paranoid model of historical awareness, the legend has been long lasting. To this day the people of the Cetina region are convinced that they set an example of heroism not only to the rest of Croatia but also to the rest of Western Europe through their determined resistance to the Turks.

It is the very same rhetoric of heroic self-sacrifice, martyrdom and moral superiority featured in the children's story that also played a crucial part in Croatian narratives of the last war. A number of accounts symbolically link the historic battle of 1715 to the Homeland War of 1991–1995 – a war in which many Croatians perceived themselves again as the violated victims of a hostile expanding power. The military offensive known as Operation Oluja was carried out in the 'Krajina' region in the immediate vicinity of Sinj, and was particularly suited to this association as the majority of the Croatian population interpreted this brief 'operation' as an act of self-defence that turned into a rather unexpected military victory. The soldiers of the Croatian Army who fought in the Homeland War and the defenders of the fortress of Sinj in 1715 were thus synonymously referred to as *branitelji*, or 'defenders of the homeland'. In the framework of this discourse, Serbian and Turkish troops become interchangeable under the label of 'attackers from the East'. This ahistorical linkage of two or more unconnected events represents a widespread strategy of constructing or highlighting the notion of cyclic (self-)sacrifice of the Croatian nation.

During the Homeland War the ancient antagonism against the 'evil-doers from the East' was significantly reinterpreted – this time not neighbouring Bosnian Muslims but the mainly Serbian-led JNA (Yugoslav People's Army) and Serbian paramilitary forces were perceived as the main threat. This fact, however, did not alter the importance of the historic battle of 1715 for Croatian self-stylisation as guards and protectors of the Occident. In Croatia and elsewhere, concrete historical presence of the Ottoman Empire has traditionally been conceived of as an Oriental and genuinely non-European element, and this still prevails in prevalent Croatian discourses linking Balkanism to the Ottoman legacy. To this day, all versions of Croatian nationalism are constructed in vehement, direct opposition to the idea that Croatia is a part of 'the Balkans' – a region strongly associated with its Ottoman, and therefore Muslim, legacy.

Sinjska Alka: Performing and Parading Superiority

Course and Tradition of the Alka Tournament

The local population of the Cetinska krajina had their own way of celebrating and commemorating their victory over the Turkish army of
Mehmed Pasha in 1715. In honour of the successful defence of Sinj,
they established a chivalrous game called Sinjska Alka, or the Alka of
Sinj.[31] Drawing upon the medieval tradition of horsemanship competitions, the Alka was first inaugurated as a parade and later established as
a veritable tournament. It is considered to be the direct descendant of
knightly tournaments that were common in the Middle Ages throughout Europe and in parts of the Near East.

> It is a unique continuation and reflection of ancient competitions, par-
> ticularly what were known as 'spearing the ring' (the Italian giostra,
> hastiludium, etc.). This type of contest, together with kindred games
> (the quintain, behourd, carousel, etc.), was widespread in many coun-
> tries of Europe, and especially in the countries bordering the Mediter-
> ranean. (Š. Jurić 1987b: 58)

The Alka takes place every year on the first weekend in August and has
traditionally been one of the main attractions and characteristics of
the Cetinska krajina and of Sinj in particular. It is one of the folkloristic events that travel writers, folklorists and ethnographers would inevitably refer to when describing the region's rich range of traditional
costumes, folk art, habits and customs. However, in present-day public
perception, the Alka is treated both as an invaluable cultural heritage
of Dalmatia and as a slightly outdated relic from ancient times signal-
ling rural backwardness. Croatian ethnologists Renata Jambrešić Kirin
and Tea Škokić write that '[t]he folklore and its values are simultaneously experienced as the source of national pride and a means of
self-representation on ceremonial occasions, but also as the object of
ridicule and the vehicle for everything that seems to hinder the sought
for adoption of modern, Western cultural practices' (Jambrešić Kirin
and Škokić 2004). Although these authors are writing in a different
context, their assessment is nonetheless greatly applicable to the Alka
tournament. Yet despite its double-edged connotation, the Alka is still
the major feature of local self-representation and self-conception in
Sinj to the present day. In a certain sense, the local population uses the
tournament as a way of dignifying its demeanour and attitude, despite

the occasional ridicule cast on it by urban compatriots. One of my interlocutors put it like this: 'Sinj – that is Alka and the Gospa (Virgin Mary)'.

In the course of the Alka's age-long history, each respective authority or state power has sought to exploit the tournament for its particular purpose and to install it as a celebratory component of its regime. The Alka, however, was never directly aligned to any government or political system, although its date has occasionally been modified in order to guarantee the games' longevity.

The fact that the costumes and the actual course of the competition have hardly changed can be attributed to the effectiveness of the strict statutes governing the games since their inception. The earliest Alka statute, dated 1833, was written in Italian and was later translated into Croatian. It contains detailed instructions regarding the order and rules of the tournament, and accurately prescribes the type and arrangement of weapons that each knight [*alkar*, pl. *alkari*] and squire [*momak*, pl. *momci*] has to carry.[32] The Viteško Alkarsko Društvo (VAD), the Alka Knightly Tournament Association, appoints the statute and also carefully monitors each contestant's compliance with the rules.[33] The current statute, effective since Croatian independence in 1991, derives directly from the original rules and changes have been kept to a minimum.[34]

Figure 1.2. Impressions of the Sinjska Alka 2005. Photo: M. Schäuble

Costumes, Masculinity and Local Pride

At first glance, the tournament is primarily a matter of knights dressed in ornate traditional costumes riding on horseback. At full gallop, the knights attempt to target an iron ring [*alka*] hanging from a rope that is stretched across a racetrack with a three-metre-long lance. However, the Alka is much more than simply a formalised dexterity game carried out in traditional costumes. First and foremost, it is an expression of bravery and regional pride. The statute dictates that only men born in Sinjska krajina (the town of Sinj and its surrounding villages) are eligible to participate in the tournament and thus secures local patriotism and local embedding of the event.[35] As a figurative performance of virtue, courage and military force, it also aims at demonstrating readiness for combat – and this certainly includes a parade of rivalry and masculinity. The Alka can thus be viewed as a performance in which manhood is emphasised and, on a more symbolic level, as something that provides a way for men to demonstrate publicly that they are capable of protecting their families (and the whole community) from threats. A fighting spirit, pugnacity and discipline, as demonstrated in the Alka, are closely related to concepts of masculinity and to the affirmation of manliness in general, and they play a crucial role in the (re-)construction of male identity in post-war Croatia. The Alka is a contest for, and a display of, male excellence. To win the tournament is thus considered to be the highest possible honour for a man from Sinj.

The notions of masculinity involved, however, are very controversial and are closely reflective of an urban–rural divide. In this context, Stef Jansen's notion of gendered Balkanist ascriptions elucidates the moral or civilisational issues implied in the common association of rural areas with traditionalism, 'machismo' and backwardness. He writes:

> In an evolutionist paradigm, particularly urbanites cherished a recursive version of Western discourses of Balkanism, further displacing the Balkan 'Other' specifically onto the countryside (including the one inhabited by one's co-nationals). A central element of this attributed primitivism was the traditionalist gender organisation amongst 'peasants' and, particularly, a posited Balkan model of masculinity. (Jansen 2007: 6; cf. Helms 2006: 343–61; Greenberg 2006)

This observation can be directly transferred to the current public perception of the Alka. Mainly young urban Croats despise or ridicule the Dalmatian tournament as an expression of 'peasant primitivism' and a display of 'archaic masculinity'. In their view, this merely confirms

Western discourses of Balkanism. The participants in the Alka themselves, however, perceive their display of masculinity and heroism as self-authentication and not as a perpetuation of outdated Balkanist attributions.

The only negative comments of locals on the Alka concerned the economic aspects of the tournament. Apparently, the Alka is a loss-making endeavour that is sponsored by private donations and the budgetary funds of the municipality of Sinj.[36] Some critics remarked that the current mayor and the town council were not treating the Alka in a sufficiently commercial manner, and one man even said, 'The Alka ruins Sinj.' Apparently, before Ivica Račan of the Social Democratic Party became prime minister of Croatia in 2000, the Alka was subsidised by the state government in Zagreb and the horses belonged to the Croatian army. Since the year 2000, however, the land, stables and horses have been privatised and are now maintained by the Viteško Alkarsko Društvo who is accused of mismanagement. These critical voices, however, become silent as soon as the meaning of the Alka for the region's self-conception and pride is highlighted.

The Folkloristic Procedure

As a traditional form of dramatic entertainment the tilting competition is an exuberant spectacle that lasts for three days. On the first day, the *alkari* compete for *bara* and on the second for *coja*, which are the prequalification rounds for the main competition. In previous times, the winner of the *bara* was awarded a piece of grazing land in Sinjsko polje and the winner of the *coja* was given a valuable piece of red homespun drapery. For the *bara* and *coja* tournaments, the *alkari* are dressed in plain clothes, simply wearing riding boots, riding-breeches and a short-sleeved white shirt. It is only on the third day, for the actual Alka competition, that they don splendid traditional costumes.

On the day of the Alka that is held on the Sunday before Velika Gospa (Assumption Day), thousands of people gather in the wooden grandstands that are erected on either side of the racing course. The adjacent houses are adorned with flags and flowers and, more recently, also with huge advertisement banners. Early in the morning a shot is fired from a cannon that is set up on the ancient fortification wall for the occasion. A brass band playing marching tunes parades along the narrow alleys of the town. Two hours before the beginning of the tournament three trumpeters and three drummers, dressed in local folk costume, call upon the competitors to assemble. At the summons, each of the squires, in full attire, goes to his appointed knight's house and helps him to prepare (cf. Š. Jurić 1987c: 114). In the afternoon the knights and their escorts make an appearance. They are awaited by the commander of the tournament, the *alaj-čauš* (the duke's deputy), and joined by the drummers and trumpeters. Divided in two lines, the company of squires marches uprightly and proudly in time to the music. The squires represent the foot soldiers who fought in the battle against the Turks. They are brawny moustachioed local men of almost two metres height, glancing neither right nor left. They wear the traditional folk costume of the Centiska Krajina that comprises interlaced linen shoes, dark blue or black woollen trousers, a white linen shirt with hanging sleeves, as well as a short sleeveless jacket of red felt. Over their felt vest they sport a mesh of silver thread with about four hundred silver buttons on each side. On their heads the *momci* wear red bonnets of Illyrian origin with black tassels that are decorated with white, red and blue flowers, resembling the Croatian national colours. Over their shoulders they carry long flintlock guns, a flint pistol and a dagger that is tucked into their waistband, called 'the serpent's nest'.

The *momci* are followed by drummers, trumpeters and the standard-bearer on horseback who carries the banner of the Viteško Alkarsko Društvo. At a short distance, following the display of ancient weapons and shields allegedly captured from the Turks, comes the *edek*, led by two squires. The *edek* is a splendidly equipped horse symbolising the Turkish Pasha's mount captured at the siege of Sinj, according to the legend. The bright red saddlecloth of the horse is bejewelled with delicate golden embroidery, as befitting a Turkish commander (cf. Alaupović-Gjeldum and Batarelo 1987: 99–109; Dalbelo 2001).

The *edek* is followed by the *alkari* on their grandly adorned horses. The *alkari*, who are led by the *alaj-čauš*, represent the knights of olden times, generally commanding personnel in the army units who fought against the Turks (cf. D. Jurić 1987a: 73). Their costumes resemble the attire of the Croatian nobility in the early eighteenth century. They wear leather boots with spurs and ribbons decorated with silver or golden tassels. The *alkari*'s riding breeches and their silk vests are embroidered and the vest is additionally adorned with little silver or golden palettes and rings. Their white shirts are held together by a silver filigree buckle and tied with a three- to five-metre-long silk belt. Over this they wear dark blue hussar jackets ornamented with silver embroideries and large silver sequins the size of coins. Each *alkar* wears white gloves and carries an antiquated sabre on his left side. Their barrel-shaped caps are made of marden fur and adorned by the feather of a white heron.

Once the splendid parade has come to a halt, the *alaj-čauš* gives the command 'mount!' to the knights, and salutes the company of squires with his lance. The *alkar vojvoda*, the Duke of the Alka, establishes the sequence in which the horsemen compete and announces the names and scores of the contestants. As the master of the tournament, he heads the pageant and carries a banner with the emblem of Gospa Sinjska, but does not participate in the contest himself. It is usually a highly regarded resident or honorary citizen of Sinj who holds this important and very prestigious office.

The game itself consists of three runs, and the *alkar* who has collected the most points in the end is announced *slavodobitnik*, the victor. One horseman after another is announced and has to ride the 280-metre-long racetrack (a street that is heaped up with sand for the occasion) at full gallop, aiming at the *alka*-ring with his lance. The *alka*-ring that gives the game its name consists of two concentric iron rings linked by three bars dividing the space between the rings into three equal parts. It is affixed at a height of 3.32 metres above the middle of the racetrack.

A 'hit' in the smallest central part (*u sridu*) gains the *alkar* three points, in the top part two points, and in either of the bottom parts one point. The spectators fiercely applaud every strike in the centre part; the brass band plays a flourish and a gunshot is delivered. At the end all the points are added up and the *alaj-čauš* announces the winner. Cannon shots are fired from the fortress and the winner salutes all dignitaries in the loge, foremost the envoy of the government. After this, a procession of knights and squires accompanies the victor to his home where the celebrations continue until the next morning.

History and Political Agenda of the Alka Tournament

The first written document mentioning the Sinjska Alka was recovered from an archive in Zadar and dates back to 10 February 1798. It is a duplicate of a letter written by the first Austrian emissary to Dalmatia, Duke Raimund Thurn, to the commander of Sinj, Jakov Grabovac, and contains the Austrian authorities' approval to celebrate the Alka on Shrove Tuesday 'as it hitherto has been the custom' (Dalbelo 2001, see also Š. Jurić 1987b: 63).[37] From 1849 onwards the Alka was held annually on 18 August, the birthday of the Austrian Emperor and Croatian King Franz Joseph I. Throughout the nineteenth and twentieth centuries, until 1940, the games took place regularly.[38]

During the Second World War the occupying powers did not organise the tournament. The bearer of the Order of National Hero, Peko Bogdan, however, reports that in the autumn of 1944, after the liberation of the Cetina March, steps were taken to revive the Alka tournament. The costumes, equipment and arms were mostly in the hands of individuals, the private, jealously guarded property of several families who kept them hidden during the war, waiting for better times. Consequently, there was a good chance of collecting the necessary equipment and reviving the competition. (Quoted and translated in Š. Jurić 1987b: 68)

The first tournament was thus scheduled for 19 August of the following year and attended by a special envoy from the President of the Socialist Federal Republic of Yugoslavia, Marshal Josip Broz Tito.[39] It was then decided that in commemoration of the glorious defence of the fortress of Sinj, the Alka should henceforth be held in the first part of August.

Historically, the Alka has always had a religious connotation and is inseparably linked to the celebration of Velika Gospa (Assumption Day). But under state socialism the tournament changed in its standing. Tito was well aware of the explosive potential of the Alka regarding Croatian separatist attempts, and thus tried to reduce the significance of the festival to a secular folkloristic event. Yet despite his premeditated neglect of the religious and regionalist undertone of the legend that gave rise to the Alka, Tito always acknowledged the tournament's importance as a common Yugoslav cultural asset.[40]

In 1950 Marshal Tito paid his first personal visit to Sinj and the Cetina district, and in 1978 a charter was issued proclaiming him Honorary Tournament Master, or *vojvoda*.[41] When Tito was visited by an official delegation from Sinj in Bugojno in November 1979 and presented with the emblems of his office as Honorary Tournament Master, he was allegedly very moved, and gave a speech saying:

Holding the Alka tournament as a souvenir of a victory over the Turkish invaders has profound significance for our history and represents an important manifestation not only for your region but for socialist Yugoslavia as a whole. I am glad you still celebrate regularly that victory when the people of Sinj and the Cetina March took up arms against the invader. The memory lives on among our people, always transmitted to the next generation. (Quoted and translated in Vuletić 1987: 72)

The *alkari* and their squires paid their last respects to Josip Broz Tito when they stood as honour guard by the catafalque at his funeral on 5 May 1980 (cf. Vuletić 1987: 72).

Figure 1.3. Historical images of the Sinjska Alka.
© Etnografski Muzej Sinj

After Tito's death and then after the disintegration of Yugoslavia when nationalist sentiment began to grow in the former constitutive republics, the ideals of autonomy and liberation from oppression, represented originally by the Alka, provided fertile ground for mobilisation in the emerging political situation. Local chronicles and interpretations kept accentuating the tournament's longevity and stressed that '[t]he Alka tournament has survived with few interruptions until the present day, adapted in conformity with regional characteristics, yet making a vital contribution to the formation of the ethics of heroism and self-sacrifice that have always guided the people of the Cetina district' (Grčić 1987: 17).[42] Suggesting that the 'ethics of heroism and self-sacrifice' continue to constitute a vital interpretative figure or even a frame of action for current socio-political conduct in this part of the country, the author of this statement, Marko Grčić, ascribes almost mythical qualities to the Alka. In the 1987 text *The Legend Lives On* – still quoted on the town's current website – he highlights the games' memorial function and acknowledges their significance for the formation and strengthening of local identity:

> For centuries the Alka tournament had a commemorative function that also gave the people of Sinj – who have known the blessings of peace only in the most recent times – an opportunity to engage in contests of strength and skill. These formerly impoverished peasants and shepherds, exploited by the Venetian Republic mostly as soldiers to protect its trade with the Turkish hinterland, embraced the Alka tournament as the focus of their dreams and aspirations. One might even say that the Alka gave these people, who had come from different parts of the former Turkish Empire, something in common, helped them develop their own identity. Exposed to the perils of life along the border, accustomed to taking care of themselves, the people of Sinj and the Cetina district were always ready to take arms, unwilling to let anyone else decide their fate. (Grčić 1987: 18)[43]

The emotive tone of this 'emic analysis' is a strong reminder of earlier accounts that portray the people of the Cetina district as victims, typically by stressing the physical isolation of the region, the hardship of peasant ways of life and continual political exploitation.

With the outbreak of military conflict during the 1990s, historical references to armed self-defence and readiness for combat – as they had frequently been evoked in relation to the Alka – took on a new meaning. In this way, the Alka soon became a symbol of Croatian heroism and self-defence in the country's bid for independence. The first president of the Republic of Croatia, Franjo Tuđman, revived the religious symbolism inherent in the games. From 1991 onwards, the previously forbidden song was revived:

> *Sinj celebrates its historic day today*
> *Our lady of Sinj is the queen of all*
> *Guards our faith in the centennial dream.*

The 'centennial dream' is an obvious allusion to Croatia's independence, enabling Tuđman to link this regional tradition to his nationalistic political programme in the newly created nation-state. Tuđman was declared *vojvoda*, Master of the Tournament, and under his HDZ government the Alka was officially promoted as independent Croatia's pre-eminent folkloric display of martial virtue. The idea of 'national liberation' inherent in the legend that has given rise to the Alka was 'successfully' reassigned to political discourse following the end of Socialist Party rule in Yugoslavia. Tuđman thus evoked a 'historical imagination' based on the memory of collective Croatian victimisation and resistance-based suffering. The strategy to turn affliction under foreign rule into 'moral capital' (Verdery 1996: 106ff.) and use it as a political resource has since been employed by many nationalist leaders – particularly in the Balkan region and in relation to nation-state formation after socialism (cf. Verdery 1996: 107f.).

Tomislav Z. Longinović, although in a different context, describes this process as follows: 'The destiny of small peoples is thus a symptom of the imaginary hypertrophy of their collective identity, which results from the memory of historical victimisation. This unhealed injury is then covered with stories of one's greatness, which perpetuate the historical imagination and reverberate in the literary and cultural narratives of oppressed people' (Longinović 2005: 41f.). Using the Alka as a key cultural narrative of this kind, Tuđman succeeded in constructing a Croatian imaginary of a small, victimised country with the greatness to overcome oppression and to fight heroically for its independence. This mechanism is crucial not only in understanding the national rhetoric and symbolism that facilitated the violent break-up of Yugoslavia, but also in helping to decipher the language and rationale concerning the resurgence of nationalism in current political debates on Croatia's role within Europe.

The fact that Gojko Šušak, then Croatian Minister of Defence, visited the Alka in 1994 in the midst of the Homeland War and greeted the crowds with the same salute used by the Fascist Ustaše during the Second World War illustrates the games' susceptibility to political commentary and manipulation. After the end of the Homeland War in 1995 the Alka continued to be associated with right-wing nationalist politics, although the martial tone softened over the years. The most recent Alka tournament I visited, in 2012, was very moderate in terms of the political declarations that traditionally accompany the event. So it seems that the tournament's myth of historical foundation is transferred, and adjusted according to contemporary socio-political developments.

A Local Scandal

From 2001 to 2005 former Croatian general Mirko Norac was the honorary Duke of the Alka games. Norac was the first Croatian general to be convicted of war crimes and crimes against humanity during the Homeland War. In 2001 he was sentenced to twelve years' imprisonment by a court in Rijeka. After being pronounced guilty of involvement in the 'Gospić massacre' in which more than a hundred local Serb civilians were murdered by men under his command in October 1991, powerful political anti-cooperation groups and war veteran organisations organised huge rallies in his support. Born in Otok, a small village near Sinj, Mirko Norac is closely connected to the region. After his trial, Norac reputedly said that the first thing he would do after his expected release was to participate in the Alka tournament. This statement illustrates the significance of the games as a key symbol of (military) honour and regional pride.

In consideration of the indictment of Croatian generals, the Visteško Alkarsko Društvo decided to stage the 286th Alka in 2001 as a nationalist rally in support of Mirko Norac. That February, a protest rally against the arrest of Norac was held in Sinj and thousands of people from all over Croatia and Herzegovina gathered to urge the government to stop his persecution. The *alkari* and *momci* gathered at the command of the *arambaša* and participated in the protests in full ceremonial costume – something that had happened only once before in the century-old history of the Alka, namely in 1991, at the outbreak of the Homeland War – and honoured their Duke, Mirko Norac, by announcing that they would defend him, with their own blood if need be. Under the slogan *Mirko, ne damo te, čekamo te na alci!* [Mirko, we don't hand you over, we await you at the Alka] supporters of Norac protested against his persecution and extradition to the ICTY and accused the government of treason (Paštar 2001; Vukušić 2002). The town council of Sinj proclaimed that it 'fully supported the popular rage that the indictments provoked', and the mayor of Sinj declared that the people of Sinj and the Cetina region stood under the special protection of Our Lady of Sinj who had led her knights in the war so that the Croatian nation could finally gain freedom. In these protests, a very strong anti-government sentiment prevailed and, referring to then Prime Minster Ivica Račan and President Stjepan Mesić, the crowd sang '*Oj, Ivice i Stipane, pojest će vas crne vrane*' [Hey, Ivica and Stipe, the black crows will feast on you], thus famously discrediting the politicians. Other speakers referred to the Račan government as 'Khmer Rouge', thus hinting not only at their alleged communist agenda but also indirectly accusing them of betrayal and of performing criminal acts against their own people by extraditing heroic Croatian 'defenders'.[44]

In the summer of that year, declarations of solidarity with the general were omnipresent, and the slogan *Svi smo mi Mirko Norac* [We are all Mirko Norac] confirmed that large parts of the population – headed by the people of the Sinjska krajina – supported his case and did not consider him a war criminal, but a hero. Before the actual tournament started, placards with the slogan 'We are all Mirko Norac' were handed out to the audience; and whenever the name Mirko Norac was mentioned, the crowds chanted 'Mirko, Mirko!', whereas thousands of people in the audience booed whenever the name of then president Mesić was mentioned.[45]

Figure 1.4. Sinjska Alka held in honour of ex-general Mirko Norac in 2001. Photo: courtesy of Brigita Malenica

The local newspaper *Slobodna Dalmacija* wrote that 'the first Alka in the third millennium was characterised by Mirko Norac, who was not physically present, but nevertheless ubiquitous ... The games will stick in our memory because of the public demonstration of dissatisfaction with the present state authorities' (*Slobodna Dalmacija*, 6 August 2001). In the opening speech, the Duke of the Alka, Ante Kotromanović, dedicated the 2001 tournament to the *branitelji* (lit. defenders), by name to Mirko Norac, whom he addressed as 'my personal friend, the Alka Duke General Mirko Norac', Lieutenant General Ante Gotovina and Major General Rahim Ademi. He said:

Waiting for the moment of the creation of an independent, autonomous Croatian state, the Croatian people have suffered terribly through history and endured several different rulers. But we have never given up hope of welcoming a free and independent Croatia, for which our best sons have sacrificed their lives ... How many times have we experienced them shelling our Sinj and surrounding villages, when those, who were neighbours until yesterday – some of them even *alkari* – broke the dam Peruča in a unprecedented insane and hysterical manner in an attempt to destroy everything downstream from the source of the Cetina. But, like in 1715, a miracle occurred and the Croatian people, led by their *branitelji*, led by the present Croatian martyrs Norac, Gotovina, Ademi, at great cost of life succeeded in beating the enemy from Vukovar to Dubrovnik, although they were poorly armed and unprepared for battle ... On the very day that we should celebrate and be proud of the glorious victory of the Croatian people, on this day we persecute the Croatian generals, defenders of the homeland, we denounce them as criminals, false invalids, false defenders. As the Duke of the Alka, today I say 'no', it is not true ... We are not the ones who are false. From 1991 to 1995 we did our duty to the pride and delight of the Croatian people. Croatia is liberated and a state has been created upon our blood, upon our dead, our wounded, our missing. False are those who condemn us, who pulled us into quicksand, those who make promises, but do not keep them, hypocrites, demagogues – we also call them politicians ... A people who liberated their country cannot be perpetrators. And therefore I call on the Croatian nation, who already in 1715 resisted their occupiers and in 1991 decisively supported the defence of Croatia's independence, to oppose the criminalisation of the Homeland War and the criminalisation of legitimate rescue missions of the Croatian Army ... Simply be Croats![46]

The audience enthusiastically received this heated speech that quite bluntly and unscrupulously names culprits and innocents. Its rhetoric and tone are paragons of nationalist agitation, based on militarised narratives of historical (self-)victimisation and local heroism. The general atmosphere was very agitated and anti-government. During the Alka festivities the attending representative of then President Mesić, General Milivoj Petković, was repeatedly insulted: at first, the *alkari* refused to be photographed with him. Then, every time his name was mentioned, the audience whistled and booed. And after the games, the winner of the tournament refused to accept the golden ring and sword that are traditionally handed to the victor by a government delegate. In a closing remark Mate Jukić, then president of the Viteško Alkarsko Društvo and mayor of Sinj, explained that presidential gifts could not be accepted while honorary Alka Duke General Mirko Norac remained in jail.[47] Instead, the winner of the tournament donated his prize money to a monetary fund established to cover the costs of the defence of Mirko Norac.

According to numerous conversations with interlocutors and friends in Sinj, the reasons for nationalists' antipathy to Mesić's government, but even more to him as a person, are manifold. In September 2000 Mesić dismissed seven active Croatian generals who had written open letters to the public accusing the government of 'campaigning to criminalise the Homeland War' and 'denigrating and neglecting the Croatian Army', reproaches that were almost literally repeated during the 2001 Alka speeches. These measures clearly did not win him the sympathy of people who revere the generals as heroes in the country's struggle for independence. Another grievance was that Mesić had testified at the International Criminal Tribunal for the Former Yugoslavia (ICTY) that implicated the Croatian army in the war in Bosnia and Herzegovina. In reaction to this testimony (which many also see as full of falsehoods) several nationalists branded him an *izdajnik*, a traitor, willing to put his own people's head on the block for the sake of Croatian membership of the European Union and NATO. He was widely insulted as a 'Croatian Judas' who betrayed the Croatian people by associations of war veterans and other nationalist groups. During the Alka in 2001, the audience thus celebrated Norac as a personification of virtue, but scolded '*Mesiću, cigane!*' [Mesić, Gypsy!], a racist reference that was meant to indicate that the president was a shifty and dishonest character – a hypocritical, demagogic politician *par excellence*, as described in Kotromanović's inauguration speech. Since this scandal, the Alka's reputation as a gala of regional resistance to state authority and a stronghold of ultra-right-wing attitudes consolidated in the years to follow.

A Changing Game

The Alka Tournament in 2005, 2007 and 2012

To this day it is impossible to visit the town of Sinj without noticing references to the Alka everywhere. Not only does the town bear an Alka horseman on its coat of arms, but numerous sculptures, statues, reliefs and other depictions throughout town serve as a visual memento of the legendary battle underpinning the tournament. One of the first things one sees on the road from Split is a dark cast iron sculpture of an *ulkar* on horseback (*Spomenik Sinjskoj Alci*) by the local artist Stipe Sikirica dating from 1965. It is located at the start of the Alka racetrack. Another rather conspicuous Alka representation can be found in the municipal park where a massive stone fountain is composed of three larger-than-life *momci* who jointly carry a huge *alka*-ring above their head, symbolising local unity and strength (*Fontana Tri Momka*). The town also hosts an Alka museum, while a number of shops, restaurants and hotels are named after allusions to the Alka. During the summer, children play with lances and *alka*-rings in the streets. Even flowerbeds in the park are planted in the shape of an *alka*-ring. In short, the lived-in environment of Sinj and the Sinjska krajina is visibly linked to the Alka.

It is therefore not surprising that I was very excited when in the course of my fieldwork in 2005 the date of the actual games approached. I had heard countless stories about the event and its significance for the locals, and thus anticipated that attending in person would be one of the highlights of my research. And indeed, in the midst of the summer heat of August 2005, the sleepy little town turned into an arena of colourful folkloristic performances and re-enacted history. The images of grim-looking extravagantly bearded *momci* and proud *alkari* in traditional costumes that commonly feature on postcards, websites and in tourist guides of the region were awakened. A celebration of regional tradition and virtue, the 290th Alka grounded itself in the dramatic or dramatised self-presentation of Dalmatian manhood, and culminated in a contest of (male) excellence and skill.

On 7 August I positioned myself in the first row of the spectator stand with my video camera, trying to capture some of the visual richness and vibrancy of the performance. And although it proved impossible to record the actual sensory versatility of the performance, I still managed to catch a glimpse of the general excitement caused by the event. The atmosphere was enormously charged, and a spirit of insubordination and historical self-importance seemed to reign in the town. Four years after the No-rac scandal the games were still performed in honour of the imprisoned ex-general. Days before the actual event, posters and placards of Norac on horseback wearing the traditional Alka costume were put up all over town. They featured slogans that not only proclaimed solidarity with him but also declared him a national liberator and hero. I also learned that the profits of the Alka were paid into a fund launched to finance a legal appeal on behalf of Norac (*Slobodna Dalmacija*, 8 August 2005).

Figure 1.5. Poster with the slogan 'The truth and the people are on your side – Mirko Norac, Croatian General', displayed in Sinj in 2005. Photo: M. Schäuble

After the impressive opening parade of the horsemen, the Croatian national anthem was sung. The audience was asked to pay tribute 'to the first Croatian president Dr Franjo Tuđman, defence minister Gojko Šušak, and all those who died in the Homeland War fighting for Croatia's independence', followed by a minute of silence. A representative of the Alka Association delivered the following speech (in excerpts):

> At this historical moment when some try to [stain] our history and when all the basic values of man and homeland are being trampled on, it is good to be reminded of these words by a dear unknown poet of the Cetina district:
>
> 'We have been what we are / We are what we have been'
> [*Mi bili smo što jesmo / Jesmo što smo bili*]
>
> We could ask ourselves: What is the value of everything that has been done through the centuries? What is the value of the victims and of all that has been achieved through the blood of [our] martyrs – that which is now destroyed and despised and which should be sacred to us? Without respect for the permanent values and without [acknowledgement of] the real truth about us and our past, there is no way to build a future ...
>
> A couple of days ago we celebrated the tenth anniversary of the military operation Oluja, which was another demonstration of what it is to love, honour and defend our country and its freedom. Like the *bura* from the Dinara, our defenders chased away the bloody clouds of evil that came over Croatia. With a rosary around their necks and under the watchful eye of the first Croatian president and honorary Alka Duke, Dr Franjo Tuđman, they fulfilled the millennial Croatian dream [and] returned unity and dignity to the Croatian people. On this festive day we should all pay tribute to the Croatian *branitelji*, and their sacrifice for the homeland.

A round of gunfire from the fortress marked the end of the speech.

Like Kotromanović's speech four years ago, this address also paradigmatically exemplifies the systematic blending of past and present forms of subjugation that is employed to substantiate the image of a victimised Croatian nation in need of protection and self-defence. The image of suffering evoked here shows how a people can draw on an experience of repression over the centuries and deploy it as an argument in favour of preserving ancient values and practices. Further, in crediting the heroic

sacrifices and martyrdom of the Croatian *branitelji* with the people's escape from continual oppression to independence, this Alka spokesman
contributes to a widespread scheme of 'organised innocence' (Jalušić
2004: 40–67) that ultimately sustains the legitimacy of war and violence.

The moment the national anthem was solemnly intoned, it became
clear that the Alka's scope cannot be fully grasped unless its prevailing political agenda is noted. Holding a minute of silence for 'Dr Franjo
Tuđman, defence minister Gojko Šušak and all those who died in the
Homeland War fighting for Croatia's independence' set the political tone
and revealed the underlying nationalistic character of the event. In this
context it is relevant to keep in mind that it was mainly due to Šušak's
extremist ideas that Tuđman's regime aspired to annex parts of Bosnia-
Herzegovina with a majority Croatian population – including Western
Herzegovina. Šušak's radical political course initiated the proclamation
of the wartime entity Hrvatska Republika Herceg-Bosna (Croatian Republic of Herceg-Bosnia) on the territory of Bosnia and Herzegovina in
1991, and eventually led to war between Bosnian Croats and Muslims,
who had been previously allied against the Serbs.[48] Even members of
their own party considered the politics of Tuđman and Šušak in Bosnia
and Herzegovina to be too radical, and in 1994 a group of officials consequently left the HDZ. One of them was Stjepan Mesić who did not
support Croatia's expansionist plans in the early 1990s.

The fact, however, that Tuđman and Šušak are honoured in the Alka
address and mentioned along with those who died 'fighting for Croatia's
independence' rehabilitates their extremist political aspirations. They
are treated as the founding fathers of the independent Croatian nation-
state and thus symbolically transformed into heroic ancestors, on whose
'sacrifices' the country has been built. The reference to Mirko Norac
then puts the imprisoned ex-general on a par with these 'historical figures' and promotes him as a local dignitary of nationwide importance.

The speaker's mention of the rosary 'around the neck' of the Croatian
branitelji during the Homeland War is an allusion to the well-known
saga according to which every soldier of the Hrvatska Vojska (Croatian
Army) wore a blessed rosary on his uniform as he went into battle. The
role of the Virgin Mary as advocate and military patron saint is symbolised by the rosary as an 'ancient weapon of Catholic Christianity' (cf.
Scheer 2006: 358).[49] The rosary is thus a key symbol not only of the Catholic faith but also of politicised Marian veneration and Marian support
of Catholic military forces in general. In the Croatian case, the soldier's
rosary has become a renowned symbol of the divine protection of the
Croatian army, and is habitually invoked in all depictions of Croatia's
victory in the Homeland War as reflecting the will of God.[50]

Containing almost every motif, metaphor and argument that typically features in nationalist narratives, this speech not only conveys a victim-turned-victor's sense of history but also evokes a mythological past in order to create a collective sense of identity among the addressees. One of the key concepts recurrently mentioned is 'truth', or rather 'the real truth' about Croatia's history. In the slogan 'We have been what we are / We are what we have been', the speaker declares tradition and historical awareness of the core elements of 'Croatianness'. In the politics of truth employed here, however, historical facts are stretched to match an emotional state. And within this frame of mind, tradition is seen as a representation of the 'real truth' that reaches beyond mere facts; that is to say, the 'divine truth'. To underline this point, the speaker employs a discourse of constant threat to the 'real truth' and constructs a figurative opposition between pollution (by those who 'stain' the history and 'trample on the values of the homeland') and sacredness of the homeland (marked by those who have 'regained honour and liberty'). This assumed threat – posed by unspecified external as well as internal enemies – particularly concerns the depreciation of tradition and traditional values, explicitly 'honesty, integrity, heroism and courage'. The speech thus appeals to a constant need for vigilance and (militarised) self-defence, and declares local values and rituals to be elements of a 'pure' national Croatian culture, thereby promoting the (re-)enactment of autochthonous tradition.

It is in this context that the speaker then also refers to the historical battle against the Turks in 1715. However, the most astonishing element of the 2005 Alka speech, at least in my perception, is neither the indication of century-long victimisation nor the mention of Croatia's finally fulfilled 'thousand-year-old dream' of independence, but the reference to the naturalistic character of history as represented by the wind, water and soil of Sinjsko polje. By calling the source of the River Cetina a source of inspiration for the future and by comparing the past to the wind blowing from the Dinaric mountains, the speaker links the region's history with its landscape, with its environmental features. In this respect, he adopts and re-evaluates earlier ascriptions according to which places and natural phenomena are metonymically and metaphorically ascribed and tied to identities. The Serbian aggression is metaphorically compared to 'bloody clouds of evil that came over Croatia' that have been chased away by the cold north wind, the *bura* – the *bura* being used both as a symbol for the 'sounds of the past' as well as the Croatian *branitelji* during Operacija Oluja. It becomes clear that the speaker is far from acknowledging any attack on Serbian civilians or eviction of them that might have occurred but is, on the contrary, ostensibly recounting the 'real truth' that involves exclusively the suffering and consequent courageous self-defence of Croats. 'Croatianness' is not only constructed as real and placed alongside an imagined pantheon of heroic ancestors but is also directly linked to territory, thus indicating that 'Croatian soil' is the exclusive national homeland of Croats.

After this agitated inaugural speech, the actual tilting competition was held in strict accordance with the statute. The audience enthusiastically supported the contestants, and occasional cannon shots and fanfares accompanied the ovations whenever one of the *alkari* managed to hit *u sridu*, the central ring. The whole event was vibrant and ornate, but because of a sudden heavy thunderstorm the concluding prize-giving ceremony was kept rather brief and the audience quickly dispersed after the winner had been announced.

During the tournament I had noticed an elderly women sitting on one of the wooden benches of the spectator stands. She was dressed in black and held up two posters attached to a wooden handle. One of the placards was a replica of the Gospa Sinjska with the inscription *Čudotvorna Gospe Sinjska moli za nas!* [Miraculous Lady of Sinj, pray for us]. The lower one depicted General Norac, and provocatively said

Figure 1.6. Lady attending the Sinjska Alka in 2005, displaying posters of Gospa Sinjska and of Croatian ex-general Mirko Norac. Photo: M. Schäuble

Ako smo slobodni, ne dajmo osloboditelje! [If we were free we wouldn't extradite our liberators!]. This was one of the posters distributed during the Alka in 2001 in support of Mirko Norac.

This combination of creed and political commentary points towards the close connection between the veneration of religious figures and militarised hero-worship in post-war Croatian society. It can be understood as an example of local protest by which a community – represented through a number of individuals – stresses its complaint at what is communally perceived as political marginalisation and systematic sidelining. Along with ethnicist and traditionalist speeches like the one quoted above, such expressions of dissent articulate severe critique and ultimately imply the rejection of official authorities. 'Removed from the urban centres of power, resentful of what they see as their systematic neglect at the hands of politicians, [the villagers] express hostility to any source of authority outside the local community … In short, they use the argument of inequality to represent their rebellious actions as a redressive form of reciprocity' (Herzfeld 1985: 19). What Herzfeld describes here for the case of 'outlaw' Crete mountain villages equally applies to Sinj: the rejection of official authorities or officialdom is largely expressed as an act of defiance in response to marginalisation and global invisibility. And just like the Cretan highlanders described by Herzfeld, most Dalmatians do not compromise their 'loyalty to the principle of national identity (as opposed to loyalty to the bureaucratic state)' but claim moral excellence above all other Croats instead. The current formation of protest against state authority and supra-regional influences draws back on the long tradition of political, and also military, resistance in the Dalmatinska Zagora; and the 'campaign' of the elderly woman against the legal prosecution of General Norac is but one demonstration of the power that religious images, narratives and cults can develop when they are mobilised and reinterpreted in a context of political events.

The Alka as a Barometer of Political Change

Two years later, in August 2007, and five years after his delegate was hissed down in Sinj, the then Croatian president, Stjepan Mesić, visited Sinj and personally attended the 292nd Alka. Despite the absolute political dominance of the national HDZ in this region and widespread disapproval of the presidential political course, Mesić thanked the residents of Sinj for their invitation and he assured the audience that his presence reflected the radical changes within the Visteško Alkarsko Društvo. For the first time there was no commemorative silence held for former defence minister Gojko Šušak, although President Tuđman was still honoured as he had been in previous years. However, the tone and obvious importance of the speech Mesić delivered at this occasion gives ground for speculation that he may have strategically launched his 'entrance' in order to propagate and promote his pro-European political agenda.

Mesić was extremely unpopular in Sinj and I have repeatedly observed people spitting spitefully at the television set when he appeared on screen. I have also heard frequent 'death threat' wishes whenever conversation turned to him (for example: 'If only I was a good sniper, I would have shot him a long time ago', or 'If he came to Sinj he would not only be booed at but assassinated'). Yet despite this open hostility, Mesić decided to visit Sinj, and what is more, he came to visit during the Alka – a time when the unruly nationalist spirit in the region is customarily at its height. It is thus quite obvious that Mesić used this symbolically charged occasion to blaze a trail and to give a clear political signal that he was not intimidated by nationalist threats seeking to sabotage his political course.

In his speech he first of all acknowledged that the Alka tournament had always been recognised as a knightly competition symbolising the heroic town of Sinj and region of Cetina. Subsequently, however, he declared that it was now time for the Alka to overcome its localised political significance and to strive to become an event of much larger scope:

> [The] Alka symbolises the freedom-loving spirit of Sinj, the Cetina region as well as of all Croatia, and a spirit that we reaffirmed in the antifascist struggle and in the Homeland War, and that we are reaffirming today by building a free and democratic Croatia. That's why [the] Sinjska Alka doesn't and cannot have significance only for locals, but for us all, for the Croatian people and all Croatian citizens ... [The] Alka is the holy day for all of us who respect the courage, patriotism and sacrifices of all our ancestors in the struggle for justice and freedom. Today [the] Alka is part of the Croatian cultural heritage, and in the future, as a non-material monument of culture, it should become part of the European and world cultural heritage as well.

By acknowledging and honouring the local significance of the Alka while simultaneously decoupling it from its rebellious tendency and separatist connotation, Mesić intended to defuse the explosive potential of the games as a publicity campaign of the political Right.[51] His strategic inclusion of the Alka into a communal network – by emphasising the unifying rather than dividing character of the games as a tradition shared by 'all Croatian citizens' – aimed primarily at averting 'political divisions'.

At first sight, he used the same rhetoric and catchwords commonly applied in nationalist speeches (i.e. 'courage', 'patriotism', 'sacrifice', 'struggle for justice and freedom'). In contrast to the speech given two years earlier, however, Mesić connected these catchwords neither to 'ethnicity' nor to apprehensive notions of Croatian (self-)victimisation. Instead, he mentioned them in one breath with the 'anti-fascist struggle', the 'Homeland War' and a 'free and democratic Croatia'. This (rather unanticipated) attempt to create a more optimistic climate is also mirrored in Mesić's appeal to Croatian citizens – and in this speech, to the citizens of Sinj in particular – to participate actively in current processes of transformation and democratisation, and to contribute to shaping Croatia's path to Europe. In doing so, he also included and deliberately challenged those who were most opposed to these processes and who had most audibly been blaming the state and state politics in general for their unfavourable situation.

Promoting this forward-thinking perspective, Mesić was in my view also trying to de-essentialise notions of 'identity', 'ethnicity' and 'the homeland', among others. This provides a potentially liberating reaction towards the Alka's oppressively collectivist ideology that ties an ethno-national group to a common origin and identities to a specific territory. (Ethno-)nationality is territorialised and thus entails an essentialised notion of belonging. Mesić's speech can thus be interpreted as an attempt to oppose the territorialising efforts of nationalist movements and to de-couple territoriality and nationality. He promoted a move towards a deterritorialised, non-national citizenship compatible with a form of liberal globalisation – or 'global liberalization', as Jansen and Löfving pointedly put it (Jansen and Löfving 2007: 8).

In this context, Mesić's mention of the Alka as a part of European and world cultural heritage referred to the attempts of the Visteško Alkarsko Društvo to include the Alka in UNESCO's protective register of non-material cultural world heritage – a plan that was realised in 2010 when the Alka was finally inscribed in UNESCO Intangible Cultural Heritage lists. By not reducing the Alka to a mere folkloristic spectacle but speaking of it as an event with the potential to represent the country's international image, Mesić tried to revive the tradition in a different, if not even a diametrically opposing, direction. He consequently closed his address with the words: 'Croatia's future is a united Europe founded on anti-fascism, democracy, tolerance, [and] respect for and exercise of human and minority rights. Croatia's future is a Europe in which borders connect, not separate, a community of equal states and peoples' (ibid.). According to these concluding remarks, the intention of his speech was to re-signify the symbolic potential of the Alka and link it to EU politics, to NATO membership and to more general attitudes towards globalisation. Mesić countered the 'ethics' conventionally associated with the Alka, such as readiness for combat, military courage and national unity, with an ideology of anti-fascism, democracy, tolerance and equality. Attempting to redefine the Alka without discounting the 'freedom-loving spirit' of the region, Mesić rather skilfully managed to link the games with his vision of a European Croatia that has permeable national borders 'that connect and do not separate' – a vision that eventually indicates concepts such as transnationality and multiculturalism.

Furthermore, his plea for the enforcement of human and minority rights appealed both to Croatian domestic policy and to the European Convention on Human Rights that all EU members must sign. Human rights narratives, however, are commonly ridiculed and rejected by Croatian nationalists and juxtaposed to an allegedly more enduring set of values, such as love of native soil. Mesić, on the other hand, implicitly advocated egalitarianism by invoking the universalist principle that all people are equal by virtue of human rights. However, it is evident that the Alka has become the site of a discursive battle in which different sides compete for entitlements to interpret the past and to define the 'real truth' – represented by 'the truth about [the] Alka's past as well as future' – and link it to a particular set of political convictions and aims.

Five years later, in 2012, I attended the Alka again, and once more I was surprised at how much the tone of the speeches had mellowed and at how the atmosphere during the games had changed. By coincidence, in 2012 the day of the Alka tournament was held on 5 August and hence fell on the same day as the seventeenth anniversary of Operation Oluja. But instead of using this occasion for further tirades of hate against 'evildoers from the East' and invoking threats to Croatia's integrity, the organisers staged a relatively undramatic event. Up to the opening of the actual tournament it was not clear if ex-general Mirko Norac would participate in the games, and many people eagerly anticipated his appearance. In November 2011 he was released from prison on probation and so the 2012 Alka was the first opportunity for him to make good on his promise that the first thing he would do after serving his sentence would be to ride the Alka. Therefore it came as a surprise that not only was he not present in person but that no mention of his name was made throughout the entire tournament. The speakers omitted any reference to his participation in Operation Oluja and hence avoided any allusions to the supposedly unjust conviction of Croatian generals and any rants of hate against the ICTY. Instead, the Turkish ambassador visited the games as the first representative from Turkey in nearly three hundred years. His presence was enthusiastically acclaimed by the audience and was highlighted as a sign of reconciliation and settlement of century-old animosities.

Ivo Josipović, who had taken office as Croatian president in 2010, was also greeted very warmly, despite the fact that he, a Social Democrat, had previously delivered a speech to the Parliamentary Assembly of Bosnia-Herzegovina in which he expressed deep regret for Croatia's involvement in efforts to divide Bosnia and Herzegovina in the 1990s – a speech that amounted to a confession of Croatian war guilt in Bosnia and was condemned by the members of the Croatian Democratic Union (HDZ).

None of this caused any disturbance to the procedure of the tournament, and no protests were voiced. As in previous years, the national anthem was sung and a minute of silence was held for the victims of the Homeland War. In his address, the *vojvoda* referred to the Alka as 'a living image of the past' whose 'message empowers us in the times of the present economic crisis that calls for so many sacrifices from Croatia, from Europe and from the world. The heritage of the Alka is an inspiration to us: we have learned to never give up … therefore we will contribute to a fast denouement of this present crisis'. He ended his speech with the words, 'We run this tournament for all those who lost their lives for Croatia', which was concluded by cannon shots. In his closing speech, after the tournament had finished and the winner announced, President Josipović called it 'fortuitous' that the Alka and the 'Victory and Homeland Thanksgiving Day and the Day of Croatian Defenders' fell on the same date so that 'Croatia could spread the message of peace through the Alka tournament'. He referred to the presence of the Turkish ambassador as a sign for this new direction pursued by Croatia in general and by the Alka of Sinj in particular.

Interestingly, my host family, who followed the games and the speeches on television, were quite pleased with Josipović's comments and rated his address as 'apolitical'. Although most people in Sinj are strongly opposed to the president's centre-left political course, he is perceived as a 'cultured man', and he does not provoke the same aggressive reactions as Stjepan Mesić did. Josipović's speech at the 297th Alka in 2012, however, can be seen as a direct continuation of the changed direction initiated by Mesić in 2007 in which the latter defined the Alka as a nationwide – not regionally specific – tradition signifying the overcoming of borders (in a symbolic as well as a material sense) instead of a drawing and/or defence of boundaries, as initially designated.

In just over ten years, between 2001 and 2012, the prevailing tone at the Alka tournament has changed from an openly right-wing and nationalist propaganda platform to a plea for peace and reconciliation. Considering these recent developments, it seems appropriate to view the Alka as a paradigmatic indicator or barometer of the political atmosphere in Croatia. The excerpts of the four different speeches briefly presented here denote the clash between the government's move towards Europe and a genuinely nationalist worldview in which Croatia is constructed as potentially threatened and in need of protection from foreign influences. According to public opinion in Sinj, Mesić belongs among those who, as the representative of the Alka Tournament Association put it in his speech in 2005, side with the international aggressors and thus potentially 'stain' the history and 'trample on the values of the homeland'. Due to his earlier political about-face and his later pro-European politics, during his period of office Mesić was commonly accused of betraying Croatia and/or of being a puppet of international politics. He himself, on the contrary, was eager to reassure the people of Sinj that he was opting for an alternative form of 'globalisation' and integration into Europe that is anchored in traditional local practices. In this context, I would interpret his speech as an attempt to emphasise the optimistic possibilities that democratisation and participation in political processes could provide for everybody – not just for the political elites. And in direct continuation of this message, Josipović's appearance must be understood as a plea for a new (social-democratic) imaginary that is consciously set off against nationalist populism. It has become quite obvious that the Alka's radical political impetus and its tendency towards cultural fundamentalism have started to decline.

The reactions of my host family in Sinj indicate that – contrary to all expectations and despite all previously uttered threats directed at Mesić and other 'pro-European' opinion leaders – the locals are overall quite pleased with the official attention the Alka has received in recent years. Since the Alka is under the protection of UNESCO as a 'world intangible heritage', it has come to represent the whole of Croatia and obtains an important status as a symbol of Croatness [*hrvatstvo*]. This visibility increased when a parade of *alkari* and *momci* in full attire represented Croatia upon the country's entry into the European Union in July 2013. It was agreed that an Alka procession would march on Luxembourg Square in front of the European Parliament in Brussels and, as the newspaper *Slobodna Dalmacija* reported, even the possibility of heaping up a sand racetrack in the town centre to hold a tournament was seriously discussed. According to the news report, members of the Alka Association refrained from this idea, however, on the grounds that according to the Alka statutes only a tournament held in Sinj on the original track could be considered a proper Sinjska Alka.[52]

It is, of course, a rather ironic twist of history that a tournament that epitomises rebellion against foreign domination and state authority is now to represent the Republic of Croatia within the European Union. As I have shown, the tournament has been used as a platform to articulate fierce nationalist and anti-European sentiment in the past, and has fuelled rather than appeased existing antagonisms in the region. Only recently did the Alka Association, with the backing of pro-European politicians, reinvent the games as a festival through which 'Croatia could spread the message of peace', as Josipović expressed it. Now the small, hitherto insignificant town of Sinj is all of a sudden vaulted into the centre of Croatian political power where the heads of state, the prime minister and members of Parliament gather to represent the unity of the government and to discuss the future of Croatia within Europe.

These developments give reason to believe that a wider recognition of the Alka might promote a further defusing of the subversive and potentially volatile political capacity of the event. On the other hand, notwithstanding the suspicion and disdain cast on the Alka so far by urban middle-class Croats, the fact that the festival is planned to serve as a prime example of Croatia's cultural and folkloristic wealth does simultaneously reaffirm the conservative notion that the future of the country lies in a return to its traditions and history. Furthermore, this singularisation of Dalmatia's and Sinj's folkloristic heritage, and the message that the Alka is considered exemplary for Croatia's new public image in Europe, might strengthen the already prevalent conception that the region is 'authentically traditional' and thus superior to other parts of Croatia.

Notes

1. A newspaper report including the heated political speech by Ante Kotromanović, the *vojvodin* or 'duke' of the 286th Alka in 2001, can be found at http://arhiv.slobodnadalmacija.hr/20010806/novosti1.htm, last accessed on 10 October 2012.
2. Due to a deed of donation of the Hungarian-Croatian king, Ludwig I, the 'fortress of Sign' and the whole of the Cetinska krajina were assigned to Count Ivan II Nelipić in 1354. This document contains the first written mention of what is today known as the town of Sinj. For a detailed historical account of the Sinjska krajina from the thirteenth to the mid-twentieth century, see Stulli 1967/68: 5–93.
3. In his *History of the Roman Provinces in Dalmatia*, J.J. Wilkes identifies the fortress of the citadel of modern Sinj as a settlement of the Dalmatae south of the Dinaric Alps. The settlement was called Osinium by the Romans and is identical to the Late Roman castle Asinio (Wilkes 1969: 347, 396).

4. The Venetian chronicler Sanuto noted that in March 1511 the fortress of Sinj was set on fire by the Turks (see also Jurić 1965). In 1513 two further attacks on Sinj were recorded.

5. Written in Italian, this eye-witness account kept presently in the archive of the Franciscan monastery in Sinj, contains a detailed description of the events from the appearance of the Turkish army on Mt. Prolog on 23 July 1715 until its withdrawal into Bosnia on 15 August 1715.

6. Letter to Signor Marsili, Professor of Botany in the University of Padua, Fellow of the Royal Society, etc. (Fortis 1778: 223).

7. For a selected overview of printed sources as well as travel books on Dalmatia from 1485 to the present day, see Masturzo and Colognola 2005.

8. Fortis's anthropological approach and his account of the rural Slavic Dalmatians was of general interest to philosophers of the Enlightenment, particularly in the context of Voltaire's emphasis on 'custom' in 1754 and Rousseau's notion of the 'noble savage' in the *Discours sur l'origine de l'inégalité* of 1755 (Masturzo and Colognola 2005: 23; see also Wolff 2001: 156–57), as they were commonly described as strong, tough, hearty, but also sincere, hospitable, honest, noble and reliable (see Gulin 1997: 84). As early as in 1775 Goethe's 'Klagegesang der edlen Frauen des Asan Aga', rendered as a translation 'aus dem Morlackischen', was incorporated in Herder's *Volkslieder*-collection published in 1778 and 1779 (Wolff 2001: 130, 190). The epic that is widely known as 'Hasanaginica' had originally been collected, transcribed and translated into Italian by Fortis. The first novel based on Fortis's description is *Les Morlaques* by Giustiniana Wynne (1788).

9. The English translation of *Travels into Dalmatia* was published in London (Fortis 1778).

10. Comparison between the Dalmatians and North American Indians became a widespread cliché and feature prominently in many nineteenth- and twentieth-century travel accounts. In *Dalmatia, the Quarnero, and Istria*, Thomas Graham Jackson, for instance, described Morlacchi women as 'half-savage looking creatures [wearing embroidered leggings] that give them the appearance of Indian squaws' (Jackson 1887: 203). Alice Moqué also referred to Dalmatian women's 'embroidered leggins, which are worked in colored thread and adorned with many beads like the leggings and moccasins of an American Indian' (Moqué 1914: 60). And Maude Holbach remarked, of Dalmatian women she photographed in the market of Zadar, that 'at the first glance they seemed to me more like North American Indians than any European race' (Holbach 1908: 31).

11. In a Croatian census in 1991, twenty-two people declared themselves 'Morlachs' by ethnicity – most probably a subversive way of avoiding ethno-nationalist classifications that were heavily on the rise in Croatia in the early 1990s.

12. When the first elementary school in Sinj was to be opened in 1798, the Austrian governor in Zadar Pietro Goess opposed this initiative and wrote in an official report to the minister that 'there is no need to build schools for

the Vlachs, it is enough if they know their duties as Christians and subjects. One need only encourage among them the heroic and fighting spirit necessary for populations living on the borders of the Turkish Empire' (quoted and translated in Jurić 1987a: 35f.). This illustrates that the population of the Dalmatian hinterland was basically considered to be cannon fodder whose role in the Empire was restricted to guarding the border region.

13. Fortis was also the first to collect and record the rich variety of folk tales of the Sinjska Krajina (see Bošković-Stulli 1968).

14. This observation corresponds with Lovrić's remark in 1776 that '[t]he errors of certain illustrious writers often obtain such dominion over the minds of many men, that it takes centuries, and not years, to eradicate them' (Lovrić [1776] 1948: 6, quoted and translated in Wolff 2001: 237).

15. Fortis's book is widely known and very popular in Croatia, and I had been referred to it several times as a source of still valid information about Dalmatia. In August 2005 the newspaper *Slobodna Damlamcija* published a Croatian-language reprint of *Put po Dalmaciji* which sold out within hours.

16. One of my interlocutors once said: 'The English have not produced anything apart from imperialism and slavery … They don't have their own culture and stole everything from elsewhere – mainly from the colonies. The English are like the Serbs – they don't have their own culture'.

17. The Croatian expression *praviti se Englezom* that literally translates as 'to behave English' is a periphrasis for 'to play dumb' and illustrates how prejudices about the English even show up in figures of speech and popular sayings.

18. The best-known is the Split-Sinj-Livno caravan track connecting Bosnia with the Adriatic Sea.

19. Whilst Tuđman was busy writing a new constitution, many Serbian families began to find that the disparaging term 'Četnik' had been smeared on their front doors. The journalist Misha Glenny writes: 'Although some 200,000 Serbs lived in Zagreb, they had become disenfranchised from society, just as the Croats in the Krajina had been' (Glenny 1992: 162).

20. Jerry Blaskovich reports that 94% of the region's 158 Roman Catholic churches had either been destroyed or damaged during this time (Blaskovich 1997).

21. The international community imposed a weapons embargo, which hardly affected JNA-backed Serb forces, but heavily weakened the young Croatian army.

22. A year later, in April 1992, the Bosnian Croats in Herzegovina set up their own militia, the Hrvatsko Vijeće Obrane (Croatian Defence Council), or HVO.

23. The United States, which had an interest in pushing the Serbs to negations in Dayton, played an important role in Operation Storm under NATO's flag. They assisted the Croatian Army with logistical and communications issues and in clearing Serb blockades. On 4 August 1995, a United States Air Force plane bombed two Croatian Serb surface-to-air missile radar sites near Knin and Udbina.

24. In Croatian public discourse it is highly disputed whether the Serbian civilians were forced out or left of their own accord. By November 1995, however, UNPROFOR, the UN peacekeeping force in Croatia, had documented the deaths of more than two hundred people in the area.

25. The Croatian Colonel General Ivan Čermak, Colonel General Mladen Markač and Brigadier (later General) Ante Gotovina were indicted on the grounds of personal and command responsibility for war crimes carried out against Serb civilians in the Krajina. In April 2011 Ante Gotovina was sentenced to twenty-four years and Mladen Markač to eighteen years in jail for crimes including murder, persecution and plunder. Ivan Čermak was cleared of all charges. The verdicts on Gotovina and Markač caused huge protests among the Croatian government and public, as the men are regarded as heroes by many. In November 2012 the initial 2011 verdict was overturned, and Markač and Gotovina were acquitted by the ICTY.

26. During the war, up to 2 million landmines were laid in Croatia, and 1,888 people have been involved in mine incidents since 1991, out of which 492 were killed and 1,103 have suffered major bodily injuries. A decade after the end of the war, in January 2006, the Croatian Mine Action Centre (CROMAC) estimated that there were still 250,000 mines in the ground. By then, an area of nearly 1,200 square kilometres with a population of 1.1 million was still contaminated by mines and other explosive remnants of war. Although the de-mining was planned to be completed by 2010, more recent reports state that there were still 90,000 mines remaining in 2012 and a complete de-mining of territory will not be achieved until 2019. For further information see the *National Mine Action Strategy of the Republic of Croatia* at http://www.hcr.hr/pdf/Strategija%20eng.pdf

27. Croatia passed a General Amnesty law pardoning everyone who did not take an active part in the war.

28. In the afternoon of the 15th of every month, a mass is held at the chapel that is mainly attended by women who pray ecstatically and move around the Marian altar on their knees.

29. For a good overview of folk customs, traditions and folk beliefs in the Sinjska Krajina, see Miličević 1967.

30. Dinko Šimunović's novel *Alkar*, first published in 1908, is the most widely known literary account of the Alka tournament. Born in Knin and educated in Zadar, Šimunović spent most of his life as a schoolteacher in the Sinj region and was well versed in local traditions. In recent times, the writer Ivan Aralica – a member of the Croatian Academy of the Sciences and Arts as well as a Croatian nationalist extremist – has taken up regional historical motives like the battles against the Ottomans in Dalmatia and the Sinjska Alka in his novels to illustrate the Croats' fateful entanglement in the 'clash of civilisations'.

31. In the winter following the battle of 1715 the Cetina region suffered a terrible famine caused by massive plundering, burning of houses and destruction of food supplies by the Turkish troops. The first actual Alka therefore

might not have been held until 1717. For a detailed ethnographic description of the Alka and other 'folk games', see Bonifačić Rožin 1967–68, and Kretzenbacher 1963.

32. For a detailed description of the Alka weaponry, see Gamulin 1987.

33. The highest body of the Viteško Alkarsko Društvo is the Assembly, composed of all the members, that meets at least once a year. Every four years a presidency with eleven members, a supervisory committee, a tournament master, his deputy, the leader of the company of squires [*Arambaša*] as well as the Court of Honour is elected (see D. Jurić 1987a: 73).

34. The full array of statutes can be seen online at http://www.alka.hr/dokumenti/statut/, last visited 30 January 2009.

35. A few years ago the local hospital in Sinj was to be closed and transferred to Split due to it lacking patients and financial resources. However, this practicable proposal caused major protests amongst the population of Sinj – not because the locals insisted on having their own clinical centre nearby, but for the simple reason that if no more boys would be born in Sinj then nobody would qualify to participate in the Alka anymore. And instead of changing the respective statute, the municipality decided to further fund the local hospital in Sinj (see Widmer 2004: 93). This anecdote illustrates that changing one of the statutes of the Alka is not seen as a feasible option.

36. According to rumours, however, the safe of the former Yugoslav national bank supposedly administers 40 kilograms of gold and silver bars that the Viteško Alkarsko Društvo has gathered. The access to this fortune is suspended, because the successor states of the former Yugoslavia have not yet agreed on the distribution of the state assets. The Sinj branch of the Splitska Banka, on the other hand, is said to store gold and silver items owned by the Viteško Alkarsko Društvo worth more than two million Euro (Widmer 2004: 94).

37. Šime Jurić mentions sources documenting that the Alka tournament was also supported by the French general Molitor and was held in the years 1806–1809 and in 1811. These documents invalidate earlier statements claiming that the tournament had been discontinued during the period of French occupation (Š. Jurić 1987b: 64).

38. In 1922, at the time of the Kingdom of the Serbs, Croats and Slovenes, the Alka is reported to have been held in Belgrade in honour of the coronation of King Aleksandar Karadjordjević.

39. Thirty to forty suitable riding horses had to be specially requested from the Army stationed in Ljubljana for this purpose.

40. One of my interlocutors told me that in the years after 1945 only members of the Communist Party could be part of the Alka Tournament Association.

41. In 1954 Josip Broz Tito was proclaimed honorary citizen of Sinj. And on this eightieth birthday a delegation from the Alka Tournament Society visited him in Belgrade to express their best wishes, in full uniform (see Vuletić 1987: 71).

42. See also http://www.dalmacija.net/sinj/sinj_1.htm, last visited 15 August 2008.
43. See also http://www.dalmacija.net/sinj/sinj_1.htm and http://www.tzsinj. hr/alka.php, last visited 15 August 2008.
44. Reports on the 2001 protests in Sinj published in the newspaper *Slobodna Dalmacija* are accessible at: http://arhiv.slobodnadalmacija.hr/20010210/ novosti.htm, last accessed 20 November 2012.
45. Personal communication with the political scientist Brigita Malenica who was present at the 2001 Alka games and kindly provided me with a very informed and vivid account of the atmosphere of the tournament.
46. A detailed report on the 2001 Alka games and the whole of Kotromanović's speech can be found at http://arhiv.slobodnadalmacija.hr/20010806/novo-sti1.htm
47. In an interview in 2010, when asked if he would repeat his comments of the 2001 Alka today, Mate Jukić answered that he would still say the same thing and that he is one hundred per cent convinced that he struck the right cord with the people of Sinj and the Cetina region regarding general Mirko Norac. See http://tjednik.ferata.hr/ferata5/45-intervju-ferata-mate-jukic (last visited 18 October 2012).
48. The previous leaders of the Croatian Republic of Herceg-Bosnia, namely Jadranko Prlić, Bruno Stojić, Slobodan Praljak, Milivoj Petković, Valentin Ćorić and Berislav Pušić, are presently on trial at the ICTY. Their charges include Crimes against Humanity, Grave Breaches of the Geneva Conventions, and Violations of the Laws or Customs of War.
49. The significance of the rosary as a spiritual weapon in the battle against non-believers and political enemies traces back to the legendary battle of Saint Dominic against the Heretics, as well as to the miraculous victory of the naval battle of Lepanto in 1571 (see Scheer 2006: 306; Schreiner 1994).
50. The use of the rosary features prominently in everyday religious worship in Croatia, and during the Homeland War its significance increased even more. Many people, including the members of my host family, used and continue to use the rosary on a daily basis like an amulet or a magic charm against vulnerability. 'It is something to hold on to', I was told. To the present day, almost every car in Sinj is adorned with a rosary that is attached to the interior mirror. The Bosnian equivalent to the Catholic rosary is called *tespih*, a string of prayer beads of Persian origin that is traditionally used by Muslims to keep track of counting during prayer.
51. After the tournament, Mesić presented the winner with a sabre and a gold ring with a Croatian coat of arms, which was accepted this time.
52. In its entire history, the Alka has only been held outside of Sinj three times, namely in Split in 1832, in Belgrade in 1922 and in Zagreb in 1946.

Chapter 2

Marian Devotion in Times of War

Travels of a Miraculous Painting

'Sinj – that is Alka and the Gospa (Virgin Mary)'. This widely used maxim elucidates that beside the Alka tournament, the most revered institution in Sinj is the 'Svetište Čudotvorne Gospe Sinjske', the Sanctuary of Our Miraculous Lady of Sinj. As a pilgrimage site well known throughout the region, Sinj annually attracts hundreds of thousands of pilgrims.

In this chapter, I emphasise the significance of religion and Marian devotion for the (re-)construction of local, regional and national identity in post-socialist and post-war Croatia. Starting from a delineation of the historical context and genesis of the Marian sanctuary in Sinj, I elaborate the role of the Franciscans as the largest and most influential order in the region so as to understand the administration of religious belief in a context of current power structures regarding local religious and political elites. My main focus, however, lies on the everyday practices of religious devotion and the ethnographic description of the major pilgrimage in Sinj, Velika Gospa (lit. 'Great Lady' or 'Great Madonna') on Assumption Day. Taking the example of Velika Gospa, I work out material, commemorative, political as well as gender aspects entailed in Marian devotion, and highlight their connections to pan-societal transformation processes. In order to explore the contemporary role of the Virgin Mary as a Croatian national saint, I trace the role of Marian devotion in the region during communism and analyse the revival and increasing politicisation of the Marian movement after the violent break-up of Yugoslavia. In this context, I examine the phenomenon of Marian apparitions in Dalmatia and the Catholic-majority regions of Bosnia-Herzegovina in the early 1980s.

Finally, I give an account of a Marian apparition that allegedly occurred in 1983 in the small village of Gala, near Sinj. Despite all parallels, this apparition site did not develop into an internationally acclaimed pilgrimage location like Međugorje in neighbouring Bosnia-Herzegovina, but remained a locally constrained and highly contested site of worship, persisting as a constitutive element of local and regional rooting in Dalmatia until the present day.

The painting of the Gospa Sinjska, to which pious locals attribute miraculous powers stemming from the legend of the historic liberation of Sinj, constitutes the pilgrimage shrine. The sanctuary is located in the eponymous church and affiliated to a monastery that is administered by the Franciscan Order. The church and adjacent *Franjevački Samostan* [Franciscan monastery] are situated in the geographical centre of town and provide a major contact point for local worshipers as well as for all the pilgrims who visit the Marian shrine annually.

The miraculous painting itself is an undated work by an unknown Venetian artist, but most probably originates from the early seventeenth century. It was brought to Sinj in 1687 by a group of approximately seven hundred Catholic refugees from Rama, a small town in Central Bosnia, who – led by the gvardijan of Rama's Franciscan monastery, Fra Stipan Matić – fled Ottoman attacks. It was in the course of this exodus that the painting first acquired a reputation for miraculous powers and for protecting the refugees from further perils.[1]

After the legendary battle of 1715 when the prayers of Marian intercession were answered, the painting reached the height of its fame as an icon of divine protection. Out of gratitude for the victory the military officers of the army of Sinj collected eighty gold ducats and donated a golden crown and a cross to be placed together with the painting of Gospa Sinjska. In September 1716, Archbishop Stjepan Cupilli officially placed the crown over the miraculous image, and the words *in perpetuum Coronata triumphat* [the Crowned triumphs eternally] were inscribed at the bottom of the painting.[2] An altar was built, while, as a further sign of gratitude, the people of Sinj and the Cetina district donated a wreath of twelve silver stars.[3] These ornaments adorn the painting to this day, and the 'Slika Čudotvorne Gospe Sinjske' [Painting of Our Miraculous Lady of Sinj] is commonly depicted as endowed with a golden crown and an opulent silver necklace.

In 1723, restoration work was completed on the 'Crkva Čudotvorne Gospe Sinjske' [Church of Our Miraculous Lady of Sinj], which the Turkish attack had almost burnt down. Its present form dates from 1771; the Franciscan monastery was attached to it at the end of the eighteenth century. When Pope Benedict XIV granted a plenary indulgence to those visiting the Church of Our Miraculous Lady of Sinj in 1752, the popularity of the sanctuary as a site of pilgrimage was secured.[4] Throughout the centuries – and despite severe damage from

Figure 2.1. The painting of *Our Miraculous Lady of Sinj*, with adornment.
© Franjevački Samostan Sinj

fires, earthquakes[5] and air raids by the German Luftwaffe in 1944 – the altar of Gospa Sinjska has remained a place of worship to this day and is widely regarded as a source of divine protection.

The people of the region retain the belief that no harm will befall the place where the miraculous painting is kept. During the Homeland War locals thus swarmed to the shrine of Gospa Sinjska to pray for divine protection. The frontline of the fighting lay only eight kilometres from Sinj and cut the nearby village of Hrvace in half.[6] But in Sinj itself, only one grenade hit a residential house, and no civilians in town were directly killed.[7] Many people credited the sparing of Sinj from calamity to the direct intercession and miraculous protective powers of Gospa Sinjska, and the fame of the painting consequently increased in the immediate post-war years.[8]

Alongside the Marian sanctuaries in Marija Bistrica and Trsat, Sinj counts among the main pilgrimage sites in Croatia.[9] It is one of the leading spiritual centres in Croatia, and the 'Svetište Čudotvorne Gospe Sinjske' is the most frequently visited shrine in Dalmatia. The main gate of the church, a bronze relief crafted by Stipe Sikirica in 1987, tells the history of the Miraculous Painting of Our Lady of Sinj. In an upper segment the portal is divided into four panels each depicting a station in the life of Christ: the Annunciation, the Nativity in Bethlehem, the Crucifixion at Golgatha and the Ascension. The massive folding doors comprise two parts of the depiction. The left wing represents the Marian apparition in the year 1715. In the background, the relief embodies the image of a lady in a wafting robe floating in front of the ancient fortress of Sinj. In the foreground, the artist portrays Ottoman equestrians wearing turbans and swaying scimitars that are put to flight by the local troops. The right wing of the portal displays the dates 1687–1987 in its upper-right corner, and below this is a procession of believers carrying the painting of Gospa Sinjska, headed by a bishop. Considering that 1687 is the year in which the miraculous painting was brought from Rama, the portal was most probably made for the tercentenary of the flight from Central Bosnia. The images of the hilly landscape in the background – presumably signifying the Dinaric mountain range – and the procession of the painting in the foreground suggest that the relief depicts the exodus from Rama as well as the annual parade at Velika Gospa when the miraculous painting is carried through the streets of Sinj. The Velika Gospa procession can therefore be interpreted as a reminder, if not a re-enactment, of the exodus of Catholic Croats from Rama to Sinj in the seventeenth century.

The mini-replica of the miraculous painting of Gospa Sinjska is shinier than the rest of the bronze relief, indicating that people frequently touch the small image of the Virgin. The portal opens towards the central market square of Sinj and is a (visually) ubiquitous component of the townscape.

Another prominent sign of the omnipresence of the Gospa Sinjska in the local commemorative topography is a 2.7-metre-high bronze Marian statue [*kip*] that had been erected in 2008 (cover photo). The Archbishop

Figures 2.2 and 2.3. The church portal in Sinj depicting the miraculous salvation of Sinj and the Marian apparition in 1715. Photos: M. Schäuble

of Sarajevo, Vinko Cardinal Puljić, inaugurated the Marian statue during the 2008 Alka tournament in the presence of then president Stjepan Mesić, then prime minister Ivo Sanader, high-ranking delegates of the Croatian Parliament and other domestic as well as foreign dignitaries. The statue is positioned *u gradu*, on the hill where the Marian apparition of 1715 allegedly took place, overlooking the whole of Sinj and the Cetinska krajina.

Reminiscent of the oversized crosses on the hills of Mostar and Skopje, the Marian statue now dominates the townscape of Sinj when illuminated at night. Fra Mirko, an elderly Franciscan, told me that the statue had been commissioned and erected as a reminder of the approaching 300-year jubilee in 2015, at which the municipality of Sinj will celebrate the historic victory over the Ottoman troops. As the siege of Sinj in 1715 had lasted seven days, the seven years leading up to 2015 function as an emblematic number in preparation for the celebration that symbolises the town's prolonged resistance to foreign invaders.

The erection of yet another replica of Gospa Sinjska – along with the somewhat disproportional seven-year preparation for the 300-year jubilee of the historic battle of Sinj – indicate that the narrative of the town's heroic defence against the Ottomans and the concomitant legend of the Marian apparition do not abate but only increase in importance. The massive Marian statue is a visible memorial marker in the landscape that connects the present to the past and moreover signifies that divine protection is more sought after and required than ever before. In other words, the Marian statue helps to maintain a sense of continuity across time and therefore plays a vital part in shaping the narratives of national as well as regional susceptibility to attacks and victimhood. This politico-spatial maintenance of historical time evokes strong emotional ties, and reveals that local identity continues to be heavily rooted in the region's past and in the historical role of the town as a fortification against (foreign) intruders.

Administrating Belief: The Franciscan Hegemony

The inhabitants of Dalmatia and the Franciscan Order have been closely connected for centuries. The Franciscans established their first monasteries in the early thirteenth century during Saint Francis's lifetime. As early as 1357, Pope Innozenz IV permitted Count Nelipčić of Sinj to build a Franciscan church in the Cetinska krajina.[10] Thereafter, numerous Franciscan clergymen migrated from nearby central Bosnia, where they had earlier begun to proselytise in the country through newly established monasteries (cf. Tanner 2001: 18). The Franciscans practised in Sinj and the surrounding areas until 1536 when the Ottoman troops conquered this part of Dalmatia and started to persecute the Catholic population. In the territories acquired by the Ottomans, Franciscans and the Catholic clergy were regarded as 'emissaries of a foreign, hostile power' (Tanner 2001: 42).[11]

> The oldest and most prestigious Franciscan monasteries in central Bosnia gained a written charter of toleration from the Sultan. But this applied only to a few individual buildings. Outside of Bosnia the Catholic Church was virtually a Catacomb church, especially in the 1520s and again in the 1590s, when persecution of Catholics raged most intensely. (ibid.)

Around 1687 many Catholics were forced to flee Bosnia and resettled in the Dalmatian hinterland, an area belonging at that point to the Venetian Republic. Šime Jurić recounts that several Turkish strongholds and settlements had been plundered and set on fire in a 'punitive mission' by reinforcement cohorts of the Venetian army after the Turks had tried to attack Sinj in 1687. The Christian population in Bosnia feared a counter-offensive and were urged by Venetian representatives to migrate to trans-Dinaric regions under army protection.

> In these events a decisive role was played by Franciscan monks from the monastery in Rama, who also abandoned their sanctuary. Reports of the large-scale migration from Rama spread throughout Bosnia, and more and more groups began to flee other districts … The refugees, mostly Croats, settled sparsely populated areas of the Dalmatian hinterland, thus contributing to their present-day ethnic composition. (Š. Jurić 1987a: 26f.)

A glance at the town chronicle of Sinj reveals that the majority of families or *pleme* [lit. tribe, clan] who set up their homestead in the Cetinska krajina originally migrated from Central Bosnia, particularly from the town of Rama, whence they had also rescued the miraculous Marian painting.

Members of the Franciscan Order have traditionally cherished very close ties with the local population. In the case of Dalmatia and nearby Herzegovina, most of the friars administer parishes in the region of their origin and are known to be very attached to their native soil. In contrast to diocesan priests, the Franciscans in rural Dalmatia and Herzegovina often grew up in the parishes they serve and know many members of the congregation personally. They are considered approachable, down-to-earth and entertaining preachers who would prefer a meaty joke or saying over a lengthy intellectual bible exegesis. They speak the language of the rural population and are known for their firm sense of regionalism and nationality – attributes that also gained them a reputation of consistently defying episcopal authority.[12] And when Ivo Andrić writes, apropos of Bosnian Franciscan monasteries, that 'throughout the centuries of Turkish rule [they] constituted a kind of storage battery of popular energy, and monks enjoyed the people's sympathy and respect far more than did the diocesan clergy', this also holds true for the Franciscans monasteries in Dalmatia (Andrić 1990: 65). A young friar in Sinj also told me that the Franciscans were particularly popular among the population because they stayed in Sinj during the Homeland War and never left the population behind. The Franciscans' closeness to the rural population is also reflected in their belief systems and religious practices where Marian devotion plays a crucial role. Franciscan prayers, chants and sermons are strongly influenced by pictographic contemplation plates depicting the Virgin Mary – practices that form the centre of Franciscan Marian mysticism (cf. Egger 1982).

In the long-standing military history of the region, the Franciscans excelled not only as fierce guardians of Catholic faith but also as advocates of a Catholic Croatian homeland. It almost goes without saying, therefore, that the Franciscans opposed the incorporation of Croatia into the multi-ethnic and multi-religious Yugoslav state after the Second World War. They constituted a strong anti-communist force on the local level that in turn was countered with severe retaliations and sanctions of both an ideological and economic nature.

In the course of my fieldwork I frequently heard stories of friars and/ or their families who suffered from systematic discrimination in the Socialist Federal Republic of Yugoslavia (Schäuble 2014, forthcoming). Considered as ringleaders of subversive movements by the Socialist authorities, many Franciscans were sent to prison or work camps, and some of them had also been tortured. As a consequence, they were widely considered political martyrs.

While the Croatian branch of the Catholic Church for a long time pursued a policy of non-interference in domestic political affairs in Yugoslavia, and some of the bishops even collaborated with the regime, the Franciscans always opposed the political structure unequivocally (cf. Perica 2002: 57f.). Their unperturbed nationalist positioning and subsequent persecution resonated with a conviction of persecution felt also by many 'common believers', thus strengthening the

Franciscans' ties with the local population – especially with the nationalistic and rebellious peasants and shepherds from small villages.

'The Franciscans are the carriers and guardians of our history and our tradition. If it were not for them we would have long forgotten who we are', one of my interlocutors once said. This comment reflects a close affinity between the people and the clergy, and illustrates that the friars act as both role models and representatives for lay people.[13] As religious advisors and frequent advocates of nationalistic movements they have a significant effect on ethno-religious identity formation in Croatia. Due to their access to higher education and literacy they are considered the 'carriers and guardians of history and tradition' and are thus expected to preserve the cultural memory of the Croatian people.

At present, the Franciscan monastery in Sinj accommodates twenty-five consecrated padres, which makes it the second biggest Franciscan monastery in the whole of Croatia. Besides their spiritual tasks, a responsibility for national education and tutoring, particularly in rural areas, constitutes a vital part of classical Franciscan pastoral care. In the case of Sinj, the Franciscans run a classical grammar school [*Franjevačka Klasična Gimnazija Sinj*] and provide first-class humanistic schooling. The *gimnazija* was founded in 1838 and was the first Croatian-language school in Dalmatia. Under state socialism, however, the teachings and graduation certificates of non-state schools were not officially recognised; but since 1992, the Franciscan grammar school in Sinj has been privatised and has now transformed itself into a reputable and fully recognised secular co-educational institution.

The monastery also accommodates an ample archive as well as a museum that is run and curated by local Franciscan friars. The exhibition comprises a small but unique collection of regional ethnographic and archaeological objects. In addition, the Franciscan monastery in Sinj is affiliated with a boarding school for novices, a so-called seminary, which at the time of my fieldwork accommodated fourteen boys aged 14 to 18.[14] The boys are taught alongside their lay peers at the in-house grammar school.[15] The order has no difficulties recruiting seminarians, as a still quite widespread tradition holds that a son from almost every local family joins the Franciscans; the majority of the novices come from neighbouring parishes or from rural Catholic areas in Bosnia-Herzegovina.

The Order of Friars Minor (O.F.M.), commonly called simply 'the Franciscans', is by definition a mendicant monastic order and the friars live according to the three vows of obedience, chastity and poverty. References to these vows are a common source of joking amongst the friars of the monastery in Sinj. Although they do not transgress the vows, they gladly exercise their right to interpret them freely. For instance, they follow the principle that obedience to God is more important than obedience to state or episcopal authority; and the vow of poverty seems to be negotiable as well. The younger friars own smart mobile phones and occasionally gold watches, and I saw fashionable trainers visibly peeking out from beneath their robes when I met them. The monastery's car park also boasted a number of rather impressive cars. When I carefully mentioned my astonishment at this, a 32-year-old priest replied to me in a tone of self-irony: 'The Order provides for our needs, you know. But the needs differ considerably from person to person here'.

Because of their traditional brown habits, the Franciscans are easy to identify and their visible presence all over town signals approachability and unpretentiousness.[16] However, the popularity of the Franciscans among the local population does not prevent them from also being objects of criticism and frequent ridicule. It is quite common in Sinj, for example, for people to believe devoutly in the Gospa and her miracle-working powers while simultaneously being rather critical of the Church and the Franciscan Order, objecting to their wealth and/or political influence in the region. These remarks, however, are mainly meant as a critique of the priests' worldly activities but do not cast any doubt on their religious integrity or authority.[17]

The Shrine of Gospa Sinjska and Everyday Practices of Religious Devotion

For the majority of people in Sinj, the shrine of Gospa Sinjska constitutes a vital part of their everyday (spatial) world and lived-in reality. It not only provides a source of religious comfort but also signifies a localised sense of identity and belonging. Marian veneration is a distinct component of individual and communal life that is self-evidently incorporated into everyday conversations and routines. It thus shapes a moral geography that dominates both the visible and invisible realms.

The shrine itself consists of a massive Marian altar that is located on the left side of the church. Four brownish-red mottled marble columns support the structure, at the centre of which sits the miraculous painting of Our Lady of Sinj. The painting itself measures 58 by 44 cm, and could, according to art historians, be a detail of a previously much larger painting. Four white putti border the opulently silver-framed piece that is traditionally adorned with a golden crown and silver necklace. The altar table is decorated with an embroidered cloth, candles and flower arrangements. Through a small passageway that runs around the altar, the devout usually move around the altar clockwise as they pray the rosary – some of them even on their knees. Others kneel on one of the three steps that lead up to the altar. On the lateral sides four confessionals are located on a corridor that links the church to the monastery and connects the latter to the shrine via doors. A small donation box next to the altar, decorated with a small image of Gospa Sinjska, is frequently touched or kissed by the believers as they leave the shrine.

In contrast to other pilgrimage sites or places of Marian worship in Croatia, such as Maria Bistrica, Krasno, Trsat or the Kamenita Vrata [stone portal] in Zagreb,[18] there are no marmoreal or metal plaques depicting a vow, and there are no publicly displayed expressions of gratitude at the shrine in Sinj. All of the above-mentioned places possess walls covered with engraved plaques, votives and/or personal gifts and notes left by indebted believers or by pilgrims in search of Marian intercession. In Sinj, by contrast, no such donations are on show, and only a small collection of votives are exhibited in the small museum.[19] And although I do not know the exact reasons for this, I gather from various comments by local clergymen that the pilgrimage site is meant to be kept as humble and non-commercial as possible. One of the priests, Fra Mile, told me that pieces of gold and silver jewellery donated by pilgrims and local believers have recently been melted down and cast into a chalice for use during Holy Communion, 'so that the whole community can symbolically and literally partake of the donations'.

The modesty and commonality for which the sanctuary and parish of Gospa Sinjska is widely celebrated is also manifest in the shrine's public accessibility. The portal of the Marian church opens towards the market place and is usually kept ajar. People thus frequently step inside and pay the shrine a brief informal visit. In the course of my fieldwork I regularly observed that people dropped in on their obligatory daily way to the *kavana* [café], to school, to the market or simply in-between running errands. These would include groups of giggling high school girls, women with overflowing shopping bags, mothers with whining children, old ladies dressed in black, male teenagers wearing their compulsory leather jackets, soldiers, as well as middle-aged and older men. There are always a couple of visitors standing or kneeling in front of the shrine to pay tribute to the Virgin Mary, and at certain times of the day the church looks like a busy extension of the market place. Apart from daily passers-by, believers with specific concerns who vehemently (and audibly) pray or beg for Gospa's salutary powers also frequently visit the altar. There are continuous reports that people suffering from various diseases have been miraculously healed and the reputation of the painting for thaumaturgy steadily increases. Every now and then, small pilgrimage groups from other parts of Croatia or abroad arrive to visit the Svetište Čudotvorne Gospe Sinjske. These are usually groups on their way to the much more prominent pilgrimage site of Međugorje in nearby Bosnia-Herzegovina. Depending on the country of origin of the respective group, a Franciscan friar with the relevant linguistic skills usually extends a warm welcome, shows the visitors around, hears the confessions of the pilgrims and occasionally even holds a specific mass. As a rule, however, the groups leave on the same day and do not spend a night in Sinj. Religious tourism therefore does not provide a regular source of income for local businesses. It is limited simply to one singular event: the annual pilgrimage on the day of Velika Gospa.

Velika Gospa: Pilgrimage and Political Rally

Celebrating Velika Gospa (Assumption Day)

> Every pilgrimage has a local and regional history; responds
> more or less sensitively to a national history; and especially
> in the case of the most important pilgrimages, is shaped and
> colored by international, even world history.
> — Victor and Edith Turner, *Images and Pilgrimage in
> Christian Culture*

On 15 August each year, hundreds of thousands of people undertake a pilgrimage to the sanctuary of Our Miraculous Lady of Sinj. During Velika Gospa, as Assumption Day is commonly called, multitudinous masses of believers flock to Sinj, a huge number of them by foot or even barefoot. They come to ask for help and divine guidance, to give thanks for favours received and prayers answered, or simply to honour the Virgin Mary. And although most of the pilgrims arrive from Dalmatia and Bosnia, the Velika Gospa celebration is far from simply a regional event. Some visitors come from as far as Australia or the United States.[20] Others who fled the Yugoslav Wars of Secession in the 1990s or who left Yugoslavia in the 1970s to work as *Gastarbeiter* – most of them in Germany, Austria or Scandinavia – return for this occasion and pay their relatives a visit. The journey serves as a demonstration of local connectivity, and the religious duties involved usually entail participation in Holy Mass, receipt of the confession sacrament and Holy Communion, as well as completion of a vow.

Assumption Day is a festival in the church calendar in which a particular shrine's, parish's or memorial's history is commemorated. Smaller sanctuaries in particular experience their main pilgrimage times during such events (Dubisch 1995: 37f.). This is certainly also the case for the annual pilgrimage in Sinj that is indeed highly seasonal and embedded in a number of accompanying ritualised events and/ or canons. Nine days before the actual Velika Gospa celebration the so-called *devetica* or *devetnica* (from *devet*, nine) commences. In this period a number of small local pilgrimages from neighbouring villages such as Glavice, Hrvace or Otok take place. Each day at six o'clock in the morning, groups of pilgrims leave their respective villages and walk to the Marian shrine in Sinj on foot. A morning service is held at seven o'clock during which the believers usually make or mark the fulfilment of vows [*zavjeti*].

In the days preceding the festivities, groups of pilgrims from all over Dalmatia and Bosnia arrive in Sinj; most of them almost impalpably during the night, as I myself experienced in 2005. The following is an excerpt from my field notes:

> Thousands of people must have arrived overnight and simply slept outside. Every open space in town is populated with pilgrims, back-packs, camping mats, stoves … All over town vendors have started to put up their booths. Apart from devotional objects, such as rosaries, candles, figurines and images of Gospa Sinjska or the Madonna of Međugorje, people sell crocheted blankets, plaited wicker baskets, fabrics, clothing and underwear, sunglasses, and toy guns for children.
>
> The yard of the monastery is populated with thousands of standing, sitting, laying and kneeling pilgrims. The Franciscans provide cold drinks and sandwiches and attend to those with bleeding blisters and other injuries from walking. The Mass in church is broadcast via loudspeakers. Under a banner that says *Sv. Misa* [Holy Mass] local nuns collect money. I find out that for the price of 50 kunas (approx. 8 euros) believers can 'buy' a Mass, which means that the name of the deceased relative whom the Mass had been bought for is read out aloud during one of the countless services over the next few days.
>
> In the inner courtyard the priests have erected two rows of open-air confessionals. I meet Fra Zvonko. He is tanned, wears mirrored sunglasses and is extremely friendly. Despite the rush, he patiently

answers all my questions. Not being sure about the exact number of pilgrims, he tells me: 'We have ordered 120,000 Hosts this year. We estimate that every third person takes the Holy Communion. That is how we know the approximate number of visitors'. That would be 360,000. I have no idea if that is realistic, as I have never seen so many people in one spot before. To me they look like millions ... 80 per cent of them are youths, Zvonko says. 'That is traditionally so'. The first service apparently took place at 4 A.M.; a third of all pilgrims arrive by foot and the march from Split to Sinj takes about seven hours. He certainly knows his numbers ...

Later on I meet Fra Željko ... He tells me that the pilgrimage in Sinj wasn't really popular until the 1960s. Unfortunately, he hasn't much time and does not elaborate on that. I have to ask about that in more detail later. Instead, he tells me that he doesn't like to hear people's confessions. 'I hear about 20 confessions per hour, sometimes 30. That is less than 3 minutes per person. I would really like to have more time for individual advice'. ...

At 4 P.M. I attend the *misa na gradu* (lit. 'Mass uptown', meaning Mass in the chapel on the ancient fortification wall). It is relatively unspectacular and moderate. The Mass is held by a local Franciscan priest who in his sermon commemorates the historic battle against the *turci* [the Turks] 290 years ago, and praises the seven hundred soldiers who heroically defended the fortress. He calls the Croatian soldiers of 1715 *branitelji*! He talks about the defence of the 'Christian hemisphere' in general, but all in a comparatively restrained way. The congregation sing the song of Gospa Sinjska, exchange the greeting of peace and celebrate the Eucharist. After the Mass they pray a rosary outside the chapel together.

Downtown in the church a seemingly endless stream of pilgrims circumnavigate the Marian altar in a clockwise direction. Women with disabled children next to girls in miniskirts, middle-aged men, old women in black headscarves ... thousands of people pray and donate money. I observe that while the women usually tend to be more eccentric worshippers (loud praying, weeping and lamenting, knee bends, kissing of the altar, etc.) the men usually hold their left hand to their heart while crossing themselves three times with the right hand – to me this looks as if they pay homage to the Gospa rather than beseeching her for help or divine protection.

A young woman in the queue is writing a text message. Others kneel on towels to pray. On the other side of the monastery's inner courtyard, people queue for the open-air confession. I see Željko's troubled face from afar and feel sorry for him. Outside on the Trg

Franje Tuđmana [Franjo Tuđman Square], the tribune for the evening service is almost set up. (Field Notes, 15 August 2005)

Within a couple of days the population of Sinj had (temporarily) increased eighteen-fold from 20,000 to 360,000 and the town seemed to be bursting at the seams. The sheer logistics of the preparations for this enormous inrush of pilgrims had kept the Franciscan friars busy for weeks. All of them seemed tired but visibly moved by the innumerable believers' attestations of faith in the miraculous powers of the Gospa.

The order of events during the festive days is ritually determined and proceeds strictly according to specification. August the fourteenth is commonly referred to as *Gospin post*, a day of fasting, when fish is substituted for meat. The most important date in the preparatory phase before Velika Gospa, however, is the night of 14/15 August. It is called *Gospa Žežin*, meaning literally 'glowing Madonna', when the miraculous painting is illuminated in remembrance of the Marian apparition in 1715 when a white lady illuminated by a vast light appeared before the besieging soldiers. Thousands of pilgrims move around the altar and worship the painting all night long.

Figure 2.4. Open-air confessions during the annual celebration of Velika Gospa in Sinj. Photo: Franjevački Samostan Sinj

Velika Gospa is not only a church festival but also an important national holiday, so that at times the pilgrimage resembles a huge folk festival rather than an act of contemplation. But none of the pilgrims seemed to perceive this as contradictory in the way I did, as I recorded in my field notes:

> In the evening I go into town again. This time, it appears as if all 360,000 people are in the street at the same time. Every bar and every café plays loud Balkan pop, and everybody seems in a perfect party mood. There are countless market stalls, with suckling pigs, grilled lamb and grilled Čevapi being sold everywhere; likewise beer, rakija, slivovic and other stuff. One merchant is selling T-shirts with a *Gotovina – Heroj!* [Gotovina – Hero!] logo. The narrow streets are completely blocked and it is almost impossible to pass. On my way to the church, numerous drunks bawl and fall over me. What a spectacle! I cannot see the connection to the pilgrimage and ask myself how prayer is supposed to be possible here … But I guess that is not the point.
>
> The party almost reaches all the way to the altar, as the church doors are open all night. Joško told me that the night of 14 August is called 'Gospa Žežin' (Glowing Madonna), as the miraculous painting is illuminated – and the stream of pilgrims pouring in all night is endless. Some of them sleep on the pews. The atmosphere in the church here is very peaceful and to my astonishment people pray much less fervently in front of the Marian shrine than they usually do at other times in the year.
>
> In the municipal park a huge funfair is set up with carousels, roller coasters, auto scooters, ball-tossing stands, etc., and people celebrate all night. (Field Notes, 15 August 2005)

My host Joško tells me that the communists had tried to prohibit *Gospa Žežin*. He recalls numerous stories from his childhood and adolescence when he and his friends used to smash light bulbs with slingshots so that individual pilgrims could not be identified and arrested by the police. The youngsters, he says, came up with many more cunning ways of befooling the police in the late 1950s and 1960s: 'Those who publicly sung religious songs during Velika Gospa were immediately arrested – even though, of course, the constitution of Yugoslavia granted religious freedom; "religious freedom" – ridiculous!'

I am also being told that most pilgrims traditionally come from regions around Livno and Duvno in Herzegovina. In the past, when the pilgrimage was proscribed, they secretly crossed the mountains by foot and put up direction signs by assembling stone formations or scratching markers into the rocks along the way. This previously secret trail was known as *oputina*. Before the bridge over the River Cetina was built, the communists used to regularly shut down the riverine traffic before Velika Gospa in order to prevent pilgrims from reaching Sinj. Such and many other anecdotes about obstacles and counter-subversive actions are told during the festive days. People collectively remember the dangers they faced and the hurdles they had to overcome to participate in the pilgrimage before the 1980s.

A visible demonstration and display of faith, the annual pilgrimage was also 'staged' as an act of resistance to state communism, reflecting what Herzfeld (1997) describes as fundamental concern with display and concealment. Today, Marian veneration and pilgrimage embody a public manifestation of faith that still maintains certain distinct political and nationalistic potencies (cf. Eade and Sallnow 2000).

In the form of a procession – in which the painting of Gospa Sinjska is carried through the narrow streets of Sinj – the local population commemorate their ancestors' flight from Rama together with the Marian apparition and her divine intervention in the battle of 1715. The *alkari* are the main local dignitaries who feature prominently during the

Figure 2.5. Soldiers, policemen, and *alkari* and *momci* in traditional costumes escorting the miraculous painting during the Velika Gospa procession in Sinj. Photo: Franjevački Samostan Sinj

festivities and are a visible reminder of the historical background of this customary celebration. It is their responsibility to carry and 'guard' the painting during the procession; a responsibility they traditionally share with soldiers of the Croatian army and police divisions. The presence of military and police delegates dominates to such an extent that the three-day Velika Gospa celebration in Sinj is occasionally referred to as 'military pilgrimage'. During these days it is also quite common for the national anthem to be sung and prayers for General Mirko Norac to be uttered in church.

> The actual day of Velika Gospa starts at 7 A.M. with cannon shots '*na gradu*', from the chapel at the fortification wall – reminders of the historic battle. It seems that even more pilgrims have poured in through the night. The town centre looks shattered: rubbish, broken glass, left-over food and cigarette butts everywhere. Drunks from last night still populate the cafés. On the other side of town, however, people start gathering for the procession. I can see groups of *alkari, momci*, soldiers, marines, police divisions, an army general ... The Franciscans must have taken down the painting and put it on a stretcher by now ... The procession will start at 9.30 A.M. and I put up my tripod with the camera opposite the town hall. A couple of old people depose a beautiful bouquet on the street. Several people curiously approach me and ask if I am filming for television. Hearing my accent one man says, 'So, you are from Germany? That is very good. Germany and Croatia are sister nations [*bratinstve nacije*]. I was in the army in 1991 and Germany helped us very much back then. And Austria and Rome, too. The Vatican. But mostly, of course, we owe the victory to our Gospa Sinjska!' An old man who overheard the conversation screams 'Heil Hitler!' at me and then walks off without further comment ... Then the procession gets going. The crowd seems to be divided in two parts. At first there is a priest carrying a cross, followed by a Croatian flag and two banners ... Several tens of thousands of people follow. The painting has not yet passed by. The prayers and chants are broadcast via loudspeaker throughout town. A few minutes later the second part of the procession follows. It is a sea of people headed by a group of nuns, the Nadbiskup Marin Barišić, and a group of priests, followed by the *momci*, the *alkari*, and a group of girls in traditional regional costumes. I recognise four Franciscans from Sinj carrying the painting. Groups of soldiers in uniforms, marines and police divisions are marching behind the painting. They are followed by countless believers. A Franciscan with a walkie-talkie keeps running back and forth; he coordinates the procession and makes sure that the way for the Gospa is clear. People

bow low, cross themselves and keep trying to touch the painting as it is carried by on the stretcher. The carriers take turns as I have been told beforehand, but it is impossible to follow the whole procession … All of a sudden there is the sound of military marching. The stretcher with the painting is put down next to the town hall (probably right on the bouquet), just across from where I stand. People throw flowers and petals … To me it looks as if a blessing takes place. The painting of the Gospa is lifted, slightly turned, and put down again. This occurs until it has been turned a whole 360 degrees. I have no idea what this is supposed to signify. Do they bless the town hall that way? … Joško later tells me that the pilgrims try to stroke the flowers on which the stretcher with the painting rests, because they believe that the blessing of the Gospa is transferred to all objects in contact with the painting … The procession leads across the whole town back to the church where tens of thousands of people gather at the Trg Franje Tuđmana for the Eucharist mass. (Field Notes, 16 August 2005)

The day after the procession, on 16 August, the newspaper *Slobodna Dalmacija* published a photo of the procession in Sinj and reported that about fifty thousand pilgrims had attended Velika Gospa in Sinj. And although there are no exact verifiable numbers (except for the Franciscans' wafer-estimate), fifty thousand is clearly a crude understatement. I doubt the local clergymen's common explanation that 'the journalists are all a bunch of communists who always criticise anything to do with the church', but I am nevertheless astonished at the newspaper's immense miscalculation. The public display of religious devotion still seems to pose a threat to a large section of the population, especially to educated elites in urban centres.

The Interplay of Sacred and Secular Spheres

The complex interplay of religious devotion, political commentary, social communication and secular activities is a most striking characteristic of the Velika Gospa pilgrimage in Sinj. Like most rituals, pilgrimages are disciplines by which cognitive and bodily habits are rehearsed and by which the manifold emotions of the believers are formed, expressed and channelled (Asad 1993; see also Feuchtwang 2007: 60). Accordingly, the devotions the pilgrims perform in front of the Marian altar in Sinj are manifold. While some may be kneeling in front of the painting, others move around the shrine on their knees, kiss the altar, kiss the reproductions of the original painting and/or make extended appeals to the Gospa. These acts, along with the pilgrims' recurrent attempts to touch the painting during the procession, all indicate that the religious practice of Marian devotion is highly sensual and tactile.

The Miraculous Painting of the Gospa Sinjska is a cult-image [*Kultbild*] in the classic sense of the term defined by the art historian Hans Belting, who writes of images

> that could turn against clerical institutions if they had not passed over in their possession. They protected minorities und became advocates of the people, because they were innately beyond all hierarchies. They spoke with the voice of heaven with no need of a mediator; a voice against which all authorities are powerless ... Images whose fame originates from their history and the miracles they perform are not adopted in the theology of images. They are the core of all those images that were kissed and adored and treated like living persons – and that were approached with a personal request. (Belting 2004 [1990]: 16, my translation)

The resuscitation of the 'charismatic features' (ibid.) of a cult-image works according to the principle of analogy: an artefact, statue or image is animated in religious practice through an eliciting of powers believed to inhere it. The powers are then mobilised and transferred to the worshipper – mental power becomes a corporeal power. 'The cult-image is

Figure 2.6. Pilgrims attempting to touch the miraculous painting during the procession at Velika Gospa. Photo: Franjevački Samostan Sinj

the image of the *passio* of its worshippers if they can recognise their own moving experiences in it, writes Fritz Kramer (Kramer 2005: 220, my translation). The pilgrims also bring material offerings – usually pieces of jewellery, rosaries, flowers, candles, etc. – or donate money, which they usually place directly on the altar. The tactility and sensuality of the devotional practices are expressions of a believer's embodied perception of herself/himself as well as her/his surrounding and mediate the relationship, not only between her/his body and mind, but also between the individual and the religious community. In addition to its (corporeal) devotional characteristics, the pilgrimage at Velika Gospa entails material, commemorative, political and gender aspects.

Commemoration and the politicisation of historical tradition are key features of religious pilgrimages and the annual Velika Gospa pilgrimage in Sinj comprises and displays a particularly rich repertoire of commemorative qualities based on historical references. Apart from the obvious citation of the Marian apparition in 1715, the celebration is also a commemoration and tribute to the role the local Franciscans have played in preserving Catholic religion and Croatian culture since the years of Ottoman occupation and down to the most recent regimes, including Titoism. Victor Turner has pointed out that important pilgrimages are not only closely related to the local and regional history but also 'respond … more or less sensitively to a national history … and [are] shaped and coloured by international, even world history' (Turner and Turner 1978: 23). During the annual pilgrimage on Velika Gospa, historic events of an international scale – such as the Ottoman attacks and years of occupation and exploitation by various foreign powers, followed by oppression under communism up to the recent onslaught of Serbian military unions and the JNA in the Homeland War – are commemorated on a national and local level by way of religious pilgrimages all over Croatia. Not only in Sinj but also in the other major Croatian pilgrimage sites of Marija Bistrica, Trsat, Aljmaš and Krasno, Assumption Day is solemnised as a countrywide remembrance day of national liberation and independence. 'Although its power usually derives from specific past events, a pilgrimage site also gains power from the belief that what happened in the past might occur again, writes Jill Dubisch in extension of Turner's approach (Dubisch 1995: 37; see also Turner and Turner 1978: 6). In the case of Sinj, the miracle of 1715 had already been revitalised during the years of the Homeland War when the 'evildoers from the East' were re-signified as 'Serb aggressors', and the 'recapture of occupied Croatian territory' during the Homeland War was partly ascribed to divine intervention. My supposition here is that in future, this belief in or hope for Marian safekeeping will mainly concern the cohesion and unambiguousness of the Croatian nation-state and the well-being of the region in an era of growing globalisation and multiculturalism.

Gendered Aspects of Marian Veneration in Dalmatia and the Mediterranean

A number of anthropologists have noted the importance of Marian devotion in European – and pre-eminently Mediterranean – religious practice.[21] Pilgrimage sites such as Lourdes (France), Fátima (Portugal), the island of Tinos (Greece) and Međugorje (Bosnia-Herzegovina) are among the most renowned shrines not just in Europe but worldwide (cf. Carroll 1986; Dubisch 1995). Eric Wolf pointed out that Marian cults constitute an important marker of the 'major religious traditions found around the Mediterranean' and noted that popular expression of religious faith and 'links to the holy' of this kind are highly gendered in character (Wolf and Lehmann 1984: 4). But except for the widespread observation that the majority of believers and pilgrims are women, gender usually plays a subordinate role in analyses of the habitus and everyday practices of Marian devotion and Christian pilgrimage. Some explanatory models, however, refer to the image of the 'virgin' or the 'suffering mother' as a devotional figure and seek to link it to the concept of mother worship and mother cults in the Mediterranean and/or locate the roots of Marian devotion in the family structure of late Roman and early Christian Mediterranean society. Most notably, psychoanalytic approaches to Marian devotion emphasise the maternal configuration that is associated with nurturing, protection and self-sacrifice. In this perspective, Mary's impact as a (self-sacrificing) maternal role model and paragon of female martyrdom are causal features of the devotional cults surrounding her (Carroll 1986).[22]

Mary is often referred to as *mater dolorosa*, the sorrowful mother, and concepts of suffering, (self-)sacrifice and (self-)victimisation are important elements of Marian veneration that are often publicly acted out during pilgrimages. Dubisch notes that 'pilgrimage also provides performative and emotional space', pointing out that women who dramatically display their pain and suffering during pilgrimage produce and reproduce images of the suffering mother of Christ (Dubisch 1995: 218).[23] Pain and suffering are commonly associated with women's or mothers' experiences in general, and scholars of religious behaviour in the Mediterranean speculate that women appear to adopt and connect to the 'holy stories' more than men because they seem to know them better from personal experience and because they tend to 'relive them more imaginatively' (Cutileiro 1971: 272; Davis 1984: 38, fn 7).[24] The 'greater involvement of women in religious activities, both within and outside the church, has been noted throughout the Mediterranean', but the prominence of women in Mediterranean religious practice contrasts strongly with the formal position they are granted by official Catholic doctrine (Dubisch 1995: 211; see also Christian 1972; Davis 1984; Pina-Cabral 1986).

Pina-Cabral suggests for the case of Portugal that since women are constructed per se as more sinful by the church, they might develop a stronger need for religion or religious redemption than men (Pina-Cabral 1986). 'In addition, the restraint that the church attempts to exercise on sexuality, the institution of confession, and the necessity to submit to the authority of other men (men who are often not held in high regard) seem to be sticking points for men ... in the Mediterranean', Dubisch adds (Dubisch 1995: 211). To this extent religious activity becomes less attractive to men. Campbell even goes as far as to suggest that the example of Christ might not provide a desirable role model for men – for Mediterranean men in general and for Greek men in particular – in as much as 'modesty, meekness, humility are values only admirable for women' (Campbell 1966: 167). These studies and approaches all have commonly described religious practices in general and Marian veneration in particular as restrictive measures by which women are reprimanded, or 'disciplined and punished', to employ Foucaultian terminology. This perspective is affirmed in the assertion that the church traditionally draws on Marian devotion 'to combat forces of modernism and rationalism and in support of a conservative political agenda' (Dubisch 1995: 231). The Mother of God is associated with qualities traditionally perceived as 'feminine virtues' such as maternity, chastity, subordination and obedience, such that against the backdrop of anti-modernism a cult of Mary becomes bound to reinforce conventional gender roles and to strengthen traditional family values and structures.

When I asked why the majority of visitors to the shrine of Gospa Sinjska and participants in daily Mass were women, locals in Sinj (both men and women) would usually tell me that, generally speaking, women were the ones responsible for providing spiritual support within families and for importing religious beliefs and convictions. One Franciscan friar even said: 'Women are the ones who hold the families together and therefore they also hold our society together. Men are also connected with the church but they usually aim at the more prestigious posts, you know. Like carrying a flag during processions and being seen in public'. The visible contradiction between public female worship and participation in religious activities on the one hand, and the sequestration of women on the other, endorses the assumption that female devotion tends to be associated with a 'public demonstration of surrender', while men's religious activities are often perceived as proclamations of their social status (Davis 1984: 22). Judicious and gender-conscious comments like the friar's quote above, however, were rather rare in Sinj. Usually the parishioners would jokingly refer to the fact that women had much less work to do than men and therefore had more time on their hands to go to church. One woman inverted this (already ironic) stereotype by saying: 'We simply have a better and more efficient time management – that's why we have more time for prayer.'

From my daily observations at the shrine of Gospa Sinjska I would add that male and female practices of daily worship also differ considerably. Women pray ardently, often loudly and in an almost trance-like state, handle their rosaries, fall on their knees and sometimes even pass around the altar on their knees. With these bodily techniques they create a personal connection and (corporal) closeness to the Mother of God. Men, on the other hand, usually pray much more formally and greet the Gospa deferentially. During weekdays, men visit the altar less often than women and in general stay for much shorter periods of time. At the altar many men typically click their heels, perform a brief and sharp bow, pray quietly for a moment while standing upright with their head lowered, then cross themselves, bow again and leave swiftly. This procedure often reminded me of a military act in the course of which the devout men viewed the Gospa like a superior officer. I therefore argue that women tend to dissolve boundaries and seek to come closer to the Gospa, while men rather tend to submit to the Gospa and to create a respectful distance through their practices of worship.

In the case of Velika Gospa in Sinj, the procession and the pilgrims' accommodation are organised by the Franciscans, and the proportion of men who participate in the pilgrimage and the subsequent masses is higher than in customary church attendance. Although a few nuns and a small group of girls in traditional costumes intermittently carry the painting of Gospa Sinjska, the greater part of the procession is dominated by local (male) authorities, by the clergy and by representatives of the military and the police. I once asked my main interlocutor in a different context if he could define the concept of 'honour' [*čast*] for me, and after a brief moment of consideration he answered: '*čast* is, for instance, to win the Alka or to carry the painting of the Gospa during the procession – like my youngest son did last year.' This comment indicates that the religious procession also comprises a number of secularised, or socio-political and cultural, aspects. To participate in the procession and to carry the painting is regarded as a sign of respectability and (political) influence – and I would also go as far as to consider the procession as a parade and celebration of (masculine) honour and masculinity. The fact that the religious procession is accompanied by a pageant of *alkari* and *momci* in arms and full attire is a further indicator that some of the key values embodied in the cult of Gospa Sinjska are local patriotism and pride. The selection of those appointed to carry the miraculous paint-ing in the procession depends on social roles and status, and not only symbolises the internal – secular as well as religious – structure of the community but also allows for a parade of local culture and folklore.

Kraljica Hrvata – Virgin Mary, Queen of the Croats

From Military Defeat of the Turks to the Religious Struggle against Communism

Devotion to the Virgin Mary is of exceptional importance to both Cath-olic dogma and popular Catholic imagery, as notably expressed by the two papal decrees concerning Immaculate Conception from 1854 and Bodily Assumption from 1950. The documents of the Second Vatican Council, held from 1962 to 1965, formally recognised the status of the Virgin Mary in the Roman Catholic Church and reaffirmed her cult, as the Marian devotion decreed from above found an echo in popular pi-ety. The prayer for celestial intervention and divine protection is a key attribute of the veneration of saints, and to address the Mother of God and pray for her intercession constitutes an integral part of folk belief and tradition. As a popular form of religiosity, Marian cults have been significant throughout Europe in times of crisis, war or threat from for-eign powers. Victor Turner has pointed out that early in the nineteenth century an emphasis began to shift from Marian devotion as a system of beliefs and rituals towards 'Mary herself, as an autonomous figure who takes initiatives on behalf of mankind, often intervening in the midst of the economic and political crisis characteristic of industrialised mass society' (Turner and Turner 1978: 203). This personalisation of Mary as intermediary advanced the functionalization of Marian cults in political contexts and successively enabled various concrete nationalist mobilisa-tions of Marian devotion (Zimdars-Swartz 1991).

    In her comprehensive study *Rosenkranz und Kriegsvision – Mariener-scheinungskulte im 20. Jahrhundert* [Rosary and War Vision: Marian Ap-parition Cults in the 20th Century], Monique Scheer analyses the role of Marian apparitions and subsequent Marian cults in times of war in twentieth-century Europe. She convincingly demonstrates that only those places of apparition where the Virgin appeared immediately before or after a war to give instructions on how lasting peace could be achieved turned into genuine pilgrimage sites (Scheer 2006: 339). She finds that '[t]he application of miraculous pictures and relics of the Virgin Mary as a defence against hostile attacks gained in importance in inner-European conflicts during the Middle Ages', and also describes the central symbol of Marian intervention and protection during military action in modern times in terms of a 'Lepanto paradigm', stemming from the legendary naval battle of Lepanto in 1571 (Scheer 2006: 301, my translation; see Schreiner 1994: 374–87). This early battle initiated the close affinity between Marian veneration and the defeat of Ottoman dominance that later played an important role during the siege and Battle of Vienna in 1683 and the Battle of Sinj in 1715.

The historical development and political utilisation of Marian cults from early modern to recent times is relevant to my study of the cult and pilgrimage in Sinj for several reasons. The appropriation of Gospa Sinjska for the Croatian national liberation struggle in the late twentieth century stands in a long tradition of militarised cults of the Virgin Mary as a spiritual subject of army command. I argue that the cult of Gospa Sinjska could only be revived ahead of the Homeland War because the Virgin Mary had already been successfully established as an interventionist figure and patron saint of warfare, in accord with the 'Lepanto paradigm'.[25] The Marian cult in Sinj exemplifies Marian devotion throughout history in as much as it encompasses a whole sequence of developments, from veneration of a miraculous Marian painting in the early modern period, through resistance to Ottoman expansion, to political mobilisation of religious symbols during the two world wars, to dissociation from communism, and finally to the independence efforts and military 'defence' against Serb expansionism in the 1990s.[26] The cult of Gospa Sinjska is therefore particularly suited for reconstructing and comprehending the emergent (re-)politicisation and (re-)militarisation of Marian devotion in relation to Croatian nationalism – a process that culminates in the cult's present deployment in the rehabilitation of Croatian war criminals (Schäuble 2014, forthcoming).

Politicisation of Marian Devotion in Historical Context

Narratives attributing military victory to Marian intercession reached a point of climax in 1571 with the legendary naval battle of Lepanto. The Spanish King Philip II instituted a 'Holy League' coalition of Venetian and Papal forces against the Turkish fleet in the northern waters of the Gulf of Patras, on the western Greek coast. Against all odds, the Holy

League won the day, inflicting a devastating defeat that halted Ottoman expansion and presaged the end of Turkish supremacy in the Mediterranean. The victory of the Holy League was credited to the Virgin Mary and resulted in her invocation as *auxilium christianorum* – 'aid of the Christians'. Her intercession was elicited through the rosary, and use of rosary prayer during the Ottoman wars would notably be revived in the apparition cults of the twentieth century (Scheer 2006: 312).[27]

The victory of Lepanto vindicated Marian veneration in military battle, leading eventually to the Virgin acquiring the sobriquet 'great general' after her perceived intervention in the defeat of Ottoman forces in front of Vienna in 1683.[28] Following the example of the Spanish King, the Habsburgs had also placed their troops under the protection of the Blessed Virgin Mary to prevent the capture of Vienna and the advance of the Ottoman Empire into Europe. A Capuchin padre was called to lend spiritual edification to the Viennese troops. It is believed that the padre allegedly mobilised the troops with the battle cry '*Mariahilf!*' [Mary help!], an invocation that also refers to the sacral painting from Passau (Scheer 2006: 53; see Hartinger 1985: 27; Schreiner 2002: 110). In the resistance to the Ottoman troops, every regiment was equipped with a flag depicting the image of the Virgin. The battle marked the political hegemony of the Habsburg dynasty in Central Europe.[29]

Sixteen years later in 1697, however, the Turks threatened to launch another attack and the Capuchin padre was again called upon for spiritual guidance. He held mass prayer gatherings and the intensive Marian veneration is said to have warded off the Turks for a second time. In a sermon held during a commemoration service, the rosary was compared to a weapon of war against infidels. This image added to the militarisation of the Marian cult as a form of religious belligerence against infidels. I argue that it also served as a model for the legend of the Marian apparition and divine intervention in the battle against the Ottoman troops in Sinj. The tradition of waging war under flags and banners with an imprint of the Virgin Mary has been widely adopted throughout the Christian hemisphere (cf. Schreiner 1994: 374–409). The fact that during the official commemoration of the Battle of Sinj, the annual Alka pageant, a horseman carries a banner with the emblem of Gospa Sinjska to this very day, refers to this practice and symbolises that the battle against 'infidels' is fought in the name of the Virgin Mary and under the Virgin's protective care.

The revitalisation of Marian veneration between 1850 and 1950 reflects clear elements of the earlier religious wars. This period is commonly referred to as the 'Marian century'. Scheer sees in it a resurgence of the earlier tradition of seeking sanctuary in the Blessed Mother in

times of war and radical transition (Scheer 2006: 14, 19). As an auxiliary
to Catholic soldiers, Mary remained an important patron saint and her
cult underwent a significant revival during and immediately after the
First World War.[30] Scheer accentuates the specific significance of Marian devotion in post-war times and refers to Marian cults and apparitions in terms of crisis-induced revitalisation movements (Scheer 2006:
393–408).

In the radically changing political landscape in the twentieth century, the concept of both political and religious enemies underwent
transformation. In 1917 the Virgin Mary appeared in the small Portuguese village of Fátima, and the subsequently developing cult transformed Fátima into one of the major sites of Marian worship and
pilgrimage worldwide. The Virgin delivered a number of messages and
'secrets' whose political tone at first echoed the First World War and
the insecurities of the interwar years. With the outbreak of the Second
World War, the cult of Fátima started to trace a severe anti-communist and anti-modernist course. One of secret messages of Our Lady
of Fátima – or Our Lady of the Rosary, as the Fátima Madonna is also
frequently called – was the 'consecration of Russia'. In 1942 the message of Fátima was 'updated' (Scheer 2006: 72) and one of the seers of
the Fátima apparition, Lucia de Jesus, was allegedly commissioned to
circulate the following message:

> If my requests are heeded, Russia will be converted, and there will be
> peace; if not, she will spread her errors throughout the world, causing
> wars and persecutions of the Church. The good will be martyred; the
> Holy Father will have much to suffer; various nations will be annihi-
> lated. In the end, my Immaculate Heart will triumph. The Holy Father
> will consecrate Russia to me, and she shall be converted, and a period
> of peace will be granted to the world. (de Jesus 1995: 104)

Proclaimed in the anxious climate of the Cold War and supported by
the Pope, the messages of Fátima fervently preached and predicted
victory over communism and thus stimulated an even greater polari-
sation of the world powers. The historian Vjekoslav Perica has stated
that the Fátima myth developed into 'one of the most efficient forms
of popular anti-communist mobilisation in the twentieth century created and carried out by the Roman Catholic Church' (Perica 2002:
114). Rhetorically grounded on another threat 'from the East' – this
time not proceeding from the Ottoman Turks, but the 'Russians' – the
so-called 'Fátima movement' generated a continuation of the earlier
politicisation and militarisation of Marian cults.[31] The dreaded Bol-

shevik expansion was symbolically linked to the historic expansion of the Ottomans, and Fatima was accordingly referred to as the 'new Lepanto' (Scheer 2006: 339).

The Impact of Marian Devotion on Electorates and Gender Norms

After the end of the Second World War, Marian cults significantly boomed for a second time, leading William Christian Jr. to discern that in the period between 1947 and 1954 four times as many visions and apparitions of the Virgin Mary were reported as in the years from 1930 to 1975 (Christian 1984: 241). The anti-communist message of Fátima was received and emulated all over the world and had a particularly effective impact in those Catholic regions of Eastern and South Eastern Europe under communist rule. Utilising 'ever-popular Marian apparitions as weapons in the struggle against secularization, liberalism, liberal nationalism, freemasonry, socialism and communism, and against hostile regimes and rival religions', the Church exercised an increasing influence on socio-political change (Perica 2002: 115). The individual impact of the Marian messages, however, is intertwined with other domains and is closely connected with power inequalities based on gender, class, ethnicity and age. Visitors to Marian shrines verifiably comprise an above-average proportion of the socially disadvantaged or marginalised population groups,[32] and it remains uncertain whether Marian devotion serves in some way to improve the conditions of those oppressed by cultural and ideological hegemonies or whether it works rather in favour of the powers of religious and political conservatism.[33]

In any case it is beyond doubt that church interventionism has not only economic and political but also moral consequences that lastingly affect the social cohesion of a given community. Particularly in post-war societies, transformations towards the establishment of a 'civil society' are mainly noticeable on a family level as well as in changing gender relations. The evangelism of the church hence ostensibly aimed at exerting political influence at a family level, and the growing religious involvement of men had an immense socio-political impact on electoral behaviour. In Italy and France, for example, the implementation of women's suffrage prevented an election defeat of the conservative parties in 1946 when a majority of men voted for Communist or Socialist parties (Christian 1984: 244; Scheer 2006: 356). It thus becomes clear that the militarist language of the Fátima cult was not only addressed to women but also intended to appeal to former soldiers and/or to Catholic men involved in some way in military action. John Davis has noted that the reaffirmation of the Virgin Mary served to realign men away from the public arena of politics and dubious profiteering towards the morally unambiguous household (Davis 1984; see Wolf and Lehmann 1984: 8). Such appeals to masculine devoutness counter-balanced the increasing 'feminisation of religion' that had evolved since the nineteenth century (Scheer 2006: 357). By and large, the Fátima messages aimed at strengthening the Christian family and promoted the foundation of a civil society under ecclesiastical hegemony (Wolf and Lehmann 1984: 8).

The Politics of Marian Apparitions in Croatia and Herzegovina

In the former Yugoslavia – and particularly in the Catholic strongholds of Croatia and the Herzegovina region – the aftermath of the Second World War and the growing politicisation of Marian devotion had a significant effect not only on changing gender relations but also on ethno-nationalist discourses. The first wave of popular Marian devotion occurred in the 1940s under the fascist Independent State of Croatia and was significantly revived in the 1980s when the multinational state of Yugoslavia began violently to disintegrate – a process that Vjeko-slav Perica laconically entitled 'From Apparitions to Partitions' (Perica 2002: 109ff.). In 1987 Pope John Paul II declared a second Marian year in the history of the Catholic Church, lasting until Assumption Day on 15 August 1988.[34] This declaration has been seen by many as a gesture meant to lend moral support to the processes of opening up that were underway in Eastern Europe in the 1980s, and was certainly of immense importance in the context of post-communist transformation.

In Croatia, popular Marian religiosity is very widespread and her cult bears a close affinity to the concept of Croatia as a nation. The Virgin Mary is commonly referred to as *Kraljica Hrvata*, or Queen of the Croats, and particularly in times of war the nation as a whole has felt itself entrusted to her care (Grünfelder 1999; Schäuble 2014, forthcoming). Religious affiliation in general, and Marian devotion in particular, have traditionally played an important role in the struggle for Croatian nationhood. Zlatko Skrbiš argues that Marian apparitions and cults 'presuppose ... the existence of the very same principle that underpins nationalist imagining: *the idea of election/chosenness* and an associated perception of divinely ordained specialness' (Skrbiš 2005: 445). Convergence between Croatian nationalist discourse and Marian devotion is based on memories of Marian intervention in earlier battles of the seventeenth and eighteenth centuries – memories also invigorated and evoked systematically in the course of wars in the twentieth century.

Commencing in the early 1940s during the NDH period, Marian devotion developed into a key symbol of religious nationalism in

Croatia. The Archbishop of Zagreb, Alojzije Stepinac, undertook to establish the Marian sanctuary in Marija Bistrica in the Zagora region as a national shrine of the new Croatian state. The Croatian Catholic Church aspired to an 'ethnicisation' and 'nativisation' of Catholicism, while the regime of Ante Pavelić lent financial assistance to Archbishop Stepinac's endeavour of advancing a process of the re-Christianisation of Croatian society (Skrbiš 2005: 449f.; see also Perica 2002: 9–11, 60). Skrbiš interprets Pavelić's support for the Church in terms of an outlook of the pro-fascist Independent State of Croatia which 'had strong religious and indeed millenarian undercurrents that provided a sense that Ustasha were fulfilling a religious, as much as a national, mission' (Skrbiš 2005: 450). The salutation '*Bog i Hrvati*' [God and Croatians], which is still used sporadically in nationalist and military rhetoric today, refers to this notion of Croatians as a chosen people. After the war and under the Communist government of Josip Broz Tito, however, the reassertion of Croatian Catholic identity and unity was repressed: religious liberty was restricted and religious institutions were effectively marginalised. For more than two decades, free practice of religion and pilgrimages to Marian shrines were hindered in every conceivable way.

Catholicism, however, remained an important indicator of Croatian cultural identity and the remarkable accumulation of Marian devotion practices laden with anti-communist undertones after 1945 gradually started to affect the Catholic population and the politics of the Catholic Church in the former Yugoslavia (Christian 1984; Carroll 1986). The church started to make concessions to Croatian nationalism again during the 'Croatian Spring', a pro-nationalist political movement of the early 1970s that demanded greater civil rights, democratic reforms and a right to take pride in Croatian history. The church responded by reinforcing the cult of the Virgin Mary as the leading religious and national symbol of Croatia and resurrected the project of establishing a national Croat Catholic shrine in Marija Bistrica (cf. Perica 2002: 59). In 1971, the acting Archbishop of Zagreb, Franjo Kuharić, announced that 'small, oppressed nations worship the cult of Mary with an extraordinary piety' (*Glas koncila*, 22 August 1971; also quoted in Perica 2002: 60), and as a consequence of the Yugoslav bishops' conference in the same year, the Catholic Church 'launched the mobilization of the Croats under the aegis of "the Virgin Mary, Queen of the Croats"' (Perica 2002: 60).[35] Also in 1971, a Marian congress under the slogan 'Let Our People not Lose their Identity' was held in Sinj, and the Catholic Church obviously felt a vocation to assist in the formation of a Croatian nation and the implementation of a common Croatian identity.

In the absence of native saints prior to 1970, the Virgin Mary Queen of the Croats had become the central cult of Croatian Catholicism as well as one of the most popular symbols of Croatian nationalism. Marian statues, shrines and pilgrimages symbolically unify territories that Croatian nationalists considered historically Croatian. (Perica 2002: 60)

The tendency to mark territory as Croatian by consecrating and symbolically putting the land under the Virgin's protection has had a long tradition and the territories in question have primarily concerned contested areas such as the 'Krajina', the Croatian–Bosnian and Croatian–Serbian borderland and regions with an ethnic Croatian majority like Herzegovina. It is certainly no coincidence that a Marian sanctuary of major importance is located in each of these contested areas: the shrine of Our Lady of Biskupija that hosts the earliest known Marian figure in Croatian art is located in the 'Krajina', only five kilometres south-east of Knin. Accordingly, the sanctuaries of Sinj and Široki Brijeg are situated in the Croatian–Bosnian border region and Aljmaš is located close to the Croatian–Serbian border. The most renowned pilgrimage site, Međugorje, is located in the Herzegovina region in Bosnia-Herzegovina with a predominantly Croatian Catholic population and thus also represents a consecration of the land to Mary. After Tito's death in 1980, the Church expanded its position as a major driving force of Croatian ethnic nationalism and a number of 'secular nationalist leaders recognized the Church's leadership and became practising Catholics' (Perica 2002: 63).

Apart from the official (re-)launch of Marian cults by the Catholic Church, small shrines in south-eastern Croatia and the Herzegovina region under Franciscan administration experienced their own locally anchored revival of Marian devotion. These local cults were not directly linked to the religious awakenings instigated by the Croat episcopate but did also use the symbol of the Virgin Mary as a carrier of national as well as regional identity. It was in this extraordinarily tense political climate – characterised by mounting ethno-nationalist tension as well as church–state and church–internal conflicts – that the Virgin appeared in the small Herzegovinian village of Međugorje. In 1981, on the 64th anniversary of the apparitions at Fátima, six village children reported an encounter with a Croatian-speaking Gospa. The time and location of occurrence of the Marian apparition in a region known to be a stronghold of Croatian nationalists and militant Catholics – near the site of a Second World War Ustaša massacre – was bound to develop into a politicised movement that could be used to legitimise and endorse Croatian claims in the region. The apparitions provoked a heated dispute between the Episcopal Church of Bosnia-Herzegovina and the local Franciscans.[36] Whilst the bishop of nearby Mostar viewed the apparitions as fraud, the Franciscans in Međugorje managed to expand their religious as well as political influence. Since the first apparitions in 1981, more than seventeen million pilgrims have visited the community, and transformed the small village into an internationally acclaimed Franciscan-run pilgrimage site. Historians and anthropologists repeatedly point out that the Franciscan friars of western Herzegovina, where the parish of Međugorje is located, were closely connected to the fascist Ustaša regime during Second World War and remained committed to nationalist ideas throughout the communist period (Ramet 1985a, 1985b, 1989; Rubin 1995; Perica 2002; Skrbiš 2005). Perica even claims that 'west Herzegovinian friars, who during the war had sided with the Ustaša, labored against Yugoslavism and communism and dreamed about the restoration of the Croat state' (Perica 2002: 117). Based on their anti-Yugoslav, anti-communist and pro-nationalist agenda, the Franciscan clergy built up a reputation as advocates of militant Croatian Catholics, and are for the same reasons seen as resistance fighters by large parts of the local population.[37]

In the Marian cult and Marian apparitions of the early 1980s, religious and nationalist discourses became systematically entwined in one another and exerted a significant effect on independence efforts. With the mounting disintegration of Yugoslavia, all belligerent sides started to employ religious symbols in their nationalistic mobilisations and military efforts, and Međugorje openly displayed national Croat identity.

The Marian apparitions at Međugorje facilitated secessionist tendencies in Herzegovina, leading Perica to go as far as to label them 'a prelude to partition, war and genocide' in Bosnia-Herzegovina (Perica 2002: 122). When the Yugoslav Wars of Secession broke out, a range of political observers deemed the apparitions to be catalysts of inter-religious and inter-ethnic hatred, and the local communist county official referred to the Gospa as 'Ustaša Virgin' (Cviić 1982: 5f.; see Aleksov 2004: 4).[38] In 1993 Croatian president Tuđman stated that the apparitions in Međugorje 'presaged and ignited the "reawakening of the Croatian nation"' (Rubin 1995: 65), and the Marian shrine at Marija Bistrica became a site for 'public proclamations of universal Croatian values with heavily integrated patriotic undertones' (Skrbiš 2005: 458, n. 4). Employed in nationalist and militaristic discourse, Marian devotion increasingly diverged from the message of peace, love and harmony that the Gospa, as self-proclaimed 'Queen of Peace', had initially declared (Schaeffer-Duffy 1994). A priest in Turjaci, a neighbouring parish to Sinj, told me in an interview that a popular song emerged after the war that apparently included the line: 'Dear Gospa Sinjska, please take Stipe [Stjepan Mesić] and give us Franjo [Tuđman] back'. This story illustrates the relationship between Tuđman's church-friendly, nationalist politics, the rejection of Mesić's social democratic approach, and Marian veneration in the region.

In her study *Les Guerres de la Vierge* [The Wars of the Virgin], published in 2003, the French anthropologist Élisabeth Claverie clearly underlines the relationship between warfare and Marian veneration. She states that the local clergy perceived Međugorje as a 'second Fátima' and that the Virgin herself allegedly referred to her earlier messages of Fátima and mobilised her followers for the 'fight against the forces of evil' (Claverie 2003: 245, my translation). In the years of war, an image of the Virgin Mary prevailed as 'Woman of the Apocalypse', preaching a clash between Catholicism and 'atheist communism' or 'Serb aggression'. Instead of emphasising her initial message of peace, religious tolerance and freedom, '[t]he Virgin has been used to strengthen the morale of Croatian soldiers operating in Herzegovina and the local Croatian paramilitary forces in Herzeg-Bosnia [self-proclaimed Croatian entity *Hrvatska Republika Herceg-Bosna*, existent between 1991 and 1994]' (Skrbiš 2005: 454). This development can be seen as a continuation of the earlier militarisation of the Virgin Mary and her invocation as patron saint of soldiers in battle. Today, the close relationship between the Gospa and the military manifests itself in the visible presence of soldiers and army personnel during Marian pilgrimages and at religious commemoration services throughout Croatia and in the majority-Croat areas of Bosnia-Herzegovina.

The exploitation of the apparitions at Međugorje as instruments for anti-communist struggle and national homogenisation had a significant effect on parishes and pilgrimage sites throughout the region (Perica 2002: 118). Other devotional and pilgrimage sites started to flourish, too. The parish of Sinj, in particular, located only 120 kilometres from Međugorje, was affected by the apparitions and the awakening of nationalist imaginings related to it. Since the Homeland War the sanctuary of Gospa Sinjska has gained importance as a national pilgrimage site, and a visit to one of the numerous other Marian shrines in Croatia – be it Krasno, Trsat, Almaš or Marija Bistrica – is no longer just an expression of religious devoutness but also an experience of displaying a sense of nationality and national commitment. The Virgin Mary, Queen of the Croats, continues to play a vital part in popular religious sentiment as protectress of the Croatian people, and her veneration has increasingly developed into an 'orgy of history, local folklore, nationalism and religious ritual' (Skrbiš 2005: 453).

A Marian Apparition

Corporeality of Belief

It has been a centuries-old pattern that Marian apparitions primarily take place in remote, mountainous areas in which the Virgin usually appears to young shepherds or shepherdesses. This has been the case for the four apparitions in nineteenth-century France in Garaison, Laus, LaSalette and Lourdes, as well as for the apparitions in Fátima. And although not exactly shepherds, the four seers in Međugorje were also from humble rural backgrounds and thus confirmed the pattern that the Virgin prefers to show herself to the less powerful in the social hierarchy. Accordingly, it is usually remote parishes that tend to embrace popular piety and stimulate folk Mariology (cf. Lisón-Tolosana 1966; Christian 1972; Davis 1984). In Sinj, where community life today still remains far from secularised, the convergence of local patriotism and Marian devotion is a distinct feature; and when the apparition occurred in nearby Međugorje, the Franciscan friars in Sinj – influenced by the Church's internal dispute between the Franciscans and the dioceses of Mostar and Split – readily supported the (re-)awakening of the Marian movement in the region.

However, when on 27 August 1983 the Mother of God first appeared to five peasant children in Gala in the hamlet of Tomašević, approximately seven kilometres from Sinj, the Franciscan friars were highly sceptical. The apparitions in Gala are first mentioned in academic literature two years after the event by the historian Pedro Ramet, who clearly links them to the apparitions in Međugorje. Analysing the role of the local Franciscans, he notes that

> [s]ome observers … have suggested that the Franciscans contrived to produce reports of miraculous appearances of the Madonna first in the Herzegovinian village of Medjugorje in 1981 and subsequently in the village of Sinj in 1983. Whether or not the reports were the works of the Franciscans, it is clear that the Franciscans believed they stood to gain the most from the ensuing religious euphoria in Medjugorje, and while the Bishops' Commission of the Mostar diocese (in which Medjugorje is located) has urged a cautious attitude towards these claims, the Franciscans have openly endorsed the authenticity of the Medjugorje apparition (although the Franciscan provincial distanced himself from the reports about Gala). (Ramet 1985b: 308)

A reluctant attitude of the Franciscans towards the apparitions in Gala seems to prevail today, and so I decided to pursue this case. I had read about these alleged 1983 apparitions in the village chronicle of Gala in very few historical accounts, but had found some newspaper clippings from that time. Furthermore, I heard a number of enigmatic contradictory statements by Franciscan friars from Sinj, members of my host family and friends in Sinj. Some told me that regular Masses were still being held at the alleged apparition site, others said that a small chapel had recently been erected, while still others assured me that nothing could be found in Gala at all. This rather irritating discrepancy of facts regarding the visions in Gala as well as the reluctance of the local clergy to address this topic made me want to revisit and look for the alleged apparition site myself (see also Schäuble 2014, forthcoming).

In the summer of 2012, my colleague Duška Vranješ and I travelled to Gala by car, and not quite knowing what exactly we were looking for, we asked a local peasant who was passing by on his tractor if he could tell us where to find the chapel. The man asked 'Do you mean where the Gospa appeared?' as if this was the most conventional landmark. He explained the road to us and we followed a tiny, very steep track that all of a sudden stopped. We tried to turn around in the car thinking that we certainly must be wrong, when an elderly lady wearing an apron dress and a white headscarf came out of her house and asked if we needed any help. Upon telling her that we were looking for the alleged apparition site, she most casually told us that it was her son who first saw the Gospa in 1983. The woman introduced herself as Dinka Marija Tomašević and kindly invited us into her humble stone house that was pleasantly chilly despite the insufferable August summer heat. We sat at her kitchen table for the next two and a half hours listening to her vivid and very detailed account of the 1983 events and their aftermaths with goose bumps.

> Marija – that's how she asks us to call her – tells us that in the afternoon of 27 August 1983, on the first birthday of her youngest child Anđelko, the Gospa first appeared to four boys in the vineyard behind her house. One of the boys was her son Jurica who was then six years old. The children told that the Mother of God was sitting on a stone, dressed in black. According to the children seers she looked very beautiful and combed her long blond hair. She told them that she dressed in black because she was mourning since her children [all human beings, MS] increasingly tumbled into the abyss [because of their sins, MS]. While three of the boys ran off terrified, little Jurica

allegedly said to her 'If you are from God's side, stay, if you are from the serpent's side, go away!' [*Ako si sa božje strane, onda ostaj, ako si od zmije, onda idi*]. The Gospa smiled leniently and called him closer to her. Jurica ran home to call his sister Anita and his second cousin. Marija had been in the kitchen preparing the birthday for her youngest, and had heard the turmoil, when Anita came running to tell her that the boys had seen a woman in the vineyard. Seven children (the four boys and three girls), Marija, Marija's aunt and another woman rushed to the vineyard, where the girls also saw the Gospa. The girls said that in the meantime she looked like the painting of Gospa Sinjska and wore a golden crown ... The children seemed enraptured and when Marija's aunt walked towards them and asked what they saw, they screamed 'Careful! You walk right across her!' The adults could not see the Mother of God, but they kneeled down by a fig tree and started praying. The Gospa appeared again and called Jurica towards her, but this time he could not understand what she was saying. From this moment on, the children had regular visions and the Gospa consistently appeared in the vineyard. News of the apparition spread fast, and by the next day the first curious spectators and the devout were already arriving at the scene.

During one of the visions, the Gospa told the children that a spring would erupt in the field and at the time when the miracle would occur, the place would be become more famous than Međugorje. When Duška intervened and asked Marija why this had not happened yet and why she thought that Gala had not become as popular a pilgrimage site as Međugorje, Marija simply answered 'God's secret'. She calmly continued her narration and told us that the Mother of God in a vision had also shown her daughter Anita what the place would look like. Anita allegedly saw a brooklet in the vineyard and flowers of a kind that she had never seen before. Two little angels in patchwork dresses had played in the water, splashing and laughing. At one point, Anita had touched the hand of the Gospa and told her mother that it felt like a hand of flesh and blood. In a different vision, the Gospa declared that she would not show herself for a long while now but that she would still be present. She would, however, continue to appear in Međugorje and she asked that people in Gala continued to pray. (Field Notes, 4 August 2012)

Throughout her account, Marija was very serious, and it was very clear that she believed every word of what her children had told her. Sometimes she started crying, because she was still moved by the words of the Gospa and the grace they had received.

She tells us: 'The children have seen it all: they have seen the dead, they have seen heaven, hell, and they have seen the devil, too. But nobody believed them and helped them. Instead they were laughed at and teased'. Her son Jurica had to repeat 5th grade five times because he was so troubled and confused by the apparitions. And when he could not answer a question at school the other children would tease him and say 'Why don't you ask your Gospa for the answer?' Apparently, not even the grandparents of the children, Marija's parents, believed in the visions, but she assured us that she never had any doubt about her children's honesty.

The Yugoslav state authorities had also heard the rumours about the apparitions in Gala, and when many pilgrims started to visit the site they sent police forces to disperse the devout. Marija tells us that they retreated to a nearby meadow and met during the night for prayer. At the height of the influx of visitors, police patrolled for eight days and eight nights in a row. 'But the policemen started to see things, too', Marija assured us, and she mentions quaint things, such as an increase in snakes and disappearing walnuts. Policemen apparently picked nuts from the local farmers' trees, which disappeared before they could be eaten. Marija tells us these stories to reassure us that they were not intimidated by the state authorities and did not surrender, so that in the end even the police started to sense a divine presence. But it still becomes clear that it must have been a very daunting experience to have police and secret services in one's backyard. (Field Notes, 4 August 2012)

When we asked Marija if she could show as the site of the apparition, she took a quick shower and changed her clothes, as if she wanted to be 'clean' when visiting the Gospa.

All of a sudden she looks twenty years younger, with a modern short haircut, wearing a black T-shirt and black trousers. She takes us on a trail behind her house, and shows us the exact spot where her children had first seen the Mother of God. Today, the vineyard has made way to a rather barren-looking, steep field. Marija walks ahead of us and sits down on the stone where the Gospa allegedly sat when Jurica first saw her. She pretends to comb her imaginary long hair to show us exactly what the children had described. Later on she points to the exact spot where Anita saw the spring and the splashing angels and with her hands forms the blossoms of the flowers that Anita allegedly saw – as if the landscape itself could verify what the children had seen. (Field Notes, 4 August 2012)

Marija's own corporeal and tactile re-enactment of the Gospa's behaviour was as much an attempt to show us as it was an attempt to
understand herself what had occurred here in 1983. And although she
had not seen the apparition with her own eyes, she seemed to be able
to (re-)feel the presence of the Gospa through the sensory impulse of
imitating her. By impersonating something she had not seen herself,
Marija managed to construct and sustain her particular world view
through sensual re-enactments and moments of immersion.

> She then leads us further up the hill, into a small grove. And there, in
> a clearing, stands an altar-like construction with a beautiful Marian
> statue. Concrete steps lead up to the monument that was constructed
> as a facade with three archways sheltering the two-metre-high bronze
> statue. The altar is rather big and we hadn't expected such an impres-
> sive monument in the little grove; yet it is well hidden in the woods
> and we wouldn't have been able to find it without guidance. Marija
> tells us that pilgrims from Italy donated the statue, and as she nar-
> rates more stories about her personal encounters with the Gospa, she
> softly caresses the hand of the statue.

Figure 2.7.　Marian altar in Gala. Photo: M. Schäuble

It is evident that Marija has an intensely physical relationship with the saint. She tells us that the statue had cried: first her forehead was wet 'as if she had done manual labour'. Marija had gone to fetch paper to dry the statue's forehead, but the Gospa sweated more and more. When Marija had fetched a paper towel to dry her, she saw tears pouring out of the statue. The tears rolled over her face, along her arm and dripped from the statue's hand into Marija's hand. At that point she knew, Marija said, that the Virgin Mary was mourning with her because she already knew that she would have to take Marija's son. And actually a few days after this incident, in January 2008, Marija's son Jurica, the boy who had first seen the Gospa, died at the age of thirty. 'Jesus's age', as Marija assures us amid tears. (Field Notes, 4 August 2012)

Jurica had suffered from a severe illness for several months and on his deathbed he reassured his mother that the Gospa had appeared to him again and had told him that she would take him home. As a suffering mother who had lost her son, Marija feels a particularly strong bond with the Gospa, who had lost her son at the same age.

Praying, for her, is a sensory and an aesthetic experience: the way she touches and caresses the statue conveys a deep love and connectedness. And she keeps telling us how beautiful the statue is and how many different facial expressions 'she' has. According to Marija, the Gospa had cried a second time and her whole upper body was wet

Figure 2.8. Marija caressing the Marian statue. Photo: M. Schäuble

from tears (Marija leans over the railing to softly touch the statue and to show us, where the tears had appeared). She would come here very often, especially when she was sad, Marija told us, and most of the time the Gospa would smile at her and make her feel better. Her daughter Anita explained to her that the Virgin was there to console and strengthen her, and to cheer her up.

'How did you hear about the apparitions?' Marija asks us. When I explain that I had lived in Sinj for almost a year but had read about the apparitions in a history book because nobody in Sinj had directly mentioned the events to me, she does not seem at all surprised. She shrugs her shoulders and says, 'Of course they want Sinj to stay the main pilgrimage attraction'. She mentions the economic factors and suspects that the Franciscans in Sinj are afraid that the pilgrims would come to visit the Gospa in Gala, not in Sinj, during the annual pilgrimage at Velika Gospa. And although she is very pious and would never think of questioning church authorities, let alone doubting the authenticity of the apparitions in Međugorje, she is very critical of the commercial exploitation of the Marian apparition site in nearby Bosnia-Herzegovina. 'Have you been there? Have you seen all the houses there and the shops? Before the 1980s nobody had a house there. Now they are all rich'. Shortly before his death, Jurica had told her that he really wanted people to visit the apparition site in Gala, but if it turned out the way it did in Međugorje, he'd rather not have anyone visiting at all ... It is really fascinating that she does not slander or blame anybody, after everything she and her family went through.

She doesn't mind being photographed, although it is very clear that she prefers us to take pictures of the statue rather than her. She tells us about the 1983 apparitions because she wants us to believe in them. She is not at all a person who would push herself to the fore, although she clearly enjoys the fact that we listen to her accounts and ask so many questions.

After we return to her house, we can see that Marija has turned a corner of her living room into an altar for Jurica. She shows us some newspaper clippings from which we can see that Jurica joined the Homeland War as a volunteer when he was sixteen years old! The washed-out newspaper picture shows him in a uniform, holding a machine gun in one hand and indicating a victory sign with the other. Under the pictures he is quoted as having said '*Kakav bih ja bio Hrvat kad bih ostao kud kuće, a neprijatelj nas želi zgaziti?*' [What sort of Croat would I be if I sat at home while the enemy wants to trample us?]. She must have unfolded and looked at this clipping many times, because it is almost falling apart. (Field Notes, 4 August 2012)

Currently, Jurica's widow and their two children live on Marija's compound together with Anđelko and his family. Marija's daughter Anita and her family live in a nearby village. Marija makes a living from selling donkey milk for 300 kunas (approx. 40 euros) per litre. She breeds the donkeys in a stable behind her house, and donkey milk is said to have curative effects.

> Before we leave, Marija tells us that the children were tested by a church commission in 1983 and were found to be telling the truth. They were secretly brought to the parish hall at night, and questioned by the archbishop, because he and the parish priest were afraid of the Communist police, as Marija reassures us. With this last effort to verify her account, she blesses us and wishes us a safe journey home. (Field Notes, 4 August 2012)

This is the first and so far only ethnographic account of the apparitions in Gala. In the 1980s the Yugoslav government went to great lengths to suppress the spreading of the news about the alleged apparitions and to prevent Gala from turning into a pilgrimage site. And today it still seems as if the Franciscan priests in Sinj as well as the parish priest in Gala would prefer to maintain silence regarding this matter. Therefore, the cult of the Virgin Mary in Gala is very locally restricted, and only few people know about the place and visit on a regular basis. The parish priest of Gala, however, agreed to hold a Mass at the monument once a year on the last Sunday in August to commemorate the 1983 apparitions. This service is very popular and hundreds of people arrive from nearby hamlets to worship the Gospa.

The church chronicle of Gala, published in 2010, is less secretive about the events and makes mention of a parish archive in which reports about the apparitions are kept. Apparently, then parish priest Mile Marović reported on the events in Gala, and especially about the seers, on a daily basis between 27 August 1983 and 5 September 1985. All efforts, however, to access these records have hitherto been unsuccessful. Various attempts to attain insight into the documents have produced a number of different excuses from diverse sides. Also locals of Gala, including Marija, who tried to gain access to the reports have been refused based on the sorry excuse that the files were lost when the parish hall was moved.[39] One document, however, a report by then archbishop of the Split-Makarska diocese, Dr Frane Franić, is accessible. This report was published by the ordinariate, and verifies that Franić himself established a so-called 'small commission' consisting of six members, whose task was to follow the events in Gala and to record the testimonies of the seers. I will provide a (nearly) full-length translation of this document that was published in the church periodical *Nadbiskupijski vjesnik* [Archiepiscopal Courier]. It not only provides vital insights into the position of church authorities of the time, but also confirms and extends Marija's account. In 1984, Archbishop Franić wrote:

> Last year, in late August, a rumour spread about a Marian apparition in the parish of Gala near Sinj. I first read about it in the newspaper *Slobodna Dalmacija.* In the beginning people flocked to the site of the alleged apparition and this lasted for a while. Later the number of visitors decreased daily. Nevertheless last year in October, when traditionally Mass is routinely being held in the parish church, the service was well frequented every evening, because the children 'seers' were attending. Initially there were fifteen 'seers', now there are five.
>
> O. Provincijal Dr Šimun Šipić [because Gala was under the authority of Presv. Otkupitelja], and I as archbishop, founded a small commission of six members to follow and investigate the events surrounding the alleged apparition in Gala and to report to the provincial administration as well as to the archiepiscopal ordinariate. During this first time O. Provincijal and I collaboratively wrote a small newsletter to all parishes in the Cetinska krajina in which we explained the nature and the meanings of these private apparitions to the people according to ecclesiastical exegesis. Unfortunately, many parish priests misunderstood this letter and wrongly passed on the impression that O. Provincijal and I denigrated these private apparitions, especially those in Gala, and a priori condemned them. The reports of the small commission were in general very positive, considering that the content of the 'message' coincided with the clerical dogmas and given that the behaviour of the majority of the 'seers' appeared honest to all members of the commission – in this respect we all had the firm impression that this was a serious matter that needed to be further pursued.
>
> The commission could not detect any lies or manipulation of the children. It was clear from the beginning, however, that the Franciscan parish priest and other Franciscan friars of the province of Presvetog Otkupitelja, especially those of the nearby sanctuary of Gospa Sinjska, did not want to have anything to do with these events.
>
> Nonetheless, pilgrims started to come from far away, for instance Zagreb. Recently, a 2.5-metre-high wooden cross, cast in concrete, emerged at the site of the 'apparition'. Also the newspapers reported about it. But the cross was quickly removed by the state inspection.

All of these were reasons that led father Provincijal and me to travel to Gala to find out more. Apart from the wish to familiarise ourselves with the events described above, we also wanted to bestow our paternal love on the children 'seers' and to pray in Gala. Therefore, in the afternoon of 30 October 1984, we, the above mentioned, went to Gala where we were received by the parish priest Mile Marović. He had been informed about our arrival beforehand, but had not told anyone so that the private character of our visit could be maintained. We talked to the children 'seers' in the parish hall who seemed like 'little angels' to us. We could not educe a single bad word from them about those who do not believe them, lead them into temptation or try to discredit them in any possible way. They angelically smiled at our attempts to provoke them and said that this was nothing and that everything would be like God had said. We were surprised about such spiritual maturity and composure of the children. The children told everything honestly and naively. There were no lies, not even white lies, no exaggerations, exorbitance or deception, and the children didn't behave in an unusual or striking manner: the children remained real children in every respect. We also met two 'adult seers' whose narrative style naturally differs from those of the children. Of course, the children don't have these 'experiences', these 'apparitions' on a daily basis. Little Anita has also so-called internal dialogues. She seems particularly gifted, but we don't tell her that.

We went to the site of the alleged apparition and prayed there together with the children seers for about half an hour. The children kneeled motionless on the wet stone while we remained standing. After that we went to the parish church and celebrated the Holy Mass together – the archbishop, the parish priest and one of his companions. And after the parish priest hospitably accommodated us, we all went to our houses in the dark.

Result: the messages of the children are prayer, humility, prudence, peace and reconciliation – so the same as in Međugorje. On the basis of all this, I am now convinced that the events in Gala are of a sheer religious character, that they don't remotely have the dimension of Međugorje, that they occurred spontaneously and without connection to Međugorje but nevertheless repeat the message of Međugorje, yet in a different ambience than Međugorje, or rather in an exclusively catholic area.

Therefore, I personally and humbly consider the religious and mystic events in Gala currently as probable, and perceive them as an outgrowth of Međugorje. Hail and glory to the Holy Trinity! (Frane Franić, Archbishop, *Nadbiskupijski vjesnik*, Br. 6/1984. Str 19–20)

In this highly revealing and volatile report, then Archbishop Frane Franić recounts his personal encounter with the 'children seers' in Gala and makes no secret of his bewilderment regarding the matter.[40] Between the lines, one can also sense his fear of state authorities as well as his insecurity as to how to handle the apparitions in view of clerical dogma on the one hand and his own personal impressions on the other hand. This is a very rare and valuable document in the sense that it provides insights into decision-making processes that are usually hidden from the public (i.e. on what grounds an apparition is declared 'authentic' or dismissed as fraud). Archbishop Franić's assessment is not automatically an ecclesiastical evaluation, of course, since neither the apparitions in Gala nor the ones in Međugorje have ever been officially approved by the Catholic Church, but neither have they been condemned.[41] The 'small commission' Franić established resembled the commission launched by the local Bishop of Mostar, Pavao Žanić, in 1982, which first consisted of four and later of fourteen members, including theologians and medical professors, who had to investigate the apparitions in Međugorje. Žanić was originally in favour of the authenticity of the Međugorje apparitions but he later denounced them, and in 1986 submitted a negative report to the Vatican. Žanić's change of mind triggered many speculations, most notably the suspicion that he was intimidated and ultimately collaborated with the Yugoslav secret police, UDBA. In view of this background, it is understandable that Bishop Franić was afraid that he would be given responsibility by the Congregation for the Doctrine of the Faith, then headed by Cardinal Joseph Ratzinger, to assess the Gala apparitions – a conceivably unrewarding assignment. But this did not happen, as I will show in the following, because he decided to keep a low profile and let the developments in Međugorje take over.

Another version of the events in 1983 has mainly been assembled and reconstructed by the Croatian historian Vjekoslav Perica. Perica's analysis of police files and court papers related to the Gala apparitions contextualise the events from an official state perspective and further highlight the political brisance of the events. At the beginning of the 1980s and at the height of the anti-communist climate, when the break-up of Yugoslavia became a realistic option, a number of Croatian clerics arranged participation in so-called 'voyage missions'. A 'voyage mission' is a kind of religious convoy in the course of which a statue or image of the Virgin Mary – normally an image of the highly politicised figure of 'Our Lady of Fátima' – is carried from parish to parish with the intention of sanctifying and stabilising a country in times of political or economic crisis, and proselytising the population. Previously these missions had been carried out in Spain, Italy, Poland, and even in South American

countries such as Chile and Brazil.[42] In 1983 one of these famous con-
voys reached the rural parishes in Dalmatia. Several statues of Our Lady
'Queen of Peace' of Fatima had been imported from Italy. Perica reports
in this connection that '[t]he Madonnas were packed into polished altar-
like boxes, with the Fatima's message on the 'conversion of Russia' typed
on a sheet of paper attached to the box' (Perica 2002: 119). A number
of parishes, among them the sanctuary of Our Lady of Sinj, had put the
statues on public display when all of a sudden a miracle occurred:

> In the Marian shrine of Sinj and surrounding villages, apparitions of
> the Madonna were reported during the 'voyage missions'. A 16-year-
> old girl from the village of Gala announced that she had seen the Vir-
> gin Mary. The familiar scenario of Međugorje and other apparition
> sites was repeated. Thousands of pilgrims flocked to the apparition
> site, and many buses carrying pilgrims to Međugorje turned from the
> Split–Mostar highway to take a look at the sight of the newest miracle.
> (Perica 2002: 119)

Perica further reports that '[t]he police surrounded the site, searched
houses, arrested the visionary and the local clergy, and repeatedly dis-
mantled wooden crosses erected on the apparition site, until the faithful built a six-foot-high concrete cross which the police finally let stand
there' (Perica 2002: 119). According to his version, the young seer from
Gala was accused of 'disseminating false news' and 'alarming the public',
and was subsequently sentenced to two weeks' imprisonment. Additionally, charges were brought against three local priests who had initiated
the 'voyage missions' and supported the seer's story.

> Alojzije Bavčević, the rector of [the] Catholic seminary in Split, who
> purchased the Madonnas in Italy and imported them to Yugoslavia,
> with two parish priests from the Sinj area who organized the 'voyage
> missions', were charged with violating the federal criminal code by al-
> legedly 'insulting a foreign country [Russia]'. (Perica 2002: 119)

The girl's lawyer allegedly argued that the news was not false and insisted that the judge should prove that the Virgin Mary does not exist
and that the girl did not really see the apparition. 'In the local press the
whole affair was used to ridicule both the Church and the authorities'
(Perica 2002: 278).

Marija, on the other hand, told us that this girl, Anđela, was not one
of the initial 'seers' and was only arrested by the authorities because she
was the oldest and already went to secondary school. She was suspected

of having instigated the younger children, but, according to Marija, never had any visions herself. There was no mention of the 'voyage missions' in Marija's account of the 1983 events, and it is doubtful whether the local village population even realised the political topicality of the message inherent in these missions.

Perica further provides a translation of the original indictment against Bavčević and the Franciscan friars from Sinj, filed in the 'Office of the Commission for Relations with Religious Communities of the Association of Municipalities of Dalmatia, Split, Croatia.' The indictment alleged that:

> in the period from October 1983 to April 1984, the suspects received, planned, and carried out a ceremonial tour of the statue of the so-called 'Our Lady of Fatima' – an icon revered by the church-going people as sacred and capable of performing miracles – throughout the parishes and villages of Trilj, Košute, and other places ... The statues were purchased and imported from Italy by the indicted Bavčević, who retyped and attached to the box with the Madonna's statue a text titled 'Mary's Words from Fatima to the World', in which a foreign country, the USSR, is ridiculed and insulted ... Bavčević handed out incriminated statues to the indicted Milan Vrdoljak and Vjenceslav Kujundžić, who exposed them in parish churches and organized their circulation among believer's families and homes. (cf. Perica 2002: 119)

In the end, however, none of the three accused was sentenced, as the indictment never reached the court. According to the correspondence between Archbishop Frane Franić and the municipal Commission for Relations with Religious Communities, Franić decided to discontinue the Madonna's voyage missions and replaced the word 'Russia' with the expression 'the world', thus rewriting the intention of the Fátima message as 'conversion of the world' (Perica 2002: 119, 278). According to Perica, the message of the alleged Marian apparition in Sinj gradually disappeared after the interventionist rebuke by state authorities in the face of the much more turbulent developments in Međugorje.

Local narratives, however, differ. Marija told us that when Anđela was in prison, her daughter Anita had another vision, in which she saw that Anđela was beaten and maltreated by police. She also saw that Anđela was doing something with her hands that she could not recognise. After Anđela was released she was missing a tooth and was told about Anita's vision. However, she was reluctant to talk about what had happened to her in prison, because she had promised to herself and to the Mother of God to observe silence. But when asked what she had done with her hands, she explained that she had pulled threads from her bed cover to braid a rosary for prayer. Whether she or any of the other children denounced the apparitions at any point remains unclear, but it is apparent that Anđela was interrogated, arrested and ill-treated by the police. Apparently, she now lives abroad and does not talk about the 1983 incidents.

The Gala parish chronicle also mentions that, even if quietly, believers continued incessantly to assemble at the apparition site for prayer, especially on Sunday afternoons. The devout from other parts of Croatia, and also from Italy, undertook pilgrimages to the site. On 16 May 1988 a Marian statue, a votive offering from Italy, was consecrated at the parish chapel to be erected at the apparition site. According to the chronicle, Gvardijan Fra Luka Livaja performed the blessing of the statue. But it was not until 15 September 2001 that the memorial chapel was consecrated at the site of the alleged apparition in the hamlet of Tomašević. This background information adds to Marija's account, who did not mention that the statue had been kept in the local parish church for thirteen years before it was relocated. The fact that a statue was erected and a memorial built almost twenty years after the first apparition provides grounds to believe that the local cult of the Gospa in Gala all but dissipated. Even if locally restricted, people continue to visit and pray at the site of the apparitions, and Marija affectionately takes care of the memorial.

I have already mentioned that it is widely accepted in academic literature that apparitions of the Virgin Mary tend to happen in times of personal, social, political and/or economic crisis. This certainly holds true for the apparitions in Gala in the 1980s when, after Tito's death in 1980, Yugoslavia was going through a period of great uncertainty, both in its political and its economic systems.[43] The increasing resentment between the republics and the fear of a rocky future were certainly noticeable even in the most remote corners of the country, such as the Dalmatian hinterland. However, it is rather unlikely that the children seers were manipulated by church or other authorities to announce their visions publicly. In the 1980s in a small village in the Dalmatian hinterland nothing was to be gained from the miraculous accounts on a socio-political or economic level apart from ridicule and persecution by Yugoslav state authorities.

When Jeffrey S. Bennett writes for the case of Fatima in 1917 that the ensuing apparition cult was not a Jesuit invention but 'the offspring of ordinary women and men, who were primarily concerned with the productivity of their smallholdings, the protection and moral cohesion of their families and villages, and the availability of resources to cope with existential crises of various sorts' (Bennett 2012: 19), his assessment can be directly transferred to Gala in 1983. Despite the imminent political turmoil, Dalmatian village life in the 1980s was still dominated by physical hardship and concerns about economic subsistence as well as the continuous underlying refusal to accept the state-decreed socialist image of humanity. The majority Catholic population desperately tried to hold on to their religious beliefs and practices, despite the imposed reprimand and disadvantage that came with exercise of religion in the Socialist Federal Republic of Yugoslavia. This also includes moral values, mainly in relation to Christian family cohesion and traditional gender arrangements. Viewed from a political perspective, the Marian apparitions in Gala were part of a conservative, 'popular anti-communist mobilisation' and the accounts were utilised to shield the local community from liberal and secular influences, and defend it against hostile influences (Perica 2002: 114f.). On another, more personal and locally grounded level and taking the long-standing restriction of religious worship into consideration, accounts of the apparitions can also be seen as a reserve of the disadvantaged and marginalised village population that was mobilised in view of the emerging prospect of political change.

In my analysis of the event, I am not so much concerned with the actual credibility of the visionaries or in providing pseudo-psychological interpretations of their visionary experiences, but rather with incorporating the local devotional practices and socio-political consequences in the aftermath of the apparitions, as described in my field notes above. From an emic point of view, the accounts of the children seers are narratives of local and personal suffering that contain the possibility of eventually overcoming suffering. A large part of the Gala apparition narrative is constituted by the fact that the visionaries and their families did not give in to threats by the state police and were not intimidated by the critical scrutinising of church authorities. The local villagers managed to withstand the overwhelming police presence in their backyards that lasted for days, if not weeks, and they continued to gather and to worship the Gospa at the alleged apparition site. In this respect, the apparition narratives are to be understood as tales of resistance and insubordination in a marginal place.

When Yugoslavia fell apart and the war broke out in the 1990s, Jurica, the first child seer, volunteered to join the Croatian forces as a volunteer when he was only sixteen years old. In the eyes of many Croats, this willingness to fight and possibly die for his homeland had made Jurica a hero already. Like a number of volunteers, he saw his military deployment not just as a national duty, but as a quasi-religious vocation to defend Croatia against intruders, as his mother Marija reassured. After the war, however, he shared the destiny of so many *branitelji*, especially those who had joined the armed forces at a very young age before they could finish school or professional training and became unemployed, with occasional jobs as an unskilled labourer or farm hand. When he then died of a severe illness at the age of thirty, Marija managed to turn her son Jurica into a proper martyr-hero. The corner of her house that is dedicated to Jurica and adorned with photographs, a rosary, candles and flowers resembles a religious house altar. On the other side of the wall, Marija had also hung up a picture of General Gotovina, who she reveres as a national hero. This blending of personal family and national history illustrates the convergence between Croatian nationalist discourse, Marian devotion, and private commemoration. Marija's altar makes it almost look as if Jurica sacrificed his life for God and Croatia on the battlefield, rather than losing his life to (presumably) cancer. The mere fact, however, that her son died at such a young age turns Marija herself into a *mater dolorosa*, and the concepts of suffering, (self-)sacrifice and (self-)victimisation that are such potent elements in Marian apparition, are symbolically transferred to Marija's own life, too.

Today, the villagers in Gala and the Dalmatian hinterland no longer live in fear of reprisal because of their religious, moral or political beliefs. However, most of them still live in fear of poverty, unemployment and an insecure future, and have little hope that the EU membership of Croatia will contribute to their personal well-being. Instead, a conservative political agenda in conjunction with religiously inspired attitudes to morality consider the traditional Christian family as a value per se, and (re-)construct it as the basis of communal as well as individual stability in the region.[44] For Marija, the visionary experiences of her children in the 1980s and her own ongoing corporeal relationship to the Gospa provide a durable source of moral comfort and support – support that she, as the head and sole provider of a three-generation family cannot expect from elsewhere, either from the church parish (which remains highly critical of the apparitions) or from the Croatian state (on which she does not want to be economically dependent). In this respect her religious beliefs remain a reserve to the present day that allow her to orient and define herself in meaningful ways. As a rural woman who underwent more hardship and suffering in her life than most people, and as the present guardian of a Marian memorial, she constructs herself as 'authentically' chosen by the Virgin, which provides her with a powerful status helping her to shape her immediate social reality and the future of her family. Due to the miraculous reputation of her hamlet and the produce of her farm (i.e. the curative powers of her donkey milk) she manages to uphold not only an economic, but also a moral independence and integrity that is above social and political marginalisation.

But why could Gala, as an 'outpost' of the sanctuary of Gospa Sinjska, never become an internationally acclaimed pilgrimage site like Međugorje? At first sight, the parishes of Gala/Sinj and Međugorje are very similar: they are both located in a mountainous and extremely barren area and the majority of the population live from subsistence farming, livestock raising and semi-transhumant pastoralism. Poverty made a large percentage of the male population of both places emigrate during the 1960s to work as *Gastarbeiter* in Western Europe, most of them in Germany. The Sinjska krajina as well as Međugorje were Ustaša strongholds during the Second World War, and both communities are located in the immediate vicinity of massacre sites. Moreover, Franciscans, who have a very close connection to the local population and take a clear patriotic stance, administer both parishes. The fact, however, that Sinj, or rather Gala, never became nearly as famous as Međugorje suggests a conclusion that the 1983 apparitions in Gala were discredited as a side effect or as an emulation of the earlier apparitions in Bosnia-Herzegovina. I can only assume that the Franciscan friars in Sinj did not like to mention these incidents of 1983 to me because they were embarrassed that the local clergy had surrendered to the communist authorities' ban on a developing apparition movement.

I once asked an elderly Franciscan friar in Sinj why, in his opinion, Sinj and Gala never gained the same reputation or status as Međugorje. He told me that the local Franciscans in Sinj always wanted the sanctuary to 'stay true to itself'. Furthermore, he elaborated that since the sanctuary of Gospa Sinjska has never been commercialised and has remained an unpretentious place of daily worship, it has succeeded in establishing a more authentic and 'purer' site of Marian devotion. As a down-to-earth local shrine, the sanctuary of Gospa Sinjska has nonetheless developed into a pilgrimage site of supra-regional and even national salience that attracts annually over half a million pilgrims – the majority making their pilgrimage on Assumption Day, Velika Gospa. Compared to the pilgrimage site at Međugorje, however, the pilgrimage to Sinj is much more territorially rooted and more closely linked to local memory and to the specific centuries-old history of the miraculous painting of Gospa Sinjska. The apparition site and the Marian altar in Gala are also locally rooted, but bear no direct reference to the contested history of the region at the crossroads between empires. The fact that the Marian statue in Gala was produced in Italy and bears no resemblance to the painting of Gospa Sinjska disconnects the 1983 apparition from the popular mythology of the legendary battle against the Ottoman troops in 1715, and might contribute to the wilful neglect of the Gala site by Catholic Church officials and Franciscans from Sinj alike.

The apparitions and miracles at Međugorje, on the other hand, have been extremely commercialised over the years and thus attract huge crowds of international visitors with diverse individual concerns that are entirely unrelated to the history and politics of the region. Today, the pilgrimage site at Međugorje still has a huge economic impact, but the initial political impetus has decreased since the apparitional phenomenon began to develop along its own independent lines. In contrast, the annual pilgrimage to and daily veneration of Gospa Sinjska has preserved and revived its significance as a site of the Croatian people's resistance to foreign intruders dating back to the times of the Ottoman invasion – and is hence best suited as *the* location for commemorating and celebrating the idea of Croatian chosenness.

In 1972 William A. Christian suggested that the process of long-term decline in cults of regional and local pilgrimage saints after the reformation period might be partly due to changes in territorial rooting and to a fading sense of connection to socio-geographical regions that are associated with particular saints. Mobility and the mass media, he suggested, broke down boundaries and brought localised (Catholic) communities into contact with a wider world (Christian 1972; see Turner and Turner 1978: 207). In the former Yugoslavia, however, the violent contestations over territory that accompanied the breakdown of the multi-ethnic state revived people's association to places that they considered their 'homeland' and 'sacred soil'. And less than ten years after Christian's prognosis, cults of regional saints and – in the case of Catholic regions – local Marian cults, experienced a major resurgence. Christian's predicted 'de-emphasis' of local saints' shrines and minor pilgrimage shrines has proved particularly incorrect in the Balkans, where Marian devotion has become a symbol of the struggles between official Church doctrines and popular beliefs, between tradition and modernity, and between the local and the global. Marian shrines and venerated images are resources through which localised norms and value systems are currently recharged (Schäuble 2007a). I argue that with the increasing importance of regions in the context of ever-advancing Europeanisation and globalisation, regional religious cults will take on even greater significance in the future – and will again be heavily politicised. In the case of Croatia this implies that Marian devotion and folk religiosity continue to provide an idiom with which to promote (moral) conservatism and increasing regionalism as valuable local resources or reserves that facilitate resistance to centralised, supra-regional political and economic influences.

Notes

1. On the arrival of the emigrants in Sinj, the painting was not at first publicly displayed for veneration as the Pre-Ottoman medieval church in Sinj had been destroyed in one of the many battles against Turkish troops. In 1698, however, the church was reconstructed beneath the ancient fortress, and this and the adjacent Franciscan monastery were the first structures to be built outside the ancient fortification walls.
2. The inscription is taken from the following verse of *The Book of Wisdom*: 'Cum praesens est imitantur illam et desiderant eam cum se duxerit et in perpetuum coronata triumphat incoinquinatorum certaminum praemium vincens' [When it is present, men take example at it; and when it is gone, they desire it: it weareth a crown, and triumpheth for ever, having gotten the victory, striving for undefiled rewards] (Book of Wisdom 4:2).
3. Up to the present day, the wreath of silver stars is laid out on the altar on 2 July every year for public veneration.
4. According to Roman Catholic theology, a plenary indulgence is the full remission of temporal punishment due for sins committed up to that time.
5. Due to the seismic instability that is common in many Mediterranean regions, Sinj had three serious earthquakes in the eighteenth century (in 1709, 1768 and 1769), with the last one destroying the fortress. In 1898 another earthquake caused great damage in Sinj and its surroundings.
6. To begin with the Serbian troops seized Potravlje and later tried to push forward to the Peruča hydroelectric dam near Sinj. They threatened to blow up the dam, which could have flooded the whole Cetina valley, leaving Dalmatia without power. The disaster was prevented at the last minute by a UN task force.
7. In Sinj only one 'civilian' was killed, in August 1991, when handling a self-made nitro-glycerine bomb that exploded in his hands. A memorial stone in the town centre of Sinj with the plain inscription *Suborci* (from *soborac*, 'comrade in arms') commemorates his death.
8. An elderly Franciscan friar, who was ordained to priesthood in 1961 and lived, taught and preached in Sinj for almost all his life, told me that during the Homeland War the 'Miraculous Painting of Our Lady of Sinj' was kept in Split, for security reasons.
9. Prof. Dr. Adalbert Rebić of the Theological Faculty at Zagreb University called the three pilgrimage sites of Marija Bistrica, Trsat and Sinj 'a triangle that covers the whole of Croatia – except for Slavonia' (personal communication 30 Oct 2004).
10. The church architecture in Croatia features hardly any Byzantine influence as the Franciscans adopted churches with one nave and a rectangular chancel according to the decree in the year 1220, and they also propagated this architecture in Dalmatia (Badurina 1982: 403).
11. Due to the failed papal crusade of 1443 the Ottoman rulers tended to tolerate the Catholic Church much less than the Serb Orthodox Church.

12. The Franciscans constitute the largest and most influential religious order in Croatia today. They are divided into the Order of Friars Minor, Conventuals, Capuchins and monastic Third Order Franciscans. Spread over three provinces in Croatia with headquarters in the municipalities of Zagreb (15 monasteries), Split (13 monasteries) and Zadar (5 monasteries), the order of the Friars Minor is the most prominent branch. The Franciscan Conventuals have twelve monasteries throughout Croatia with headquarters in Zagreb. Also with headquarters in Zagreb, the Third Order Franciscans have fourteen monasteries whilst the Franciscan Capuchins have one province with ten monasteries.

13. The Albanian studies scholar Stephanie Schwandner-Sievers, for instance, reports that in the northern Albanian town of Skhodra (Skutari) the Franciscans published the first Albanian version of the *kanun*, a collection of proverbs and sayings which codified an autochthonous Albanian customary law in 1933. In this sense the local Franciscan order contributed to the preservation and protection of traditional local custom despite the *kanun*'s official obliteration during state communism. In the 1990s the Franciscan Seminary apparently published a second edition and made the texts accessible to a wider public, thus indirectly supporting the withdrawal from state power and making them guardians of local tradition (Schwandner-Sievers 2004: 111f.).

14. The boarding school was completely renovated in 1991, during the war.

15. The grammar school [*gimnazija*] teaches 180–200 pupils, and thirteen of the twenty teachers are Franciscan priests.

16. Fra Željko told me that the robe was formerly regarded as *signum diferentiatium*, but today it was every friar's free decision if he wanted to wear the Franciscan habitat in public or not. He jokingly added: 'It's like a role play, our life in the monastery'.

17. The Franciscans reputation of being fond of worldly goods has made them the subjects of ridicule and many jokes. One of them directly refers to the greediness of priests and was told to me in a coffee bar in Sinj: 'A man comes running to the *gvardijan* of the monastery and screams "A priest has drowned! Oh my God! He drowned!" The *gvardijan* is totally shocked and asks "But why didn't you rescue him?" The man replies, 'But I tried! I kept shouting, *Give* me your hand! *Give* me your hand! But he didn't respond.' The *gvardijan* looks puzzled and replies: 'Of course not. You should have said: "*Take* my hand!"'

18. The Kamenita Vrata ['stone portal'] is one of four archways into the walled Gornji Grad ['Upper Town'] in Zagreb. In 1731 a fire destroyed much of the town, and legend has it that a vision of the Virgin Mary could be seen in the burnt ash that remained in this entry. Kamenita Vrata was reconstructed in 1760 and has not changed since. Today, the devout light candles, kneel in the church pews that are put up in the archway and pray to the painting of the Virgin Mary. The people who pass through the archway cross themselves or quickly bend their knees as a gesture of silent

worship. The walls are adorned with stone and marble brasses depicting vows and expressions of thanks.

19. During a personal tour of the museum by one of the Franciscan curators, I was shown a small collection of cast-iron, lead and/or silver reproductions of cured body parts, mainly eyes and legs, that believers have donated in the course of the past centuries.

20. Most of the visitors from the United States are members of the St Jerome Croatian Catholic Church in Chicago, a subsidiary parish of the order of Our Lady of Sinj overseas. There is a frequent exchange between the two parishes, and every year groups of American-Croats from Chicago travel to Sinj to participate in the festivities at Veliku Gospu.

21. Most studies focus on Marian devotion and the veneration of saints in Catholic religious practice; references to Marian devotion in Orthodox Christianity are for the most part under-represented in academic discourse. However, ethnographies like for instance Jill Dubisch's study on the Church of the Madonna of the Annunciation on the Aegean island of Tinos, *In a Different Place: Pilgrimage, Gender, and Politics at a Greek Island Shrine*, convey the importance of the veneration of the Virgin Mary in Greek Orthodox religion (Dubisch and Winkelmann 2005).

22. Feminist scholars like Eleanor McLaughlin have been pointing out that Marian devotion does not necessarily constitute a liberating force for women, but, on the contrary, confirms the inferior and submissive role of women. She writes that '[t]he medieval cult of the Virgin ... rather than deepening an appreciation of the bipolarity of God's creation ... underlined the weakness, inferiority, and subordination of real females' (McLaughlin 1974: 246).

23. This view is closely related to approaches suggesting that religion provides a space for women to socialise as well as to publicly articulate and/or perform needs and emotions that would otherwise go unheard (see Lewis 1988; Boddy 1989).

24. I argue that the figure of the *mater dolorosa* is of particular importance in the context of pilgrimages in post-war Croatia where mothers had to worry about sons or witness their death during the Homeland War.

25. A comparable phenomenon takes place in the small village of Krasno in the Velebit region. The well-known Sanctuary of St Mary of Krasno is located in a mountain village in the vicinity of Gospić. During the Homeland War, Gospić was a site of heavy skirmish. The town was repeatedly shelled by the rebel Serb forces of the Republic of Serbian Krajina but eventually, control of the area devolved to the Croatian government. Today, the sanctuary attracts tens of thousands of pilgrims every year, many of them soldiers and policemen who had been stationed in Gospić or nearby during the war. The Velika Gospa pilgrimage to the Sanctuary St Mary of Krasno is one of the most popular and best-attended pilgrimages in Croatia, as I saw for myself when I attended it in 2004.

26. In this context it is interesting to note that the parish 'branch' of the Dalmatian Franciscans in Zagreb is called *Gospa Lourdska*, named after the Marian apparation in Lourdes. The construction of this monastery started during the Second World War but could not be completed. After the war the communists did not accede to the initial construction plans because the church tower had allegedly been designed too high. I have been told that, as a subversive act, the building was completed nonetheless, but without a construction plan.

27. Pope Pius V instituted the commemoration of the battle as early as 1572 that is now honoured by the Catholic Church as the celebration of 'Our Lady of the Rosary' on the first Sunday of October.

28. In September 1623, shortly after the victorious Battle of White Mountain (1620) in Bohemia in the Thirty Years' War, the Italian Capuchin friar Hyacinthus of Casale sent the following blessing to Maximilian I, Duke of Bavaria '*[N]el nome di dio sempre benedetto e della nostra gran generalissima*' (cited in Schmidt 1993: 309; see also Scheer 2006: 309). His diction 'gran generalissima' documents the tradition to refer to the Virgin Mary as 'military support' and characterise her as 'great general'.

29. In commemoration of the victory, the Feast of The Holy Name of Mary was inaugurated and later extended to the entire Church by Pope Innocent XI.

30. It is reported that French soldiers, for instance, habitually wrote petitions or thanked the Lady of Lourdes for her protection and her support during battle (Becker 1994: 60–62; Scheer 2006: 340).

31. In relation to the apparitions at Fátima, organs of the Catholic Church founded the 'Militia of the Immaculate Conception' in 1917 and the 'Legion of Mary' in 1921 (see Perica 2002: 115).

32. The Virgin Mary is commonly referred to as *Consolatrix Afflictorum* and associated as protectress of the vulnerable, hopeless and the poor (Skrbiš 2005: 444).

33. Emphasising the socio-political claim of what he classifies as post-industrial pilgrimages and cults, Victor Turner has also noted that '[t]he Virgin's message is identified with lower-middle-class interests, and both big business and international socialism are condemned as major causes of humankind's sins, the sins we are called upon to repent' (Turner and Turner 1978: 209).

34. The first 'International Year of Mary' was proclaimed in 1975/76. Previous to that, however, Pope Pius XII had already proclaimed a Marian year in1954, commemorating the centenary of the declaration of the dogma of the immaculate conception.

35. The sanctuary of the Black Madonna of Marija Bistrica remains the official Croatian national shrine to the present day and is a popular pilgrimage destination, albeit much less integrated into daily routine business than for instance the sanctuary in Sinj.

36. Comparable to Sinj and the whole of Dalmatia, the Catholic Church never fully controlled Bosnia-Herzegovina, and the Franciscans established a firm regime in the rural areas where the Catholic communities outlasted, mainly around Franciscan monasteries. The Bishop of Mostar 'was convinced that members of the Franciscan Province of the Assumption, who had disobeyed the episcopal authority for over a hundred years, had engineered the miracle in order to forestall the bishop's plan for a redistribution of parishes in favour of diocesan clergy' (Perica 2002: 110). This dispute went to the lengths of the bishop collaborating with the communist secret police to denounce the friars, who, in turn announced through one of the visionary's messages that the Gospa considered the Franciscans to be in the right in this matter (Perica 2002: 110ff.; Claverie 2003: 186ff.; Skrbiš 2005).

37. Aleksov calls attention to the fact that Partisans had killed twenty-nine Franciscans as war criminals at the end of the Second World War, because they were suspected of hiding Ustaše at the monastery of Široki Brijeg near Međugorje. In the decades after the war, the communist regime tried to conceal the crime, but the local population nonetheless regarded the murdered friars as martyrs (Ramet 1982, 1985a; Aleksov 2004).

38. In this context it is quite revealing that the hill of the apparitions had previously been a commemoration site for the victims of an Ustaša massacre in 1941 (Aleksov 2004: 4).

39. I will continue to pursue this matter and hope to be able to present an in-depth study of the Gala parish chronicle and other documents in the parish archive during the coming years.

40. Marija also told us that the 'children seers' were later taken to Split to be tested for a whole week, but could still not be convicted of lying. An account of this second test is missing from Franić's report.

41. In April 1991, the Bishops' Conference of the former Yugoslavia published the following declaration: 'The bishops, from the very beginning, have been following the events of Međugorje through the Bishop of the diocese [Mostar], the Bishop's Commission and the Commission of the Bishops' Conference of Yugoslavia on Međugorje. On the basis of the investigations so far it cannot be affirmed that one is dealing with supernatural apparitions and revelations. However, the numerous gatherings of the faithful from different parts of the world, who come to Međugorje, prompted both by motives of belief and various other motives, require the attention and pastoral care in the first place of the diocesan bishop and with him of the other bishops also, so that in Međugorje and in everything connected with it a healthy devotion to the Blessed Virgin Mary may be promoted in accordance with the teaching of the Church.' Since this 1991 declaration, the status of Međugorje has not changed and the Holy See has allowed this status to remain as it is.

42. A replica of the Black Madonna of Marija Bistrica constantly toured Poland for nine years, from 1957 to 1966, to mobilise anti-communist forces

(Perica 2002: 115f.). The 'travelling Virgin' was also a major feature of Cold War Marianism; the Fátima Madonna travelled through almost all the Catholic regions of Western Europe between 1945 and 1955. The precursor for this was the 'Grand Retour' organised by the French episcopate in 1943.

43. The introduction of fuel limitations, food shortages and rising inflation made Yugoslavia's massive foreign debt and Western trade barriers immediately perceptible on all levels of society.

44. The fact that my companion Duška Vranješ and I each had a young baby surely helped in gaining Marija's trust, and she related to us as mothers.

Chapter 3

Re-Visions of History through Landscape

Dead Body Politics in the Dalmatian Hinterland

A Croat, a Bosniak and two Serbs arrive on the moon. The Croat points to the lunar mountains and says, 'Those are like the Dalmatian Hills. This must be Croat land!' The Bosniak argues that the cratered surface resembles the shell-scarred roads of Sarajevo, 'so it must be Bosnian'. One of the Serbs pulls out a gun, shoots the other Serb and says, 'A Serb has died here. This is Serb land'.[1]

This morbid and admittedly rather biased joke that is widely recounted in post-war Croatia illustrates the importance of landscape and particularly of burial grounds and graves to notions of national identity and belonging. It is not only the Serbs, however, who believe that Serbia is 'wherever there are Serbian execution pits and graves', as Vuk Drašković – dissident nationalist writer, founder of the Serbian National Renewal Party and later Serbian foreign minister – famously claimed in 1989.[2] The graves of the ancestors are an important factor in the politics of territory and likewise generate a sense of belonging to a particular *nacija* (nation, people) or region throughout the whole of the former Yugoslavia. Above all, places and landscapes of war, conflict and violence – such as ancient battlefields, front lines, vestiges of military constructions and memorials to commemorate them – are significant historical markers that constitute 'fundamental parts of the national iconography of modern states' (Raivo 1999).

Battlefield relics not only contribute to the materiality of historical landscapes but also bear national genealogies that have become important vehicles of separatist and nationalist politics over the past decades in the former Yugoslavia.[3] In this chapter I will take a closer look at the role material remnants of previous violent conflict play in contemporary Croatia, and more specifically in the Croatian-Bosnian border region. I emphasise the centrality of the immediate environment in which accounts of past battles and atrocities become grounded temporally and spatially.

Dalmatia is often referred to as both 'Balkan' and 'Mediterranean', and in either case the region is marked by its dense fragmentation and fractal character, influencing not only the dominant cultivation techniques, channels of trade and the 'political and ethnic untidiness' but also the religious topography (cf. Horden and Purcell 2000: 25, 622). Notions of locality and landscape play an important role in the process of (re)shaping national ideologies and identities in Croatia today and contribute to the composition of the nation's history and heritage. I use the term landscape following Susanne Seymour's understanding that, '[l]and-scape does not simply mirror or distort "underlying" social relations, but needs to be understood as enmeshed within the processes which shape how the world is organized, experienced and understood, rather than read as its end product' (Seymour 2000: 214). By focusing on my interlocutors' embodied relations with the surrounding environment, I attempt to better understand how they position themselves not only within their natural habitat but also, more generally, how they assess their role as inhabitants of a marginal place within the framework of the new Europe.

Besides affecting the way people organise their livelihoods, the physical conditions of the landscape also have an impact on the configuration of historically experienced and constituted space and time. Accordingly, I examine nationalist historiography in relation to territory, and consider examples of how memories of past atrocities in the Croatian–Bosnian border region generate a sense of rootedness and belonging, and how they – at the same time – are currently used to promote immediate political interests and to comment on political developments with regards to Croatia's role in the Homeland War.

Particularly after the breakdown of Communist Party rule, rumours of various massacres committed during the Second World War and later concealed under Tito's regime fuelled public resentment about suppressed memories of past atrocities. When unidentifiable corpses and bones of massacre victims – victims of communist Partisans, Serbian nationalist Četniks as well as of the Croatian fascist Ustaše – were rediscovered, excavated and partly reburied in their respective 'native soil' in the late 1980s and early 1990s, a hitherto disclaimed version of history became literally tangible. The anthropologists Bette Denich and Robert Hayden first showed how the uncovering of mass graves and massacre sites led to a drastic re-evaluation of notions of ancestry and territory and the increasing escalation of previously suppressed ethno-national tensions in the former Yugoslavia (Denich 1991, 1994:

367–90; Hayden 1994: 167–84).[4] Drawing on these anthropological studies to analyse the role of dead bodies in the context of post-communist nation-state formation, Katherine Verdery has addressed the nationalisms that emanated from the respective Yugoslav republics in terms of forms of an ancestor cult (Verdery 1999: 104).[5] The place occupied by the dead in both time (genealogies) and space (territory) is closely linked to national sentiment in so far as references to kinship rooted in particular soil is one of the core metaphors for nationhood (ibid.: 105, 160).[6]

Drawing on my interlocutors' own notions of locality and belonging, this chapter will show how their personally felt marginalisation and oppression during the years of communism, their sense of being under threat during the Homeland War and the life-historical narratives of subjugation (and fierce resistance) experienced by their predecessors are environmentally situated experiences. I argue that these people's relationships to their physical surroundings encompass much more than 'symbolic inscriptions' of values onto the environment. I contend that landscapes constitute mnemonic agents and sites of historic revisions. 'To perceive the landscape', writes Tim Ingold 'is ... to carry out an act of remembrance, and remembering is not so much a matter of calling up an internal image, stored in the mind, as of engaging perceptually with an environment that is itself pregnant with the past' (Ingold 2000: 189). Delineating the relation between practices, conceptions and imaginations of place in rural Dalmatia, this chapter will illustrate how the landscape of the Dalmatinska Zagora literally incorporates historical knowledge and helps to rematerialise hitherto hidden or suppressed versions of the past. Local inhabitants' sense of belonging, their relation to and identification with the Dalmatinska Zagora, springs mainly from practical and experiential involvement in the environment and is accompanied by a deep emotional attachment to the region (and its landscape). Such a localised mode of life goes hand in hand with a regionalisation that is openly and intentionally opposed to present globalising tendencies. In the Dalmatian hinterland, a perception of historic (spatial) marginalisation and neglect by ruling powers over the centuries is at present being massively remobilised and declared a local asset in the 'resistance to the utopia of globalization' (Müller 2002).

If one follows Edward Soja's express aim to 'spatialize the historical narrative, to attach to durée an enduring critical human geography' (Soja 1989: 1), it is salutary to investigate ways in which historical narratives and memories are embedded in physical surroundings and thereby made visible. A historical landscape is 'both material and meaning'

(Baker 1992: 3) and defined through phenomenological interaction and experience. It is shaped by visible historic interpretations as well as by meanings and interpretations related to them (ibid.). I argue that both individual and collective memories are attached to specific landscapes and thus have the potential to become sources for (re)writing the local histories that have been ignored or neglected by the historiography of the nation-state. 'Although memory is surely a temporal phenomenon, the ... metaphors [that are necessary to imagine memory] tend to transform the temporal into the spatial and are intensely visual. Layers are excavated, veils lifted, screens removed' (Antze and Lambek 1996: xii). This chapter is accordingly concerned with deciphering the inscriptions and attributions of historical narratives in local, regional and national landscapes in the context of post-socialist and post-war transformations.

In *War Memorials and Landscapes as an Experienced Heritage*, Petri J. Raivo states that

> [t]he historical landscape is thus part of memory made visible by somebody, and usually for a purpose. The sense of place is never created by place itself, for alongside its meanings and imaginations related to the site are created, represented and maintained. The spirit of a place, genius loci, depends on what spirits, or in the case of battlefields perhaps ghosts, we are willing to see, hear, and feel. (Raivo 1999: 3)

Over the months of my fieldwork, it became increasingly apparent to me that this 'spirit of place' in Dalmatia was deeply embedded in personal connections to local history. The longer I lived in Sinj and became involved in local narratives, the more I too was not just willing but able 'to see, hear and feel'.

Memorial Landscapes

Today, almost twenty years after the end of the Yugoslav dissolution wars, the practice of commemorating atrocities committed during the Second World War is being resumed. In the case of Croatia, nationalists adhere to the practice of commemorating crimes committed against Croats decades ago rather than facing more recent events. Atrocities that took place during the Second World War (and before that) and had been concealed in the Socialist Federal Republic of Yugoslavia still constitute the template to which the violence endured during the Homeland War is emblematically linked. With reference to my recent research findings I argue, however, that the meaning and political intentions of commemoration ceremonies at Second World War massacre sites has changed significantly since the unearthing of mass graves in the early 1990s. Taking the works of pioneering authors such as Denich, Hayden and later Pamela Ballinger into account, I draw on more recent commemoration ceremonies and thus actualise their analyses for the case of post-war Croatia (cf. Ballinger 2004b). I claim that present-day commemorative rituals at massacre sites in the Bosnian–Croatian border region are less intended to sustain or revive inter-ethnic animosity than to establish a version of history in which Croatia plays the role of an unprivileged and victimised nation that cannot be held responsible for the war waged in the 1990s. This historical self-conception is backed by the Catholic Church and above all by the even more influential Franciscan Order, who in addition have a traceable interest in rewriting the years 1945–90 as a 'litany of suffering' (to use Nancy Ries's term) for the Croatian people (cf. Ries 1994: 38–53). On the basis of a detailed analysis of ritual commemoration I seek to show that Croatian clerics actively support the denial of any Croatian war guilt in the Homeland War by referring to prior injustices suffered by Croats during the Second World War as well as under the communist regime – thus deliberately distorting historical facts and/or circulating one-sided accounts. Furthermore, the Franciscans manipulate the emotional weight of previously endured atrocities to support their reactionary political and 'moral' stand on processes of democratisation and liberalisation in the light of Croatia's recent membership in the European Union.

It is important to note that in contrast to the exhumations of mass graves and limestone caves that took place in the late 1980s and early 1990s, the sacralised commemoration that is taking place today has a different agenda: it is not part of an openly voiced political re-territorialisation process and is not linked to any direct territorial claims. The battle that is currently being fought over massacre sites is rather a rhetorical battle over the prevailing version of the past – over who is and who is not a perpetrator, who suffered the most during the communist period, who made most sacrifices, who has to bewail most casualties, and, eventually, who will emerge as the victor of history. Through the back door, this rhetorical showdown addresses the delicate question of guilt for waging war and committing war crimes in the context of the violent dissolution of Yugoslavia and the Homeland War. It is further intended to reassess and to possibly strengthen Croatia's role within Europe. In other words, I will show that the same atrocities and the same dead, dating back to the Second World War, are now reutilised in a new line of argument and adapted to current political events.

Martyred Villages: Landscapes, Legends and Commemoration

The dominant characteristics of the steep-sided limestone mountains of the Dalmatian hinterland are greyish-white karst rocks and arid tree-less slopes. This karst topography – comprising the southern parts of Lika, Dalmatinska Zagora including Sinjsko polje (the fertile karstic field that Sinj and adjacent settlements are situated on) and the larger part of Herzegovina – is riddled with hundreds of crevices and karstic grottoes, which became burial sites for innumerable victims of massacres in the Second World War. My interlocutors and friends told me that in the ar-eas surrounding Sinj, large numbers of Ustaša fighters and civilians were killed by Partisan troops. In the civil war of 1941–45 Tito's communist-led Partisans fought fierce battles with Croatian Ustaša troops govern-ing the fascist Independent State of Croatia (NDH, *Nezavisna Država Hrvatska*), as well as against Serbian royalists or Četniks. During these years cruel mass murders took place on all sides. The Ustaša committed genocide against Serbs, Jews and Gypsies, the Četniks killed thousands of civilians, mainly in Bosnia, and the Partisans slaughtered tens of thou-sands of Ustaše, Četniks and other opponents. In the majority of cases the dead were simply thrown into the numerous crevices and pits in the karst mountains. Referring to the adjacent Herzegovinian mountains, Vjekoslac Perica writes:

> The area is full of mass graves. Natural pits (*jamas*), trenches, ravines, and underground cracks in the Herzegovinian limestone karst were burial sites of the Ustaša victims but also harbored relics of the Cro-ats – victims of the communists' and the Serbian militant Četniks' re-venge. According to a map of mass graves and execution sites based on research by a Serbian author, there are 17 jamas and mass graves in the zone around Međugorje. (Perica 2002: 118)

Throughout the former Yugoslavia, local villagers who survived or wit-nessed the massacres of the Second World War secretly remembered the dead and the locations of their execution, even though they were prevented from publicly mourning and honouring the memory of their dead. Accounts of Partisan massacres of Ustaše, Četniks and civilians as well as Ustaša crimes continued to circulate in secret. The re-emer-gence of these suppressed memories is a key to understanding how past atrocities were revived and fuelled the emotions and (ethno-)political consciousness that accompanied the violent dissolution of Yugoslavia. Moreover, in post-war Croatia these memories are currently being mo-bilised anew to support what I refer to as a politics of (self-)victimisation:

memory politics that aim at highlighting recurrent suffering in order to divert suspicion from one's own people's wrongs and, in the case of commemoration ceremonies at massacre sites, at underlining the physical and hence tangible reminders of crimes endured at the hands of others.

In late- and post-communist Yugoslavia, the secret history of massacres committed by communists in 1945 gradually became open public knowledge. Along with the rediscovery of Partisan atrocities, propaganda that reinforced the memory of Ustaša massacres also increased and nationalists of diverse orientation made political use of the explosive force inherent in these previously silenced accounts. When the first free elections were held in 1990 in the republics of Slovenia (April) and Croatia (May/June), hitherto suppressed information about executions and mass burials was massively publicised by nationalist factions. Major media networks reported on excavations of bones and skeletons in mountain caves, and publicised details about public funerals and commemoration ceremonies at massacre sites, while recurrently naming locations of newly discovered mass graves. Denich mentions pictures of a forty-metre-deep cavern called Jazovka, published in the Croatian media. According to reports in the emigré publication *Nova Hrvatska*, the cave was 'full of bones of innocent Croat post-war victims of Communist savagery' (*Nova Hrvatska* 1990, quoted in Denich 1994: 378). Hayden cites a political cartoon in Zagreb's weekly newspaper *Danas* (17 July 1990: 2) depicting two figures in a bone-filled grotto, with one asking: 'Do you really think this is an inspirational place for discussions on constitutional changes?' (Hayden 1994: 175).

Images of exhumations were broadcast on national television, as in the case of Serbian remains found in limestone caves in Croatia, televised in Serbia in 1991 (cf. Verdery 1999: 100). Bones of the massacre victims were dug up and passed among lines of spectators composed of local residents, who were thus literally 'handed down' the bones of their ancestors and directly placed in touch with personal yet unidentifiable deceased associates, friends or even family members. Such 'dead body politics', as Katherine Verdery calls it, could only be successful because eyewitnesses and their descendants cautiously kept knowledge of the massacres alive despite official disownment by the Communist government. The re-emergence of these suppressed memories is key to understanding how past atrocities were revived and how they fuelled the emotions and (ethno-)political consciousness of the late 1980s and early 1990s.

> Finding the skeletons of those whom communist partisans had killed,
> for instance, was instrumental in building the anti-communist senti-

ment that assured the victory of Franjo Tudjman's nationalist party in
the first Croatian elections. Initially the arguments aimed to rewrite
the history of relations between the political categories 'fascists' and
'communists', both of whom had existed all over Yugoslavia's territory
… All sides strove to transfigure anonymous skeletons into their own
martyrs. Those skeletons then served in the historical revisionism by
which new nationalist histories emerged for newly emerging states.
(Verdery 1999: 100f.)

The fact that newly emerging national histories were partly built on
unidentified dead bodies and unsettled memories resulted in growing and emotionally highly charged ethno-nationalist sentiment in the
diverse republics of the former Yugoslavia. The literal and symbolic
exhumations provoked 'competing nationalist histories of violence and
injustice' (Hayden 1994: 173) in which every ethnic group seemed to
perceive itself as the major victim. Historical grievances fuelled the
renewal of previously repressed inter-ethnic conflict, and traumatising memories of repeated suffering provided motives for revenge that
could be easily manipulated by nationalist demagogues. Robert M.
Hayden writes:

One of the most potent weapons for building nationalism seems the
uncovering of (semi-)hidden massacres. The transfiguration of the
dead into martyrs is perhaps the most powerful mechanism of symbolic politics, and funerals provide a supreme moment for transforming ritual into political theatre (see Esherick and Wasserstrom 1990).
The discovery and celebration of martyrdom have thus taken prominence in nationalist politics in Yugoslavia in 1990–91. (Hayden 1994:
172f.)

The commemoration of massacre victims and their association with
loss, victimisation and martyrdom provided not only a powerful reservoir of nationalist sentiment but fused with an intensifying susceptibility to religious engagement. Thus proper burial rites were performed
according to the respective Christian Orthodox, Roman Catholic or
Islamic customs, and the symbolic power of the anonymous dead and
gravesites were linked to the reconstitution of religious freedom. With
the post-Titoist revival of religious symbolism and the declaration of a
new era, history again had to be rewritten.

Against this backdrop, the orgy of historical revisionism since 1989 is
seen as a rectification of communist censorship and lies … The people

whom the communists airbrushed out are particularly apt symbols for
deleting the communist era itself from the new histories, thus signifying its death. Reburials accomplish this by revisiting the bodies of persons the communists mistreated, resurrecting them, and placing them
in a new light. (Verdery 1999: 113)

In the words of Jan Assmann, '[t]he present is "haunted" by the past
and the past is modelled, invented, reinvented, and re-constructed by
the present' (Assmann 1997: 9). The phantoms of the past that haunted
the late-Yugoslav present were 'ghosts' in the classic sense of the term.
As restless dead not properly buried, the massacre victims forcefully
returned to the realm of the living to demand appropriate burial and
recurrent commemoration. The communist past, however, has equally
been reconstructed after its replacement by nationalist party politics,
and has itself also been turned into a 'ghost'.

Indeed, in his remarkable essay *The Ghosts of Place*, Michael Mayerfeld Bell develops a phenomenology of place based on the observation
that landscapes are filled with ghosts – that is 'the sense of the presence
of those who are not physically there' (Mayerfeld Bell 1997: 813). He emphasises that ghosts of place should not be reduced to mere memories
– be they individual or collective – and not simply located in the past.
According to this understanding, the spirits (or ghosts) of the previously
unacknowledged dead in the former Yugoslavia populate not only graves
and geographical sites of mass murder but equally inhabit people's present imagination of cohesion, and thereby provide for a feeling of temporal and spatial connectedness. Mayerfeld Bell here refers to the social
component of ghosts that guarantees the aliveness of particular places.
In his words: '[w]e also experience objects and places as having ghosts.
We do so because we experience objects and places socially; we experience them as we do people. Through ghosts, we re-encounter the aura of
social life in the aura of place' (ibid.: 821). In my analysis of local identity
and nationalist – or rather regionalist – sentiment in the Dalmatian hinterland, I draw upon Mayerfeld Bell's notion of ghosts as a social construction that people deliberately engage when imagining a territorially
situated common past.

In Sinj and the surrounding villages, narratives of dead bodies are
vivid and influence politics to this day, although no immediate exhumations or reburials of war victims from the Second World War took place
after Franjo Tuđman became the first president of Croatia in 1990. My
interviewees in the Cetinska krajina did not know about specific mass
graves or ossuaries, but as recently as August 2008, sixty-one corpses
were exhumed in the Bosnian-Herzegovinian town of Livno, in the im-

mediate vicinity of Sinj. A local Franciscan told me that the remains of
the exhumed bodies had been sent to Banja Luka for identification, as
they were expected to be Serbian massacre victims from the Second
World War. The forensic analysis, however, revealed that the corpses
were Croats who had been killed during the 1991–95 war. Discoveries
like this cause great agitation in Croatia, as even now, almost twenty
years after the end of the war, not all mass graves have been exhumed
and thousands of people are still missing. Each exhumation of massacre
victims not only revives painful memories of the war but also triggers
renewed narratives of Croatian victimisation.

During my fieldwork I was also frequently told about a *jama* [crevice],
located a few kilometres into the Herzegovinian mountains north-east
of Sinj, where an unknown number of locals had allegedly been killed by
Partisans and tossed into a ditch. During communism, scrap iron from
the local spinning mill Dalmatinka had been dumped into the ditch, with
the result that neither exhumations of massacre victims nor estimates of
casualty figures could be made after the demise of communist rule. The
fact that there was neither visual nor physical evidence, and therefore no
exact numbers of dead, made the *jama* even more susceptible to legendary or quasi-mythological accounts of past mass executions.

Gospa Sinjska in the Mountains

In January 2005 the son of my host family, Marko, a thirty-five-year-old
former soldier, agreed to accompany me *u planinu* [into the mountains]
to show me where the *jama* is located. To get there we had to cross
the border into Bosnia-Herzegovina and follow a steep unpaved path
into the mountains. The landscape turned bleaker and increasingly barren. Clambering over piles of stones and making our way through the
undergrowth, we suddenly came upon a recently built Marian shrine,
consisting of an altar approximately six feet high in the shape of a stone
house with a saddle roof, and a small brazen relief of the Gospa Sinjska
in the middle.

According to the inscription, the shrine was built in 2000, and flowers,
candles, coins and rosaries had been left there. Close to the altar, steep
stone stairways, which also appeared to have been constructed quite recently, led down to the *jama*. The crevice in the rock was approximately
twenty feet wide and surrounded by a protective waist-high stone wall,
in the middle of which there was a small marble cross in commemoration of the massacre victims. A few withered wreaths decorated with
ribbons in the national colours lay against the stone wall. To the left, a
marble Pietà relief had been erected, depicting Mary receiving her son's

Figures 3.1 and 3.2. The miniature replica of the altar of Gospa Sinjska in the Croatian–Bosnian mountains, built in the year 2000. Photos: M. Schäuble

dead body for burial. To me, the relief looked like a gravestone without an inscription. The crevice itself was so hidden that I would never have noticed it if it were not for the more visible altar.

On the way back we passed another monument that looked much more massive and official. I was told that it was the Memorial to the Victims of War and Fascism, which apparently hardly anyone ever visited 'except for a few shepherds', and that the locals preferred to commemorate their dead at the *jama* and not at the official war memorial. Erected in Titoist Yugoslavia as a material and symbolic reminder of the Partisan struggle against fascism, the Memorial for the Victims of War and Fascism, like innumerable other Partisan monuments all over the country, was intended to appeal to the (officially prescribed) collective memory of the entire Yugoslav nation. The memorial was admittedly located in a very out-of-the-way place, but I still noticed that it looked very rundown and that there were no flowers or wreaths or any other signs of recent visitors. The fact that the inhabitants of Sinj and the adjacent hamlets did not seem to acknowledge this memorial either as a private or a public commemoration site signifies that local historiographic narratives and memories differ significantly from the official version symbolised by the monument. It further suggests that here, in the heartland of Croatian nationalism, a shared Yugoslav memory or even nostalgia for the socialist past is deemed as highly suspicious and almost obsolete. The *jama*, on the other hand, provides a location – a landmark within a memorial landscape – for local memory as it is embedded in people's engagement with their immediate surroundings.

As a commemoration site of historic atrocities, the *jama* has become a politically and religiously charged location – if only of local significance. Michel de Certeau makes a clear distinction between space (*espace*) and place (*lieu*) and concludes that 'space is practised place' (de Certeau 1984: 117). According to this distinction, the *jama* is no longer a mere geographical *place* but has been transformed into a sacralised *space* that plays an important role for the region's history and constitutes a highly visible part of the local cultural landscape. The erection of a Marian shrine and other sanctified icons instead of a classic war memorial further indicates the religious re-signification of this historically most fraught ground. Built in 2000, five years after the end of the Homeland War and the 'liberation' of Croatia, the Marian shrine is a visual and material manifestation of divine presence at the *jama*.[7] Marian veneration and nationalism are closely linked, both in Croatia and in the parts of Bosnia-Herzegovina with a Croatian majority. The Gospa (Our Lady) is considered a divine supporter not only of Croatian independence but also of 'ethnic homogeneity' and of renewed claims to possession of land that once belonged to Croatia. The Gospa Sinjska is furthermore said to have traditionally helped the people of the region during wars, and against the plague, droughts, earthquakes and floods. As a remote subsidiary of the altar at the pilgrimage centre of the main shrine of the Gospa Sinjska in Sinj, the mini-memorial in the mountains marks and extends the zone of divine protection.

The choice of setting for the mini-replica of the shrine in the mountains at the *jama* highlights the nexus of spatial and temporal aspects of the events commemorated.[8] By claiming the place of the *jama* for 'their' war victims and erecting a religious shrine there, Croatian Roman Catholics exert power not only over a spatial site but also over the narratives and historic accounts related to it. As a visible marker of historic injustice, the Marian shrine draws attention towards the region's role in both recent and past wars. In these mountains, local warriors have frequently fought fierce battles since the fifteenth century in the effort to block Ottoman expansion into Catholic Europe and avert access of Ottoman troops to the Adriatic Sea. In this sense the Dinaric mountain range as a historic landscape of war and conflict constitutes a fundamental part of local iconography and provides a space in which public and private commemoration are openly acted out and overlap.

Pits, Ravines and Graves

Ritual Commemoration: The Mass for the Victims of the Communist Regime

A few months after I had first been to the mountains I saw posters in the town announcing the celebration of a 'Mass for the Victims of the Communist Regime' at the *jama* on 3 September 2005. I was very eager to attend the commemoration ceremony and made plans to join the festivity with Marko and his friend Predrag, a native of Sinj and one of the very few youngsters who had left the town to study law in Zagreb. In the early morning of 3 September the local radio station, Radio Sinj, announced that there would be shuttle buses to the *jama*. I imagined the ceremony in the mountains to resemble a pilgrimage in the sense that worshipers from throughout the region would travel through the landscape, gather at a cult place, mourn their dead together, remember their common violent past – beyond communist times as far back as the Ottoman attacks – and celebrate the community to which they feel they belong (cf. Turner 1969). As a sacred site, the *jama* is indeed a culturally, religiously and politically significant landmark, but the annually celebrated mass took a slightly different twist, as I described in my field notes of the following day:

> By the time we arrive by the *jama* four coaches and several cars with local licence plate numbers are parked all over the rocky terrain. Approximately 1,000 people have gathered in the shrubby field surrounding the Marian shrine. A dozen Franciscan priests from Sinj and many more from the Bosnian side (as I am later told) have come up here to celebrate the mass and have erected an additional altar decorated with flowers and candles in front of the stone memorial. Ten to twelve wreaths are laid out in front of it. The atmosphere is festive and at the same time lively.
>
> On the way there Predrag whispers: 'The main problem of our country is that we always look back. It's all about history, never about the future. The past, the past … and we are always the victims' …
>
> The service starts with a rather politicised speech by the former Franciscan provincial minister (*provincijal*), the head of the Franciscan Order of Bosnia. Croatia, he says, has been a victim of imperialistic forces for centuries and had to suffer great injustice. The slogan '*mali narod, velika nepravda*' (small people, great injustice) describing Croatia's historical destiny is on everyone's lips anyway and it does not really come as a surprise to hear it here, too. The former *provincijal* names the Bleiburg massacre,[9] the manipulated numbers of victims at Jasenovac,[10] Goli Otok,[11] and Vukovar,[12] and itemises them as a litany of injustices against the *Hrvatski narod* (Croatian people/nation). The tone is accusatory and very bitter as he goes on and on to list all the atrocities that Croatia and Croatians have had to endure. 'But the worst tragedy of all was the communist regime. Worldwide communism has brought about millions of casualties.'
>
> 'Here at the *jama*,' he continues, 'the Partisans claimed to be "antifascists", but fascism never generated as many victims as communism did.' Later in his speech he names Josip Broz Tito alongside dictators such as Hitler, Stalin and Ceauşescu, and he ridicules the so-called 'Yugo-nostalgics' who still consider Tito a popular and successful politician. Here, Tito is regarded as a criminal and Yugoslavia is perceived as a ferocious dictatorship. 'This *jama* was not the only one, but there were 400 more of its kind in Croatia', he says. 'And nobody knows or will ever know how many victims there really were!'
>
> Predrag rolls his eyes and whispers to me, 'Do you know what country could be a role model for us? Spain! They had Franco, they had a fascist period, a communist period … And look at them today. Today Spain is a normal country where people have the right to be

born, to live, and to die. Here in Croatia everything is always about politics. It is about looking back and politics' ...

In a subsequent sermon, a Franciscan from Sinj talks about politics too: 'It is no disgrace – no disgrace! – what our *branitelji* (defenders) and our generals, our Mirko Norac and our Ante Gotovina, did. They defended our homeland and our people.' ... After his heated appeal for solidarity with Norac and Gotovina, the priest starts mocking contemporary values. First of all he ridicules 'left-wing' claims for human rights that have been increasingly discussed in public of late. 'What are human rights today? They are rights for homosexuals and rights that promote the splitting up of families.' I am quite shocked by the bluntness and open bigotry of his speech. I turn around but no one else seems to object or be distressed by his polemics. ...

After the Eucharist the official wreath-laying ceremony is announced. The whole congregation is invited to follow the priests down the narrow and steep stone stairs to the *jama*. A huge jostle starts and people try to elbow their way close to the crevice. I can only catch a glimpse of the scene from afar, but I can tell that the priest is praying for the people killed here. Some of the women attending the service start weeping out loud. One of them has brought a plastic bag full of flowers and starts to strew yellow petals into the crevice. After a brief prayer the priest announces the names of the parishes, associations and political parties that have donated a wreath in honour of the anonymous victims of communist atrocities, while representatives bring their wreaths forward and place them by the small stone wall.

'Općina [Municipality] Hrvace', 'Općina Otok', 'Općina Trilj', 'Općina Sinj', 'Hrvatska Demokratska Zajednica [Croatian Democratic Union] HDZ Sinj', 'Splitska-Dalmatinska Županja [Split-Dalmatian Parish]', 'Udruga Hrvatskih Veterana domovinskog rata [Association of the Croatian Homeland War Veterans]', etc., etc. The wreaths are all dedicated to 'Hrvatskim Mučenicima [the Croatian Martyrs]', and are decorated with blue, white and red ribbons, the Croatian national colours. ...

After a final blessing and the sprinkling of holy water, the Mass is officially over. But many people stay behind to light candles and utter private prayers at the crevice. After a while everyone is gone and I can already smell grilled meat from several fires around.

When I arrive back at the *vikendica* [the weekend house of my host family in the mountains] one of the men is about to skin the lamb that they have just slaughtered. ... I can hear laughter and *klapske pjesme* [traditional singing] from other compounds nearby. ... We spend the whole afternoon together, eating, drinking and laughing. The men complain about current EU politics and its bad influence on the local economy. At one point, one of the uncles asks me, 'What did you think of the Mass?' Not knowing what to say I simply answer 'quite political.' They all laugh. 'Yes, it's the priests who do the politics here nowadays. (Field Notes, 4 Sep 2005)

My field notes illustrate how spatial, temporal, political and social perceptions of place are interwoven and affect the way locality and belonging are currently negotiated in rural Dalmatia. The landscape and the Marian shrine at the *jama* constitute what Halbwachs called the material framework (*cadre matériel*) in which the memories are embedded, while the religious ceremony provides the commemorative practice or event necessary for the dynamic remembrance of things past. The 'miniature sanctuary' at the *jama* has been created as a spatial and spiritual realm in which all the grief and painful memories that have long been forcibly suppressed are allowed to surface. By actively evoking past atrocities committed by the communists, a hitherto silenced yet emotionally highly charged period of history is reawakened and a sense of communal belonging among the victims and their descendants is evoked. The religious ceremony, the patriotic and political speeches, and the wreath-laying ceremonies can be understood as ritual practices that on different layers contribute to visualising the performative nature of collective memories, and simultaneously constitute communal commemoration. It becomes obvious that religious and national identities are closely connected and that the local Franciscans administer and foster a view of regional as well as national history that is constructed in direct opposition to the communist period and which consequently overlooks atrocities committed on the Croatian side.[13]

Belonging to a place is constituted and expressed by remembering the particular history of that place, and the visitors' feelings of collective allegiance are anchored and mobilised through shared religious activity (cf. Connerton 1989). This process is noticeably implemented during the ceremony at the *jama* where the 'political' rhetoric and religious practices performed appeal to the congregation's common experience of past atrocities and injustices – and the formerly repressed memories thereof – while simultaneously evoking a sense of regional loyalty. At this point it is important to note that the people who travelled to the *jama* for this occasion knew very well what to expect from the ceremony. Only those who appreciated the political tone of the speeches and sermons attended the Mass (except, maybe, for Predrag

Figures 3.3 and 3.4. The 'Mass for the Victims of Communist Atrocities', held in autumn 2005 at the *jama* in the mountains surrounding Sinj. Photos: M. Schäuble

who only went to accompany me and who left early because he was so annoyed). The others, who did not want to participate in this particular form of politicised commemoration, did not attend the service. The majority of men and women, however, attended the ceremony. The rest retreated to their weekend houses, prepared the food and used the occasion as a 'day out in the mountains'. It was they who, even if they never openly challenged the sermons' content, ironically commented on the priests' political agenda. Their retort that 'it's the priests who do the politics here nowadays' is both a realistic assessment of the situation and a sign of criticism towards the Church and the Franciscan Order regarding their wealth and/or their political influence in the region.

The ground on which the Franciscan clergy actually manage to exert their interpretive power over local notions of identity and belonging is the shared regional history of political disadvantage and suffering. The speeches given during the service appeal to identification with the recurrently mentioned victim status of Croatia and Croats (including Bosnian Croats) throughout history, rather than invoking the audience's common ethno-national origin. Hence, the celebration at the *jama* is not accompanied by political claims over territory but can be seen as expressing a political claim over a specific version of the past in which atrocities were committed exclusively by communists, Serbs and other people considered enemies. Neither my informants nor the speakers at the commemoration ceremony ever voiced any direct right to the terrain on which the *jama* is located. The fact, however, that they refer to the war fought in this region as the Homeland War suggests that while this part of Herzegovina may be officially and legally part of Bosnia and Herzegovina, and not Croatia, it is still part of their *domovina*, and thus of Croatia.[14]

An unambiguous portrait of one's own *nacija* as victim or victimised is a salient device in these narratives. During my fieldwork in Sinj I hardly ever heard accounts of atrocities committed towards any group other than Roman Catholic Croats. This is in line with each ex-Yugoslav ethno-religious group's perception of itself as always being the victim, not the perpetrator, of atrocities – not only under communism but also throughout the three Balkan wars (cf. Jalušić 2004: 40–67). I argue, however, that at this moment in time the legend of the *jama* functions primarily to strengthen, direct and validate personal as well as collective memories of casualties and discrimination during the communist period. Narratives related to places and landscapes of victimisation – whether personally remembered or imagined – are processes by which meaning is produced and represented for the present.

In a comparable manner, the 'litanies of suffering' that the former provincial minister utters at the *jama* exclude disreputable aspects of the Croatian past and the rhetoric used is a powerful device for forgetting Croatian war crimes while condemning others (cf. Ries 1991). Contingent feelings of guilt or remorse regarding either Ustaša crimes or atrocities committed by Croats during the Homeland War are avoided by proclaiming narratives of heroic resistance to previous oppressors as well as through distorted discourses of self-victimisation. Such narratives, whether referring to real or imagined events, aim at connecting people durably to history and territory. Simon Harrison has pointed out that '[p]eople inhabit terrain, and interact with it, always in particular embodied ways which are also – among many other things – ways of structuring memory, forgetting and the political control of knowledge' (Harrison 2004: 149). Seen from this perspective, structuring memory as well as forgetting is a powerful means of controlling the circulation of knowledge. In rural Dalmatia, knowledge of the past has become a valuable political resource that priests as designated ritual experts control and insert at appointed times and places.

It goes without saying that there is no such thing as a unitary 'cultural memory of the Croatian people' or a uniform 'Croatian tradition'. The reactionary nationalistic attitudes frequently spread by the Franciscans or radical politicians and demagogues is not consistently absorbed and shared by the entirety of the Croatian population; and even in unusually homogenous regions like the Dalmatinska Zagora with an extraordinarily high proportion of traditionalists and nationalists, there are clearly dissenting voices. Commentaries such as Predrag's statement, that '[t]he main problem of our country is that we always look back. It's all about history, never about the future … and we are always the victims', suggest that younger people in particular do not necessarily share the obsession with history and ethno-national antagonism of some of their compatriots. But although Predrag's comment is meant as a criticism of a backward-looking understanding of history and self-pitying attitude, it confirms the view that such a thing as 'national identity' is most efficiently constructed via the commemoration of communal suffering.

The Franciscan parish priests preserve the memory of the victims of communist atrocities and what they frequently refer to as the 'Croatian Holocaust' by celebrating the memorial service and presenting the stories of the anonymous dead as cases of innocent suffering. When examining the ceremony at the *jama*, it is clear that individual as well as collective memory is constituted, acted out and gradually transformed into historical memory. Henri Bergson distinguished between collective memory and historical memory by describing the former as representing

lived experience, and the latter as preserving lived experience and medi-
ating 'between one's own sense of having an experience and an external
representation of that sense which is presumed to be valid for others as
well as yourself' (cited in Crane 1997: 1375). The 'lived experience' that
is remembered and enunciated at the *jama* is one of individual as well as
collective grief due to either loss of family members or political and/or
religious persecution during communist times, or the more general be-
moaning of anonymous massacre victims. Efforts to rectify the previous
suppression of mourning and open articulation of experienced injustice
are crucial for validating these experiences for the whole community.
In the distressing phase of acknowledging their earlier concealed pain
and publicly mourning their dead, the bereaved and/or persecuted are
supported and authenticated by official dignitaries as well as by fellow
parishioners. And although the official commemoration act is highly
ritualised and no individual 'testimonies' are recited at the *jama*, I had
the impression that the ceremony allowed for the release and revitalisation of strong emotions related to painful personal memories, as people
not only lit candles and strewed flowers in the crevice but stayed behind
long after the ceremony had ended to pray and mourn in silence. The
numerous individual recollections were subsumed in the quasi-religious
speeches and transformed into a polemical and politicised narrative that
was at the same time very affecting.

By exclusively highlighting the enduring violence, the former provincial minister rejects Croatian responsibility for war crimes in the Second
World War and the Homeland War in his speech. In this sense he proclaims an amnesty. The cleric's memory is heavily politicised, evidently
seeking to name and conjure up past atrocities as an attempt to anchor
their status as Croatian national traumas. In his recently elaborated theory of cultural trauma, Jeffrey Alexander comments that 'social groups
can, and often do, refuse to recognize the existence of others' trauma,
and because of their failure they cannot achieve a moral stance. By de-
nying the reality of others' suffering, people not only diffuse their own
responsibility for the suffering but often project the responsibility for
their own suffering on these others' (Alexander 2004: 1). Such or similar
dynamics of denial are to be found on various levels of private and public
discourse in all parts of the former Yugoslavia.

The feminist critic Žarana Papić, who has described comparable
phenomena in post-war Serbia, for example, labels strategies of self-
depiction as victims and persistent denial of others' suffering as the 're-
invention' and 'fictionalization of a chosen trauma' (Papić 2003: 133; see
also Volkan 1988). While I am reluctant to adopt the expression 'chosen
trauma' for any side involved in the (post-)Yugoslav conflict, I neverthe-

less think that in his speech the former provincial minister deliberately reawakens 'old ghosts' by calling upon the unsettled memories and the unpacified dead of previous battles. In this sense his words are directly linked to other narratives in which the rhetoric of dead bodies is applied and used in favour of a nationalized ideology.

Jonas Frykman has illustrated the 'painful phase of publicly acknowledging the … dead in order to put the past to rest'. In post-communist times, he claims, 'crimes have to be made visible so that what has been a partly averted past can be worked on and thereby turned into manageable history'.[15] This, however, is a euphemistic assessment of the process of coming to terms with the past if one considers the nationalistic rhetoric of previously concealed atrocities that has been – and still is – used in many regions of the former Yugoslavia. The visualising and conjuring of previous crimes has not solely been used to work on the past, as Frykman's commentary might suggest. The speech at the *jama* is only one case that paradigmatically exemplifies how unsettled accounts of past crimes can be manipulated in order to obstruct appeasement rather than to transform painful memories into 'manageable history'.

The fact that Predrag mentioned Spain as an alternative model of dealing with the past is of particular interest in this connection, as it implies conscious avoidance and pleads for a politics of memory that did not exist in the Spanish case until very recently. In Spain, the Civil War (1936–39) was followed by almost four decades of one-party rule under the Nationalist, General Francisco Franco, who had been supported by Fascist Italy and Nazi Germany. The Francoist regime was responsible for continual serious human rights violations and mass executions. After Franco's death in 1975 the country moved quickly to a constitutional monarchy organised as a parliamentary democracy. Until recently, however, Spain made little effort to account for its past, instead following a policy that has become emblematic for official concealments of violent history. Yet this 'historical memory hole', or 'memory void', also enabled a comparatively efficient transition in Spain from dictatorship to a democratic state.[16] Transferring this principle, Predrag's comment thus implies a plea for Croatia's transition from 'dictatorship to democracy', including inevitable EU membership, without further indulgence in any retrogressive politics of memory. This statement can be understood as manifesting a weariness of dealing with the past that is typical of many young people in Croatia today, who would rather prefer to 'move on and forget about the past'. On the other hand, this attitude is diametrically opposed to simultaneously prevailing beliefs and practices that locate the past in the present, with the backing of prominent political and religious forces.

Ancestors and Haunted Spaces

> Religion expresses the relationship between the Mediterra-
> nean landscape and its inhabitants.
> — Peregrine Horden and Nicholas Purcell,
> *The Corrupting Sea*

Recollections and memories of ancestors, past events and personal experiences are linked to places and landscapes (cf. A. Assmann 1999). The
Dalmatian limestone mountains are commemorative landscapes that
are seen through traces of struggle and self-defence.[17] And even though
the landscape itself seems immutable, the memories attached to it have
a capacity to vary widely and to change over time. While a (former) Partisan might perceive the mountains as a site of fierce fighting and victory
over the fascists, a Serbian dweller might rather be reminded of Ustaša
crimes and the eviction of Serbs. In turn, many Croats who have lost
family members or friends in executions or mass killings perceive the
place primarily as a site of Partisan atrocities and – depending on context – one of historic threat from Ottoman Turks followed by eventual
victory. Hence, the region bears a particular aura of historical revision
that inheres in the process of contextual memorialisation.

Dalmatia's distinctive character is less rooted in fixed notions of ethnicity than in the texture of the environment and related modes of land
use as well as spatialised historic accounts. The barren mountains shape
and are crucial to concepts of belonging and micro-nationalism, as illustrated, for instance, by the joke cited at the outset of this chapter about
the lunar Dalmatian mountains as typical feature of 'Croatian land'.
In writing on the relation between physical landscape and collective
memory, Maurice Halbwachs stressed the stable and timeless quality of
geographical commemoration sites, pointing out that '[t]he collective
thought of [a] group … has the best chance of immobilizing itself and
enduring when it concentrates on places, sealing itself within their con-
fines and moulding its character to theirs' (Halbwachs [1950] 1980: 156).
Comments by urban Croatians such as 'Dalmatians are like the landscape they live in: tough and obstinate', or references to Dalmatians as
'stone people', rest admittedly on highly questionable ethno-geograph-
ical deterministic assumptions. Nevertheless they support Halbwachs'
theorisation of the geographical anchoring, adaptation and durability of
a community. Elaborating on Halbwachs' approach to the role of collective memory in common identity, Pierre Nora suggests that a people or a group who perceive themselves as having been marginalised in

traditional history are habitually 'haunted by the need to recover their buried past' (Nora 1989: 15). This central proposition in memory theory resonates with present-day Croatia and forms the starting point of my argument that a crucial part of national as well as regional Croatian identity is based on a perceived marginalisation that is geographically situated and continually linked to personal recollections and official historiography. The shared experience of disadvantage and continual performance of victimisation result in the creation of a communal memory that is not only of major retrospective importance but also decisive for the future coherence of a group – be it Dalmatia on a regional level or the whole of Croatia on a national level.

In his seven-volume collection *Les lieux de mémoire*, Pierre Nora creates an encyclopaedic inventory of sites and objects that embody the national memory of France, illustrating his theory that 'we speak so much of memory because there is so little of it left' (Nora 1989: 7). However, contrary to Nora's generalising argument that due to the dialectic of modernisation and historisation, *milieux de mémoire* (or real environments of memory) have entirely transformed and degenerated into *lieux de mémoire* (or sites of memory), I seek to show how in contemporary Dalmatia the existence of *lieux de mémoire* does not inevitably induce the annihilation of a distinct *milieu de mémoire*.

Assuming a universal 'acceleration of history', Nora distinguishes between 'real' or 'true memory', as exemplified and retained in what he calls 'primitive' and 'archaic societies', and 'history' (Nora 1989: 8). He writes of a process by which history or mere historical traces, residing in *lieux de mémoire*, steadily and irreversibly eradicates the kind of memory that subsists in and generates *milieux de mémoire*. In contemporary Croatia, however, references to the past in the form of repetitive personal memories, enumerations of previous atrocities, and/or reinterpretations of historical facts, are ubiquitous and are continually linked to actual political developments. These narrative accounts constitute vital and integrated parts of the present and are constantly interwoven with allusions to ancestors, mythical times and ancient war heroes. Contrary to Nora's much criticised argument, however, the prevalence of 'memory' over 'history' as I encountered it in Dalmatia by no means excludes a local historiographical consciousness.[18] My interlocutors were all well aware of the representational character of 'history' and knowingly (re)constructed distinct 'environments of memory' with reference to and often in opposition to official historiographies.

After the historical rupture of memory and the forced amnesia about Partisan atrocities under communism, techniques and media of memorialisation that would otherwise be retrogressive are at present reactivated in Croatia, generating *milieux de mémoire* in Nora's sense. Official state suppression of renegade political, ethno-national and religious beliefs led repeatedly to the secretive conservation of these beliefs and the formation of multiple reserves of memory. These reserves, maintained on a personal or family level by religious communities (predominantly the Franciscans) and by specific dissident political networks at home and abroad, have since been revitalised and successfully transformed into historical capital. Today such alternative memories are crucial for the formation of so-called 'folklore genres such as atrocity tales and belief legends' (Heimo and Peltonen 2003: 42).

Moreover, the previously described Mass for the Victims of Communist Atrocities at the *jama* conveys the emotional charge and political stance of public commemoration that follows after a lengthy period of 'forced amnesia'. Recently transformed into a private as well as public sanctuary of religious devotion and pilgrimage, the *jama* is not so much a typical 'site of memory' but rather corresponds to what Nora calls the 'living heart of memory' (Nora 1989: 23). In this function the location of the *jama* is symbolically embedded in a much wider commemorative context and contributes to the sustainability of an entire landscape inhabited by memories. I argue that what is experienced in the commemoration ceremony and kept alive beyond it on an everyday level is the actual phenomenon of lived and experienced connectedness with the past. In their speeches the Franciscan priests skilfully draw on the reserves of memory aggregated under communism and 'spontaneously actualise' them by linking them to the immediate political situation. The speakers appeal to a group's feeling of solidarity whose beliefs have previously been discounted; and although they use the national history of Croatia in their rhetoric of referring to the Croatian people's suffering and global victim status [*mali narod, velika nepravda*], they in fact install the *jama* as a platform for the articulation of distinct regionally embedded memories. In this sense the *jama* is constructed as a local niche of heavily politicised (religious) commemoration, thus perpetuating regional belief legends and atrocity tales.

The risk, however, that accompanies the revival of previously repressed memories is their susceptibility to manipulation. Nora points out that memory, in contrast to history, is characterised by its lively nature, being 'open to the dialectic of remembering and forgetting, unconscious of its successive deformations, vulnerable to manipulation and appropriation, susceptible to being long dormant and periodically revived' (Nora 1989: 8). These very characteristics and dynamics have made, and still continue to make, processes of remembering and

forgetting of atrocities, of loss and suffering, tools of exploitation for political propaganda in the whole of the former Yugoslavia. Negative and
bitter memories are particularly vulnerable to bias or omission, as they
are deeply charged with emotion.

The immediacy of memory makes it a very powerful yet volatile force,
particularly with regard to the reconstruction and representation of a
contested past, as in the case of post-war Croatia. The commemoration ceremony at the *jama*, for example, corresponds closely to Nora's
description of memory, or a memorious event, in so far as it is highly
'affective' and 'magical' (Nora 1989: 8). As past atrocities are publicly
conjured up and emotionally bewailed during the ceremony, their memory is considerably invigorated and revived. This makes the ritual event,
the locality of the *jama* as well as the narratives that surround it, particularly vulnerable to manipulation. The *jama* has in my opinion recently
(re)-gained importance as a setting and signifier for regional commemoration, and as a performance venue of local identity, because of its very
capacity to accommodate the facts that suit it. The erection of the miniature altar of Gospa Sinjska and the restoration of the *jama*-site in the
year 2000 demonstrate the relevance of remembering communist atrocities to the present socio-political situation and at the same time reveals
the need to install this remembrance within the realm of the sacred.

The evocation and recital of memories, especially of angry memories,
at the *jama* is accompanied by what Stjepan Meštrović has termed 'displaced emotions from history' (Meštrović 1996: 2). Affect is probably
the most important catalyst and fortifier of remembering, as memories and affect coalesce on an individual level. In other words, affective
memories are not correctable, as they are not about 'the truth' but about
authenticity. On many occasions, my interlocutors insisted strongly on
the truthfulness of their narratives and local legends, even if the events
in question occurred long before they were even born, or when documented evidence clearly disproved their accounts. If the memories that
are publicly articulated at an occasion like the ceremony at the *jama*
correspond to people's individually felt emotions – and moreover enable
the identification with a group who suffered injustice, injury or trauma –
they enter into authenticated political narratives.

Returning to Nora's distinction between memory and history, I claim
that in rural Dalmatia the tradition of memory is continued and currently revitalised – albeit with the support of material icons, such as the
miniature altar of the Gospa Sinjska or the Pietà figurine at the *jama*. In
contrast to the nearby official war memorial – a typical *lieu de mémoire*
in Nora's sense – which is much less frequented and has no direct impact on people's affective memories, the memories and emotions that

are evoked at the *jama* not only influence people's engagement and relationship with the past but also secure the emotional weight of the past in the present. The memories of past atrocities cannot be separated from the soil where they 'took place'. Nora points out in this connection that '[m]emory takes root in the concrete, in spaces, gestures, images and objects [whereas] history binds itself strictly to temporal continuities' (Nora 1989: 8). It is exactly in the 'concrete', the material environment and space of the *jama* that the passed-down local memories are located. The aura that sacralises the *jama* and the memories related to it cannot be adequately represented by an abstract memorial. Especially in places where people were denied the right to mourn their losses and to tell publicly of their suffering, official commemoration sites are not sufficient to compensate for the deprivation.

My accounts in the preceding chapter illustrate that Nora's conceptualisation of memory crisis is not applicable to the case of the Dalmatinska Zagora, and I assume that it is just as unsuitable for a number of other regions in Croatia and elsewhere. I even assert a tendency moving in the opposite direction to his prediction of disenchantment following the substitution of history for memory. One of the main factors to which Nora attributes 'the fundamental collapse of memory' is industrialisation and the concomitant disappearance of peasant culture as a 'quintessential repository of collective memory' (Nora 1989: 7). In Dalmatia, however, the persistence of peasant culture in the form of subsistence farming and small-scale agriculture might contribute to the preservation or reinvigoration of collective memories. An increasing reliance on local resources and a (virtually imposed) tendency of some bucolic communities to resist the ever-increasing industrialisation and market monopolisation that confronts their devastating economic situation is in any case closely related to local politics of memory and commemoration. Yet another vital aspect contributing to the niche structure of the Dalmatinska Zagora and furthering the continuation and rise of local memories on a micro-political level is religion. The fervent religiousness and folk spirituality that prevails in the region provides a basis for plentiful belief in legends, and guarantees the numinous aura that Nora presumed to be a prerequisite for the flourishing of memory.[19]

In view of the recent revitalisation of religion and the amplified turn to local practices of commemoration in Croatia, I argue that the secular memory of the nation is at present not superseded but supplemented by regionally bound and religiously marked memories. In summary I therefore claim that the restoration of 'peasant culture' as well as the revival of religiosity in present-day Croatia – and even more in poor rural regions like the Dalmatian hinterland – are intrinsically connected and contribute to the formation and implementation of resourceful *milieux de mémoire* that Nora saw as irretrievably lost. Today, official *lieux de mémoire* and underlying *milieux de mémoire* coexist and shape a type of memory that is effectively marked by religion.

The Politics of Martyrdom and Self-Victimisation

Dismissing the Communist Past

At the *jama* the grave of the nameless dead is collectively honoured by the pilgrimage of the living to the execution site. This annual visit is a way of commemorating and paying respect to those who have died for what is widely considered a political cause; a sacrifice on which the present Croatian nation-state is built. Through the ritualised ceremony and the speeches at the *jama* they are made into martyrs, and 'keeping their memory alive has been a significant step in reshaping the nation in contrast to the "barbaric" communist times' (Frykman, unpublished manuscript: 2). In other words, the Mass for the Victims of the Communist Regime is an occasion for publicly acknowledging the dead and simultaneously strengthening the emotional bond between the living and the dead. A tangible connection to the forefathers and to the land in which they rest constitutes a sense of (temporal as well as spatial) continuity and belonging that almost assumes the form of an ancestor cult. The rewriting and re-visioning of history is a strong emotional force and it is the pain of the mourners that keeps the memory of the dead as well as the memory of past atrocities alive. In the case of the commemoration ceremony at the *jama*, the women who publicly weep and strew flowers in the crevice to honour the deceased are in charge of and represent this emotion-laden process. Through their emotional engagement the absent are made present, and this guarantees the undisturbed cohabitation of the living and the dead. The presence of the dead conjured in this way leaves mythic traces in the present and plays a vital role in the way local actors situate themselves in their environment.

Interrogating the powerful influence of 'imagined communities' on individuals, Benedict Anderson points out that nationalism potentially has the capacity to offer citizens a means of converting their own deaths into a shared immortality (Anderson 1983: 10). I argue that it is the very idea of shared immortality that has facilitated, and continues to facilitate, concepts of a homogenous population that is unified and anchored in a common mythological past and identified with a particular place and territory to the present day. The notion of immortality, however, has a strong religious implication and, at least in the context of Croatian memory politics, it cannot be separated from the suffering that is related to the self-sacrifice of Christ. The symbolism implied in Christian eschatology enables the identification between personal suffering and the (historical, present, as well as anticipated) suffering of one's nation, and provides a potential for manipulation to political effect. Katherine Verdery writes in this connection:

> Like saints, ancestors engage deep feeling when their biographies can be cast in that most common of all nationalist tropes: suffering. The revival of religion has intensified this imagery. When it can be said of a dead person that, like Christ, he suffered – for the faith, for the nation, for the cause – then that gives his corpse both sanctity and a basis for empathic identification. (Verdery 1999: 114)

In the specific case of the Mass for the Victims of the Communist Regime, the dead are sanctified and invoked as carriers of memory with whom the community of the living empathise. The suffering of the victims of the communist regime makes them martyrs of an independent Croatian nation-state[20] – and these victims-turned-martyrs become sacred figures who embody and provide a link between personal and communal suffering. An icon that personifies this suffering is the stone Pietà next to the *jama*, the sculpture of the Virgin Mary holding her dead son on her lap. The Pietà is a visual reminder of the martyrdom of Christ as well as of (maternal) suffering, and points towards the Christian dogma of death and resurrection.

Vis-à-vis this forceful evocation of martyrdom and anticipation of divine justice, the speeches delivered at the *jama* devaluate and ridicule secular, and above all, international jurisdiction. The priests portray secular values such as human rights as corruptible and inferior to a more enduring set of divine values within which love for one's homeland is emphasised as the prime religious duty. The Christian concept of 'absolute and eternal truth' is perceived as incompatible with what T.G. Ashplant, Graham Dawson and Michael Roper call 'human rights narratives'. These authors argue that '[o]ne significant effect of the growing power of the human rights narrative and its various legal and quasi-legal agencies has been a strengthening of the transnational arena, as a domain where war memories previously unrecognized in the arena of the national state might be articulated' (Ashplant, Dawson and Roper 2000: 68). These, however, are exactly the reasons for which human rights narratives are rejected by right-wing Croatian nationalists, for whom not human rights per se but the political implications of a unitary judicature and a new post-Cold War ordering of international relations seem to pose an immense threat. This attitude is a direct continuation of Tuđman's policy, who 'considered human rights a Western fabrication, and [arrogantly discarded] the idea of a constitutional state respecting civil rights in favour of sovereignty and national independence' (Hedl 2000). In the concrete case of the sermon at the *jama* in 2005, the polemic of the priest is in my view obliquely directed against the Convention for the Protection of Human Rights and Fundamental Freedoms, also known as the European Convention on Human Rights (ECHR), that all EU member states are expected to ratify. And with their renunciatory attitude, the adversaries of a superordinate set of laws, who are by and large also opposed to Croatian EU membership, intend to rebuff any imposed legal or supra-national state authority. By insinuating that they refuse to submit to the jurisdiction of the International Court of Justice, they also refuse to accept the International Humanitarian Law (IHL), a legal corpus that is composed of the Geneva Conventions and the Hague Conventions, as well as subsequent treaties, case law and customary international law.

Church representatives in particular often justify such radical notions by stating that, as devout Catholics, the Croatian people are accountable to God alone and therefore not compelled to bow to international jurisdiction. I argue, however, that at bottom, all of this comes down to the rejection of a common war crimes law, of which the International Criminal Tribunal for the former Yugoslavia (ICTY) is part. In this context, the main reservation of the Eurosceptics and ICTY objectors concerns the role of Croatia and Croatian soldiers in the Homeland War. Their refusal to cooperate with the ICTY and to accept the tribunal's indictments of Croatians rests on an apprehension that any admission of war guilt would create an equivalence of responsibility among Croats and Serbs, and challenge the legitimacy of the Homeland War and of Croatia as a nation (Peskin and Boduszynski 2003: 2). The fact that the *jama* is chosen as a site for this highly controversial proclamation illustrates how many nationalists stress and invoke the victim status of Croatia and Croatians in order to argue that they cannot be perpetrators or be held responsible for crimes committed during the Homeland War. It is through this perception of continual victimisation that war crimes charges and verdicts imposed by international jurisdiction are vehemently rejected.

I have mentioned earlier that the *jama* is part of a religious geography that accumulates many layers of meaning and provides a stable framework of national narratives and memories that are allocated to a specific place. The material space of the homeland is imagined as being founded on relics and bones, and the *jama* as a mass grave grants a sense of connectivity and continuity that reaches beyond linear concepts of historicity. It becomes clear that the significance of territory is linked to the reconfiguring of time, and secures the realignment of the local population with their ancestors. Ancestral and family graves impart to individuals a rootedness in time and space, and simultaneously consolidate the cohesion of a community, most especially when a community uses mythic topologies as geopolitical markers to define its entitlement to a particular place or territory.[21] Whereas in the immediate post–Second World War years the dead haunted the (forcibly repressed) memories of the living, since the late 1980s the living seem to haunt the dead in an attempt to secure them as allies for their changing political endeavour.

Official Commemoration Sites: Local War Memorials and Monuments

In the previous section I illustrated the significance and symbolic connotation of the *jama* for local and regional memory in its embedding in people's engagement with their immediate surroundings. The *jama* provides a location – a landmark within a memorious landscape – for private mourning as well as for public ceremonies of commemoration. However, as an official site of commemoration it does not exceed the scope of regional relevance. Sites that claim to appeal to the collective memory of an entire nation, on the other hand, tend to pursue a politics of representation that provide mnemonic aids by visualising and materialising history. Collective memories or collectively relevant versions of the past are generated by and through symbols, institutions and media – and commemoration sites, monuments and memorials that are located within a shared public space are the main deposits or carriers of such shared (and often decreed) memories. According to Gillis, monuments are expected to comprise the 'power to commemorate, to forge and sustain a single version of the past' (Gillis 1994: 3). War memorials and monuments in particular are classic *lieux de mémoire* that encompass three coexisting aspects: a material, a symbolic and a functional aspect (cf. Nora 1989: 19). This implies that memory sites are not fixed or static spaces but instead gain their meaning solely through ongoing interaction with the people whose memories they are meant to symbolise and maintain – an interaction that not only manifests itself in reinvigorating commemoration or wreath-laying ceremonies but also possibly in violations and vandalism as forms of protest against decreed version(s) of the past.

The Partisan Monument in Glavice, a neighbouring village of Sinj, for example, was blasted in the early 1990s. The remnants of the destroyed memorial are still visible and I have heard a number of conflicting stories as to who was responsible for the sabotage. But it became clear from the tone of the narratives that none of my various interlocutors bewailed the memorial's destruction. On the contrary, people prided themselves on their 'subversiveness'. Furthermore, in the ancient town of Solin, located between Sinj and Split, a Partisan monument in the form of a bridge parapet containing all the names of the men of Solin who were killed in the Partisan fighting was blasted at the end of the Homeland War. And for months on end whilst I stayed in Sinj in 2004/2005, the sole Partisan monument in Sinj was 'adorned' with the graffito '*smrt partizananima*' [Death to the Partisans] before it was silently whited-out one day. This list could easily be continued, since, according to the 2001 study *Rušenje Antifašističkih Spomenika u Hrvatskoj 1990–2000* [Demolition of Anti-Fascist Monuments in Croatia 1990–2000] published by the Union of Anti-Fascist Combaters, 731 Partisan monuments had been destroyed and 2,233 monuments demolished in the 1990s in Croatia alone (cf. Frykman, unpublished manuscript: 7).[22] But I chose these comparably recent examples from Sinj and its immediate vicinity to illustrate how the clamour against the country's communist past takes shape on various levels and in various forms, and occurs even – or maybe pre-eminently – in remote areas. By proudly pointing at a destroyed monument more than twenty years after the break-up of Yugoslavia, the locals not only accentuate their resistance under communism but still seem to feel the need for retrieving hidden or suppressed memories – almost as if they could change the past itself by changing its official representation.[23] Frykman argues that the Partisan monuments that were erected after the Second World War became part of the rhetoric that hid the 'real truth'. 'They increased consciousness about the fact that there was a truer truth that everybody knew about, but which nobody could speak of' (Frykman, unpublished manuscript: 18). In this regard, the monuments for many became markers of a fraudulent regime; and when the war broke out in the early 1990s, several of these monuments were destroyed to signify that the communist regime no longer had a raison d'être and that a shared Yugoslav memory had become obsolete.

But it is not just communist monuments that are destroyed or vandalised because of the version of history they transmit. In contemporary Croatia, contestations over historical truth regarding most recent events, such as the Homeland War, continue to be fought out by erecting, renaming, removing, demolishing, or defacing a variety of war memorials on all sides. A vivid example is a massive monument ded-icated to the victory of Croatian *branitelji* in Operation Storm that was erected in the main square in Knin. The association of war veter-ans, *Tvrđava Knin* [Fortress Knin], had initiated the construction of the monument that was inaugurated on the 'Victory and Homeland Thanksgiving Day and the Day of Croatian Defenders' [*Dan pobjede i domovinske zahvalnosti i dan hrvatskih branitelja*] on 5 August 2011. Only a few weeks later, in September 2011, an unknown person (or persons) scribbled 'Ratko Mladić' and 'Serbia' in Cyrillic letters at the new monument, and reportedly also demolished lamps and candles symbolising the fallen Croatian soldiers of the Homeland War. This act of vandalism can be understood as a (symbolic) protest against the se-lective remembrance of Operation Storm as heroic military action that led to the liberation of Croatia. In Knin, where the population before the war consisted of approximately 82 per cent Serbs and 15 per cent Croats, today the population ratio is almost entirely reversed. After 1995, Knin's demographic composition changed greatly with the influx of Croatian refugees from Bosnia and former Croat militia members, who to a great extent replaced those Serbs who either fled, were ex-pelled or killed during Operation Storm. As of 2011, approximately 77 per cent of the inhabitants of Knin are Croats and only 21 per cent are Serbs. Viewed in this light, it might be easier to understand why the remaining (or remigrated) Serbian population find an exclusive depic-tion of Operation Storm as a victorious recapturing of Croatian ter-ritory problematic, to say the least. This does, of course, by no means justify the crude display of Serbian nationalism at the monument, which did not even flinch from glorifying Mladić to whom some of the worst war atrocities in the Yugoslav wars are attributed.

Ratko Mladić had been arrested in Serbia and extradited to The Hague in May 2011, shortly before the monument in Knin had been vandalised and smeared with his name, and his arrest can conceivably be linked to the appearance of the graffito. Whether the vandal(s) attempted to symbolically charge Mladić's war crimes up to the crimes committed during Operation Storm, aimed at protesting against a biased historical interpretation epitomised by the monument, or whether it was simply intended to provoke the public by scrawling nationalist Serbian slogans, is not known. It is certain, however, that the erection on the main town square of such a colossal monument celebrating Croatian victory was bound to cause upset amongst those who experienced the very same historical event as an exodus of the Serbian population.

The monument covers the whole of Ante Starčević Square in the cen-tre of Knin and consists of a large quadrangular marble bridge behind a split stone cuboid sculpture. One side of the marble bridge construction hosts a wall that is decorated with empty cartridges that were used in the shelling of Knin in 1995. The wall is adorned with a brass cross, and along each side displays a number of lights. By donating money through a slot, the lights that symbolise candles for the fallen Croatian soldiers start glowing. On the opposite wall, a documentary film on the 1995 military action is screened on a loop, thus combining monumental architecture with multimedia presentation (although the sound of the film is hardly audible). In front of the monument illuminable glass tops are embedded in the ground, each of which contains either facts and figures about the Homeland War (including monetary costs of the war), or descriptions of the various military actions, or alternatively, nationalist poems. They are lit at night and glow yellowish-green on the ground. The whole monument is framed by a brass banderol on which the names of the brigades that participated in the Homeland War are engraved.[24]

The desecration of this monument brings to mind another incident, in which a memorial, or rather a memorial plaque, was removed in Knin in 2010. In an attempt to establish an alternative, critical memory of Operation Storm, the regional 'Youth Initiative for Human Rights in Croatia' placed a marble plaque on the town's northern exit that contained an inscription 'offering an apology to the thousands of exiles who fled via this street for their suffering in place of a missing apology on the part of those responsible'. The plaque, that was allegedly funded by the Government Office for Human Rights in Zagreb, was removed a day after it had been placed, on the grounds that the youth organisation had no permission to set up the plaque and that 'the association of a dozen people cannot apologise on behalf of all citizens'.[25] Despite its outcome, this incident illustrates that contesting versions of history – regarding Operation Storm and the admission of Croatian war guilt – exist and continue to compete.

As Janine N. Clark has also convincingly shown for the case of Vukovar, recently erected war memorials tend to cement one particular version of the past and obstruct the repair of relationships and the rebuilding of trust (Clark 2013a).[26] Apart from selective memory it is also 'too much' or 'excess memory' that prevents society from moving forward, she argues. In areas such as Knin, where the cohabitation of Croats and Serbs is inevitable, it is essential to find common ground, and the example of the youth initiative in Knin raises hope that the younger generation are readier to acknowledge the suffering of Serbian civilians in the region, not just that of Croats. This acknowledgment could be the starting point for a 'shared truth' through which competing and contradictory ethnic narratives might be settled and upon which a shared future can be built.

In Sinj, which is located only seventy kilometres from Knin, cohabitation and reconciliation are not such pressing topics since the population is almost exclusively Croat, and hence commemoration politics are much more oriented towards the distant local past. During my fieldwork, in the summer of 2005, a new memorial, a massive bronze statue of the Franciscan Fra Pavao Vučković (1658–1735) was erected at the entrance to the old town.[27] Fra Vučković had been a leading figure in the exodus of Croatians from Rama to the Cetinska krajina in 1687. Besides being a clergyman and the *gvardijan* of the Franciscan monastery in Sinj, he had also fought in the legendary battle of 1715 and acted as a diplomatic figure in the negotiations with the Turkish attackers. When, in mid-summer 2005, the president of the local 'Matica Hrvatska', Igor Zidić, revealed the statue, he stressed the importance of this historic figure for present-day political conduct.[28] His inauguration speech included the following remarks:

> Fra Pavao Vučković is the living image of the man we need today as we did several centuries ago. To this day, nothing has changed. We are still surrounded by those bigger than us, and the big and the bigger continue to want what is ours. And alongside our faith we still have to, metaphorically speaking, hold a cross, a rosary and a gun under our pillow. God forbid we should forget that. This man, Fra Pavao, comes to us from the past, but he is alive, he is with us. He lives as an example, as a calling invitation, as a sign of how to fight and how to live both in war and in peace ... We have no illusions that the current peace will last forever. That's why we won't allow ourselves to fall asleep. Because, when a small one falls asleep, a big foot will step on him – and that's it. A people as small as ours can trust no one but God. Everything else is constantly questionable, and I want this statue to remind us of that.

This speech is another example of an attempt at resuscitation of a historical figure who in my view illustrates a widespread hesitation amongst Croatians (and Dalmatians in particular) about transforming the past into history. The statue of a cleric who has excelled as a warrior calls into being a local 'hero' and 'resistance fighter' – a man who, in the name of God, had fought for liberation from occupying powers. Fra Vučković's historic persona is transferred to the present and politically functionalised as he is honoured in place of all courageous locals who oppose foreign intruders and foreign authority. His memorial, in which a community celebrates its own bravery and militarism, is also intended to serve as an encouragement for those who intend to maintain this opposition in the future, whatever the circumstances. The speaker appeals to the public to be watchful and to distrust neighbouring countries as well as the Great Powers, thereby stimulating an atmosphere of fear and terror. By referring to unspecified outsiders as *velika stopa* (big feet) who always threaten to trample on Croatia, he constructs an image of Croatia and Croatians as constantly being menaced, and employs the classic trope of Croatian self-victimisation. Calling on the citizens of Sinj to doubt that the current peace will be a lasting one, he indirectly discourages disarmament and endorses a continued militarisation of society under the pretence of indispensable self-defence.

It is also interesting to note that the decision makers involved in choosing a new cenotaph for the town centre of Sinj opted for yet another monument in memory of the historic battle of 1715. The townscape of Sinj holds numerous monuments, all of which epitomise or display a cultural heritage that is exclusively related to local history. It thus becomes evident that local history plays a much more vital role in people's daily lives than national history does. Particularly the insignia of the Alka, the historical battle against the Turks and Gospa Sinjska are omnipresent in public places and signify that memory is highly localised. I understand this as a sign of the growing regionalisation and particularisation of memory practices that result from the increasingly important role of the region as a place of cultural identification in the new Europe.

In shaping modes of historical perception, people draw more and more on 'traditional neighbourhoods' grounded in everyday experiences and the physical environment, rather than on 'architectural monuments' that represent a version of history advocated by the nation-state (cf. Herzfeld 1991: 6, 46). This might be due to the fact that in this part of the world the borders of the nation-state are perceived as shifting and unstable; the historical self-understanding of the nation-state is therefore not seen as a reliable frame of reference. The townscape of Sinj thus turns into a contested cultural topography in which popular (regional) understandings of history prevail over official (national) understandings. The fact that recent politics of memory tend to strengthen regional belonging and identity rather than national or European self-conceptions can further be ascribed to a deep-seated rejection of state-supported constructions of the past as previously practised in the Socialist Federal Republic of Yugoslavia.

The Militarisation and Masculinisation of Public Space

An important aspect of commemoration is the visual omnipresence of particular historic events, historiographies or one-sided worldviews in public space. Such commemorative impositions on people's lived-in surroundings not only involve monuments and memorials but also the naming of public spaces such as streets, squares, shops, restaurants and cafés. In contrast to landmarks that exude a certain sense of timelessness (Halbwachs [1941] 1971), the naming of streets and places expresses a conscious choice that creates and shapes public memory. I have already shown that in Dalmatia, and especially in Sinj, commemoration is highly localised, and is founded on everyday experiences rather than solely on official monuments. Studying the micro-politics of naming, I illustrate how the townscape of Sinj forms an arena in which municipal authority and private individuals put their conception of history on display and publicly comment on political events by choosing a particular designation for their venture such as a street, a town square or a quarter. The popular naming of public spaces in Sinj shows itself to centre on images of military force, war, and the celebration of Croatia's independence. This again affects the public awareness of soldiers and veterans in Croatian society and has repercussions for notions of masculinity within the local community.

Referring to the period from immediately after the Second World War until the mid-1950s, Renata Jambrešić Kirin speaks of a Yugoslav era that was primarily characterised by the domination of military and veteran culture. 'It was a politics of memory that militarised and masculinised history, glorified acts of physical heroism, worshipped the cult of the president-marshal, and eliminated "undesirable elements" from the collective memory' (Jambrešić Kirin 2004: 128). This specific *Erinnerungskultur*, or memory culture, that prevailed in the decade following the Second World War has experienced a revival in Croatia since the mid-1990s, and I argue that it prevails to the present day. In contrast to the post-war period, the current phase is dominated by nationalist undertones, but the militarisation and masculinisation of history and the concomitant glorification of physical heroism are definitely comparable. The socialist personality cult, however, has been replaced by a more general reinforcement of hegemonic masculine role models and finds its expression in the public approval of ex-generals Mirko Norac and Ante Gotovina, as well as in the high regard for Croatian soldiers in general. The material manifestation of an increasingly 'militarised and masculinised history', as noted by Jambrešić Kirin, occurs in public space and becomes visible in urban features, such as in the (re)naming of places.

Periods of transition are often initiated or accompanied by the removal of symbols of the previous era, such as the renaming of streets,
buildings and public places, and the dismantling of statues, memorials
and walls (cf. Verdery 1999). In Croatia, the transition to national independence was also accompanied by a number of historical 'rewritings',
many of which concerned the symbolic renaming of public places. In the
weeks following the official election of Tuđman as the first president of
Croatia, streets and squares in the capital Zagreb reminiscent of Tito's
Yugoslavia were renamed. One of the earliest changes concerned the 'Trg
Republikska' [Square of the Republic] in the centre of Zagreb, which was
restored to its former name 'Trg Bana Jelačića' [Ban Jelačić Square]. Josip
Jelačić (1801–1859) was a noted Croatian army general of the Habsburg
dynasty who fought the Ottoman Turks and Hungarian revolutionaries.
And whilst the revolutionary Left and the communist government of
Yugoslavia considered Jelačić an Austrian collaborator, Tuđman managed to turn the fallen hero of the revolution of 1848 into a mythologised
national leader and a symbolic figure of Croatian independence. The renaming of the main square in Zagreb and the re-erection of the Jelačić
statue were clear signs by the new Croatian government of parting from
the country's communist past. Much more controversial was Tuđman's
later decision to rename the 'Trg žrtava fašizma' [Victims of Fascism
Square] in Zagreb the 'Trg hrvatskih velikana' [Great Men of Croatia
Square]. This step signified that the memory of the county's fascist past
was officially replaced by the glorification of Croatian statesmen and heroes. Being a military historian, Tuđman was well aware of the significance of such denominations and he readily utilised them as symbolic
acts in favour of his nationalist political course.

These rewritings of history not only occurred in the capital but
spread throughout the whole country. After 1991, symbols of Croatian
sovereignty that had been forbidden during socialism and considered
insignia of separatism or Croatian fascism – such as the *šahovnica*,[29] the
red and white checkerboard that has been a symbol of Croatian kings
since the tenth century, or photographs of Ante Pavelić, the Ustaše
head of the Independent State of Croatia – were eagerly put on public
display to assert the existence of the new nation.[30] Particularly in areas
that had been directly affected by the conflict, public commemorations
of the Homeland War and celebrations of Croatia's independence replaced earlier Socialist imagery. In Sinj, the memories and interpretations of reality are grounded in heroic ideals of national unity and
regional bravery – an attitude that is visible in the townscape. Apart
from the obligatory 'Ulica Domovinskog Rata' [Street of the Homeland
War] in Sinj, one can also find an 'Ulica žrtava rata' [Street of the War

Victims] and a 'Trg Gojka Šuška' [Gojko Šušak Square], named after the minister of defence during the Homeland War. The public space is strongly dominated by local feelings of pride and sorrow for the sacrifices Croatian citizens made in fighting for independence. And while the monuments and memorials in Sinj are for the most part commemorations of the battle against the Ottoman Turks (like the Alka tournament and the belief in the intervention of Gospa Sinjska), public place names mainly refer to the country's recent past, or alternatively to the country's legendary history.

One example of how recent historical events and personas are mapped onto the physical environment is the plaza 'Trg Franje Tuđmana' [Franjo Tuđman Square] in the centre of town. Tuđman's radically nationalist political course and his fundamental rewriting of Croatia's past (and present) has always been very popular in this region, and it is not surprising that the municipality of Sinj declares its belief in Tuđman's political ideals by naming a busy public place in the heart of town after him. Public memory is inseparable from discourses of national identity (Hodgkin and Radstone 2003a: 170), and shared narratives of the national past often draw on a country's mythologised or glorified history – a strategy that Tuđman amply utilised during his presidential term. This policy was also at stake in Sinj, when in 1992 the main square in front of the church was renamed 'Trg Kralja Tomislava' [King Tomislav Square] by no lesser a figure than Franjo Tuđman. It was under the rule of Tomislav I (910–928) that Croatia became one of the most powerful kingdoms of Medieval Europe and he is celebrated as the founder of the first united Croatian state.[31] Naming the central square in Sinj after him is a clear reference to the medieval glory of Croatia, meant to authenticate and strengthen the newly created Republic. As a guest of honour of the 277th Alka, Tuđman inaugurated the square and unveiled a memorial plaque bearing the following inscription:

> King Tomislav Square. In the year of the anniversary of the thousand-year-old Croatian Kingdom (1925), the people of Sinj and the Cetina region erected this memorial plaque at the front of the sanctuary of Gospa Sinjska in honour of King Tomislav. In the year of hatred (1944) the façade and the plaque were destroyed. In the year of the renewal of the Croatian nation the memorial plaque is newly erected and unveiled by the President of the Republic of Croatia, Dr Franjo Tuđman.
>
> Sinj, 30 August 1992, on the day of the 277th Alka

The inscription gives the impression that the new Croatian nation is the continuation or realisation of the 'thousand-year-old dream' of a Croatian nation, covering the fact that the fame and magnitude of the Medieval Kingdom of Croatia faded not long after its formation, when Croatia entered into a personal union with the Hungarian kingdom in the year 1102. The dream of a thousand-year-old Croatian kingdom, however, has always been a key element of Croatian nationalism, and it featured prominently in Tuđman's rhetoric, part of whose imperialistic political concept was to conjure up the reincarnation of the lost Croatian state and to restore Croatia's 'natural and historical borders' (cf. Hedl 2000). The inauguration of the square in Sinj thus not only involves a re-naming ceremony but constitutes an active rewriting of history. Several layers of historic events are blended while other less honourable periods are concealed, distorted or reinterpreted. The time of the Croatian kingdom (925–1102), the battle against forces of the Ottoman Empire (represented by the commemoration of the Alka), and Croatian independence in 1991, are depicted as linear sequential historical developments. They all converge in the main square of Sinj and anchor the place in Croatian history. The placing of the memorial plaque on the façade of the sanctuary of Gospa Sinjska further ties this version of national history to regional history and makes it accessible or more 'tangible' for the local population.

The understanding of history that is conveyed in this memorial plaque replaces the previously valid 'official memory' and is highly nationalistic. The 1944 'year of hatred' [*godina mrženje*] therefore does not refer to the reign of the fascist Independent State of Croatia but to the increasing victory and eventual takeover by Tito's Yugoslav Partisans. In this sense, the version and evaluation of history that officially prevailed in the So-cialist Federal Republic of Yugoslavia (1945–1992) is not only redefined but directly reversed. Both the act of renaming the square and the text of the inscription mythologise the past and lay 'claim to something more ancient and authentic', as described by Hodgkin and Radstone. By revis-ing the official historical narrative, the authorities of the new Croatian state legitimise what is 'theirs' by drawing on an ancient past that long preceded the previous regime.[32]

The naming of streets and places also serves as an indicator for the socio-political climate in a given environment. In Sinj, the parting from socialist Yugoslavia is not so much marked by aspirations towards Eu-rope but by a reversion to a more ancient past in which the country's nationalist ideals are believed to be grounded. The fact that not a single public place in Sinj is called 'Evropa' – in contrast to something that according to the Croatian writer Slavenka Drakulić (1996) has become a tradition throughout the whole of Eastern Europe – indicates that a critical attitude to 'the West' is particularly pronounced in this part of the world, where people feel deceived by Europe and the international community.

In nearby Mostar in Bosnia-Herzegovina, for instance, a huge number of small businesses and shops are called 'Fenix' [phoenix], evoking the image of 'rising phoenix-like from the ashes'. This denomination indicates a hopeful spirit and points towards the projected reconstruction and prospering of a town that had largely been destroyed during the war. In Sinj, on the other hand, the names of public places are less directed towards the future or the prospect of rebuilding than to the region's glorious past and Croatia's recent independence. The general atmosphere is dominated by patriotism and a sense of righteousness after years of subjugation.

Commentaries on the most recent past can also be found in the names of small enterprises and shops. A *kavana* on Trg Kralja Tomislava in Sinj, for example, was called 'Café Gensher' – a misspelled homage to the former German foreign minister Hans-Dietrich Genscher, who was one of the first international statesmen to publicly recognise Croatia's independence in 1991.[33] Genscher is very popular throughout Croatia because of this early concession, whereas people in the neighbouring republics disapprove of his pro-Croatian political course. A Bosniak interlocutor of mine, for example, who lived in Mostar during the war scornfully exclaimed: 'Genscher? He was more of a Croat than Tuđman!' The fact that a café is named after Genscher in Sinj can be understood as a sign of gratitude and a political statement highlighting the importance of the German recognition of Croatia.

Other *kavanas* in the centre of Sinj are called Alkar, Alcatraz and Westpoint. The name of café Alkar is a clear reference to the Alka tournament and I assume that Alcatraz may have been chosen for the same reason. However, the fact that two of the main public gathering places in the small town are named after a prison island and a military academy give good reason to suspect a certain fascination with the exertion of discipline and control. In both military academies and in prisons, (primarily) male bodies are disciplined and inmates' or cadets' behaviour is rigorously controlled and sanctioned. As custodial places within which activities are 'imposed from above by a system of explicit formal rulings and a body of officials' and where activities are tightly scheduled, prisons and military academies are 'total institutions', in Erving Goffman's initial sense of the term (Goffman [1961] 1968). Such institutions also idealise 'masculine qualities' such as toughness, discipline and fearlessness, and proclaim belligerent men as the norm. The unconcealed attraction such institutions hold for young men is in my view a sign that in a society in which social mobility is radically restricted, the longing for directives and conventions prevails.

No matter if I visited Café Alka, Alcatraz or Westpoint, the sight was always the same: the majority of the customers were groups of young men, many of whom wearing Croatian army uniforms. The *kavanas* are mostly located on either side of the *korzo*, a small boulevard in the centre of town where people meet acquaintances, exchange news and gossip, or simply stroll. People can usually sit outside on white plastic chairs throughout the year, and even during the chilly winter months all try to catch a few rays of sunshine. It is a daily ritual for men sitting in the cafés to gaze at (and audibly comment on) the girls who self-confidently walk up and down the *korzo* and occasionally throw a spicy remark back. Despite the playfulness of this scenario, the townscape is visibly dominated by the presence of uniformed men and the conversations one can overhear at the various tables are dominated by complaints about the never-ending victim status of Croatia and anecdotes about the war.[34] To be sure, talk about Croatia's violent past and visits to cafés named after Westpoint or Alcatraz do not alone make people military or criminal in outlook. Nonetheless, I argue that the omnipresence of army personnel in public space, the dominance of war-related topics in public discourse, along with regular declarations of solidarity with then indicted Croatian ex-generals, gradually leads to a militarisation of everyday life that confirms and naturalises hegemonic masculinities.

In their introduction to *The Politics of War Memory and Commemoration* Ashplant, Dawson and Roper note that 'in the context of national imaginaries, dominant memory is often centred around the idealized figure of the masculine soldier' (Ashplant, Dawson and Roper 2000: 21). In many post-war societies veterans are celebrated as soldier heroes and their willingness to fight and to die for their country dominates the official memory and shapes the narratives in which the identity and symbolic continuity of the new state are grounded. In the case of Croatia, the commemoration of the Homeland War also centres on the heroic sacrifices of Croatian soldiers, the ex-generals Mirko Norac and Ante Gotovina becoming personifications of the idealised masculine soldier figure. Statements of solidarity with the former generals in the form of slogans, pictures or graffiti and placards in commemoration of 'successful' military operations during the Homeland War – such as a poster celebrating *Dani Ponosa i Slave* [Days of Pride and Glory] and the twelfth anniversary of the military operation 'Operacija Maslenica' in January 2005[35] – are displayed on advertisement columns, walls, and in shop windows, creating unequivocal public statements in support and honour of the *branitelji* on behalf of the citizens of Sinj. The symbols and practices of commemoration highlight the successful self-defence of Croatia and the public imaginary draws on the figure of the intrepid male defender.

Military historians such as Gillis argue that national commemoration practices in general changed greatly after the Second World War in various countries. In the United States in particular, one change was that the cult of the fallen soldier was replaced by a new emphasis on veterans (Gillis 1994: 13). In present-day Croatia, however, the role of veterans is highly ambivalent. Although official memory is expressed through a calendar of ceremonies such as military parades, as well as commemoration days, military pilgrimages and commemorative services, public and private remembrance collides in many cases. This visibility and public recognition of ex-servicemen stands in marked contrast to the psychosocial situation of those who suffer from the repercussions of the war. Traumatised ex-combatants in particular, do not feel like heroes, and have difficulties reintegrating into mainstream society. For a large number of *branitelji*, the official memorial narrative of triumph does not therefore concur with personal experiences and memories. But veterans who feel victimised, helpless and confused have no space to communicate their suffering in a society that considers war the quintessential proving ground of masculinity and that glorifies the imaginative figure of the soldier hero. War-affected communities such as contemporary post-war Croatian society often lack a climate of compassion for, and understanding of, what combatants have experienced, and the result of this neglect is a phenomenon of masculinity in crisis (Živković 2006).

Notes

1. A shorter version of the chapter has been published in *History and Memory* (Schäuble 2011). Also cited in *The Guardian* (U.K.), 27 December 1995, page 2.
2. Speech at the Extraordinary Meeting of the Serbian Writers' Union, Književne novine, 15 March 1989 (Čolović 2002: 36).
3. For a comprehensive analysis of how war violence is socially remembered in relation to the materiality of place, with a particular focus on the destruction of landscapes and builtscapes during the First World War, see Filippucci 2010: 159–83.
4. For a more recent study on the Istrian case, see Ballinger 2004b: 145–59.
5. Especially in Chap. 3, 'Giving Proper Burial, Reconfiguring Space and Time', Verdery primarily draws on ethnographic material on exhumations and reburials in the former Yugoslavia as described by Denich and Hayden.
6. In this context, it is interesting to note that the relative strength between 'genealogies' and 'territories' in constituting national sentiment is gradually

changing and that the Serbian 'blood and soil' ideology, for instance, is putting a greater emphasis on 'blood' rather than 'soil'. The most noteworthy indication of this shift is probably Radovan Karadžić's remark of 13 September 1995, at a time when he was president of 'Republika Srpska': 'We will not become a nation until being a Serb is more important than living where your ancestors lived' (quoted in Hayden 1996: 783).

7. In their account of the relation between religion and the physical environment, Horden and Purcell note that 'out of an estimated 3,248 active pilgrim shrines in Europe, 18 per cent are connected with cities of more than 25,000 inhabitants ... 30 per cent of those are "suburban" (peripheral rather than central to the city landscape). Most of the shrines which are related to landscape features – the familiar trees, springs, rocks, summits of our survey so far – are remote from cities, and very few are in their centres.' In addition, they stress that it is precisely because of their remoteness and their detachment from normal conditions of life that cold mountain tops 'have been linked with the time of origins, suitable places for the abode of the divine' (Horden and Purcell 2000: 422, 413). In this sense, the shrine at the *jama* represents a rather typical specimen of remote pilgrimage sites. (Cf. Turner 1973: 191–230.)

8. It also underlines the interrelatedness of culture, power and place, as noted by Gupta and Ferguson (1997).

9. In 1945 Yugoslav Partisans killed thousands of Croatian Ustaše and Home Guards [*Domobrani*], Serbian Četniks and Slovenian White Guards along with a large number of civilians who had fled ahead of the advance of the Partisans in May 1945. Hoping to surrender to and gain protection of the Allies, these fugitives tried to cross the border into Austria where British infantry brigades were stationed. The British troops, however, forcibly returned the fleeing militia and refugees to Yugoslavia, where the Partisans executed most of them. The question of how many people were actually killed at Bleiburg remains controversial. While some Croatian nationalists insist that up to two hundred thousand were killed, others have put the final death toll at thirty thousand. The Bleiburg massacre has become paradigmatic for the betrayal of Croatians by the Allied troops and is commonly deployed as *the* trope of Croatian victimisation.

10. Jasenovac was the largest concentration and extermination camp in Croatia during the Second World War. Set up in August 1941 and run by the Ustaška Narodna Služba UNS [Ustaše People's Service] of the NDH, Jasenovac was constructed in a manner similar to Nazi concentration camps. Victims included mainly Serbs, Jews, Gypsies, and opponents of the Ustaša regime. Estimates of the numbers of victims murdered in the Jasenovac camp vary tremendously due to the lack of exact and reliable records. Many Serbs use Jasenovac as a metonomy for genocide and the Ustaša campaign to expel them from Croatia, whereas a number of Croatian historians in turn sought to 'correct' or to downplay the number of actual victims.

11. Goli Otok (literally 'barren island') is an island off the northern Adriatic coast that was converted into a high-security prison in 1948. Run by the authorities of Socialist Yugoslavia, the entire island was used to incarcerate political prisoners, mainly Stalinists and/or Yugoslav citizens who sympathised with the Soviet Union. Later, mainly nationalists were imprisoned and forced to do heavy labour in a stone quarry. A large number of political prisoners were never released, and died on the island. The prison camp was shut down in 1988.

12. Located on the border between Croatia and Serbia on the Danube, Vukovar was attacked by the Yugoslav People's Army (JNA) and Serbian paramilitary troops in July 1991. During a devastating three-month siege, the town was almost completely destroyed. The Croatian population of Vukovar was partly exiled and a large number were killed. In a nearby field called Ovčara, mass executions of Croats took place and the actions of the JNA and Serb paramilitary forces are widely regarded in terms of ethnic cleansing. Croatians saw the battle for Vukovar as a life-or-death struggle for the survival of their nation, which they compared to the Soviet Union's decisive Battle of Stalingrad. Today Vukovar remains largely destroyed, the surrounding fields still covered with landmines.

13. The strong anti-communist sentiment of the Croatian Catholic Church and the Franciscan Order is based on the severe repressions the Yugoslav communist regime exercised against the Church. Large numbers of clerics were subjected to ruthless persecutions, and many priests and monks were killed during and after the war. Tomislav Jonjić notes that '[t]he Shepherd's Letter of the Catholic Bishops of Yugoslavia dated 20 September 1945 especially pointed to the unprecedented persecutions of Catholic priests: 243 killed, 169 in prisons and camps, and 89 missing. There were also 19 killed clerics, 3 killed monks and four nuns' (Jonjić 2007: 136).

14. In this sense, the commemoration comprises an emotional (but not a political) claim over the Croatianness of the territories and victims in question. Similarly, the border between Croatia and Herzegovina is never referred to or taken seriously as a state border, but is instead either ridiculed or verbally disparaged.

15. Frykman refers particularly to the *ensuli*, the Italian-speaking population of Istria, who were heavily persecuted under Tito's communist regime and fled into exile [*esuli*]. See Frykman unpublished MS: 2. For a comprehensive ethnographic study of the repercussions of the displacement of up to 350,000 ethnic Italians from the border zone between Italy and Yugoslavia, see Ballinger 2003.

16. Cf. Narotzky and Moreno 2004: 273–93. For a detailed study of the historical memory of the Spanish Civil War, see Aguilar 2002.

17. The description of a wounded space that continually fails to heal corresponds to Aleida Assmann's definition of a 'traumatic place' (Assmann [1999] 2006: 338). I would, however, refrain from considering the *jama* a classic 'traumatic place', as the notion is habitually used with reference to concentration and extermination camps whose excess of horror exceeds

all powers of imagination. The extent to which the *jama* represents local trauma is in my opinion quite significant, yet not comparable to classic traumatic places.

18. Critics of Nora, such as Paul Antze, for instance, argue that his approach is 'Eurocentric' and 'romantic' (Antze and Lambek 1996: xiv).

19. The folk belief in this region also features quite imaginative curses and swear words. Most of the curses contain a reference to Gospa Sinjska, and in a personal conversation Prof. Dr Adalbert Rebić said, 'The people in Sinj swear by and at the Gospa Sinjska. But this only shows how deeply their religious belief is rooted' (personal communication 30 Oct 2004).

20. The majority of those Croats who died in the battle against the Partisans had fought for the fascist Croatian NDH-state. Today, these dead are reinterpreted as victims in the fight for the independent Republic of Croatia.

21. The literary critic Tatjana Pavlović notes that '[a]llusions to nature, animals, stones, earth, trees, etc. are common Croatian metaphors illustrating the "profound" connection of the people to their historical roots. These allusions are also found in many of our pop groups that tie their belonging to the nation to a particular tree, which they envision as a pillar of nationhood' (Pavlović 2001: 140–41). This analysis illustrates that closeness to nature is seen as rootedness in place and connected to the territory that marks a nation and constitutes nationhood.

22. Ludwig Steindorff and Wolfgang Höpken have both pointed out that in Croatia hardly any monuments were erected for those killed in the First World War (Höpken 2001: 381; Steindorff 2003: 165). According to the new state, the soldiers had fought on 'the wrong side' and were thus for the most part devoid of official honours.

23. The Croatian word *spomen* translates as 'memento, memorial, monument' as well as 'remembrance', and thus signifies the material manifestation of memories as well as the process of remembering.

24. In 2012 the festivities surrounding the 'Victory and Homeland Thanksgiving Day and the Day of Croatian Defenders' were held around this monument on Starčević Square in the form of a folk music event that was broadcast on national television for hours on end.

25. For the respective news report, see http://www.index.hr/vijesti/clanak/grad-knin-skinuo-spomenplocu-izbjeglicama-oluje-inicijativi-zaprijetio-hcsp/505578.aspx (last visited 30 Oct 2012).

26. Vukovar is another 'divided' Croatian town in which Croats and Serbs coexist, but unlike Knin that came to symbolise Croatia's victory in the Homeland War, Vukovar has become synonymous with Croat suffering and victimhood.

27. There was some disagreement as to where the statue should be put up in town. In the end it was decided to erect it at the entrance to the historic ancient town next to the barriers of the toll parking collection for cars.

28. Matica Hrvatska is the major cultural organisation in Croatia, founded as early as 1842. Its local branch in Sinj is very active in publishing books on local history and organising various cultural events.

29. The *šahovnica*, literally 'chessboard' from *šah* for 'chess', is a checkerboard that consists of thirteen red and twelve white fields and is traditionally considered a distinctive feature for Croats and Croatia. In 1919, it was included in the coat of arms of the Kingdom of Serbs, Croats and Slovenes to represent the Croats. Later, the Ustaše also used the *šahovnica* (with the upper-left square white in contrast to the present upper-left square red) as the official national symbol and superimposed the letter 'U' as their ideological trademark. After the Second World War, the *šahovnica* was included in the new socialist coat of arms, this time adorned with the typical communist symbols such as wheat, an anvil, a rising sun and a red star. During the change to multiparty elections in Croatia and prior to the establishment of the current design, the *šahovnica* got rid of the communist symbols and simply consisted of the red and white checkerboard. The present coat of arms of the Republic of Croatia consists of a *šahovnica* as well as five smaller shields that represent the five historical regions from which Croatia originated.

30. In Sinj, this public display of fascist paraphernalia continued during the course of my fieldwork. In the interior of a café whose holder is known to be a member of the ultra right-wing HSP, I have even seen Ustaša emblems and pictures of Ante Pavelić on public display.

31. Tomislav I of Croatia first reigned as Duke (*Dux Croatorum*) of Croatian Dalmatia in 910–925 and then united the Croats of Dalmatia and Pannonia into a single kingdom. He subsequently became the first king (*Rex Croatorum*) of the Croatian Kingdom until his death in 928. His empire covered the territory from the Adriatic Sea in the south to the Drava River in the north, and from Istria in the west to the Drina River in the east. To this day, some radical nationalists time and again claim this area to be Croatian territory.

32. The name of my host family's eldest son is also Tomislav. When he was born in the late 1960s and his parents went to register his name, they were suspected of being dissidents, and questioned by the secret service. To call a child after the first king of Croatia was considered a subversive act and an attempt of Croatian separatism by the socialist Yugoslav authorities. My hosts were intimidated but in the end did not suffer any repercussions. A street in the old town of the idyllic seaport Trogir was renamed 'Ulica Kohl Genscher' (Kohl Genscher Street) in honour of the German chancellor Helmut Kohl (in office 1982–1998) and his foreign minister Hans-Dietrich Genscher (in office 1974–1992) who decisively supported the international recognition of Croatia's independence in 1991. The 'Caffe bar Gensher' in Sinj, however, had been renamed by the time of my visit in 2012.

33. Although many of the people I talked to or interviewed claimed that they were sick and tired of talking about the war and would rather 'move on', narratives about the war are omnipresent in public discourse. During my fieldwork, the television show 'Dva u devetu' on OTV held an opinion poll where viewers could call in on the question: 'Should the media report more

about the Homeland War or less?' It did not really come as a surprise that 98.92% of the viewers pleaded for 'more', and only 1.08% for 'less'.

34. Opercacija Maslenica was a Croatian army offensive launched on 22 January 1993 in the course of which occupied territory in Northern Dalmatia and Lika, including the strategically important Maslenica area, was reconquered. The military aim of the operation was to push the Krajina Serb forces back from approaches to Zadar and Maslenica Bay, and to secure a strategically important land route between Dalmatia and the rest of Croatia. Opercacija Maslenica was the first and only instance of Croatian naval and air forces acting together in a single major operation, and in Dalmatia it is considered a particularly important military success, because it stopped the advance of Serb troops into Zadar. After the initial success, the 126th Home Guard Regiment of the Croatian Army conducted its own offensive operation against the occupation of the Peruča dam near Sinj so that a detonation and massive flooding of the Cetina valley could be prevented. In Sinj this operation is thus celebrated as *the* most significant military victory of the Homeland War in the region. The general in charge of Opercacija Maslenica was Janko Bobetko, a man who is considered a national hero in Dalmatia to the present day.

‹· Chapter 4 ·›

Of War Heroes,
Martyrs and Invalids

Present-day gender relations in Croatia – especially the strengthening of patriarchal gender constructs and traditional role allocation – prove an additional battleground for different ways of remembering, understanding and restructuring the past in the light of a ruptured present. Individual as well as communal identity construction in the peripheries is constituted by the mutual embeddedness of gender, ethnicity and (marginal) political status. Ana Lowenhaupt Tsing has pointed out that state politics shape ethnic and regional identity, and are, in turn, informed by them. 'State and ethnic politics are gendered just as gender difference is created through state and ethnic discourse. Yet each of the three creates divided dispositions that destabilize the communities of interest formed by the other two', she writes (Lowenhaupt Tsing 1993: 34). It is exactly in this area of tension that my analysis of the role that gender plays in narratives of Croatian (self-)victimisation is anchored. As I have shown so far, nationalism, religion, the increasing importance of so-called 'authentic Croatian/Dalmatian tradition', even the embodied perception of landscape and space, are highly gendered categories. My concern in this chapter is less with gender inequalities as they exist today in the republics of the former Yugoslavia than with the interplay between gender [*rod*] and nation [*narod*] in post-war Croatia, which is engrossed by a patriarchal, martial and masculine heroic cultural imaginary, and by this imaginary's constitutive counterpart, the trope of (self-)victimisation.

The study of transitional processes, especially in times of raised national awareness, involves a detailed analysis of local notions of gender and personhood as situated positionings vis-à-vis other segments of the social, political and cultural life of a community as well as vis-à-vis urban centres of power and visions of the nation itself (Herzfeld 1985; Jambrešić Kirin and Škokić 2004). (Ethno-)nationalism and the construction of an (imagined) community based on a common ancestry with a shared historical fate, however, are far from being purely

symbolic classifying processes. They are also material, corporeal practices, leading Gal and Kligman to point out that '[o]ne's relation to the
future and to history is understood in generational terms, through stories of physical, biological reproduction' (Gal and Kligman 2000: 25).
The procreational element underlying this line of reasoning and its effects on postsocialist politics is also emphasised by Katherine Verdery.
In a comparable manner, she points to the gendering of nationalist imagery and to the gendered nature of postsocialist discourses on citizen
rights and democracy.

> Anthropological work on nationalism is revealing it to be quintes-
> sentially about kinship, something that is organized around ideas of
> youth and age, male and female, shared substance, blood and bone,
> and exclusion. If nationalism is kinship, then these same axes will or-
> ganize nationalism as well. We might therefore expect nationalist ideas
> to bury the socialist past and reshape the postsocialist future in part
> through notions of gender and substance. Gendered images of kin –
> images of 'brotherhood', 'forefathers', and 'mother-' or 'fatherland' – are
> at the very heart of nationalist imagery. (Verdery 1996: 233)

To a certain extent, the emerging nationalisms in the respective republics
of the former Yugoslavia built themselves on the unsuccessful attempts
of socialism to redefine national identity and erase ethnic as well as gender difference. The socialist claim for a social reorganisation of gender
was not fulfilled and did not have any effect on ending the persistent
gendering of power and of the workforce. Instead it ultimately reinforced
patriarchal family structures. By applying a kinship-familial metaphor to
characterise the relationship between citizens and the socialist state, and
thus producing dependency rather than agency, 'paternalist socialism'
can be understood as having a certain affinity to ethno-nationalism and
eventually even paving the way for gendered nationalist rhetoric as a
prelude to war (Verdery 1996: 63).

The personified depiction of the nation as a woman or as being endowed with female virtues, and (hence) in need of masculine protection,
is a well-known propaganda strategy that featured prominently in the
late 1980s and early 1990s, during the war in which Yugoslavia disin-
tegrated (see also Žarkov 2007). This policy of gendering of the nation,
and mobilising the potential for ethno-national 'othering' contained in
it, continues to inform current strategies of creating national solidarity throughout all the republics of the former Yugoslavia. My analysis
demonstrates that Cynthia Enloe's sharply worded observation that it is
masculinised memory, masculinised humiliation and masculinised hope

that lie at the beginnings of nationalism certainly holds true for national-ist politics in post-war Croatia, and also finds its most ostensive expres-sion in narratives of Croatian victimhood (Enloe 1989: 44).

Forgotten Women, Contested Masculinities

It was not for their deeds but for their being that women were remembered.

— John R. Gillis, 'Memory and Identity'

My empirical analysis of micro-politics and everyday practices of mem-ory has found that memories are not only connected to processes of identity formation in time and place but also that they are gendered. The gender categories that take effect on individual as well as collec-tive memories and commemorations are mostly connected to notions of victimisation, suffering and belonging. Especially memories related to war and violence in the former Yugoslavia employ gendered metaphors that tend to naturalise historic events and reveal the interconnected-ness of gender and ethnicity – showing how victimisation, suffering and belonging are ethnicised through gender discourses and vice versa (Žarkov 2001). I will, however, not put the main emphasis on male and female forms of memorising. Although I have noticed that women and men remember different events, narrate different stories, and recount or understand the same events in different ways, I am much more in-terested in the ways that gender and gendered representations are uti-lised in shaping and denoting collective memories and commemoration practices. Simultaneously, this approach also raises the question of in what ways memory discourses and commemoration practices construct gender roles and generate ethnic exclusion.

In her study on *Nationalism, Gender, and Race* Anne McClintock ar-gues that in national scenarios men tend actively to access and achieve 'national agency' and play a 'metonymic' role whereas women are more likely to adopt a 'metaphoric' or 'symbolic' role, and in this sense are more likely to represent an 'imagined community' (McClintock 1996; see also Wenk and Eschebach 2002: 28). It is noticeable that this 'meta-phoric' female role is inseparably connected to the female body and as-sociated with the demarcation of boundaries of ethnic and/or national groups. A number of feminist scholars have pointed out that the female body symbolically represents and delineates the body of the homeland (cf. Theweleit 1977/1978; Yuval-Davis and Anthias 1989: 6–11; Enloe 1988, 1989, 1993, 2000; Seifert 2001, 2004, 2007; Žarkov 2007). In the case of Croatia, the imagined community of the Croatian nation used mainly symbols of victimisation of these violated – 'real' as well as meta-phoric – female bodies during the war to mobilise ethno-national antagonisms in order to justify military intervention and to 're-historicize the "holiness" of their own nation' (Kašić 2001: 198).[1]

Describing nineteenth and twentieth century commemoration politics in general terms, John. R. Gillis notes that 'women remembered the men, while their own contributions were represented largely in terms of sacrifice, a traditional female role that only reinforced gender stereo-types' (Gillis 1994: 12). Women themselves are hardly ever remembered as 'heroines of the nation', and particularly in the case of the former Yugoslavia the 'female heroine' is generalised and mainly represented as an unknown suffering mother or waiting bride. The symbolisation of women through motherhood is based on maternal fecundity and additionally ethnicised by common expressions such as 'Croatian mother', 'mother Croatia' or 'mother Homeland' (Kesić 2001: 65; Žarkov 2007: 69). In times of violent conflicts and wars, women are appreciated most for sacrificing their sons to the national interest by sending them off to defend the homeland.[2] They are thus constructed as supporters of the male soldiers whose main task it is to defend helpless and vulnerable children and women – who, in turn, represent the nation. Appropriated in this way by national interests, the maternal body is 'either victimized and put in the service of othering, or militarized and put in the service of (justification of) violence' (Žarkov 2007: 69; see also Elshtain 1995; Enloe 2000). Such is the entire maternal-filial relationship. The ethno-nationalist discourse on womanhood and motherhood also strongly influences modes of (national) commemoration that ascribe to women a role of general keepers of memory, tradition, family and the home.

Gillis's analysis underlines the gendered nature of national commemoration practice and illustrates the tendency that it is commonly perceived as the women's task to restore and preserve the past, while the image of men at the spearhead of progress and modernisation prevails. In other words, it is men who write history while women are expected to remember and embrace their deeds. He adds that '[w]omen and minorities often serve as symbols of a "lost" past, nostalgically perceived and romantically constructed, but their actual lives are most readily forgotten' (Gillis 1994: 10). This observation very much corresponds to my own findings during fieldwork in which the history and achievements of real women are almost systematically forgotten or concealed. Even the case of the female Partisan fighters during the Second World War is considerably downplayed in contemporary public discourse – even though a quarter of the one hundred thousand women fighting in regular Partisan military units were killed in action, and another forty thousand wounded (Milić 1993). These women are nowadays hardly ever mentioned, and if they are remembered they are not individually remembered for their deeds or for their military bravery but for the unspecified sacrifices they have made. Official war narratives, monuments and renderings, by contrast, are primarily dominated by masculine heroes.

Katherine Verdery describes this official history-writing as an 'endless sequence of male heroes, strung out one after another, almost like a series of "begets", and producing the impression of the nation as temporally deep patrilineage' (Verdery 1994: 238; see also Kesić 2001: 70). The same mechanism was at stake after the Homeland War, when female *branitelji* did not receive medals like their male compatriots from the trenches, their actions as front-line fighters being instead largely forgotten soon after the end of the war. Accordingly, female civilians are mainly remembered as anonymous victims of war violence or described as safeguards of unofficial and highly emotionalised collective memories. As sainted victims they became a key figure for metaphors of the victimised Croatian nation (Kašić 2001: 197).

The commemorative role assigned to women is traditionally that of chief mourners and mediums (Gillis 1994: 12). Mourning and suffering is a sentiment, role and/or a cultural practice that is still mainly attributed to women. In Serbia (and in certain parts of Croatia, too) the custom to commission professional mourners is still quite widespread and a woman whose function is to lament at funerals on behalf of the family is called *narikača* (from *naricati*, to lament). A *narikača*'s ritual function is to recount the life story of the deceased in a highly poetic way and make him or her appear a glorious person whose loss is gravely felt by the bereaved (cf. Žarkov 2007: 29f.).

In the case of the ceremony at the *jama*, described in the previous chapter, for example, women are also assigned the role of chief mourners who publicly bewail and bestrew the dead with flowers. And although the whole pilgrimage to the *jama* is not exclusively considered a female affair, the gender roles are clearly marked: the men deliver public speeches, achieve 'national agency' and restore the 'official memory' of the deceased, whereas the women are expected to act as mediums via their emotional engagement with past atrocities, injustices and suffering. Standing at the *jama*, my companions repeatedly told me to 'think about all the mothers who have lost their sons here'. This reminder points not only towards the gendered notion of commemoration but also to the politicised glorification of motherhood. As literal and symbolic reproducers of the nation, mothers and motherhood have become interchangeable with national suffering in the sense that personal suffering of mothers in times of war is portrayed as a (voluntary) sacrifice for the nation. The suffering mother thus signifies the suffering of the homeland and the maternal body serves as a marker and maker of the nation and national territory (Žarkov 2007: 69). In the Christian tradition, the most powerful visualisation and key signifier of ultimate (maternal) suffering is the iconographic motif of the Pietà, the tormented mother of Christ. An established 'commemorative figure' (J. Assmann 1988: 12) or 'memorial formula' (Weigel 1996: 258), the Pietà serves as a paradigmatic representation of mourning and bereavement as the most painful act of remembrance. It is thus no coincidence that the recently erected monuments at the *jama* comprise a Marian shrine as well as a Pietà relief that correlate the commemoration of Partisan atrocities with maternal suffering. Mourning and suffering are constructed as gendered commemorative activities that are ascribed to the female sphere. As a memorial, however, the Pietà de-historicises the actual historic event it is supposed to represent and incorporates it into a much larger framework of sacralised iconography.

A 'sculpture of compassion' (Ziegler 1992) the Pietà encompasses the universal memory of human suffering beyond a specific historical event and represents the readiness to make sacrifices. In the context of war memorials where the Pietà motive is most common, this sacrifice usually refers to the 'honourable sacrifice' of a soldier who is willing to give his life for his homeland as well as to the sacrifice of a mother who has to bewail the loss of a child. The religious symbolism of the Pietà sculpture at the *jama* thus suggests an analogy between the suffering of the atrocity victims and the suffering and death of Christ, as well as the affliction of the Mother of Christ and the affliction of the bereaved family members, in particular the mothers of the victims. The depiction of the suffering mother is a symbolic representation of all Croatian mothers who have lost their sons during the war as well of 'mother Croatia' herself, the homeland that has sacrificed its sons in battle. My host once told me at length about the similarity between the love of a mother and the love of one's homeland. He said:

> We have a saying that the love of one's land is like the love of a mother. This is very philosophical if you start to think about it. The love of a mother is boundless. Almost like the love of God or the love of the Gospa. A mother does everything for you and you are forever connected to her. And if she needs your help at some point, you have to be there for her. And if you need something, you will get it from her. You don't even have to ask for it – she usually knows by herself what you need. That's how the love of your country works.

This notion of maternal devotion and self-sacrifice, which is expected equally of Croatian mothers and Croatian soldiers fighting for the motherland, is embodied in the figure of the Pietà.

In identifying with this mother figure, the (female) visitors at the *jama* confirm the victim status of the 'victims of Communist atrocities' as well as the victim status of the whole Croatian nation. The Christian notion of sacrifice of an innocent victim, however, also always implies the promise of redemption. Therefore I argue that – with particular reference to the suffering of Mother Mary – the Pietà icon also incorporates the idea or possibility of surmounting earthly suffering and pain vis-à-vis the anticipated resurrection of the deceased son. Transferring this religious imagery to the profane political context of the Partisan atrocities committed at the *jama* during the Second World War, it seems that the mothers (and the motherland) are perceived as having sacrificed their sons for a higher purpose, namely the defence and liberation of Croatia. In summary, one can say that the Pietà icon of the *mater dolorosa* constitutes suffering women as 'mothers-heroes' (Borić 1997: 40) or 'heroic "nation-victims"' (Kašić 2001: 198). Dubravka Žarkov describes the maternal body as a body 'vested with the power to give birth to the nation'; that is, 'both vulnerable and powerful, a potential target of attacks and a focus of protection, a fierce defender of its honor and its offspring' (Žarkov 2007: 19). In this sense, female vulnerability and the maternal willingness to suffer are glorified mainly as prerequisites for the later construction and acknowledgement of heroic masculinity.

The quasi-religious notion of redemption qua sacrifice is generally based on women's suffering and culminates in the epitome of female willingness to sacrifice – and ultimately even implies the Christian ideal of forgiveness of one's enemies or of those who do one harm. During my fieldwork I led numerous conversations and interviews with priests and other (male) representatives of the church, and it was interesting to note that at some point in the conversation (usually towards the end), almost all of them presented me with what I would call a 'reconciliation narrative'. And although these narratives varied in length and detail, they usually included that it was the Croatian women who had suffered most, but that they did not despair and were not filled with bitterness. 'They say "No, I don't hate the Serbs. Why should I hate the Serbs?" We all have to learn from these women's capacity to forgive.' And one priest even said: 'Our women are very devout. During confession a woman told me that she prays that no member of her family will take revenge, because she couldn't answer for that on Judgement Day. I sometimes think that you wouldn't hear such docile words even from a priest.' Such narratives, exclusively told by men, turn Croatian women into victim-heroines who are expected to promote sentiments of forgiveness and reconciliation despite their own suffering and the sacrifices they have made. In this sense, an almost larger-than-life female Croatian (mother) figure is constructed as a feminine paragon of virtue who is responsible for the emotional well-being and restoration of a peaceful and stable society.

After various periods in recent Yugoslav history in which women were successively conceptualised as strong 'comrade workers' during socialism, then functionalised for nationalist propaganda in the early 1990s and either exploited as victims of war rapes or heroic mothers willing to give birth, raise and sacrifice their sons for the homeland, they are now expected to foster the rebuilding of a war-torn society. There is a distinct tendency in current post-war Croatian society to reinforce traditional gender roles and return to conventional family structures. Mainly in rural areas where women are traditionally relegated to the domestic arena and the role of motherhood, traditional gender constructs and normative concepts of femininity and masculinity have been increasingly propagated and (re-)installed since the end of the war. Speeches by conservative government and church officials, like the one held at the Mass for the Victims of the Communist Regime, illustrate that the (heterosexual) nuclear family is constructed as a primordially Christian institution and turned into a battleground over the transmission and conservation of collective values. The traditional family model is perceived as the core unit or 'spine' of the ethnic nation-state. In opposition to the new Western/European alignment in post-Yugoslav and post-war society, the Croatian nationalist project seeks to (re)construct its own standing through the reinforcement of new/old gender stereotypes.[3]

Summoning categories like 'nature' and 'normality', these argumentations essentialise the inequality of men and women as natural and proclaim procreative heterosexuality as the norm. This has, amongst other things, led to an intensified and openly decreed anti-gay climate in Croatia, and homophobic comments like the ones voiced in the speech at the *jama* are nothing unusual. In mocking human rights as 'rights for homosexuals and rights that promote the splitting up of families', the priest at the Mass reveals his polemic's underlying motive. It becomes evident that homosexuality is perceived as a threat to the 'Christian family' mainly on grounds of demographic concerns, jeopardising the whole 'Croatian nation'. Considering homosexuality as an inversion of traditional gender relations and therefore as a menace to 'intact' and reproductive family life, the priest's remarks aim to entrench patriarchal gender hierarchies, hetero-normativity and ultimately ethnic homogenisation.

Such attempts to exert control over sexual orientation and reproductive behaviour – supported by powerful ecclesiastical and/or nationalist institutions and ideologies and circulated by conservative media organs – is not only directed at women. Male bodies are equally gendered, sexualised and ethnicised, but the mechanisms and representations by which (hegemonic) masculinity is produced operate in a different way than in the construction of femininity. In this chapter I analyse how masculinity is constructed in war and post-war contexts in relation to ethnonational and sexual identity. The cultural code that 'masculinity equals heterosexuality equals power' (Žarkov 2007: 169) features particularly prominently in militarised societies in which 'able-bodied' and fortified virility is seen as guaranteeing a community's defence and safety. In simplified terms, dominant notions of masculinity are nourished by the pronounced opposition between (male/heterosexual) militancy and (female/homosexual) vulnerability.

Embodying Painful Memories: Illness and Suffering

> The incoherence of lives is equated with illness.
> — Vieda Skultans, *The Testimony of Lives*

A few months into my stay in Sinj I noticed that the members of my host family were continually complaining about health problems and fell ill conspicuously often. I decided to draw up a list of all the health issues that arose within one family in the course of one month and took note of the following. The youngest son Petar (28) was in hospital for two weeks because of high fever when a kidney disease was diagnosed. Petar's wife Vanja (25) had frequent migraines, caught a heavy cold and had to call in sick. Their daughter Eva (4) had a fever three or four times and had to be sent home from day care several times. The second son, Marko (32), also caught a cold, and in addition to his recurrent war-related suffering (including insomnia, hyperreflexia, palpitations and anxiety attacks), he crashed into a tree on one occasion when he was tobogganing drunk at night and was bruised all over. The father, Joško (66), had a chronic heart disease and continually fell ill. He caught a bladder infection as well as a kidney infection, had palpitations, severe headaches, was nauseous and was in and out of bed for two months. The mother, Nada (66), caught a cold twice within four weeks and developed a heavy cough. She also complained of stomach aches and high blood pressure, developed a rheumatic fever and was eventually diagnosed with diabetes. As a quasi-permanent guest of this family (with no health issues of my own during this time whatsoever) it was puzzling for me to be confronted with persistent complaints and narrations of disease and suffering by all members of the household.

Those affected, however, clearly interpreted their illnesses as bodily symptoms and signs of emotions related to painful (historical) events and personal memories. And although this certainly does not hold true for the symptoms of ordinary colds and sports accidents, physical suffering was regularly described as psychological pain or put down to psychosomatic causes, and was usually expressed in connection with narratives on social suffering and deprivation. Some of my interlocutors used the term 'trauma' when referring to their illnesses and afflictions, without me suggesting this terminology. This (conscious or unconscious) practice of narrating the troubles of one's own body and connecting it to painful memories or 'traumatising' experiences is not limited to one family in the Dalmatian hinterland, but constitutes a rather widespread public discourse throughout Croatia. I frequently came across sentences like 'due to trauma he/she cannot put his life in order', or 'because of constant anxiety during the war he/she developed a heart disease/high blood pressure/diabetics/cancer', or 'because of the war, he is not interested in women or marrying' – thus indicating that the cause of a particular disposition, illness or 'deficiency' was directly instigated by anxiety and distress. The syndrome as well as its symptoms is usually described as a form of *nervoza* – nerves, or nervousness by those who experience such debilities. *Nervoza*, the phenomenon of nerves or rather nerve damage, was acknowledged as an embodied emotion by my interlocutors and was used to express individual pain as well as feelings of loss of control and perspective. A young Franciscan told me, 'During communism a lot of people here were very poor and had no future prospects. That's why so many left for Germany as *Gastarbeiter*. But they managed to survive somehow. Today it has become even worse. The people are very nervous – very nervous and uncertain'. This widely diagnosed and stated nervousness often goes hand in hand with heavy smoking as well as alcohol and drug abuse (cf. Bašić 2004a, 2004b).[4]

In medical anthropology, research on 'nerves' has developed into a significant field of study, and 'nerves' are commonly interpreted as an 'expression of distress resulting from familial, social and cultural disruption' (Lock 1991: 89; see also Davis 1988; Guarnaccia, De La Cancela and Carrillo 1988; van Schaik 1988). In her study on the medical condition of female Greek migrants to Canada, Margaret Lock examines *nevra*, the Greek term and concept for nerves, as a medical condition and develops a specific anthropology of nerves that she calls 'Nerves and Nostalgia' (Lock 1991). She illustrates that 'nevra functions as a metaphor around which narratives about distressful and painful events can be elaborated',

and goes as far as to interpret the various discourses on nerves and nervousness as 'products of and reactions to the dominant ideology of the
Circum-Mediterranean honour and shame complex ... and ... to the development of labor in capitalistic society' (Lock 1991: 89, 90). Like the
majority of recent anthropological work on the experience of illness and
pain (cf. Devisch and Gailly 1985; Lock and Dunk 1987; Kleinman 1988;
Kirmayer 1989, 1992; Kleinman and Kleinman 1991; Pandolfi 1991; Ots
1991; Kleinman, Das and Lock 1997) Lock describes the symptoms as
predominantly experienced by women. In Mariella Pandolfi's study on
women's narratives and identity in a southern Italian village, she notes
that 'the particular way "feeling bad or ill" is expressed is not just individual but is actually the genre the women use in describing themselves' (Pandolfi 1991: 59). In similar ways, Jill Dubisch in her study on
Marian devotion in Greece refers to 'suffering as an aspect of womanhood' (Dubisch 1995). The idea that *nervoza* or nerve damage originates
from a 'lack of self-esteem and [the] lack of political power' of women
(Lock 1991: 89) has a long tradition – and particularly in research in
circum-Mediterranean areas, 'nerves' are commonly identified as part
of a specifically female way of expressing marginalisation and alienation
via bodily symptoms (cf. Lewis 1988; Boddy 1989).

In contrast to these studies, however, the narrations of suffering and
everyday complaints I encountered in Croatia are not limited to women.
Although I principally agree that 'nerves' can be interpreted as a metaphorical expression of the 'structural inequalities of gender, class and
ethnicity inherent in the societies under study' (Lock 1991: 89), I still noticed that in present-day Croatia feelings of inequality and disadvantage
are experienced across all levels of society. Relegating bodily processes
to psychological mechanisms has almost become a 'mainstream' incident, regardless of gender, class and ethnicity. The present socio-political
stagnation and ubiquitous uncertainty is experienced as bodily unease.
At times of radical change and severe crisis '[t]he risk of fragmentation
is preceded by [a] proliferation of symptoms', as Pandolfi observes, and
these symptoms can be experienced by women and men alike. But concepts of illness and health are nonetheless gendered in post-war Croatian society and I argue that they are closely linked to normative notions
of masculinity/femininity as well as prevailing discourses of self-victimisation. I understand some of the symptoms described above as a form
of emotional engagement with social and political realities. A 'sore body
that hurts and expresses the discomfort of living' (Pandolfi 1991: 62)
is a somatic metaphor for the discomfort of one's living conditions in
general and a feeling of socio-economic and political disadvantage in
particular.[5] The decline of living standards, high unemployment rates,

growing poverty and an increased perception of powerlessness leave people feeling (psychologically and physically) vulnerable, insecure and lacking control – an embodied experience that defies the ideal of dynamism, strength and vigour. People suffering from *nervoza* and related symptoms do not perceive of themselves as active actors who are self-determined and in control of their fate. They 'perceive life as something *felt* rather than *accomplished*' (Pandolfi 1991: 60, italics mine) and feel excluded from the 'masculine world of "doing" and "making"', as Pandolfi puts it (ibid.). In gendered hierarchies a weak body and 'lack of power over the present' (Bourdieu 1999: 185) are commonly assigned to women and associated with positions such as subordination, passivity, and violability (Žarkov 2007: 164). The resulting 'demasculinisation' is considered highly alarming and humiliating. And particularly in areas like Sinj and the Dalmatinska Zagora, where notions of manhood and masculinity are conventionally equated with safety and protection against intruders and external influences, the experience of vulnerability and defencelessness appears to endanger the cohesion and safety of not only individuals but the whole community. I argue that this perceived 'feminisation of society' is closely related to the 'crisis of masculinity' presently at stake in Croatia, and ultimately promotes efforts towards remasculinisation and remilitarisation within society to facilitate the transformation from powerless to powerful citizens.

Narrations of illness, feelings of distress, or profound suffering are inseparably intertwined with narrations of historic events and narrations of distressful personal and family stories (cf. Pandolfi 1991: 61). While Pandolfi interprets the narrations of suffering as ways of establishing a 'new identity' (Pandolfi 1991: 61, 63), I claim that they, in the case of Croatia, are transformed into emotional capital (Skrbiš 2003; see also Mihaylova 2006: 55) and promote the concept of self-victimisation. People who experience themselves as marginalised (and thus 'feminised') by political and historical events use narratives about this marginalisation to call attention to their own incorruptibility and moral superiority. By declaring themselves victims – whether victims of war and post-war events, of various policies, of international power politics, of socio-economic and political transformation, of market economics, of Europeanisation, globalisation and/or 'history' in general – large numbers of Croatians draw on a strategy of 'organised innocence' (Jalušić 2004: 42) to create a comforting reassurance about their own situation, by directing guilt towards 'Others'. These discourses on a victimised and weakened nation legitimise the upsurge of strong nationalist sentiment and are gendered in so far as they lead to a belief in the need for (militarised) masculine protection.

In the mid-1980s Jean Comaroff noted that socio-cultural conflicts are often apprehended metaphorically in terms of physical illness (Comaroff 1985; see also Crapanzano 2004: 71). In a comparable manner and at around the same time, Lutz and White pointed out that emotions help to form an 'actor's sense of his or her relation to a social world' and serve as 'a primary idiom for defining and negotiating social relations of the self in a moral order' (Lutz and White 1986: 417). Emotions thus generate a connection between the personal and social worlds. In most anthropological studies, however, expressions of emotions – and expressions of suffering in particular – had hitherto been either disregarded, discounted as irrelevant statements of individual feelings, or largely been restricted to the study of women (cf. Rosaldo 1987; Dubisch 1995: 213). In the late 1980s most studies on emotions and social suffering focused on the marginalisation of women, 'not because women are "naturally" more emotional, but because cultural factors often lead women to construct and express their identity through emotional statements and acts' (Dubisch 1995: 213). Yet in recent times another shift in the study of the 'language and the politics of emotion' (Lutz and Abu-Lughod 1990) and 'social suffering' (Kleinman, Das and Lock 1997; Bourdieu 1999) is noticeable. The turbulent political and economic transformations that followed the collapse of the Soviet Empire and the wars in the former Yugoslavia caused strong feelings (Svašek 2006). This has generated a new field of study that is particularly concerned with the analysis of the political dimension of emotional processes in postsocialist states (cf. Skultans 1998; Svašek 2002, 2006; Mihaylova 2006; Rakowski 2006, 2007; Schäuble 2006, 2007a, 2007b). The radical changes that left whole nations, communities and/or ethnic groups distraught and marginalised have even been categorised as 'social trauma' by a number of social scientists (Sztompka 2004; see also, Kideckel 1995; Halpern and Kideckel 2000; Hann 2002; Šuber 2006). An astonishing number of accounts of people who live through processes of restructuring in formerly socialist countries of Central and Eastern Europe show common characteristics.

In her account of narratives about damaged health in post-Soviet Latvia, Vieda Skultans for instance, states that her interviewees 'present illness as a breakdown of values, purpose and meaning … Narrators locate illness at the point of intersection of memory and present experience, at the point where images of the past converge with and are undermined by the reality of everyday life' (Skultans 1998: 102). This observation also exactly applies to Croatia, where a perceived recent decline of moral values is deplored and held responsible for physical degeneration. Memories, whether nostalgic or distressing, along with disappointed expectations and hopes, are conceptualised as the major source of resignation and frailty. Further, Skultans detects a 'widespread feeling that history and society are to blame in general as well as quite specific ways for ill-health' (ibid.: 103). The tendency to blame others and to reject responsibility for one's own malaise is also prevalent in present-day Croatia where seeming historical disadvantage and wrong political decisions are directly linked to individual suffering and emotional distress. A further crucial parallel occurs with regard to Skultan's observation that '[p]olitical repression is one aspect of the past which narrators link to nerve damage' (ibid.: 104). I have already illustrated that the motif of *nervoza* or nerve damage is also very widespread in Croatia, and the main sources of this condition are usually seen as repression under communism, the war, painful memories of the war, as well as hard physical labour and poverty. For women, the bearing and raising of children, as well as worrying about the well-being of the whole family, were named as additional sources of exhaustion and distress. More generally, people complained about the hardships of peasant life, the hostile and barren surroundings, nepotism as well as corruption, and claimed that these were the causes of their physical as well as psychological maladies.[6]

The feature that all of these narrations have in common is their radical emotionalisation and personalisation of historical and political developments. In concordance with Pandolfi, who states that '[t]he emotion is the event that generates the narrative, but the event is linked to an historical event and the history of the family' (Pandolfi 1991: 62), I argue that emotions have a considerable effect on the ways in which socio-political and historical events are experienced, embodied and handed down. Especially the embodiment of painful experiences and memories tends to generate somatic symptoms and finds expression in narratives of injustice, subjugation, damaged health and bodily harm. The Croatian anthropologist Maja Povrzanović has analysed different narrative modes in relation to the Homeland War, and stresses:

> Although the war-induced rooting of identity in spatial categories (from neighbourhood to state territory) is a persistent theme in the narratives quoted in Croatian war ethnographies, they also reveal a multiplicity, diversity, and complexity of experience that often challenge the official uniqueness of the 'prescribed' national narrative. People's firsthand knowledge of suffering is retained as bodily memories, and this gives them an authenticity that does not need to borrow ready-made phrases. (Povrzanović 2000: 155, italics mine)

This statement confirms the assumption that history is inscribed into people's bodies and that individuals experience themselves as historical subjects through embodied suffering and (painful) memories. In a comparable manner, Pandolfi explains that '[t]he experience or recollection of a strong emotion immediately shifts the narrative from the normative or common sense plane to an inner subjective plane that is hidden from the outer world and sealed within [the] body' (Pandolfi 1991: 62). The subjective emotional power of these 'sealed', embodied recollections, however, may be triggered and mobilised for political ends and become an important identity marker. I have tried to show that especially narratives of somatic pain, social suffering, and (self-)victimisation have a capacity to radicalise identity processes and either endorse resignation (primarily associated with victimised femininity) or, alternatively, to evoke impulses of rebellion against 'unjust' circumstances or an entitlement to militant revenge (primarily associated with omnipotent masculinity).

The extreme emotionalisation and personalisation of history – particularly after wars, violent conflicts, oppression, and ethnic cleansing – tend to impede mutual understanding and processes of conflict resolution. In Croatia, as in all other republics of the former Yugoslavia, discourses of (self-)victimisation have created a 'unity in suffering' through a continual conjuring up of collective discrimination. These processes were aggravated by the fact that in socialist Yugoslavia the affected groups were not allowed to mourn their losses publicly. The resultant acts of competing for victim status and emotional uncovering of past wrongs have become an integral part of the respective national identities. Jalušić argues that '[t]his pushes existing mutualities into the background and makes it difficult to find viable political solutions and to construct a common future' (Jalušić 2004: 47). The more often these emotional or emotionalised narratives are repeated, the more likely they turn into one-sided mythologised versions of the past that increasingly replace comprehensible historical facts (cf. Volkan 1988: 176). For precisely this reason, a number of peace activists in Croatia have started to object to the prevailing emotionalisation of the past. The former head of the 'Antiwar Campaign Croatia', current head of 'Documenta – Centre for Dealing with the Past', and holder of the Alternative Nobel Prize for Peace, Vesna Teršelić, told me that she is nowadays working towards a 'factualisation' of the war. Only the reconstruction of facts and the establishment of concrete numbers, she said, could help to prevent further emotionalisation and instrumentalisation of differing versions of the past – and only a non-emotionalised commemoration could provide a lasting base for the peaceful coexistence of different ethnic groups in the region.

Before the Law

Što bolje pucaš, bolje tucaš / The more you shoot, the better you fuck.[7]
— Goran Marić, alias Malkolm Muharem, *Duga*

Accounts of atrocious acts of male violence not only committed on the battlefield or in notorious prison camps, but also directed against civilians, particularly women, have dominated media coverage of the wars in the former Yugoslavia. This subsequently informed a number of (feminist) studies on the gendered nature of war violence in 'the Balkans'. Men – in most cases regardless of their ethno-national background – were frequently portrayed as having been eager to join paramilitary units and partake willingly in cruel raids, thus confirming the essentialist stereotype of the Balkans as flaunting a 'culture of violence'. The link between violent warfare and male sexuality as indicated in the aphorism of a Serbian fighter quoted above seems to confirm the image of militant combat as performance of patriarchal Balkan machismo. Retrospectively, however, post-war nationalist discourses of all parties involved in the conflict tend to justify the violence committed by asserting the necessity of (military) self-defence. With reference to the protective dimension of masculinity, soldiers are thus inclined to be reinterpreted as national heroes or martyrs of an almost epic quality in their respective home countries. My primary aim is to explore the relationship between nationalism, masculinity and militarisation, and to delineate the current challenges this correlation poses to stability and democratisation in the region.

As a concept, as well as in the practices of femininity and masculinity, gender constitutes a significant category for nationalist discourses in war and post-war settings and lastingly affects the way people experience, envision and relate to the world around them. I therefore use gender as a central idiom to 'ethnonational imaginings' (Živković 2006: 258) that helps to understand better the transformation of categories of political and social belonging in present-day Croatia. Primarily concentrating on notions of masculinity, a category that has often been taken for granted or over-simplified in the past (Bracewell 2000), I am particularly interested in the construction models for masculine heroic characters and how these are related to nationalist Croatian identity politics.

A fundamental premise is that one cannot understand the debates about the role of combatants during the Homeland War without examining the history and current resurgence of ethno-nationalist sentiment in relation to militarised notions of masculinity. At the outset I will therefore briefly delineate the strategies of gendering and sexualising nationalist discourse in the preparation for, and during, the Homeland War. War propaganda and the recruitment of soldiers largely hinged on the notion that 'war is sexy' and claimed that readiness for combat was a key attribute of masculinity. The concepts of masculinity employed, however, significantly differed between the warring parties, and the ensuing dichotomy between 'civilised' and 'barbaric' masculinity came to serve as an important ethno-national discrimination marker in Yugoslavia.

When the International Criminal Tribunal for the former Yugoslavia (ICTY) accused former Croatian generals of having committed war crimes during the Homeland War, a wave of nationalist sentiment seized the country and revealed that the army generals were perceived as national heroes and not war criminals by large parts of the Croatian population. By closely analysing the public debates in relation to the ICTY indictments and verdicts against Ante Gotovina and Mirko Norac, I demonstrate that post-war strategies of dealing with war crimes are greatly influenced by the sexual imagery employed during the war. I thus use the cases of Gotovina and Norac as paradigmatic examples to analyse the political consequences of the present revival of gendered notions of heroism as well as ethno-nationalism.

On 15 April 2011 the ICTY in The Hague declared the military actions of Operacija Oluja [Operation Storm], the August 1995 Croatian offensive to 'liberate' the Krajina region from Serb control, to be a war crime. Two Croatian military leaders, Ante Gotovina and Mladen Markač, were sentenced to extensive prison terms: Gotovina, who commanded the operation, was given twenty-four years; and Markač, the commander of police paramilitaries, was jailed for eighteen years.[8] The third accused, Ivan Čermak, was acquitted. Operation Storm lasted less than four days and resulted in the expulsion of Serb armed forces from over ten thousand square kilometres of Croatian territory, the deaths of between 1,600 and 2,200 people (among them between 500 and 1,200 civilians), and the creation of between 90,000 and 250,000 Serb refugees. The proclamation of the sentence was broadcast on giant screens in the large Jelačić Square in central Zagreb, and thousands of people, among them many veterans and former military personnel, attended and reacted with shock and outrage. The broadcast, which can also be seen as a solidarity protest rally, was organised by the veteran organisation 'Stop progonu hrvatskih branitelja' [Stop the persecution of Croatian defenders]. The crowd booed and hissed when the verdicts were announced, waved Croatian flags and portraits of ex-general Gotovina, and showed placards on which President Ivo Josipović, his predecessor Stjepan

Mesić, the then prime minister Jadranka Kosor and other leading politicians were labelled as 'Croatian traitors'.

The night before the verdicts were announced, fifteen hundred Croatian war veterans marched through Zagreb in support of Gotovina and the two other generals, and several other veterans associations announced that they would hold a peaceful parade through the city and a public prayer. A statement from the Croatian Bishops' Conference announced: 'Just as we have called on believers to pray and fast for a just verdict, we now appeal to Croatian citizens to be calm and dignified … The Hague tribunal has not justly assessed the fact that Croatia was a victim of Serbian aggression'. After the guilty verdicts were announced, Croatia's then prime minister, Jadranka Kosor, said the government found it unacceptable that the UN court considered Croatian wartime authorities responsible for the persecution and expulsion of Serbs from Krajina. She called Operation Storm a legitimate military action and publicly announced, 'We are not afraid of the truth. We are proud of our victories and of all those that made them possible', she said. As reported by the daily Croatian newspaper *Jutarnji List* several days before the announcement of the verdicts, Kosor had already met with veterans' organisations loyal to her Croatian Democratic Union (HDZ) party in an effort to pre-empt any extreme reactions, such as protests, that a negative verdict could provoke. In her meeting with the veterans, she promised to elevate the law on veteran benefits to a constitutional right that would thus be safeguarded from any future changes.

A week after the verdict, a group of five war veterans launched a hunger strike in Jelačić Square in protest at the conviction of the ex-generals. The protesters, who were later joined by ten more veterans, said there was no political organisation or association behind their decision to go on hunger strike but that they had received the support of many citizens. Their action included claims to suspend cooperation with the ICTY tribunal in The Hague, withdraw the EU membership application, abolish the general amnesty for what they maintained were twenty thousand proven Serb terrorists, obtain a release of Croatian generals and soldiers from foreign and domestic prisons, and give priority to the interests of the Croatian state and the Croatian people.[9] Eventually, after thirty-one days without food, they ended their protest action at the express wish of ex-general Gotovina himself, who had sent an according message through his wife.

It is quite obvious that the generals are considered to be war heroes by many in Croatia who believe that the military offensive was a legitimate military action taken to regain territory that had been seized by Serb forces. Equating the indictments of the ICTY with an attack on the legitimacy of the Homeland War, they always feared that a guilty verdict might excite doubts regarding the legitimacy of Croatia as a nation. Thus they saw the conviction of Croatian former military officers as submission to blackmail and as sacrifices that Croatia was forced to make in order to join the European Union. It should be noted that this trial forced the Croatian government to deal with the allegation of Croatian war crimes in full view of the world. This, however, was *the* central national taboo issue and many feared that the tribunal's indictments of Croatians would not only put the dignity and legitimacy of the Homeland War in question, but also equate the war guilt of Croats with that of the Serbs. The comment of Branko Borković, a former Croatian army commander, who in response to the 2011 conviction said: 'This is a verdict against the Croatian state; all of us have been convicted, including the Republic of Croatia', thus confirms that the verdict was perceived as a continuation of 'historical injustice' in the course of which the international community has wronged and repeatedly victimised Croatia.

It is in this context that one has to understand the enthusiasm and sense of victory that seized the whole of Croatia when in November 2012 the initial verdicts against ex-generals Ante Gotovina and Mladen Markač were overturned. In a very surprising decision, by a 3–2 majority in the UN court's five-judge appeals chamber, that not even the fiercest supporters of the ex-generals could have hoped for, Gotovina and Markač were acquitted of all charges on the basis of individual responsibility for the crimes in Krajina.[10] The court ordered an immediate release of the two former military and police officers from the UN Detention Unit, and they were frenetically greeted by tens of thousands of supporters in Zagreb upon their return.

The UN appeals judges rejected the key premise on which the initial conviction had been based, dismissing the prosecution argument that any artillery shells that landed on Serb-inhabited towns more than two hundred metres from a military target amounted to an attack on civilians. This includes the finding that the original trial had erred significantly in ruling that Croatian artillery had illegally shelled four Serb-held towns – Knin, Benkovac, Gračac and Obrovac – and that the artillery attacks were 'devoid of any specific reasoning'. As a consequence, the appeal judges also overturned the original trial verdict that Operation Storm had involved a 'joint criminal enterprise whose purpose was the permanent and forcible removal of Serb civilians from the Krajina region' and concluded that there was no planned deportation of Serbs or political conspiracy by a leadership planning ethnic cleansing (Borger 2012).[11] In an immediate reply to the acquittal, Eric Gordy writes:

The appeals chamber made a strange decision on the status of the joint criminal enterprise to forcibly expel the civilian population: they decided that their adoption of the Rodney King standard on shelling makes irrelevant the documentary evidence from the Brioni transcripts and the public statements of Franjo Tuđman that indicate that expulsion of the civilian population was a goal of the military operation. Instead they decided (paras 81–82) that an examination of the Brioni transcripts does not indicate any specific order to make any specific artillery attack. So they decided that the 'circumstantial evidence' (para. 91) does not demonstrate the existence of a joint criminal enterprise, while disregarding the direct evidence. (Gordy 2012)

This refers to transcripts of talks that the late Croatian president, Franjo Tuđman, held with Gotovina, Markač and other political and military leaders (including retired Pentagon generals and advisers ensconced in the Croatian defence ministry at the time) in July 1995, a week before the beginning of Operation Oluja, on the Adriatic island of Brijuni (also known as Brioni), in which he demanded to 'inflict such blows that the Serbs will [for] all practical purposes disappear'.[12] The Brijuni transcripts were used in the first-degree verdict to prove that Gotovina and Markač were part of a 'joint criminal enterprise', whereas the appeal proceedings stated that the same transcripts provided only limited support to a finding of unlawful artillery attacks.

Gordy also argues that by claiming that there were no war crimes committed during Operation Oluja, the appeal 'invalidates the distinction between military and civilian targets in the Hague and Geneva Conventions by finding that any target can be retrospectively defined as having been military' (Gordy 2012). Gotovina's American defence lawyer, Greg Kehoe, on the other hand, used the verdict as a pretext to rhetorically ask, 'Does this vindicate that particular operation as a proper and just attempt to bring back this land under Croatia?', adding 'Of course. And more importantly it vindicates what kind of soldier General Gotovina was' (Corder 2012; Borger 2012). The latter's perception will certainly fall on fertile ground in Croatia and not only serve as a vindication of Croatia's reputation and contribute to a collective annulment of potential war guilt committed by Croatia and Croatians during the Homeland War, but also encourage the hero status of Gotovina.

'The verdict confirms everything that we believe in Croatia: that generals Gotovina and Markač are innocent', President Josipović said immediately after the verdict. 'This confirms that Croatia did not conduct ethnic cleansing.' These words of a man who is widely considered as moderate and circumspect confirm that Gotovina's status as a national hero is no longer hindered by anything since the Hague acquittal. The question remains, however, of who is being held responsible for the victims of Oluja, and so the Croatian judiciary will eventually have to address the question of war crimes committed in 1995. Neither Josipović nor Croatian prime minister Zoran Milanović denied this, and they endorsed their attempts to address war crimes in the legal, political and social spheres domestically – that is to say, by assuring that Croatia would increasingly bring lawsuits against members of its army who committed war crimes. 'The Croatian state is not responsible for crimes committed by individuals, but it is responsible for punishing each perpetrator, regardless of who that may be', Josipović said (Hedl 2012). And according to the *Telegraph*, Milanović confirmed that the acquittal of Gotovina and Markač 'doesn't mean the war wasn't bloody and Croatia will do its part to achieve justice ... Clearly mistakes were made during the course of the conflict. Mistakes for which the Croatian state should be held responsible, not Gotovina and Markač. For those wronged by the state of Croatia, Croatia will settle its debts. We should not forget in this moment that these cases also exist' (Waterfield 2012). This individualisation of war guilt is part of an important development in the enforcement of international criminal law, despite the many logistical problems it poses regarding the massive numbers of violators of human rights and perpetrators of international crimes. In the past, the four major problems with regards to issues of transitional justice in Croatia as identified by the Zagreb-based Documenta – Centre for Dealing with the Past, are firstly that 'trials of war crimes in domestic courts are still often biased against ethnic Serbs ... Secondly, many of these trials were conducted *in absentia*, without the accused being present. Thirdly, there is a complete lack of adequate witness protection ... Fourthly, there is still insufficient legal representation of the victims' (Jović 2009: 12).[13] Should the Croatian government in the future, contrary to expectations, succeed in addressing the problems of transitional justice domestically, this might contribute to a gradual deconstruction of the 'Homeland War myth' (Jović 2012: 60) as a nationalist narrative that insists on Croatia being a victim in the war, while not fully acknowledging ethnic Serb victims, refugees and internally displaced persons. And in the long run it would hopefully also facilitate the insight that the crude nationalist oversimplification that Croats are historical victims but never villains does not contribute to the process of reconciliation and cooperation in the region.

Not surprisingly, the ruling regarding Gotovina and Markač produced fury in Serbia where it was perceived as further evidence of anti-Serb bias of the ICTY. Rasim Ljajić, long-term Head of the Coordination Team with the Hague tribunal in Serbia, is cited in the *Telegraph* as having said: 'The UN war crimes court has lost all credibility. [This] decision is proof of selective justice which is worse than any injustice' (Waterfield 2012). Considering that in 2009 then Serbian president, Boris Tadić, had stated that the only ICTY sentence considered to be fair and 'contributing to the reconciliation in the region' (Ristić 2012: 37) was the one issued against Gotovina and Markač, the revision of the earlier verdict was perceived as a blow. Even liberal Serbs predict that the acquittal is likely to create a sense of injustice, might further stir nationalist sentiments and will eventually have a negative effect on Serbia's own EU integration process.

All over Croatia, however, tens of thousands of people, including Croatian war veterans, celebrated the release of the two generals – fifty thousand on Zagreb's Jelačić Square alone – waving Croatian flags and setting off fireworks. 'Finally, we can say to our children that we are not war criminals', a veteran identified as Djuro Vec said. 'We fought for justice, and that our fight was righteous and just' (Corder 2012). For Croatian veterans the acquittal of the two ex-generals is likely to be perceived as a personal acquittal, especially since many of them have still not come to terms with their status in post-war Croatian society.

In my own fieldwork, I often came across the notion that although the case of the *branitelji* is widely recognised in the media, and although various (mostly nationalistic) political parties use their fate for party politics and propaganda, very little is actually done for ex-combatants in terms of social and professional reintegration, financial support or health care. Although veterans in contemporary Croatia are eligible for numerous benefits and material privileges, and their pensions are many times more than those of civilians or ex-combatants in other former Yugoslav republics, the majority of the Croatian *branitelji* still feel disregarded. The situation is made worse by the fact that there is little or no outreach in terms of psychological assistance for *branitelji* in rural areas. After the end of the Homeland War around 330,000 veterans were registered, and the social reality of the majority of them is embedded in the contradictory context of rhetorical glorification on the one side, and low social status as well as suppressed feelings of guilt on the other side. Due to their indeterminate state between publicly acknowledged heroism and social oblivion, many Croatian ex-soldiers feel like 'radical losers of the war' and are particularly susceptible to political manipulation. Gotovina himself had refused to acknowledge the tribunal's legitimacy and went into hiding after a warrant for his arrest was issued in 2001. Already his capture on Tenerife in early December 2005 and the extradition to The Hague had caused widespread protests amongst the Croatian population and revived the controversy concerning Croatia's moral role and responsibility for war crimes committed during the Yugoslav Wars of Secession.

The protests, primarily led by Croatian war veterans and right-wing associations, were subsumed under the pervasive slogan *Heroj a ne zločinac!* [Hero, not (war) criminal]. The assertion of Gotovina's 'unjust indictment' and the consequent refusal to cooperate with the ICTY[14] contained therein, are closely linked to a more general Eurosceptical attitude. Despite the Croatian government's increased efforts to collaborate with the tribunal and their ambitious promotion of EU membership negotiations, large parts of the domestic population continued to oppose this political course. Powerful anti-cooperation groups, defending the sanctity of the Homeland War, continued to challenge the coalition's authority and advance a fierce anti-Europeanism. The continual decline in living standards and the rise of unemployment rates in postwar Croatia have helped to revive the political strength of the right and stoke people's fears that the political and economic pressure induced by the admission criteria of the European Union will further impair the country. However, during the celebrations of the Gotovina and Markač acquittal in November 2012, one of those present said 'the EU is likely to be much more popular now', and time will tell what influence the ICTY verdict has on the overall approval of EU politics in Croatian society (Bell 2012).

Strategies of 'Man-Making'

Up to the revision of the guilty verdict, the case of Ante Gotovina was paradigmatic for Croatian nationalists' insistence on the unjust and exploitative conducts of the international community vis-à-vis the newly founded Republic of Croatia. In their view, the (enforced) surrender of individuals to foreign jurisprudence tended to parallel the subjugation of the entire Croatian nation; a humiliation that could only be countered by the restoration of a powerful, proud and potent, in short, masculinised self-conception. The association of heroic masculinity with Croatian national identity[15] is far from a recent occurrence. As a long-standing feature it has traditionally been revived whenever the integrity of the nation seemed to be endangered and in need of protection. I thus argue that these categories can be mobilised as resources 'to produce a sense of continuity and belonging in times of drastic social, political and economic change', as Jessica Greenberg puts it (Greenberg 2006: 321). It is within this context that the debates about the role of Croatian combatants were and continue to be orchestrated and linked to the underlying 'master narrative' of the historic necessity for Croatian self-defence against foreign intruders. As I have shown, this notion dates back to the times of the Ottoman invasion and continues to impact the local understanding of history and to inform national warrior-myths until the present day.

The official term for Croatian war veterans, *branitelji*, translates literally as 'defenders' (from *braniti*, 'to defend') and reflects the official perception of the Croatian military actions during the Homeland War as mere defence operations. Highlighting the defensive character of Croatian warfare is a viable strategy of distancing oneself from the committed crimes, since self-defence is considered the most legitimate of all acts of violence.[16] As a backlash to an assault or external threat, the notion of self-defence, however, necessitates masculine protection not only of the homeland, but also of freedom, honour, tradition, and, more concretely, the women of the nation (cf. Enloe 1989; Papić 1994; Žarkov 1995, 2000, 2007; Yuval-Davis 1997; Nagel 1998; Olujić 1998; Pavlović 1999; Seifert 2001, 2004). The instrumentalisation, if not militarisation, of gender involved in this process significantly helped in making the various ethnonationalisms a potent political force in the Yugoslavia of the late 1980s (Bracewell 2000: 578; see also Jones 1994; Lilly and Irvine 2002). A number of scholars have highlighted the important role that gender-related aspects of nationalism have played and continue to play in the development and outbreak of violent conflicts and wars. In his work on soldier heroes in the British Empire, Graham Dawson, for example, notes that,

> [w]ithin nationalist discourse martial masculinity was complemented by a vision of domestic femininity, at home with the children and requiring protection. The nation came to be conceived as a gendered entity, analysis of which is necessarily bound up with the theorizing of dominant, hegemonic versions of masculinity, femininity, and sexual difference. (Dawson 1994: 2)

The concept of the nation as a 'gendered entity' is a vital part of nearly all ethno-national and patriotic political ideologies, and featured particularly prominently in the Yugoslav Wars, where an analogous gender image of adventurous soldiers on the one hand and anxiously waiting brides, wives and/or sacrificing mothers on the other hand was successfully employed by the respective nationalist factions. 'The battle for the nation is not only something patriotic but something very masculine', writes Ivan Čolović (2002: 48). The image of the warrior-hero still plays a vital role in the contemporary Croatian national myth and forms the basis of male self-conception as guardians of the homeland. Based on the equation between manliness, national honour and militarism, these notions exclude all those who do not straightforwardly correspond to hegemonic models of masculinity and traditionalist gender regimes.

Some authors such as Karl Kaser and Stjepan Meštrović tend to perceive aggressive manliness as a specific regional trait, and ascribe the recurrent resort to violence to a somehow uniquely 'Balkan character' (Kaser 1992a, 1992b; Meštrović 1993; Meštrović, Letica and Goreta 1993; see also Bracewell 2000: 567). Essentialist and cultural determinism notions, however, are not very constructive in helping to understand the reasons for the mobilisation and politicisation of gender constructs in times of radical change, and they furthermore fail to explain why the majority of ex-combatants retrospectively attempt to legitimise or justify war violence through the assertions of (self-)defence and protection of the homeland. In the case of former Yugoslavia it seems much more feasible to examine how nationalist rhetoric brought neglected normative notions of masculinity and masculine ideals (back) into play. The warrior image of masculinity is not a given cultural constituent in the Balkan region, but was skilfully manipulated to precipitate and justify armed conflict in the early 1990s. With comparable means, nationalist agitators on all sides succeeded in monopolising and militarising masculinity, (re-)installing unambiguous gender hierarchies and eventually establishing a regular cult or culture of manliness with patriotism and heroism – combined with the willingness to sacrifice one's life – as the highest masculine virtues.[17]

In *The Image of Man*, George Mosse classifies modern masculinity as the centrepiece of all varieties of the nationalist movement (Mosse 1996). Observing that nationalism made its appearance parallel to the emergence of modern masculinity in the nineteenth century, he notes that masculine stereotypes are a central means of nationalist profiling (Mosse 1996: 4). The expansion of patriarchal masculinity that accompanied and determined the rise of nationalisms in Yugoslavia illustratively validates Mosse's assumption that concepts of manliness are closely connected to the defining images and ideals of a nation. In 'legitimating and encouraging violence as a way of recuperating national dignity and masculine honour' (Bracewell 2000: 585) – Croatian as well as Serbian, and to a lesser extent also Kosovo Albanian, Bosnian and Slovenian – nationalists managed to mobilise large parts of the male population to partake in armed warfare. Soldiers were increasingly glorified as epitomes of both manhood and patriotism, and the opportunity to become a hero along with the desire for adventure provided a particularly strong motive for many young men to join the army (cf. Čolović 1993: 60ff.).

The nationalist strategies of 'man-making' survived the war and are now transformed to meet the conditions in the respective Yugoslav

post-war societies. For the most part, however, the newly formed nation-states are still struggling with the disastrous economic, political and
psycho-social consequences of the violent break-up of Yugoslavia.[18] In
this climate of insecurity and uncertainty, in which many men have for-
feited their traditional roles as breadwinners and face difficulties living
up to normative standards of masculinity, every seeming threat to the
nation – such as the sentence of Ante Gotovina, for example – is inevitably perceived as an immediate threat to manliness itself. In an effort that
is evocative of the rhetoric applied in the early 1990s, post-war nationalist politics continues to present 'militarism as a way of winning back both
individual manliness and national dignity' (Bracewell 2000: 567).

Wendy Bracewell has pointed out that the recent work of feminist
political theorists, analysing the gendered character of the modern state
together with the 'importance of the hegemonic masculinity in legitimating' this state, paradoxically tends to make men as such invisible
(Bracewell 2000: 566). Her argument that masculinity cannot be treated
as a stable, undifferentiated category and her observation that not all
men benefit equally within nationalist frameworks entirely correspond
with my own assessment of the situation in post-war Croatia. While a
few people improved their economic and social status tremendously
during the Tuđman era, the majority of the population, particularly in
the rural areas, are destitute. Hardly any of the regular (predominantly)
male ex-combatants can be counted as wartime profiteers, and those
who were severely injured, disabled and/or traumatised feel increasingly
emasculated because they are incapacitated for work today.[19] The social
reality of the majority of veterans in post-war Croatia is thus embedded
in the contradictory context of rhetorical glorification on the one side,
and low social status as well as suppressed feelings of guilt on the other
side. It is, in my opinion, this very discrepancy between the traditional
ideal of manliness – based on economic self-sufficiency, dominance and
rather abstract virtues such as honour, courage and heroism – and the
currently experienced emasculation in post-war Croatian society that
necessitates the reaffirmation of manhood and generates the wish for
unimpeachable heroes.

Wartime Dandies, War Romantics and 'Real Warriors'

The salutation 'za dom spremni'

Salute: Za dom!   [For home(land)!]
Reply: Spremni!   [(We are) ready!]

was used as an equivalent to the Nazi salute 'Sieg – Heil' by the Croatian fascist Ustaše during the Second World War. In the late 1980s and early 1990s, however, this politically tainted salute gained in popularity, indicating that it was an obligation for every Croatian man to be prepared to fight for his homeland. It has recently been revived a second time in relation to the controversies surrounding the trials of the Croatian ex-generals – this time to rehabilitate the reputation of the convicted and to emphasise that they carried out a national duty rather than committed a crime.

Readiness for combat was the central attribute of masculinity at the outbreak of the Yugoslav wars, and Ivan Čolović in his analysis of the symbolism inherent in war propaganda alludes to the 'somewhat clumsy, but provocative' slogan 'Tiger, respond if you are a man' by means of which the Croatian army attempted to recruit soldiers (*Hrvatski Vojnik*, Zagreb 10 September 1993, quoted and translated in Čolović 2002: 48f.). The fixed idea that 'war is sexy' was seemingly more popular and widespread in Croatia than in the other Yugoslav republics (Čolović 1993: 60), and a number of young men who were confronted with these appeals readily responded to them. Without prior military experience or even training they did not know what to expect and so experimented with their new roles as defenders of the homeland, performing in ways they imagined would constitute being a 'real warrior.'

The ethnologist Reana Senjković (1995; 2004) refers to a particular group of war volunteers who identified and labelled themselves as 'Croatian War Romantics.'

> At the beginning of the war, the mass media represented [the young men who voluntarily joined the Croatian military forces] as the representatives of a generation growing up with rock n' roll music and ideology, shipshape and strong, wearing modern haircuts and even so-called Iroquois hairstyles. They sported Ray Ban glasses, an earring, a little cross at their necks, a black ribbon around their foreheads and sang, not patriotic songs, but Brothers in Arms by Dire Straits. Their look could be attributed to the influence of popular culture disseminated by films, TV and video. The Serbian soldier was shown as 'stinking in medieval darkness' – toothless and sloppy half-uniformed men, apparently drunk. (Senjković 1995: 59)

In her article 'Romanticising Rambo: Masculinity and Social Perception of War in Croatia 1991–1995', Senjković continues to interpret the details of the outfits as iconographic motifs of American soldiers and war heroes as represented in films such as *Top Gun*, *Rambo* and *Deer*

Hunter. While fashion and style played an important role as insignia of masculinity in Croatia, others perceived this attitude as rather effeminate. In an interview that was published in *Nedjeljna Dalmacija* in May 1992, a regular of the French Foreign Legion who was stationed in Croatia complained about the lack of manliness and respectability of the local troops:

> People here think that war is a kind of fashion. Here I can see Croatian soldiers wearing rosaries, sunglasses. What is it? It's insane! ... It's twenty degrees below zero and they're cutting the fingers off their gloves. Do you know what they are? They are wartime dandies, nothing else. (Quoted and translated in Senjković 2004: 298)

These 'wartime dandies' did not see a contradiction in looking 'cool' and simultaneously being ready to fight (and possibly die) for the homeland. Based on this attitude they disdained the Serbian soldiers who were commonly associated with uncultured machismo and backwardness.

It was a widespread practice on all sides during the war not only to ridicule but also to denigrate the respective opponent due to his

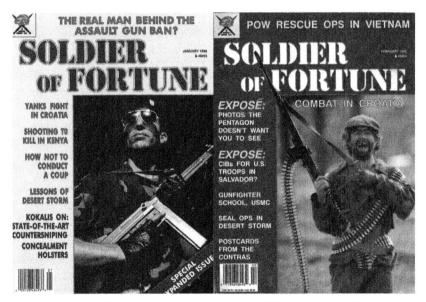

Figures 4.1 and 4.2. Shortly after the outbreak of the Homeland War, in January 1992, the U.S. magazine *Soldier of Fortune* depicted a fashionable 'cool' Croatian soldier on its cover. In February 1992 the follow-up issue of the same magazine showed a run-down 'wild' Serbian soldier. © Soldier of Fortune, 1992.

supposedly deficient or missing masculinity (cf. Senjković 1996, 2002; Ugrešić 1998; Bracewell 2000; Žarkov 2001, 2007; Čolović 1993, 2002). Natalija Bašić has been analysing how war narratives and memories of *branitelji* reflect underlying concepts of masculinity and gender identity. She quotes the example of a Croat ex-combatant who claims that, due to a genital amputation, he turned into 'a genuine Serb'. 'I am 90 per cent invalid,' the veteran says, 'I was blown up by a grenade – and now I am a genuine Serb ... I am totally fucked up.' Accordingly, Bašić concludes that '[t]his comingling of sexuality, gender and national identity is a recurrent motive that illustrates the theoretically asserted link between gender, nation and military conflict on a subjective level' (Bašić 2004a: 108, my translation). In this account the 'castrated Serb' is constructed as the personified opposite of the virile Croat, whereas the Serbs, on the other hand, would claim manliness and potency as genuinely Serbian traits. 'Testicles are a national symbol, a trademark of the race; other peoples have luck, tradition, erudition, history, reason (but balls belong to us alone)', as Danilo Kiš puts it in an ironic commentary on Serbian masculinity (Kiš 1990: 68).[20]

The sexual imagery inherent in these ethno-national ascriptions had already been employed as discrimination markers in Yugoslavia and escalated with the manipulation and militarisation of masculinities that preceded the outbreak of violence.

> Even in the eighties, one could see derogatory images of a presumed Balkan and uncivilized enemy throughout Yugoslavia: on the one hand 'Balkan man' was depicted as lazy, indifferent and violent; on the other hand there were images of a diligent, hard working, honest, civilized non-Balkan man. West–east and north–south divisions played a very active part in these boundary drawings within former Yugoslavia and paved the way for the Europe–Balkan dividing line which divided Yugoslavia itself. This division, too, was gendered, showing masculine and feminine features. (Jalušić 2004: 49)

The myth of the Serbian soldier as the prototypical Balkan warrior hero was largely based on the systematic effeminisation of opponents, in the main Croatia and Slovenia who are traditionally associated with Europe and were therefore perceived as showing more 'feminine features'.[21]

Analysing gender patterns in Croatian and Serbian popular music during the war, Natalija Ceribašić notes a much more frequent representation of Croatian soldiers defending their families and homes, while the Serbian soldier is primarily depicted as defending Serbian symbols and Serbian soil.

> On the Croatian side, soldiers' personal stories also contain descriptions of fear, justification of retreats by the army, descriptions of their being unaccustomed to military skills, and pleas for lenience for deserters. As opposed to that, the Serbian side identifies the deserters with mother's lads. They are not only cowards, and bad Serbs, but also non-men. (Ceribašić 1995: 95)

In some of these Serbian war songs Croatia was also frequently ridiculed as a loose, masochist woman who lends herself to Europe but is badly rejected or being played games with.[22] These accounts are of course mocking allusions to Croatia's aspirations towards independence as well as her 'flirting' with West European countries.

The image of Croatia's alleged 'femininity' and 'loose servility' evoked in the Serbian war songs seems to have survived and occasionally breaks into the recrimination discourses in the post-war scenario. The ways in which war crime accusations are confronted in today's Croatia and Serbia differ significantly, as do the prevailing concepts of masculinity. The notorious Serbian paramilitary commander and warlord Željko Ražnatović Arkan, for example, said in a newspaper interview: 'I never said that I used to be a good-for-nothing or an angel when I was young; I was very mischievous, and I can say that my past was stormy. I don't want to defend myself' (*Stranka srpskog jedinstva*, 6 November 1994; quoted and translated in Čolović 2004: 255). Arkan, like many other Serbian warlords with mafia backgrounds, takes pride in not wanting 'to defend himself'. This attitude is very different from many Croatian soldiers' approach, claiming that they are not responsible for the crimes they committed because they had been attacked first. In this context it is interesting to note that Croatian media reports, both during the war and after, made extensive mention of Serb perpetrators and Muslim victims, whereas Croatian soldiers were never labelled as perpetrators nor as victims. Victimisation in the context of such highly sexualised and masculinised realms as combat and warfare would inevitably be equated with rape, and the rape of men, in turn, would be associated with homosexuality and constructed as morally reprehensible and a sign of weakness. Hence, the possible rape of Croatian soldiers would threaten the entire notion of the heroic, able-bodied male defender, and was (and largely still is) a taboo issue in public discourse (see also Žarkov 2007; Schroer-Hippel 2011: 99). Concurrently, Croatian combatants are never referred to as perpetrators, as this contradicts the whole notion of the Homeland War as a defensive war. Many Serbs despise this defensive argumentation as unmanly and they accordingly refer to the Croats as 'sissies' or 'milksops'. Whereas in Serbia the image of the war veteran as an impregnable outlaw tends to predominate, discourse on ex-combatants in post-war Croatia is rather tied up to the figure of the Croatian 'Mr Clean' – figuratively as well as literally (Schäuble 2009).

In contrast to the Serbian fighters, who have traditionally been depicted and often continue to self-perform as tough, habitually bearded 'bandits' with grim looks on their faces, unwilling ever to renounce the rightfulness of the war, Croatian ex-generals, such as Ante Gotovina and Mirko Norac, perpetuate a self-image as rather boyish and ingenuous defenders of the homeland. Their appearance contradicts the classic image of the brute war criminal and neither would, for instance, ever publicly appear unshaven or unfavourably dressed. Their media profiling as respectable men who prefer not to 'get their hands dirty' is carefully orchestrated and visually transmits the appropriate political message.

The majority of the Croatian population recognises the icon of the spotless, innocent ex-general as a symbolic representative for all the thousands of *branitelji* who were heroically 'ready for the homeland'. Accordingly, the government's decision to surrender the commanding officers to a foreign court is conceptualised in terms of gendered attributes and is widely considered to be cowardly, weak and corrupt. Perceived as an insult to the veterans' honour, this position necessitates a reclaiming of the ex-generals' manliness and recuperation of the masculine virtues associated with their military deployment.

The Croatian Gentleman Hero

Mirko Norac and Ante Gotovina as Personifications of the Croatian 'Mr Clean'

The mechanism by which several former Croatian generals are currently linked with and transfigured into mythic heroes raises a number of questions. How is it possible that convicted war criminals such as Ante Gotovina and Mirko Norac[23] are conventionalised as national idols and serve as a role model for large sections of the population? What understanding of history is this credo based on and what gender concepts does it imply? And why does the destiny of a whole nation seem to depend on the guilty/innocent verdict of a single person?

First of all, it has to be noted that the trial of Ante Gotovina forced the Croatian government to deal with the allegation of Croatian war crimes in full view of the world. This, however, was and to a certain extend still is *the* central national taboo issue, and many fear that the tribunal's verdict not only puts the dignity and legitimacy of the Homeland War into question, but would also historically equate the guilt of Croats and Serbs. The refusal to deal with the subject of war debt on an individual as well as on the national level poses one of the central challenges for a lasting consolidation of the situation in the former Yugoslavia.

It is within this context that Ante Gotovina's arrest, his extradition to The Hague and his eventual guilty verdict are perceived as a continuation of 'historical injustice' in the course of which the international community has ostensibly wronged and repeatedly victimised Croatia. Vlasta Jalušić has characterised the refusal to take responsibility for war crimes as 'organized innocence' and labelled it collective 'victim identity' (Jalušić 2004: 56). Her appraisal that in the Slovenian case '[t]his presumed innocence, the self-image as an eternal victim and the radical distancing from the Balkans created a condition for non-responsibility to spread and paved the way for a politics of blaming' (ibid.: 60) is equally, if not more, applicable to Croatia. The politics of blaming the others goes hand in hand with a self-mythologisation as defenders of the homeland. Čolović has pointed out that the technique of representing the present war as a continuation of past wars has the effect of transferring previous wars' legitimacy to the present and endowing the Homeland War with 'a mythic dimension' (Čolović 2002: 253). As part of this mythologisation process, 'the complexities of social and historical experiences are simplified and compressed into the action of representative individuals or heroes' (Slotkin 1992: 13). Needless to say, the resulting cult of new national heroes was built on notions of Croatian victimhood as well as on idealised versions of masculine protection and resistance. Placed 'within the pantheon of martyrs fighting for the Croatian state' (Pavlaković 2004: 734), heroes like Ante Gotovina and Mirko Norac 'join the continuum of abstract and romanticised Croatian heroism' (Baker 2006: 25). As personified representatives of the *branitelji* community they prolong the line of heroic ancestors and ensure the historical continuity of the Croatian people as well as of Croatian nationhood.[24]

As Čolović has remarked, constructions of the new national Croatian and Serbian heroes are closely linked to the *hajduk* (highwayman) narratives. In the Balkan folkloric tradition the *hajduks* are romanticised hero figures who traditionally fought against Ottoman oppression. Referring to Christian Giordano, Čolović links the current heroes to the legendary outlaws and rightful avengers who rebel against unjust authority, and thus situates them at the interface between history and mythology:

> [T]he notion of people outside the law as popular folk-avengers is particularly common in Mediterranean societies, where long-lasting foreign rulers created enduring mistrust towards authority and law, thus

opening the way for admiration of all those who offered resistance.
(Čolović 2004: 257; see also Giordano 1996)

The personae of Ante Gotovina and Mirko Norac have become heroes of songs and stories praising their military achievements; the
public attention they are granted is closely linked to constructions of
masculinity and martyrdom. A number of Croatian nationalist sing-
ers – amongst them Marko Perković Thompson,[25] Miroslav Škoro and
Niko Bete – have used their music to support the cases of the indicted
Croatian generals and to articulate the viewpoint that the 1991–1995
war was solely a defence operation (cf. Baker 2010 and 2006). Their patriotic lyrics deal primarily with images of a timeless hero responding
to a timeless threat, and have been a rallying call for those in support
of the indictees. Miroslav Škoro's song *Sude mi* [They're trying me]
(2003), whose title is a direct allusion to the martyrdom of Christ, tells
of an unspecified 'knight' [*vitez*] who has been betrayed by his brothers and is 'locked up in a distant land' [*u dalekoj zemlji okovan*]. The
evoked image of a misjudged messiah contains an unmistaken reference to Gotovina's ordeal in 'a far-off town' (The Hague) as well as to
his trial for the defence of 'the walls of the white town' [*zidine grada
bijeloga*], presumably Zadar.

Niko Bete's songs *Na zapovijed, generale* [At your command, general!] (2002), *Mirko Norac* (2003) and *Ante, Ante, svi smo za te* [We're all
with you, Ante] (2002) regularly feature at gatherings in support of the
two generals. Catherine Baker has pointed out that '[t]he lexical trope
of *Ante, Ante, svi smo za te* is repeated on protest placards and posters,
and in punning newspaper headlines as an emergent figure of speech'
(Baker 2006: 24). In *Na zapovijed, generale* and *Mirko Norac*, the hero
[*junak*] is straightforwardly identified as Norac and his cause is backed
by lyrics such as 'We won't extradite you / so that no one might judge
you' [*ne damo te / da ti neki tuđi sudi*]. In all of these songs the legendary
status of the two generals is affirmed by their respective fight against the
'Četniks' and they are both constructed as brave yet vulnerable warriors
who have cherished their homeland more than their lives and will thus
transfigure into immortal ancestors. Through this narrative composition, agony and victimhood are symbolically transported into the realm
of timeless heroism – two states that mutually constitute each other.
However, to claim a collective 'victim identity' or 'victim status' without
forfeiting all conventional attributes of masculinity is a rather delicate
tightrope walk. In my view, the martyr is the only figure who simultaneously embodies notions of victimhood and of (male) heroism, and effectively manages to combine the two.[26]

Many Croats refer to the Gotovina and Norac convictions as submitting to blackmail and perceive them as sacrifices Croatia is forced to make in order to join the European Union. This perception makes them not only scapegoats but martyrs in the classical sense. The lyrics of *Sude mi*, in which the hero Gotovina is betrayed by his brothers, thus not only alludes to Christs' extradition, but directly refers to the general's fellow Croatian countrymen who were willing to hand him over to an international court as a prerequisite for EU accession talks. The notion that the ex-generals and their comrades had fought for the country's independence and have now been let down is frequently linked to religious concepts of treachery and martyrdom, and the two men are even assigned messianic qualities by some right-wing pseudo-religious groups.

'We are all Mirko Norac'

Mirko Norac was a high-ranking Croat military officer who had been sentenced by a Croatian court for war crimes committed by the Croatian side during the 1991–1995 Homeland War. After Norac had turned himself in 2001, he was sentenced by the Rijeka County Court in 2003, and the original verdict in the case of the so-called 'Gospić Group' was confirmed later by the Supreme Court. Mirko Norac, Tihomir Oresković and Stjepan Grandić were sentenced to twelve, fifteen and ten years of prison respectively, for war crimes committed against Serb civilians in Gospić. In July 2004, Norac was transferred to an ICTY courtroom in The Hague where another indictment for crimes committed during 'Operation Medak Pocket' in 1993 was issued against him. In 2008, in what was the first ICTY case to be transferred to a local court, he was found guilty of failing to stop soldiers under his command from killing and torturing Serbs, and was sentenced to an additional seven years imprisonment. Altogether, Norac served ten years in prison in Croatia and was released on probation in November 2011.

Norac was born in Otok, a small village in the Dalmatian hinterland, in the immediate vicinity of Sinj. In the public and private conversations I overheard during my research, Norac was regularly referred to as 'hero' [*heroj*], 'liberator' [*osloboditelj*], 'defender' [*branitelj*] and 'true Croat' [*pravi Hrvat*]. These terms point towards the entanglement of masculinity and ethnicity, and the gendered image of the fighter hero goes hand in hand with the legitimation if not the glorification of war violence.[27]

After Norac was convicted for his role in the killing of approximately forty Serb civilians in the defence of the strategically important town of Gospić in October 1991, powerful political anti-cooperation groups and war veteran organisations organised huge rallies in support of his case. After the first verdict in 2003, war veterans halted traffic at nineteen spots in nine counties, including major towns such as Zagreb, Split and Dubrovnik. Police estimates suggest that fifteen hundred people took part in the demonstrations, using about two hundred vehicles to block the roads. Mirko Čondić, the head of the largest veterans' association in Croatia, threatened that he would file lawsuits against Račan and Mesić for 'intimidating the public and comparing [Croatian] war veterans to Serbian bandits and killers who seek to destroy democracy' (Kozole 2003). And Dražen Pavlović, the president of Sinj's branch of the Croatian Disabled Homeland War Veterans Association (HVIDRA) and president of the committee for the defence of Mirko Norac, said that the president and prime minister should 'join comrade Zoran Đinđić [the Serbian prime minister assassinated on 12 March 2003] for breakfast as early as possible because that is the only way to save the Croatian state for which we fought' (ibid.). Although Pavlović later apologised for his indirect death threat to Račan and Mesić, the radicalism of his comment illustrates the outrage of war veterans at Norac's conviction, especially in his home county Sinj.

The protests were largely based on former president Franjo Tuđman's anti-ICTY legacy, and caused a major governmental crisis.[28]

> Tuđman's persistent non-cooperation and criticisms of the ICTY as an anti-Croat institution primed public opinion against the court and established the rhetorical strategy that the right wing would use to undermine the new government's moves toward increased cooperation with the tribunal. (Peskin and Boduszynski 2003: 16)[29]

The nationalist right torpedoed the new government – a pro-democratic and pro-Western coalition, elected after Tuđman's death in December 1999 and led by the reformed communist Ivica Račan – as soon as the court in Rijeka issued the arrest warrant for Mirko Norac.[30] In Split alone, 150,000 people protested against the pursuit of Norac and the government's presumed readiness to give in to international pressure. One of the placards displayed at the Split demonstration announced 'Croatian Judas – remember that you cannot betray all Croats'. This menace was unquestionably directed at Milan Levar, a key witness in the Gospić investigation, who had testified against Norac. The slogan contained several messages; among other things it is clear that Norac was seen as a representative for all Croats and that any harm done to him would affect the whole nation. Furthermore, calling a perceived traitor a 'Judas' automatically elevates the betrayed to a

Christ-like, messianic figure. The fact that Milan Levar was later killed by a car bomb illustrates how ruthless, self-administered justice was achieved in the early post-war years.

In the aforementioned contemporaneous protests in Sinj, ultra-radical HVIDRA president, Dražen Pavlović, pleaded to 'remove the stigma and stop the chase of the generals', claiming that if it had not been for Norac, the town Gospić would have met the same destiny as Vukovar. This reasoning implies that preventive defence is justifiable, irrespective of the potential war crimes that might be committed in the course of such an action. Mentioning Norac's and the other indicted generals' 'stigmata', Pavlović deliberately employs a charged vocabulary that emblematically links the generals to the martyrdom of Christ. 'Therefore through his status and fate Norac reflects the status and fate of all Croatian defenders', he added, thus unanimously glorifying the deeds of all *branitelji* and indirectly demanding a general amnesty for all of them. Furthermore, his comment brings home the message that the indictment of Norac would be tantamount to the condemnation of all Croatian soldiers and the Homeland War in general – an implication that was bound to cause turmoil. At the same gathering, the mayor of Norac's birthplace, Otok, announced that the parents of Norac had allegedly said that they would have been happiest if Gospić and the whole of Croatia could have been defended by holy water and prayer alone, instead of being involved in a bloody war (*Slobodna Dalmacija*, 10 February 2001). Such sanctimonious remarks are intended to reinforce the public image of Norac as God-fearing 'Mr Clean' who never intended to harm anybody and must hence be innocent. All speeches delivered during the rally in Sinj were evocative of the image of Norac and the other indicted generals as hero-martyrs who sacrificed themselves for the homeland, trying to avoid further bloodshed by beating off the Serb aggressors.

Despite the protests and despite being accused of selling out the Homeland War, the Račan government initially maintained a firm stand in the Norac crisis. But gradually they also partly adopted the nationalist rhetoric and ceased to cooperate fully with the ICTY (Jović 2009: 2). In December 2000, the Croatian parliament enacted a special declaration which defined the character of Croatian participation in the war as 'just and legitimate, defensive and liberating' (ibid.: 7; see also Peskin and Boduszynski), with Article 5 of the declaration inviting the state to 'provide full protection, respect and welfare' to all *branitelji* – an appeal that clashed with the declaration's invitation to Croatian courts to process individual crimes.[31] In the Norac case a preliminary settlement was eventually reached when Norac – on condition that he would not be sent to The Hague – turned himself in to the Croatian police and announced that he had never planned to defy the Croatian legal system.[32] 'Fighting for this country', he said after he surrendered, 'I also fought for its legal institutions' (Crčić 2001; see also Peskin and Boduszynski 2003: 24).

His perception as a hero, however, prevails to the present day in certain parts of the country and in fascist Croatian internet forums, such as 'stormfront.org', Mirko Norac is still celebrated as a martyr. One recent entry reads: 'Norac is from my hometown and I don't think he'll ever ride a horse again, at least not in the Alka. He was sold for thirty pieces of silver and entry into the Rothschild EU.'[33] This contributor from Sinj (or Otok) symbolically links Norac to Christ, who was betrayed by Judas Iscariot and 'sold' for thirty silver coins. Norac, in his view, was sold out in exchange for Croatia's qualification for EU accession. The first comment, that Norac would never ride a horse in the Alka again, refers to Norac's alleged statement that the first thing he would do after his release from prison was to participate in the Alka to confirm his affinity to Sinj and the Dalmatian hinterland. The author of the forum entry must have been well aware of the recent policy shift within the Alka Association, and obviously deplores the fact that Norac is no longer a desirable flagship for the tournament. Referring to the European Union as 'Rothschild EU', however, is meant to express his contempt and hatred for the EU as a confederation solely principled by monetary interests. The allusion to the Rothschild banking dynasty is part of rather widespread, anti-Semitic conspiracy theories in the Balkans, according to which 'Jewish family money' controls the world's financial institutions and has the power and intention to encourage or discourage wars between governments. This rather confused, abbreviated and distorted comment nonetheless implicates scepticism towards the economic and financial policy as well as the advocacy of the European Union that is still quite pervasive in some parts of Croatia, above all in Dalmatia.

Its tone stands in the tradition of the nationalist songs about Mirko Norac that were released between 2000 and 2004, and refer to the ex-general's Dalmatian origin. Especially the aforementioned song, *Na zapovijed, generale*, is a hymn about Norac's deep local rootedness and the heroic strength and divine protection that results from his descent. The song opens with the sound of wind, the legendary *bura*, and the ritual opening of the Alka tournament in which the *vojvoda*, the Duke of the Alka, ritually welcomes the horsemen. The traditional trumpet fanfare is followed by the sound of galloping horses and an electric guitar riff. The lyrics highlight Norac's 'heroic lineage' by linking him to the mythical defenders of Sinj and their patroness:

From Otok in the Cetina region, by the town of Sinj
A mother bore the hero of the Alka
Mirko, you're the pride, Mirko, you're the honour
Your mother imbued you with the Croatian milk.

[*Iz Otoka cetinskoga, pokraj Sinja grada / rodila je majka
alkarskog junaka/ Mirko, ti si ponos, Mirko, ti si dika /
Hrvatskim te majka mlikom zadojila*].

The mention of the mother is probably both a reference to Norac's real
mother and hence an ode to the Croatian family, and also an allusion
to the mythical lineage of Croatian martyr-heroes in the Cetina region.
In songs and narrative discourses like this, the image of the tormented
mother who has sacrificed her son(s) usually features more frequently
and is used as a personified depiction of the homeland. This imagery
is also often applied in religious contexts where Croatia is symbolically
equated with Mother Mary who bewails her martyred son. The fact,
however, that Norac was not killed in action, prohibits this imagery; instead the narrative implies that his life was saved because he was granted
divine protection:

May our lady of Sinj protect you from all evil
May Croatia always be in the first place
(Through) Vukovar, Dubrovnik, through the lightning and
the storms
You led your people, General, hear me, hear me.

[*Od svakoga zla čuvala te Gospa sinjska / Hrvatska tu uvik
na prvome mistu bila / Vukovara, Dubrovnika, kroz bljesk-
ove i oluje / Vodija si svoje ljude, generale, čuj me, čuj me*].

The mention of Vukovar and Dubrovnik paradigmatically points to Croatian suffering, since these towns were sieged and massively destroyed
when they came under fire early on in the war. Lightening and storm are
allusions to the eponymous Croatian army operations in 1995, and the
mention that Norac led his people through these battles portends his
role as heroic general and commander in the defence of Croatia. The
song continues to invoke the Croatian national colours and directly assures Norac that the people of the Cetina region would forever celebrate
him. In the end, Norac is depicted as a martyr, vicariously for all martyrs
who lost their lives in the Homeland War. The verse, 'It is an honour to

die young and to give one's life for the homeland' [*Čast je mlad, mlad umriti / život dati rodnoj grudi*] is an unmistakable glorification of male self-sacrifice and martyrdom.[34] The assertion that even the dead would rise from their graves and render homage to the Duke of the Alka [*i mrtvi bi iz groba ustali / pokloni se alkarskom vojvodi*] finally positions Norac in the pantheon of the immortal ancestral heroes.

Bete's second Norac song that is simply entitled *Mirko Norac* similarly features hordes, gangs and Četniks who started a war, destroyed and plundered everything not sacred to them, and took it with them to Serbia. Its 'semi-historical, semi-magical narrative' (Baker 2010: 113) establishes Norac as the saviour of Croatia who was assisted by the Fairy of Velebit. In Croatian folklore, the fairy of Velebit is a good spirit, an ethereal nymph who is the patron of the Velebit mountain range. In the song, the fairy asks Our Lady of Sinj to send her a soldier and in call-and-response style the Gospa answers the fairy: 'I'm not sending you a soldier / but a duke / and I imbue him with my holy blessing!' [*Ne vojnika, ne vojnika / vojvodu ja ti šaljem / i svoj sveti i svoj / sveti blagoslov mu dajem!*]. In epic Slavic poetry and folk tales fairies often watch over heroes, and the fact that Norac in the lyrics to this song is guarded by both, a nature spirit and the Mother of God, all the more signifies his divine chosenness and his connection to the realm of the immortal.[35]

When I conducted my fieldwork in 2004 and 2005, placards and posters in public places all over Croatia not only exemplified people's widespread identification with Norac but also demonstrated the obstinacy of the defence discourse. Slogans such as 'Guilty – because he defended Croatia' [*Kriv je – sto je obranio Hrvatsku!*], 'We are all Mirko Norac' [*Svi smo Mirko Norac*], 'The people and the truth are on your side' [*Istina i narod na tvojoj su strani*], and 'If we were free, we wouldn't extradite our liberators!' [*Ako smo slobodni, ne dajmo osloboditelje!*] showed that Norac's conviction was not perceived as a legitimate verdict, but rather the (self-)sacrifice of a truly heroic man.

In August 2008 posters with the image of the Croatian ex-general with signs reading 'sold', 'script and directed by: čedo & veritas [innocence/virginity & truth]' and 'all rights by Croatian government' appeared first in Otok and Sinj and later in many other Croatian cities too. The posters were designed in the fashion of film placards, yet the caption 'sold' did not refer to the capacity crowd but to the aforementioned conviction of many Croats that Norac had been betrayed and 'sold' for the price of Croatian EU accession. The posters further indicated that the 'script' is based on a true story and contingent on the general's veracity and innocence, whereas the ones responsible for the denouement were members of the Croatian government. Dalmatia-based

Figures 4.3 and 4.4. Placards lending support to the case of convicted Croatian ex-general Mirko Norac. Photos: M. Schäuble

veteran organisations did not reveal who was behind these posters, and according to newspaper reports simply referred to 'friends of General Norac' and 'defenders' as the people responsible. Given that Norac was found guilty of war crimes against civilians in Operation Medak Pocket shortly before the posters were put up, however, it is very likely that his supporters attempted to protest against this second verdict and that the placards were posted in Sinj at the forefront of the 2008 Alka, where those responsible could expect increased attention and most probably approval for their message.

In contrast to Ante Gotovina, however, Mirko Norac has never been portrayed as an adventurous daredevil. He was commonly considered a rather timid, youthful man, and the Croatian writer Slavenka Drakulić notes:

> It is hard to imagine Mirko Norac shouting the order for execution. He does not look like a soldier, much less a tough war commander. Not even a general's uniform can make him look manly and capable of such a job. A plump, plain young man with a shy smile and a double chin, he looks more soft than dangerous. (Drakulić 2004: 39)

This remark, intended to ridicule the general's manliness, paradoxically fortifies the image of the stereotypical masculine fighter. Drakulić draws on hegemonic gender categories and confirms existing perceptions of masculinity rather than critically challenging them.

The fact that Norac's appearance does not correspond to the cliché of the masculine, savage butcher contributes to the popular notion that he is a victim of a judiciary pressurised by the international community – and not a brute victimiser. The actual war crimes, plundering, demolitions, evictions, executions, murders and other atrocities are hardly ever specified or directly mentioned in media reports, public accounts or private conversations. Common talk is mainly of 'injustices', endured but never committed by Croats, and anyone who dares to contradict this prevalent view runs the danger of being characterised as either a traitor, or, in the case of women, a 'whore' [*kurva*] or 'witch' [*vještica*].[36]

In 2012, however, during my latest visit to Sinj, there were still numerous posters proclaiming Gotovina as a hero, as everywhere in Dalmatia, but there were none for Norac anymore. Most probably, the evidence of his guilt – including a video tape made by the Croatian Ministry of Interior's intelligence service of a so-called 'death meeting' at which Norac was present, the rounding up and killing of Serbs, and, finally, the celebration of the executions afterwards – was too conclusive.[37] Norac's involvement in war crimes was direct and traceable, and ultimately, his case did not withstand the narrative of unconfined Croatian innocence in the Homeland War. Unlike Gotovina, who had been convicted in The Hague on the grounds of command responsibility and later acquitted, Norac was caught getting his hands dirty by a Croatian court. Because his trial contributed to the verifiability of Croatian war guilt, Norac is no longer national hero material, even if many people in Sinj and its surroundings continue to support and celebrate him.

'Gotovina: Hero not Hague'

After going on the run in 2001, Ante Gotovina travelled on a phony Croatian passport under the telling name of 'Kristijan Horvat' [Christian Croat]. This rather uncoded alias bears witness to the ex-general's ostentatious patriotism and his complacent ridicule of international criminal police cooperation. After a long-lasting diplomatic game of hide-and-seek that caused severe deferrals and ultimately endangered Croatia's application for EU membership, Gotovina was finally arrested and extradited to The Hague.[38]

His seizure, however, was accompanied by a plethora of conspiracy theories and led to a vivid recurrence of the earlier protests that had surrounded the case of General Norac; some even assert it led to a culmination of the crisis. 'The domestic court's indictment of General

Norac, although very controversial, was not seen to be as threatening to Croatia's sovereignty in the same way as the subsequent indictments of Croatian generals handed down by the international tribunal' (Peskin and Boduszynski 2003: 24). Carla del Ponte's indictment of the two former generals Rahim Ademi and Ante Gotovina had posed another serious threat to Račan's cabinet, and resulted in the resignation of four ministers. Račan turned the crisis into a referendum on his government and, although he gained the support of the *Sabor* (parliament), nationalist groups mobilised public resentment against 'a government which does not protect national values but the policy of bargaining and betraying all values achieved in the Homeland War' (HINA News Agency, 7 July 2001; see also Peskin and Boduszynski 2003: 27). Eventually, Račan conceded to the criticism of the right and declared that the indictments would unjustifiably criminalise Croatian military actions. These seesaw changes facilitated Gotovina's escape while Ademi voluntarily turned himself in to tribunal authorities.[39] The third indictee, an 83-year-old former Croatian army Chief of General Staff, Janko Bobetko, refused to accept the indictment. Since public opinion was almost unrestrainedly in favour of his refusal to surrender, Račan's government failed to assert a definite position over the case. Bobetko was declared too ill to stand trial and died in 2003 before being extradited.[40]

With the generals Bobetko deceased and Ademi in the dock, the national resistance to war crime prosecution concentrated increasingly on Gotovina. The Croatian public passionately supported Gotovina in massive nationwide campaigns and public rallies. On the displayed posters and the ubiquitous graffiti, humour plays a crucial role. The name 'Gotovina' literally translates as 'cash', which resulted in a number of more or less original wordplays and double entendres. Before Gotovina's arrest in December 2005 the most common one was 'You don't have Gotovina/cash, try Mastercard' [*Nemate Gotovine, probajte Mastercard*]. The motto '*Nemate Gotovina*' was obviously not just playing on the country's desperate economic situation, but alluded to (and rejected) the widespread assumption that Gotovina was hiding in Croatia or neighbouring Herzegovina after his indictment, whilst the Croatian government denied any knowledge of his whereabouts and deferred his extradition. In a similar manner, the slogan 'You cannot pay with Gotovina/cash for ignorance and incompetence' [*Neznanje i nesposobnost nećete plačati Gotovinom*] taunts the international community's inefficient efforts to locate the vanished general. In general, the double-meaning of the general's name is used as a critique of neoliberal capitalism by which values like national feeling, honour, bravery, loyalty, freedom and independence are invoked.

Figures 4.5 and 4.6. Placard boards in support of the case of then indicted Croatian ex-general Ante Gotovina, 2005. Photos: M. Schäuble

After Gotovina had eventually been tracked down, the veteran and invalid organisation HVIDRA, along with other nationalist factions, organised a huge protest rally in Split. Tens of thousands of people attended and carried posters with catchphrases such as 'The hero has defended us, too!' [*Heroj također je branio nas*], 'General, we are on your side' [*Generale, na tvojoj smo strani*], 'Gotovina: Hero, not Hague' [*Gotovina: Heroj ne Haag*], 'Today Gotovina, tomorrow you' [*Danas Gotovina, sutra vi*], or the word-game 'No extradition, no deal' [*Nema Predaje, Nema prodaje*]. As happened four years previously, in support of Mirko Norac, angry war veterans blocked major streets with tree trunks, and in Zadar students were allegedly wearing Ustaša caps and burning European flags (Mappes-Niediek 2005b).

The Croatian press by and large played down the charges against Gotovina – 'crimes against humanity' and 'violations of the laws or customs of war' – and still widely conceptualised him as a male role model.[41] Neither his past as a mercenary soldier in the French Foreign Legion,[42] nor the fact that he had provided training to a number of right-wing paramilitary organisations in South America, nor the rumours that he had been detained in a French prison for a jewellery robbery and extortion, seem to damage his reputation as a 'real' or 'proper man' [*pravi čovjek*]. On the contrary, the French Foreign Legion enjoys a high reputation amongst many Croats, and one of my interlocutors proudly told me, 'They have to pass demanding physical and psychological endurance tests in the legion. And Gotovina has even been a general there – that should give you an idea of how intelligent and tough this man is'. In photographs published by Croatian media, Gotovina is either depicted in uniform or as a *bon vivant* surrounded by women. Western media coverage also served the portrayal of Gotovina as chatoyant figure, or alternatively as a hero from an action movie. His 'Rambo' image seemed to fascinate a broad readership and the BBC reported under the headline 'Fighter and Playboy': '[Gotovina] spent time on a merchant ship before joining the French Foreign Legion, where he built a reputation as a fearsome soldier with a taste for beautiful women'.[43] This abridgement combines the taste for beautiful women and the taste for battle, and couples them with classic concepts of masculinity.

Nenad Ivanković's ludicrous biography of Gotovina entitled *Ratnik: pustolov i general* [Warrior – Adventurer and General] that was published in 2001 is written according to the same principle, and borders upon bizarre hero worship. The text, romanticising warfare and the cruelty of military drill, is spiced with racist and misogynist descriptions of Gotovina's brothel visits, love affairs and marriages around the world – and it soon became a bestseller in Croatia.[44] Ivanković also makes a point highlighting Gotovina's unblemished character and his meticulous appearance, thus confirming the image of the 'Croatian Mr Clean'. He describes how Gotovina met representatives of the United Nations Confidence Restoration Operation (UNCRO) in Knin, only a few hours after Operation Storm had been successfully accomplished under his command, as follows:

> When the gentlemen from UNCRO arrived around 9.30 A.M., Ante was there to greet them; clean-shaven, spit-shined, and brown from the sun, just like in the days of his youth. He was dressed in impeccable military uniform, and had the kind of suppressed smile on his face which befitted a victor who was not arrogant, but aware that from now on, new rules applied. 'Gentlemen, I am happy to be able to greet you here in Knin', he said. (Ivanković 2001: 234)

The whole book is written in this style, in an the attempt to portray Gotovina as a worldly and cultured man – amongst other things, by mentioning that during his time in the French Foreign Legion he used to buy his safari clothing exclusively from Jean Paul Gaultier (Ivanković 2001: 85).

Gotovina's unusual life story continuously fascinates and stimulates the imagination of his compatriots, and press reports always include some uncalled-for, private elements. 'The case of Ante Gotovina is unprecedented in the scope and intensity of trivialization', writes the historian Katarina Ristić, including reports on everyday life and family visits in the detention unit in Scheveningen, supportive letters and Christmas cards sent by loyal citizens, as well as reports on his firm religious beliefs (Ristić 2012: 41). The day after Gotovina's acquittal, for example, a Croatian glossy magazine published the article *Ratnik i zavodnik. Sve ljubavi generala Gotovine* [Warrior and Seducer. All lovers of General Gotovina] focusing on the ex-general's love life. The report draws heavily on Ivanković's biography and stresses Gotovina's success with women worldwide, while also favourably mentioning that he acknowledged all his illegitimate children and is on good terms with his ex-wives and ex-lovers. He is portrayed as a caring father and proud gentleman who did not want his son to see him in handcuffs, and he refused to be defended in The Hague at the expense of anybody else.[45] The mystification and romanticising of his persona continues, and since his acquittal he is even better qualified to serve as a male role model who, after a stormy past in the service of his country, turned into a loyal family man.

After Gotovina's transfer to the court in The Hague, the process of his 'sanctification' in the homeland proceeded apace. Particularly in

Dalmatia, people continued to refer to him as a messianic figure to whom they owe Croatia's independence and who has thus become the main target of Europe's malice. When asked about the then still pending Gotovina process, one of my main interlocutors in Sinj answered with the cryptic verse:

Ajmee, pravda već da nije	[Alas, there will be no justice]
kad Irudo sud tak vije	[as long as Herod administers the law]

This saying is usually associated with the dolorous Maria Magdalena who bewails the death of Jesus at Calvary. Transferring this lament to the current Croatian context, my interview partner symbolically associates the arbitrary judgment of Herod with the ICTY in The Hague and equates Gotovina with the unrecognised and thus wrongly sentenced messiah. However hubristic this analogy might seem, the image of Gotovina as redeemer has started to become a popular trope in the collective Croatian imagination. *Feral Tribune*, a satirical weekly Croatian paper, for instance, picked up on this symbolism and printed a photomontage of the crucified Gotovina wearing a general's uniform cap instead of a crown of thorns. And although the caricature is without much doubt intended as ironic commentary, it nevertheless points towards the prevailing perception of Gotovina as an ethno-national saviour. Yet the putative victim status relates not only to Gotovina, but represents the self-conception of a whole nation.

Gendered Notions of Europe

Before the acquittal in November 2012, the discussions on Gotovina's extradition and guilty verdict were above all a continuation of the battle over 'historical truth' and ultimately about the power to determine official history. Ex-general and Gotovina's former comrade Markica Rebić told the German newspaper *Die Zeit* in 2005 that the ICTY formula of the 'individualisation of war crime' in the case of Gotovina was fraud. According to him, the tribunal intended to impose a 'collective guilt' through the backdoor, thus claiming that the 'Croatian state was built on the foundation of crime' (Mappes-Niediek 2005a, my translation). Croatia's 2nd President Stjepan Mesić (in office February 2000 – February 2010), however, was in favour of an individualisation of guilt, and argued that 'when specific people are made to answer for crimes, then collective accusations will cease.'[46] Mesić's consistent support of the ICTY and domestic war crime prosecutions earned him a number of crass insults from his nationalist opponents. In Dalmatia I recurrently heard people refer to him as *izdajnik* [traitor] and *zločiniac* [criminal], or alternatively as *peder* [fag]. Such openly discriminating and homophobic defamations not only illustrate a determined unwillingness to take responsibility for acts committed and to constructively break through the cycle of blaming the other/s, but also expose the underlying concepts of misconceived honour, cohesion and masculinity.

For the Croatian public the contrast to the virtuous male national hero is constructed as a negatively connoted non-Croat female figure. This anti-hero is the former ICTY chief prosecutor, Carla del Ponte. She was frequently labelled as 'the whore in The Hague' [*kurva u Haagu*] or as 'Carla, the whore' [*kurva Carla*] by my (male) interlocutors – thus transforming a political issue into a sexualised, misogynist discourse. In some cartoons Carla del Ponte was depicted as dominatrix under whose whip Ivo Sanader and Stjepan Mesić intimidated but lasciviously crouch. It is through such comments and public images that the institution of the international tribunal is not only personified and sexualised, but its political authority is furthermore intensely devalued. In this scenario, the martyr Gotovina, who has sacrificed himself for his homeland, is opposed to a bribable – that is to say corrupt – female without honour or morals who represents Europe.[47] In an article with the revealing title *Europe is a Whore*, Boris Buden describes the bitter anti-Europeanism that prevails in the Croatian media and correspondingly concludes that Europe is constructed as an 'effete' corrupt counterpart to Croatia (Buden 2000). I understand the use of this language and imagery as it hints at Europe's assumed loose morality and lack of principles in contrast to which local identity is constructed by drawing on 'masculinised' attributes such as integrity, steadfastness and honour.

Imagined Suicide

Performing Terrorism and the Re-Formations of Manhood in Post-War Croatia[48]

Many young men in the former Yugoslavia initially shared the masculine allure for adventure and romantic excitement of war as primarily embodied by Ante Gotovina. Today, however, little of the initial thrill and excitement of participating in armed battle is left, since many of those who saw a chance to return as war heroes actually returned as war invalids. The large number of physically and psychologically disabled *branitelji* currently poses a serious problem for Croatian civil society. Traumatic war experiences are individually sensed and discerned in

Figure 4.7. A monumental size dummy of former chief prosecutor of the ICTY, Carla del Ponte, is burnt during Carnival in Croatia in 2005.
© Keystone

many different ways, but they often materialise in the form of bodily symptoms, practices or performances. In his introduction to *Tense Past: Cultural Essays in Trauma and Memory*, Paul Antze states that the individual body serves as the sole site or *lieu* of memory (Antze and Lambek 1996: xiii), and for many soldiers whose experiences during combat left them traumatised, memories have a bodily impact that should not be underestimated. The war memories and recollections of violence are locked in the bodies of the ex-soldiers and forcefully erupt from time to time. In the following I am concerned with the socio-political basis of bodily experience and will scrutinise an episode that I call 'imagined suicide'. The said incident exemplifies how Marko, a former soldier who still suffers from combat-related traumatic experiences, gives public utterance to his desolate situation as *branitelj* and at the same time symbolically imbeds the situation in post-war Croatia in the framework of global trouble spots. He playfully envisions escaping his situation by staging a suicide attack in which his socio-politically 'inscribed' body is appointed a site of agency and intentionality through (imagined) resistance and re-activity (Jenkins and Valiente 1994: 164; see also Scheper-Hughes 1992).

Militant Agency as Empowerment of Underdogs?

In early February, Marko told me that the carnival was coming up, and that the local costume ball was considered a major cultural event in Sinj. For days on end he would disappear into the tool shed and build an elaborate construction on metal racks. Using the mount of a discarded backpack, he attached two parallel gas cartridges, equipped them with pointed tips, and additionally applied small blinking green and red lamps. Soon he revealed that he would dress up as an 'Arab suicide bomber'. After he had finished the decoration of his gear, he attached a cardboard sign to the cartridges that read:

> *Bok Amerika, pozdrav vašim blizancima! Vidimo se druge godine!*
> [Hello America, greetings to your twins! See you again next year!]

When leaving for the ball, he wore his camouflage army pants, black army boots, and a loose-fitting white shirt. Additionally, he glued on an exaggerated black, bushy moustache. Carrying his 'suicide backpack' Marko underwent a visible metamorphosis. He looked utterly grotesque and funny, yet at the same time threatening. To me, the gas cartridges on his back resembled miniature twin towers as well as two missiles. He himself referred to them as 'my rockets'. Combining a Croatian army uniform with the mock 'Arab' look, and an explicit comment on the attacks of 9/11, Marko created a hybrid by which he managed symbolically to display violence and at the same time caricature it. The most paradoxical detail of his costume, however, was the *kaffiyeh*, a chequered Palestinian headdress that his parents had bought as a souvenir in Israel. The family are very devout Catholics, and in 1996 after the end of the war, Joško and Nada – out of gratitude for the survival of their sons – had gone on a pilgrimage to Israel. This background story of the *kaffiyeh* gives the whole incident an even more bizarre twist. 'I totally look like Arafat,' Marko chuckled with the scarf wound around his head.

According to his own statement, the costume was intended as a disapproval of foreign policies of the United States and the European Union, as well as an ironic commentary on global terrorism. The complexity of this episode, however, can in my view only be deciphered against the backdrop of Marko's own experiences of violence during the Homeland War. He had been one of the first volunteers to join the Croatian armed forces after the republic's government announced a general mobilisation and declared a 'war of liberation'.[49] In 1991, when the initial military actions began, he instantly returned from Germany where he had just been offered a well-paid job, in order to defend Croatian territory. Without previous military experience or any particular training, he was posted to a missile defence unit in the mountains close to Sinj, monitoring air traffic. Today, almost twenty years after the ceasefire, he still has difficulties getting a steady job due to trauma-related symptoms such as insomnia, flashbacks, anxiety attacks, hyperreflexia and lack of concentration.[50] But despite his illness he had not been granted the official status of an invalid at the time of the incident and was therefore not eligible for provision of work programmes, reintegration measures or a disability pension.

Marko is the only one of four brothers who is still unmarried and lives at home with his parents. His everyday life in Sinj is characterised by the immediate consequences of the war. Two of his brothers were severely wounded in action and are clinically classified as traumatised, while his third and youngest brother is still in the Croatian army as a professional soldier. The four of them had initially volunteered to join the armed forces, and were all stationed on one of the various front lines. Nearly all of Marko's friends in Sinj are also *branitelji* who suffer from various degrees of physical and psychological war damage. The atmosphere in this militarised masculine environment was extremely aggrieving, yet I never conceived of it as threatening or violent. As long as I was present, the young men hardly ever talked directly about the war, but they were surprisingly open about their feelings of anxiety, their avolition, their disappointment about the poor public appreciation of their military deployment, as well as the corporeal effects of their war injuries and traumas. In their discussions, however, they blamed not so much their former enemies as the U.S. government and the current foreign policy of Croatia for their desolate situation. Yet what they seemed to suffer from most was their own helplessness and impotence in the face of current political and socio-economic developments. Marko told me that he felt trapped – geographically in Sinj as well as within his own body.

This situation might not be representative for the whole of post-war Croatia, the more so as Dalmatia and the border region to the Krajina were particularly fiercely affected by the acts of war and its aftermaths. But because the narratives and memories of violence are more pronounced in Sinj than elsewhere in the country (except for maybe in Vukovar), Marko's dramatic performance is all the more inseparable from the context within which it took place. Stef Jansen has pointed out that approaches that attempt to explain the outbreaks of violence in the Balkans since the early 1990s primarily on the basis of 'historical trauma' or the systematic revitalisation of repressed memories have to be treated with caution (Jansen 1999, 2002).[51] The widespread theoretical concepts about 'historical' or 'cultural trauma' cannot sufficiently elucidate the growing nationalisms and anti-European currents in the constitutive republic of the former Yugoslavia. Instead, it is important to note that present as well as future memories and historiographies depend on changing differences of power and status, which in turn are strongly influenced by affects. Maruška Svašek has pointed out that transformation processes in the postsocialist countries of Europe have been thoroughly examined in terms of economic, political and social changes, whereas emotional dynamics have largely been neglected (Svašek 2006: 2). But especially in those regions in which the dissolution of socialist federations or multinational states has been accompanied by violent conflicts, the politicisation of emotions and personal memories plays an important part in generating and/or reconstructing national as well as individual identities.

The close relation between politics of memory and practices of identity formation leads back to the carnival episode. For Marko and his family who were considered religious dissidents in Yugoslavia and systematically bullied (if not necessarily directly persecuted), the end of state socialism was accompanied by the hope for freedom of religion and political expression, and complemented by the willingness to make personal sacrifices for Croatia's independence. But during the war years and the ensuing economic and welfare reforms the expectations that initially went along with the international recognition of the democratic Republika Hrvatska gradually faded away. The transformation processes in post-war Croatian society are marked by high unemployment rates, new class differences, poverty, corruption and scandals in connection with the appropriation and sell-off of state property, and go hand in hand with a constant disillusionment of the population (cf. Svašek 2006: 11). This climate of disappointment and general distrust in market liberalisation and the democratisation of the state provide a breeding ground for nationalist demagoguism that is characterised by the search for scapegoats and rhetoric referrals to the historical victim status of Croatia. In this context, Marko's carnival costume can be seen as an 'emotional performance' of this disillusionment with which he symbolically refers to the propensity to violence of people who also conceive themselves as underdogs or 'losers of history'. His embodiment of a suicide bomber complies with Svašek's understanding of the bodily dimensions of emotional experience as political processes that imply that 'emotions are neither completely personal inner feelings, nor purely externally imposed expositions, but experiences of "embodied sociality" that are essential to individual human agency. This approach helps to explain how individuals employ conscious and unconscious bodily behaviour to express and negotiate emotional meanings that are politically relevant' (Svašek 2006: 8). Against the backdrop of this approach I interpret Marko's performance not as a direct consequence of his traumatic experiences during combat, but as a conscious attempt to deal with his personal experiences of war and radical post-war transformation in a quasi-ritualised form. By aligning his experiences of war to the communication structure of global terror, he not only communicates his social isolation but simultaneously tries to escape it. With this emotionally as well as politically charged performance he extends his masqueraded body into a 'living bomb' and employs it as an intercommunicative social agent (Svašek 2006: 8).

The fact that Marko chose to enact a Muslim seems the obvious thing to do, as Muslims are the most apparent suicide bombers to the Western imagination. Even so, for a nationalist Croat this performance implies an important and yet again highly paradoxical element, which entails various interrelated dimensions. First of all, the hostile Other that is constructed through the Croatian self-assessment as historical *Antemurale Christianitatis* [Bulwark of Christianity], and that is likewise incorporated and revived in the mythico-history of the Sinjska Alka, are Ottoman Muslims. The concrete historical presence of the Ottoman Empire has traditionally been conceived as an Oriental, genuinely non-European element, which still prevails in prevalent discourses linking Balkanism to the Ottoman legacy. To this day, all versions of Croatian nationalism are constructed in vehement, direct opposition to the idea that Croatia is part of the Balkans – a region strongly associated with its Ottoman, and therefore Muslim, legacy. And finally, Croatian militia and armed Bosnian Croat forces fought a cruel war against Bosnian Muslims during the so-called Homeland War in the neighbouring Republic of Bosnia-Herzegovina. Yet although it seems a vital constituent of regional self-conception and self-esteem in this part of the country to forcefully maintain the border towards the adjacent Muslim Other, Marko still jokingly chooses to annul the established disassociation and even to embody the potentially threatening 'Oriental element'.

Deciphering Statements of Violence

In his article 'The Enigma of Senseless Violence', Anton Blok writes that: '[v]iolence makes statements and it is the task of anthropologists to decipher them. They are greatly helped in this because violence often has the character of theatre and performance in which things are "said" as much as they are "done"' (Blok 2000: 31). Dressing up as a suicide bomber is clearly a symbolic action and not to be understood as a real threat. One recognisable statement of this performance, however, is the public articulation of discontent directed towards the United States of America. Knowing that Marko is politically well informed and aware of the fact that the attacks on the World Trade Centre are ascribed to the al-Qaeda network and not directly connected with the suicide bombings in the occupied territories, I was even more puzzled by his 'offensive performance' (Goffman 1971). By nonchalantly linking the two realms, he constructed himself as an allegoric figure that represented a macro-community of violence. When I visited him the day after the carnival, Marko proudly showed me a fancy trophy: he had won the first prize in the costume competition.

One might ascribe this carnival episode to the boredom of small-town life, but I rather understand it – as I understand carnival on the whole – as a cultural performance that opens up space for 'an alternative mode of collective behavior' (DaMatta 1991: 62). Carnival and concealing outfits allow statements to emerge and be brought into relationship with socio-political actuality, which in the normal course of events would be invisible or marginal. They are complex manifestations of, and humorous commentaries on, the social world. As a commentary with its multiple dramatisations in which the world is reproduced, choosing a particular carnival costume is a conscious dialectical act that involves many levels and circuits of self-reflection. Victor Turner described the social operation of cultural performances such as Marko's as 'magic mir-

rors, each interpreting as well as reflecting the images beamed on it'
(Turner 1987: 24).

The fact that Marko's costume was widely discussed and awarded
the first prize indicates that he had touched on a vital topic, and communicated it in a manner that people in the town could relate to. He
recognised and creatively utilised the role played through seemingly
irrational and imaginative acts of symbolic communication, in regard
to tackling critical issues in times of socio-political crisis and severe
change. Drawing on mythological notions of martyrdom and self-sacrifice, he assigns his guise an almost sacral character, but at the same
time ironically deconstructs the threatening potential of the weapon
by dancing, drinking, and having fun with 'his rockets'. Whereas a major goal of an actual suicide bomber is to be concealed up to the last
minute, Marko visibly carries his armament on his back. His show can
therefore also be understood as a paradoxical visualisation of secrecy
that contributes to the demystification of faceless terror. For a better
understanding of this scenario of 'imagined suicide', it is important to
note that it takes place in a post-war community where violence is a
widespread means of communication, and where openly aggressive
behaviour – particularly among male youngsters – is even perceived
as prestigious.

The social context that is interpreted and reflected in Marko's performance is largely defined by war violence and its manifold consequences.
Suicide is not an unusual phenomenon in post-war Croat society. Increasing rates of suicides committed by ex-combatants, and also noticeably mounting violent behaviour against others by this group, keeps
startling the public. In Croatia, since the end of the war in 1995, more
than thirteen hundred male ex-soldiers have committed suicide.[52] The
authors of the 2004 Annual Report of the Coalition for Work with Psychotrauma and Peace in Croatia state that:

> although there are no reliable statistics available, our impression ...
> is that the number of suicides and suicide attempts continues to rise.
> This was highlighted by the suicide of the leader of the Association of
> Croatian Defenders Suffering from PTSD in November and a report
> on Croatian Television (HRT) that 18 people had committed suicide
> during the first eight days of 2005. (CWWPP 2004)

The situation is made worse by the fact that there is hardly any or
no outreach of psychological assistance or suicide prevention work
for *branitelji* in rural areas. Natalija Bašić notes that 'many combatants hoped for a post-war status comparable to those of soldiers who

had fought in the Second World War – i.e. public prestige, privileges, careers and reputable positions in the military, public sector or in politics' (Bašić 2004a: 107, my translation). Few of them, however, are now even entitled to subsidies, war pensions or other forms of public support, let alone careers or public recognition. And although the case of the *branitelji* is widely recognised in the media and various (mostly nationalistic) political parties use their fate for propaganda, very little is actually done for ex-combatants in terms of social and professional reintegration, financial support and health care.[53] The situation is made worse by the fact that there is little or no outreach in terms of psychological assistance for *branitelji* in rural areas. This neglect causes especially visible long-term harm at the family level. The most frequent socio-psychological problems associated with war-induced distress are suicide and suicide attempts, alcoholism, drug abuse and a notable increase in domestic violence (cf. Bašić 2004a; Schäuble 2006). It is known that 'structural violence – the violence of poverty, hunger, social exclusion and humiliation – inevitably translates back into intimate and domestic violence' (Scheper-Hughes and Bourgois 2004: 1). The 2003 United Nations report of the Commission for Human Rights states that, 'there is evidence to suggest that the currently high levels of family and community-based violence in Croatia are directly related to the ongoing impact of the armed conflict' (Coomaraswamy 2003: 353). A 2007 psychological study on secondary traumatisation conducted in Rijeka found that one-third of wives of Croatian *branitelji* treated for PTSD were themselves traumatised (Frančišković et al. 2007). They met the criteria for secondary traumatisation defined as 'stress by providing help, or wishing to help, and offering emotional support to a traumatized person' (ibid.: 178), developed almost identical symptoms to the diagnostic criteria for PTSD (i.e. insomnia, nightmares, irritability, chronic fatigue, etc.), and were just as susceptible to drug abuse as the veterans themselves. The number of those who continue to suffer from the consequences of war is still on the rise and poses one of the most urgent domestic problems for Croatia.

When I asked Marko's father Joško, an eloquent man in his mid-sixties, what he thought the reasons were for the increased violence and suicides amongst branitelji, he answered:

> They have fought for Croatia, you know, and now they see that the government is selling the whole country to foreigners. Our politicians are corrupt and put everything in their own pockets. Well, maybe that's not the main reason for the suicides, but it's still an important

factor. Aggression [is the main reason]. It's against our mentality to be aggressive and to kill people. And many soldiers feel their conscience (*savjest*) now and all those images emerge. I have talked to many *branitelji* who told me that they have constant nightmares. Once it starts, you can't control it.

From the first part of Joško's comment one can infer a genuine critique of current politics and the lack of public recognition regarding the achievements of the *branitelji*. In addition, Joško explicitly contests the stereotype of the Balkans as having a 'culture of violence'. The statement that 'it's against our mentality to be aggressive and to kill' indicates dissociation from violent war crimes. But at the same time, comments like Joško's form a sharp contrast to the public image of the *branitelji* as brave and intrepid defenders of the homeland. The social reality of the majority of veterans in post-war Croatia is embedded in the contradictory context of rhetorical glorification on the one side, and low social status as well as suppressed feelings of guilt on the other side.

The Mimetic Implications of 'Imagined Suicide'

In an interview that took place a few months after the carnival episode, Marko drew an utterly depressing picture of his situation. He thought of himself as unpredictable and potentially dangerous when 'those memories and feelings get out of control'. He referred to himself as a 'ticking time-bomb', indicating that he was afraid of this 'untamed power' that lurked within his body. The war, he said, destroyed his life, and he felt that he had sacrificed his health, his education and career prospects as well as his hope for a better future – all in order to recognise now that he has been let down by the very state he fought for.

In his article 'Involuntary Commemorations', Jo Stanley has pointed out that personal memories and experiences of soldiers suffering from 'post-traumatic stress disorder' often do not coincide with the official historiography or the version of history communicated in commemorative speeches. He writes:

[T]his illness that was once called shell shock or battle fatigue, is often experienced chaotically at home in the depths of the night. Clinical experience reveals that PTSD is a total bodily, intellectual and emotional experience. And this privatized and non-chosen remembrance of combat can have more to do with deeply private feelings of shame, guilt and a personal sense of defeat than with pride – however glorious the battle was, or is said to have been, in public histories and popular memory. (Stanley 2000: 241)

This analysis corresponds to my evaluation of Marko's current situation, for whom the commentaries of politicians or official commemorations praising the heroic service of the *branitelji* or Croatia's independence must sound like an utter mockery.

I am not implying that by dressing up as a suicide bomber Marko is claiming to be a potential terrorist or hinting at actually planning to commit suicide. Rather, I suggest reading his performance in terms of the concept of mimesis. Drawing on Erich Auerbach's (1967) concept of mimesis, the difference between the performer and the performed is as much a prerequisite for mimetic imitation as it is an attempt to eliminate difference, to integrate the other, or even to transform oneself into the other. The French philosopher Roger Caillois writes that in mimetic productions, and through the use of masks in general, officiants are transformed into

> all types of terrifying and creative supernatural powers ... He [the individual] temporarily reincarnates, mimics, and identifies with these frightful powers ... The situation has now become reversed. It is he who inspires fear through his possessing this terrible and inhuman power. It was sufficient for him merely to put on the mask that he himself made, to don the costume that he sewed, in order to resemble the revered and feared being and to produce a weird drone with the aid of a secret weapon, the bull-roarer, of which he alone has known the existence, character, operation, and function ... At the time of the festival, dancing ritual and pantomime are only preliminary. This prelude incites an increasing excitement. Vertigo then takes the place of simulation. As the Cabala warns, one becomes a ghost in playing a ghost. (Caillois [1961] 1979: 87)

Transferring this concept to Marko's 'play', the 'terrible and inhuman power' would refer less to terrorism itself than to the violence he has experienced during war and still experiences within his own body in the form of recurrent panic attacks.[54] By dressing up as a suicide bomber, Marko – on a symbolic level – personifies his worst fear, namely turning into a dangerous time bomb. It is also significant to note that after having served in a missile defence unit, he transforms himself into a 'living' missile. He becomes the hostile power that jeopardises his mental and physical health.

Inverting Immobility

The attacks in New York, Djerba, Madrid, London, Istanbul and elsewhere have shown that 'terrorist violence' is organised in a global network that stretches across borders and is not bound to the country of origin of the executors or the people behind the assaults. On 9 September 2001, Mohammed Atta and his fellow combatants boarded the four American Airlines aircrafts and transcended the scope of locally restricted agency. Marko, on the contrary, experiences that he is inevitably bound to the place where he is born. Due to his trauma-related symptoms, unemployment and his consequent lack of money, he is spatially as well as socially immobile. His 'missile-backpack', which startlingly resembles a futuristic 'jet-pack', seems like the materialisation of a dream of expanded mobility on an individual level.

When asked what he hoped or wished for – for himself as well as for his country – Marko simply answered, 'to be left in peace'. On a personal level this statement indicates that he feels most comfortable when wandering alone in the mountains and does not have to interact socially with other people. Large crowds of people terrify him. On a broader level, he said, he was hoping for Croatia's independence from international politics, particularly from U.S. foreign policy and from demands by the European Union.

My interlocutors in Sinj described most countries of the Western hemisphere as 'materialist, without morals, and, worst of all, without faith' – a perception that prevails not only in rural Croatia but also in vast areas of former Yugoslavia (cf. Čolović 2002). Along with the threat of the growing influence of global forces, this view is increasingly shared in many underprivileged parts of the world. I do not claim that such discontent leads in any direct way into terrorism. However, the concept of martyrdom as a 'fantasy ideology' that suggests moral superiority might at least facilitate this association. However, writes Joseph Croitoru:

> martyr status [is but] one piece of a jigsaw that facilitates the readiness to commit a suicide attack. It equally requires a patriarchal society that preserved a pre-modern war epic and a code of honour of tribal origin as well as a constant national suppression, in which the deprivation of rights and humiliation by a militarily superior enemy have become a cruel routine. Against this backdrop the suicide attack turns into a corporative ritual that is intended to signal steeliness. (Croitoru 2003: 12f., my translation)

Martyrs signify immortality and immunity. This inviolability stands in opposition to many young Croatian men's current experiences of vulnerability and 'demasculinisation' through the loss of their socially ascribed role as breadwinner. 'I can't marry and have my own family as long as I have no job and earn no money of my own', says Marko. The widespread deprofessionalisation obstructs the reconstruction of (male) identity in post-war settings (cf. Bašić 2004a, 2004b; Blagojević 2004). Marko's case illustrates that the immediate effects of the war are gendered, and so are the reactions regarding war-induced socio-economic disruptions and subsequent practices of conflict resolution.[55]

Masculinity, Combat and (Post-)Modernity

Many veterans in former Yugoslavia have reported that violence plays an increasingly important role in their personal conflict behaviour (Bašić 2004a: 107; Blagojević 2004: 77). In this respect it might be dangerous to underestimate such cultural performances as Marko's symbolic staging of a suicide mission – in which he turns his own body into a weapon – as harmless playful gestures, particularly since numerous ex-combatants in the former Yugoslavia still own different kinds of guns, along with live ammunition, as there has been no official disarmament or demobilisation in Croatia. Dozens of recently published newspaper reports refer to incidents with ex-soldiers who either used their weapons to kill themselves or to solve private conflicts violently.

Rob Nixon writes of the psychological and socio-political situation of former soldiers in post-war settings: 'The dissipation of the enemy constructs that secured their employment and the waning of the old regimes have rendered many professional soldiers violently insecure, as they ponder fates ranging from tribunals and prison to unemployment and evaporating pensions' (Nixon 1997: 80). In the case of former Yugoslavia this insecurity does not only affect professional military forces, as large parts of the male population aged seventeen to sixty-five were involved in military actions in the war between 1991 and 1995. Like Marko, the majority of young men who joined the army before finishing their education have hardly any opportunity to find qualified work today. Factors such as low economic status, financial dependency, the impression of government-sanctioned injustice as well as the lack of recognition and perspectives contribute to an aggravation of the originally war-inflicted trauma. These men are highly disillusioned and anxiously face the quickly proceeding cultural change along with the impoverishment of their home countries. At first sight they seem to be part of a group of young disillusioned men that Hans Magnus Enzensberger has labelled as 'radical losers' (Enzensberger 2006, my translation). In his essay *Schreckens Männer: Versuch über den radikalen Verlierer* [The Terrorist Mindset: The Radical Loser] he conceptualises a psychogram of people who, as a consequence of continually experienced humiliation and disappointment, eventually turn into perpetrators of violence. Without initially distinguishing between adolescent spree killers and 'organised culprits from the Islamist underground', he lists the search for scapegoats, reality loss, desire for revenge, 'masculinity-mania', despair because of one's own failure, as well as compensatory feelings of superiority, as basic characteristics of the 'radical losers'. According to Enzensberger, the eventual escalation of terror is marked by a 'fusion of destruction and self-destruction and the compulsive wish to control the lives of others as well as one's own death' (Enzensberger 2006: 45, my translation).[56]

Due to their indeterminate state between publicly acknowledged heroism and social oblivion, many Croatian ex-soldiers feel like 'radical losers of the war' and are particularly susceptible to political manipulation. Traumatising experiences in the past, along with a desolate economic situation in the present and unpromising future prospects, repeatedly pave the way for ethnic nationalism, and have proved to lower the threshold for violence – but they do not automatically turn these men into supporters of homogenous violent movements, radical ideologies or conspiracy theories. And although the list of antagonists that Enzensberger quotes – 'Ottomans, French, Britons and Russians' (Enzensberger 2006: 27, 32, my translation), 'foreigners, secret services, Communists, Americans, major corporations, politicians, non-believers …, and Jews' (ibid.: 15, my translation) – is alarmingly similar to the bogeymen of my nationalist interlocutors in Croatia, they are far from being potential 'sleepers' (ibid.). Enzensberger's approach is therefore not directly applicable to a Croatian or post-Yugoslav context, but reveals probable reasons for which politically motivated terror attacks might fascinate young disillusioned men in crisis situations and in crisis regions.

Violence – A Politically Creative Force?

Suicide is one of the loneliest acts imaginable. But for someone like Marko, whose principal wish is to be left in peace, 'imagined suicide' might seem an appealing concept. At the same time, politically motivated suicide, be it real or imagined, secures integration into a communication structure that aims at threatening and actually influencing international politics. Marko's performance can be read as a (playful and ironic) 'vision' that is inspired by previous terrorist acts, attempting to change prevailing power relations. Simultaneously, he might have been dreaming of a social prestige that he, as an unemployed *branitelj*, is denied in real life. Inverting the feeling of being powerless, place-bound and immobile, he symbolically turns himself into a missile-driven superhero. For people who experience political impotence on a daily level, and for whom the capacity to act equals violent action, suicidal terror appears to create the illusion of empowerment (Elwert 2001).

On a socio-political level, this 'vision', as I am trying to illustrate, is not limited to Islamic fundamentalism, as is widely supposed. Rather, it amounts to quasi-millennial imaginations that are grounded in a feeling of moral superiority, in a radically contrasting context of material, socio-economic and political marginality. This sentiment of moral or ethical supremacy is what Croatian and other ex-Yugoslav nationalists have in common with disillusioned, marginalised groups all over the world. Apart from commonly felt political and economic powerlessness, as well as shared feelings of moral superiority, it is the joint perception of this 'disturbing other' that increasingly brings into association otherwise unrelated communities. An additional unifying aspect is the conviction of belonging to the 'radical losers' of history and of suffering from the global hegemony of the United States and their allies (cf. Enzensberger 2006). To highlight the fact that Croatians are just as victimised as other oppressed peoples all over the world, my interlocutors paradoxically compared their situation to that of the Kurds or the Palestinians. My host once said:

> We love our country more than our own blood, more than our life. If we die, we die. So what? You know it is like with the al-Qaeda terrorists or the suicide bombers in Palestine. They hate their occupiers and love their country and their independence more than their lives. They don't care if they die. And that's what makes them so dangerous and that's why the Americans and the Jews can't do anything against them.

This commentary does not indicate that terrorism is approved or serves as a paradigm worth copying, and I am not implying that there is a public acceptance or legitimation of actual assassination attempts; the majority of Croatians are as terrified by the recent terrorist acts as everyone else. Yet the most radical amongst my interlocutors did not conceal their admiration for what they thought were indeed extremist but consequential deeds of the suicide bombers.

In former Yugoslavia, the search for the ones to blame for war and present misery perpetuates desperate visions of (self-destructive) vengeance. Focal points of these vindictive feelings are the United States and Europe, whom many hold responsible for prior wrongs in Croatia and for not having intervened early enough during the last war. Mile Krajina, a Croatian folk musician and composer of new epic songs, puts it as follows:

> *Fierce war rages waged in Croatia*
> *While Western Europe is silent ...*
> *Land of Europe, may you be damned*
> *For letting the Serbs commit crimes,*
> *Open your doors to Orthodoxy,*
> *Place a tight noose around your neck.*
> *Now you yourselves will lose your heads,*
> *The Thames and Seine will fill with blood.*
> (Krajina 1994: 42, quoted and translated in Čolović 2002: 44)

Not unlike Marko's 'message', this song expresses the bitterness that is felt vis-à-vis the supposed let down. It also contains a symbolic threat, hinting at the fact that there would indeed be enough willing personnel to take revenge for endured injustice.[57] Given a retaliatory attitude, revenge – and suicide as a vigorous means of revenge – may constitute a radical and violent response to emotions of powerlessness or futility. In order to approach the 'rationale' behind suicide missions, suicide should therefore be understood not so much as an act of self-killing, but in terms of self-sacrifice. When regarded as sacrifice, through which the suffering and discrimination of the whole community can be annulled or avenged by a hero's donation of his own life, suicide might be considered a highly sociable act.

Drawing upon an existentialist legacy, Edmund Leach described violence as a wide-ranging productive power to imagine and bring about socio-political change: '[A]ll creativity, whether it is the work of the artist or the scholar or even of the politician, contains within it a deep-rooted hostility to the system as it is' (Leach 1977: 20). Along these lines, to dream up a suicide assault can be understood as a highly violent and (self-)destructive yet resourceful, imaginative act, which aims at changing 'things as they are' on an individual psychological as well as on a socio-political level (Jackson 1996).

I argue that one of the main prerequisites for 'imagining suicide' in relation to violent terrorist action is the prevalence of mythological notions and narratives of martyrdom, based on the self-righteous assumption of moral superiority in a context of radically divergent socio-economic and political marginalisation. Self-sacrifice and martyrdom are historically developed cultural conceptions of Judaeo-Christian origin, which are recklessly underestimated but gradually prosper in societies in which the fascination with violence as a politically creative force prevails.

War Veterans, Defenders of the Homeland

The rebuilding of the Croatian nation-state since the end of the war went hand in hand with an evocation of the potency of Croatian nationhood and references to the heroic deeds of Croatian soldiers. This glorification of military fortitude is usually described in terms of gender and physical attributes. Žarkov points out that in Croatian media representations, during the war and in its immediate aftermath, the male Croatian body was portrayed as unharmed and intact, whereas the (male) bodies of enemies – Serbs and Muslims – were either bestialised or depicted as mutilated and abused.

> The Croat man's unquestionable heterosexuality and unchallenged masculine power are symbolized in his absence from the narrative of rape and castration. The absence is what renders Croat nationhood potent and the Croat state powerful; the masculine power of the merging nation state is thus preserved in the unity and permanence of the manly bodies of Croat men. (Žarkov 2007: 166)

The self-perception of many *branitelji* however, is diametrically opposed to these representations of strength and integrity in the public media. Instead of celebrated armed defenders and liberators of the homeland, many ex-soldiers like Marko feel victimised and not able-bodied at all.

Marko feels not only victimised by the war itself but also by the political and economic measures taken to reconstruct Croatia, which in his view penalise and exclude war veterans. Moreover, his statement that he feels let down by the very country he had fought for, powerfully expresses the disillusionment that the ex-combatants of all former Yugoslav republics have in common (cf. Bougarel 2007). When showing me a picture of himself in an army uniform at the age of eighteen, Marko sarcastically remarked: 'Look at him. He looks like a boy. He did not even grow a proper beard back then'. First of all, it is of course striking that he refers to himself in the third person. The 'boy' in the picture seems so distant to Marko, that he dissociates his present (more mature and more 'manly') self from him. The comment refers to the innocence and naivety of many young combatants when first joining the army that stands in stark contrast to the reality of actual warfare. On a personal level, Marko – unlike many others of his peers – acknowledges that the boy in the picture is no longer innocent and now knows what armed combat involves.

Like Marko, many other *branitelji* who had once devotedly fought for Croatia's independence feel betrayed and forsaken today. The humiliating experience that their 'sacrifice' is not sufficiently appreciated – along with the hope for social and personal regeneration – causes many of the Croatian ex-combatants to draw on figures like Ante Gotovina whose commitment to the homeland is, despite all official accusations, more than ever acknowledged as heroic by the Croatian public. Although the majority of *branitelji* might conceive of themselves as the losing party in this war, they clearly do not identify themselves as war criminals. Gotovina's subsequently annulled lawful conviction for war crimes, however, entailed the admission of a Croatian war debt and thus deprived a majority of *branitelji* of the legitimate basis for their military actions. An important decision like this was not easily handed over to a foreign court and thus constituted one of the main reasons why only very few Croats recognised the ICTY as a juridical authority. It is in this context that the desire for socially accepted heroes who are able to represent and to restore the cracked image of the 'male warrior' takes shape.

Despite the complaints of many *branitelji* that their efforts for the homeland are not sufficiently rewarded, Janine N. Clark in her article 'Giving Peace a Chance: Croatia's *Branitelji* and the Imperative of Reintegration' argues that the payment of 'generous pensions to many (but by no means all) war veterans has hampered the latter's reintegration and, by extension, their potential to play a more constructive role in society' (Clark 2013b: 1932). Referring to statistics from the Croatian Pension Insurance Agency and a report by the European Network of Economic Policy Research Institutes (ENEPRI) she discerns that the average Homeland War veteran's pension is almost three times higher than the average pension in Croatia and that the expenses for the protection system for war veterans and their family members represent around 1.5 per cent of GDP (ibid.; see also Bađun 2009).[58] And although I agree with Clark that veterans in the former Yugoslavia should not just be perceived as 'security threats' or financial burdens but have instead the potential to fulfil a variety of socially valuable roles, for example as peace builders, I do not agree with her assessment that the payment of government pensions necessarily diminishes incentives for *branitelji* to seek employment or to 'reintegrate' into society. Given that as many as 80 per cent of war veterans who are eligible for pension receive disability pensions it is self-evident that many of them are simply not fit to work. It is therefore not so much the fact that the payment of pensions pushes them out of the labour market, as a recent World Bank report suggested, but that they cannot compete in the labour market due to their health impairments (World Bank 2011: 15). The quality of life of many of them is severely reduced and their social realities very often do not allow for an independent bearing of living expenses, even if they would prefer to work rather than live off the state (see also Braš et al. 2011). But as long as there are no jobs or labour conditions suitable for invalid or otherwise impaired *branitelji*, and no incentives for employers and companies to employ potentially inoperative veterans, attempts to reintegrate them into the labour market grasps at nothing. Furthermore, not every ex-combatant benefits from the pension scheme, and the same World Bank report suggests that the number of those who actually receive pensions falls far short of the total veteran population (World Bank 2011: 15). Many of the young, unmarried *branitelji* whom I know personally had to move back in with their parents because their pension was not sufficient to pay rent, let alone found and sustain a family. Others suffered so much from chronic pains or trauma-related symptoms that they had to be looked after by their families due to a lack of (or suspicion towards) medical facilities. Still others are compensated with inappropriate arrangements. The lessor of my small studio in Sinj, for example, a 35-year-old ex-combatant, was given the apartment as compensation (instead of a state pension). His trauma-related tremor and other movement disorders, however, were so strong, that he could not live by himself and could hence not make use of the assigned place. Others, who were given apartments in the same newly constructed building, could not move in because of the lack of a disability lift and other handicap-suited features. To my knowledge, more than half of the building stands empty to the present day due to such incompetence from official quarters.

But I nevertheless argue that the fact that these veterans receive a small pension or other forms of compensation from the state – after long and often painful and absurd processes of having to prove their disabilities and/or traumatisation – has not per se reduced the appeal of re-entering the job market or actively participating in society. On the contrary, the appreciation they receive through the (albeit ever so small) pensions or commutation payments might in many cases prevent an even stronger sense of incapability and/or reduce the feeling of being let down by the very country they had risked (and often ruined) their lives for. Payment of pensions alone is not enough, of course, and the implementation of many more incentives and initiatives that meet the various differing needs of individual *branitelji* are required.

Reports on thousands of 'fake' veterans (*Neue Züricher Zeitung*, 13 April 2010; *Croatian Times*, 14 April 2010) and coverage of numerous people who had bribed their doctors to receive disability certificates and hence (higher) pensions (Hedl 2002) have not helped the cause of those *branitelji* and their families who genuinely suffer from the consequences of the war. Public trust in the veterans as well as the national budget have suffered greatly from these fraud cases, and it should be a priority of the Croatian Ministry of the Families, Veteran's Affairs and Intergenerational Solidarity to set the record straight and restore the credibility of Homeland War veterans. In my view, disillusioned and frustrated veterans, whether they are unionised or operating individually, pose a threat to the development of civil society in post-war Croatia and potentially obstruct peace-building processes in the region. As long as the vicious circle of simultaneous blame, (self-)heroisation, (self-)vindication and (self-)victimisation in discourses concerning Croatian *branitelji* and their military actions is not broken up, the perception will prevail that their military deeds and their suffering are sacrosanct sacrifices upon which Croatia's independence is built and will depend on in the future; this again sustains an atmosphere of imminent hazard and promotes the glorification of a militarised (martyred) masculinity, long after the end of the war.

I do not argue against a cut in veterans' pensions and privileges out of fear for neglect of the 'dignity of the Homeland War' (Hedl 2002), as many right-wing Croats and veterans' organisations see things. If anything, I am convinced that a further neglect of or public distrust in *branitelji* would contribute to their disillusionment and their political radicalisation. The self-victimisation discourse of *branitelji* in contemporary post-war Croatia is not only harmful to civil society and reconciliation, but is also destructive for the veterans' own self-image. However, I agree with Clark that it is not reasonable to maintain the status quo by simply continuing to pay pensions to (some) veterans but not undertake any further outreach. Agendas such as the Programme of Professional Training and Employment of Croatian Veterans, implemented by the HDZ government in 2001, were first steps in the right direction. But these initiatives were not comprehensive or systematic enough, and did not for the most part reach the veterans living in rural areas. Personally, I cherish great expectations in the new centre-left Kukuriku coalition. Their general programme, called Plan 21, contains a whole section on Homeland War veterans in which they pronounce an individualisation and decentralisation in dealing with veterans' requirements and recognise the importance of fully reintegrating *branitelji* back into society (Kukuriku 2011: 30–32; see Clark 2013b: 1942–45). The four parties that constitute the coalition are aware of the sceptical attitude of most of the currently over two hundred veterans' organisations towards centre-left and centrist politics, and Plan 21 strives to reassure veterans and the general public that their policy will 'respect and protect the dignity and importance of the Homeland War' (Kukuriku 2011). The plan stresses a number of times that veterans will be *respected* and that the assumption of collective responsibility for committed atrocities during the Homeland War is rejected; notably, however, the notion that individual Croats have committed war crimes is not denied per se. Furthermore, the coalition calls it 'unforgivable' that more than fifteen years after the end of the Homeland War many issues concerning *branitelji* remain unresolved, and criticises the untargeted subsidies of the HDZ government that, according to Plan 21, lacked a preventive character and had no long-term coherent beneficial effect for Croatian defenders. Instead, their programme focuses on employment incentives for veterans, a revised health and social care plan, as well as a modified housing scheme.

First of all, Plan 21 envisions changes in the legislation to facilitate the employment of veterans in key sectors such as agriculture, tourism and the economy, and includes plans to subsidise the private sector and small cooperatives to allow for greater employment of veterans. The employment plan includes specific training programmes, advanced education and participation in social activities which aim at reducing early retirement amongst veterans and promoting them as 'citizens [who are] truly socially integrated into a modern and European Croatia' (Kukuriku 2011: 31). Secondly, the new health-care plan includes regimes adapted for the specific needs of *branitelji* (addiction treatment, psychological support, suicide prevention, socio-pedagogical family assistance, etc.), along with the establishment of so-called 'regional socio-health centres for veterans' to reach *branitelji* in remote regions. Thirdly, the plan allows for increased budget funds for housing and co-financing schemes regarding veterans' housing units, with the objective to 'avoid the ghettoisation of veterans'. Furthermore, the policy implementation for veterans according to Plan 21 will be decentralised to guarantee a more effective coordination and to encourage the active participation of local and regional governments. Last but not least, the coalition will publish a register of war veterans to expose fake *branitelji* and to 'establish a new symbolic recognition of war heroes and victims' (Kukuriku 2011: 32). This will not only reduce the strain on the state budget but also aims at restoring public trust in the veterans. In my opinion, these suggestions are all important measures to counter the marginalisation of *branitelji* and eventually surmount a backward-looking, war-based self-conception of veterans in favour of an active participation in civil society. Clark also rightly stresses the importance of enabling veterans 'to take pride in what they are doing *today* rather than in what they did in the 1990s'

(Clark 2013b: 1944). This all sounds rather promising and time will tell if the government will succeed in implementing support for veterans that fulfils their specific needs and is widely accepted and made use of, without entirely alienating those who criticise the privileged status of *branitelji* in contemporary Croatian society.

A further strategy would be to support and promote community-based initiatives, such as that of a group of wives of veterans who first founded an unofficial club in Zagreb and later became the first registered Center for Families of Veterans with PTSD, and have about three thousand members today (Cartier 2008; see also Clark 2013b). Other promising initiatives include 'Inicijativa izgradnje mira i suradnje' (IZMIR), an initiative that generates dialogue between members of various veterans' and victims' associations on the one side and peace and human rights activists on the other. Since the mid-2000s, IZMIR has organised seminars and workshops that foster dialogue between groups whose perceptions of the nature of the Homeland War could hardly be more dissimilar. Some of the meetings even bring veterans from Croatia and from Serbia together. Miriam Schroer-Hippel has evaluated this and other initiatives involving ex-combatants, and convincingly demonstrates how veterans are successfully encouraged to take up new roles as active participants in civil society that go far beyond safeguarding the reputation of the Homeland War (Schroer-Hippel 2011). In the long term, such initiatives can not only contribute to advancing the peace-building role of ex-combatants, but also help to avert a naturalisation of militarised concepts of masculinity and provide alternative models of masculine identities in post-conflict societies.

Brothers and Sisters in Arms, or the Gender of Heroism

Male soldiers' experiences and uses of violence on the battlefield – and I understand violence not only in terms of mere physicality, but also as assaults on the dignity and personhood of the victim (Scheper-Hughes and Bourgois 2004: 1) – pose a social problem beyond the immediate period of the war, and impede the reintegration of veterans into post-war society. Nancy Wingfield and Maria Bucur write that

> [m]ale combatants participated in … wars to fulfil their traditional obligations of protecting women at home and living up to masculine norms of heroism. But their experiences of death, destruction, and disempowerment forced men to question their *own* masculinity while reinforcing the link between masculinity and violence. The intensity of their traumatic experiences – as witnesses, victimizers, and victims

– rendered at least some combatants unable to reconnect with the women and men who lived through the war on the home front. (Wingfield and Bucur 2006: 6f.)

The different levels of violence and moral degradation that soldiers and civilians experienced during the war affected the post-war reunification with returning family members and informed the differences between women's and men's remembrances of wartime experiences. As a rule, the fighting front is equated with the masculine and the home front with the feminine, thus following traditional notions of gendered division of responsibilities and substantiating attributions of heroism and sacrifice embedded in this dichotomy. The everyday reality of war at the home front, however, proved to be rather different. Women often had to take masculine roles and began to question established gender roles in civilian life, whereas male combatants saw their obligations as masculine defenders confirmed. Upon their return, however, they had to redefine their gender roles and justify their participation in the war. 'Veterans turned participation into an important element for separating "true" men from the rest, thus upending traditional masculine class and educational hierarchies. Although populist, men's combat experience narrowed the field of masculine prowess' (Wingfield and Bucur 2006: 6). In dissociation from male civilians and women's home front experiences, male soldiers tend to reinforce warfare as a masculine norm. As one of the consequences, traumatic experiences of male soldiers are often downplayed and their (self-)destructive potential underestimated, as traumatic and post-traumatic disorders are commonly associated with vulnerability and a lack of control.[59] In a comparable manner, veterans' economic vulnerability is publicly denied and social assistance refused; although male ex-combatants continue to be celebrated as war heroes in contemporary post-war Croatian society, they cease in many cases to be the actual heads of households or the breadwinners. In this sense, the gender struggles of men and women diametrically diverge and affect the post-war restoration of gender order accordingly.

The situation of women – and particularly that of female soldiers – turned out to be completely different. I have earlier mentioned the invisibility of women Partisan fighters in public post–Second World War discourse, and registered that individual heroic deeds of women did not have the same national scope as men's. This neglect recurred in the case of women soldiers who joined national armies and paramilitary units between 1991 and 1995 (cf. Žarkov 2007). Women working as military personnel in the Croatian army during the Homeland War did not receive due attention in public discourse or media reports during the war, nor are their achievements on the battlefield adequately remembered in post-war society.[60]

Dubravka Žarkov has analysed the public image of female soldiers, and states that 'beauty, serenity, and sadness follow women soldiers as [an] important element of their representation. Their decision to become – and to remain soldiers – [has] often [been] attached to their sadness at the fate of their country, their people, or their immediate famil[ies]' (Žarkov 2007: 192). Such depictions underline the victim status of Croatia and serve as an illustration of Croatian women's disposition to self-sacrifice as well as their ability to suffer (ibid.: 193f.). In preference to mentioning the combative spirit of female Croatian soldiers and reporting on women pilots and snipers, the rare press reports rather emphasised female soldiers' domestic skills and ascribed them auxiliary tasks such as nursing and administration. Women who actually fought on the front lines are generally 'poorly integrated into the popular narrative of the wars. They literally stand outside the mainstream', as Wingfield and Bucur discern. Female combatants are therefore less able to challenge traditional gender roles, and women's wartime heroism is mainly confined to their temporary maintenance activities on the home front.

In an interview I conducted in 2005 with a then 36-year-old female ex-soldier called Rajka, it became apparent that the war has had an enormous impact on gendered identities and family structures. Rajka was in her early twenties and the mother of a four-year-old daughter when she volunteered to join the Croatian army in 1992. She was positioned on the immediate front line in Pakrac and her battalion was one of the last to return after the ceasefire. Today, Rajka is engaged in feminist peace activism and she has recently been helping to set up a therapeutic centre for traumatised *branitelji*.

In the first part of our conversation, Rajka confirmed the dominance of normative gender roles during combat by drawing on the concept of the male protector. 'The commander was worried because of me. He said that he was afraid because ten men of the division were looking after me instead of looking after themselves. They could easily get killed this way. Not looking at me as a woman, as an object, I mean, but they were looking after me and took care so that nothing would happen to me,' she said. Later, however, when I asked how gender might influence modes of dealing with the effects of warfare, Rajka drew attention to the radical transformation of gender roles and responsibilities in the post-war setting.

> M: Is there also a difference in how women and men deal with events after the war – with what they have seen, what they went through?

R: It depends on the individual, not on the fact if someone is a man or a woman. Because it's – this differentiation only exists, because there were many more male soldiers … It is a personal thing much more than … But I do believe that women are subtler. This is what teaches us to think differently – to see the things that men don't see. This makes things easier … Women have other priorities than men. It makes them just more … they can manage better in their lives, adjust better. They can heal these wounds much sooner. The inner wounds, I mean. Men give themselves the right to be very disappointed. But women usually just find a way to survive. That is the main difference. Emotion-wise there is not much difference; just the way you manifest your feelings outside. These ways are different.

M: It's interesting that you chose the image of a man falling down earlier – and now you say that men allow themselves to be disappointed, because you seem to have this concept of women always getting up and keeping going.

R: I didn't 'choose' the image. It is just what I see every day. Too many men gave up. For instance, Croatia has many divorces – especially after the war. In these divorces, women take care of the rest of the family, of the children … The men might support them financially, but it is the women who survive. There are only very few men who are different … which just proves that my image is the real image.

The war created radically different social contexts for men and women;[61] the effect on family organisation and the division of labour that Rajka delineates here reveals a gender imbalance that is a common indicator for instability within post-war societies (cf. Slapšak 2004). The counterpart to Rajka's description of women as the main caretakers and providers is the physical, psychological and/or economic situation of many male *branitelji* that precludes them from accomplishing the classic masculine role, namely taking care of and supporting a family. Like most wars, the Homeland War disturbed previously valid masculinity constructions and led to a commotion of gender identities. Marko, for example, made this dilemma clear when he said that he could not marry and have a family of his own unless he earns his own money. His concern matches many young men's current experiences of vulnerability and emasculation through the loss of their socially ascribed role as breadwinner.[62] Economic crisis, rising unemployment and financial insecurity all obstruct the reconstruction of secure post-war male identities, and many men – not just in Croatia but in the whole of the former Yugoslavia – increasingly draw on the reassertion of traditionalist militarised masculinity (cf. Bašić 2004a, 2004b; Blagojević 2004, Schäuble 2006). Compensatory and defensive male identification, however, impedes the reformation of balanced gender relations and has frequently turned out to be rather self-destructive.

Referring to the 'economic emasculation' in post-Yugoslav societies, Marko Živković notes that

> [t]he road to the kind of masculinity that comes from the ability of the male to provide, to act confidently as the breadwinner, is now cut off for a sizable portion of the population. This precipitates a 'crisis of masculinity' that offers a fertile ground for nationalist re-traditionalizers advocating a return to 'real manhood' and denouncing all the sissies, fags and other emasculated men. Most ominously, such an economic emasculation means that another traditional venue for regaining masculinity gains in appeal – going to war. (Živković 2006: 259)

The erosion of the traditional male role as economic provider had already commenced earlier due to 'women's legal and social emancipation and their increased ability to earn an income' (Miličević 2006: 271) during the socialist period. This, among numerous other factors, previously facilitated nationalist retraditionalisation and recruitment devices, and Jalušić notes, that 'sustaining a warrior's and a heroic identity was a means for the "remasculinization" of men (feminized under communist rule)' (Jalušić 2004: 54). In my opinion, the 'crisis of masculinity' has currently reached another height that is comparable to, or possibly even worse than, the one in the late 1980s.

Changing Masculinities in a Globalising Context

In this chapter I have tried to demonstrate that the ways in which masculinity is experienced and expressed in post-war Croatia continue to be closely linked to notions of self-defence and self-sacrifice. Men habitually represent and identify themselves as protectors of a victimised (and thus 'feminised') nation. The rationalisation of (male) violent behaviour as self-defence operates as a comparatively effective means to quieten the dark side of collective memory and the feeling of guilt – individual as well as communal.

American sociologist Michael Kimmel has written extensively on (post-)modern masculinities and the impact of global changes on gender regimes. He is convinced that

> [g]lobalization disrupts and reconfigures traditional, neo-colonial, or other national, regional or local economic, political and cultural arrangements. In so doing, globalization transforms local articulations of both domestic and public patriarchy ... [P]rocesses of globalization, and the emergence of a global hegemonic masculinity, has [sic] the ironic effect of increasingly 'gendering' local, regional and national resistance to incorporation into the global arena as subordinated entities. (Kimmel 2002: 24)

Kimmel's notion of 'gendered' resistance to processes of globalisation and global hegemonic masculinities mainly alludes to revitalised forms of ethnic nationalism and religious fundamentalism.

> These religious and ethnic expressions are often manifest as gender revolts, and include a virulent resurgence of domestic patriarchy (as in the militant misogyny of Iran and Afghanistan); the problematization of global masculinities or neighbouring masculinities (as in the former Yugoslavia); and the overt symbolic effort to claim a distinct 'manhood' along religious or ethnic lines to which others do not have access and which will restore manhood. (Kimmel 2002: 26)

The restoration of domestic patriarchy and normative concepts of 'manhood' can, according to Kimmel, be deployed as a form of regional refusal to go along with the incorporation into the global arena. I argue that Kimmel's analysis is directly applicable to the Croatian – or moreover the post-Yugoslav – case where the resurgence of a militarised masculinity is mobilised as a resource against overbearing external influences and global change.

The mass protests against the prosecution of Croatian ex-generals as well as the severity of the anti-EU campaigns illustrate that the road to membership of the European Union posed a severe threat to Croatian national identification.[63] The fact that these campaigns were highly gendered and that the assumed opponents were frequently endowed with pejorative feminine attributes demonstrates the 'visible ethnonationalism coupled with anti-feminist ... politicking' (Verdery 1996: 79) that many East and South-East European countries have commonly featured since the end of socialism. The re-rationalisation and return to long-established values such as family life (with the women's place ideally at home) and religion contained therein also illustrates that the lost authority of men in nuclear families is closely associated with the vulnerability of the newly established Croatian state. The state's weakness and susceptibility to 'Western liberalism', then, necessitates a new patriarchy based on a quickly mobilisable masculine protection force.

It has become apparent throughout the previous chapters that Croatia is a society in which the posture of strength and indomitability tends to be a defining feature of masculine identity – although 'masculine bravado' (Kimmel 2000: 245) varies considerably from one place to another amongst the post-Yugoslav republics. The dominant role of battle and military discourses in everyday post-war reality constructs masculinity and femininity as polar opposites and excites a long-term imbalance of gender relations. This dichotomy – that implies militancy and combat readiness as a national duty of men, and reproduction as the main female civic responsibility – obstinately prevails. Although readiness for combat is only hypothetical, the impression that Croatia is potentially endangered, and in need of (male) protection against foreign influences, perseveres. Nowadays, however, the strict EU directives, the ICTY verdicts, and NATO authority are perceived to be more threatening than the antagonisms with neighbouring countries. The modern day heroes' task is to defend Croatia's national sovereignty against international aggressors who seek to 'erase our history, condemn our freedom and remove from our memories the proud days of the struggle for a free Croatia', as ex-general Janko Bobetko put it (HINA News Agency, 20 September 2002; see also Peskin and Boduszynski 2003: 39).

By and large, masculinity in Croatia continues to be constructed as militarised masculinity. The armed forces continue to play a dominant role – be it as an important employer for young men, in private discussions and public political debates on the role of the *branitelji*, or simply by its ubiquitous visual presence. Military socialisation is still perceived as a vital rite of passage into male adulthood, and conscientious objectors are habitually characterised as 'unpatriotic cowards' or 'wimps'.[64] The image of the indispensable gentleman hero, however, is a construct that neither corresponds to the social reality of the majority of the war veterans, nor to that of the numerous women who have become central figures in all aspects of reconstructing the ravaged country. And even if feminist scholars like Cynthia Enloe and Jamie Munn might be sceptical about the option of 'decoupling nationalism and masculinity when the state-building process is still fresh and yet to be completed' (Munn 2006: 300; Enloe 1989: 64ff.), I am nonetheless convinced that a sensible redefinition of masculinity – disengaged from ethno-nationalist and religious rhetoric as well as from a prescribed overdose of 'masculine bravado' – would contribute to the post-war reconstruction and reconciliation process in the Balkan region.

Notes

1. A shorter version of this chapter was published under the title 'Contested Masculinities' (Schäuble 2009: 169–97). This was of course not only the case in Croatia, but in the nationalistic currents of all other republics in the former Yugoslavia as well.

2. For a detailed analysis of the changing role of Croatian mothers – from the beginning of the war and the pacifist movements of Croatian mothers called 'Wall of Love' who demonstrated for the release their sons from JNA army barracks, through the promotion of the image of the mother-saint who willingly sacrifices her sons for the nation, to the figure of the mother-victim who has been raped, become a refugee, or lost her children in the course of the war – see Skokić 2001: 201–12 and Žarkov 2007: 41–82.

3. In a referendum held in December 2013, 65% of Croatians voted to change the definition of marriage in the constitution to apply exclusively to 'a living union of a woman and man'. The referendum was allowed parliamentary scrutiny after a Catholic group called *U ime obitelji* [In the Name of the Family] collected almost 700,000 signatures to outlaw same-sex marriage. The supporters of the referendum – backed by the Catholic Church and right-wing parties – allege that the model of the Croatian family is under threat. The discriminatory and homophobic poll results must be considered a major victory for Croatia's conservatives and religious fundamentalists.

4. A former female soldier, who went from three packets of cigarettes a day during the war to non-smoking after the end of the war, told me that 'the cigarette industry was the main sponsor of the war – we wouldn't have lasted otherwise'.

5. Phenomenological approaches are based on the observation that in everyday life experience is characterised by the non-awareness of our bodies. The return of the body into consciousness in disease, pain, distress or dysfunction automatically turns our attention to the negative (Leder 1990: 127; see also Csordas 1994: 8). In this sense, the ill or suffering body takes up a dysfunctional task of being-in-the-world in the consequence of which people associate their own bodily suffering and physical shortcomings with the suffering and disadvantages of their community and/or country.

6. Comparable phenomena have been described in Serbia, Slovenia, Poland, Bulgaria, Czech Republic, Romania and Russia (cf. Verdery 1991; Meštrović 1993, 1996; Meštrović, Letica and Goreta 1993; Heady and Gambold Miller 2006; Mihaylova 2006; Zerilli 2006; Svašek 2006; Skrbiš 2006; Leutloff-Grandits 2006b; Golanska-Ryan 2006; Müller 2006; Kalb and Tak 2006; Rakowski 2006, 2007; Šuber 2006; and many more).

7. Goran Marić, alias Malkolm Muharem, *Duga*, 30 August – 13 September 1992.

8. The court found that Gotovina and Markač planned and led members of the Croatian military forces and special police in an effort to forcibly and permanently remove the ethnic Serb population from the Krajina region of Croatia. The two retired generals were found guilty of persecution, deportation, plunder of private and public property, destruction, murder, inhumane acts and cruel treatment. They were found not guilty on only one count, that of 'forcible transfer'.

9. http://daily.tportal.hr/128810/Veterans-end-hunger-strike-at-Gotovinas-wish.html, last visited 2 Nov 2012.

10. A copy of the judgement is accessible at: http://www.icty.org/x/cases/gotovina/acjug/en/121116_judgement.pdf, last accessed 18 Nov 2012.

11. For a generally intelligible analysis of the verdict, see Ivanišević 2012.

12. An analysis of the Brijuni transcript is available at: http://www.sense-agency.com/icty/brioni-transcripts-analyzed.29.html?cat_id=1&news_id=12711, last accessed 16 Nov 2012.

13. The webpage and documentation of the activities, outreach and publications of Documenta is available at http://www.documenta.hr/en/home.html, last accessed 26 Nov 2012.

14. A public opinion poll published in February 2002 by the International IDEA Archive states that the tribunal was trusted by 8% of the population in Serbia, by 21% in Croatia and by 22% in Macedonia. In Bosnia the situation was more mixed: the tribunal was trusted by 4% in the Serbian part but by 51% in the Croat-Muslim region (http: //archive.idea.int/press/pr20020404.htm; see also Hayden 2007: 110).

15. The association of masculinity with ethno-national identity is evidently not an exclusively Croatian trait. In this chapter, however, I will mainly focus on the nuances between Serbian and Croatian notions of masculine heroism in order to delineate different strategies of reconstructing (gendered) postwar identities as well as varying policies of dealing with accusations of war crimes. For a very good analysis of the reconfiguration of Bosnian Muslim veteran identity, see Bougarel 2007.

16. Janine N. Clark has pointed out that 'the term *bivši branitelji* [former defenders] is never used despite the fact that the war in Croatia ended 18 years ago' (2013b: 1939).

17. Ivan Čolović, however, has argued, that for many soldiers throughout the former Yugoslavia, prospects of adventure and sexual escapade served as much more appealing motivations for military service than actual patriotic devotion or nationalist commitment (Čolović 1993: 60ff.).

18. In their 2006 country analysis of Croatia, the European Training Foundation (ETF) reported that in the period between 1990 and 1998 total employment in Croatia decreased by 34.3% and by as much as 59.1% in the state sector (ETF Country Analysis Croatia 2006: 5).

19. While there were 45,225 war veterans registered as unemployed in 1997, this number dropped to 26,769 in 2005. This reduction, however, was partly caused by redefinitions of the official term 'war veteran' (ETF Country Analysis Croatia 2006: 8).

20. Quoted from and translated in Bjelić and Cole 2005: 279. It goes without saying that the 'Other' of the masculine soldier is (rhetorically as well as visually) constructed as a vulnerable woman in need of protection. A well-known 1992 HDZ election poster, for instance, depicts a young Croatian woman in traditional costume who is carefully watched over by a uniformed male soldier.

21. Dubravka Žarkov reports that '[a]rticles in Serb tabloids explicitly called Muslim men homosexuals and used historically and culturally constructed arguments to "prove" that homosexuality is a natural state of Muslim men' (Žarkov 2007: 168). In the Croatian press, Muslims as well as Serbs were depicted as genuine homosexuals. Muslim men, however, are feminised through victimisation whereas Serbs are rather demonised and pathologised (ibid.: 169).

22. Of particular interest in this respect is Ceribašić's mention of the song *Što se nije Hrvatska udala* [Why Croatia did not get married] by Dragutin Knežević, in which Croatia is described as a divorcee who 'bares her calves, and sashays through Europe, but nobody wants the bride' (Ceribašić 1995: 96). Initially, this disgraceful image was intended to mock Croatia's break-up with Yugoslavia and President Tuđman's request for international recognition during the early war years. Today, however, it might be used to mock the Croatian government's desperate efforts to meet the requirements for EU membership.

23. I ignore the 2001 ICTY charges against General Rahim Ademi as well as the Janko Bobetko indictment in 2002. Although their prosecutions also caused massive protests throughout Croatia, neither of the cases proved in the long run to be as spectacularly controversial as the Mirko Norac and Ante Gotovina indictments. Because Ademi surrendered and Bobetko died before he could be extradited to The Hague, neither of them was really suited to personify Croat concepts of masculine resistance and heroism.

24. During my fieldwork, when Gotovina was still on the run, I occasionally heard people saying that Croatia would lose its *bono*, its 'good soul', if he were to be extradited.

25. Catherine Baker has pointed out that Thompson actually reserved two empty seats for Ante Gotovina and Mirko Norac at his 2002 'E, moj narode' concert in the Poljud stadium in Split and solemnly greeted the generals in absentia throughout the tour (Baker 2006; see also Krželj 2002). The name Thompson originates from the eponymous American submachine gun that was used in the Balkan Wars and favoured by soldiers and civilians alike for its compactness, its large. 45 ACP bullet, and high rate of automatic fire.

26. The original meaning of the Greek word *martyr* is simply 'witness', but as stated in the Encyclopaedia Britannica, 'the idea of suffering came by the end of the first century to be connected with the bearing of witness or being a martyr' (Encyclopaedia Britannica 38th edition, 1987, 15: 458). A martyr is 'one whose testimony to the truth as he sees it leads to and culminates in his death' (ibid.). See also Hasan-Rokem (2003).

27. For further information, see the 2005 European Commission Progress Report of Croatia, at http://www.delhrv.ec.europa.eu/uploads/dokumenti/3a 87bfc3ab7e5d6740a3a4b1aef3e26a.pdf, last visited 15 Mar 2008.

28. Franjo Tuđman, whose authoritarian and nationalist HDZ regime ruled Croatia from 1990 to 1999, was notorious for his attacks on the ICTY. However, under strong international pressure, Tuđman handed twenty-seven Croats from Bosnia and Herzegovina who had been indicted for criminal offences committed in the territory of that state over to The Hague. The extradition of Bosnian Croats proved far less controversial than the handover of Croatian ex-generals, as the military intervention in Bosnia was not part of the Homeland War fought on Croatian soil (see Peskin and Boduszynski 2003: 16). Moreover, these indictees were lower-level suspects and never really featured as personifications of Croatian victimhood or heroic self-defence.

29. In 1996 and 1999, the respective ICTY presidents officially reported Croatia's non-compliance to the UN Security Council.

30. Only a few months after the change of government, Croatia was admitted to NATO's Partnership for Peace programme. In July 2000 the country joined the World Trade Organization and signed a Stabilization and Association Agreement with the European Union in October 2001.

31. The full text of the declaration is available online in *Narodne novine* at http://www.nn.hr/clanci/sluzbeno/2000/1987.htm, last accessed 20 Nov 2012.

32. In the detailed analysis *The Domestic Politics of State Cooperation with the International Criminal Tribunal for the Former Yugoslavia*, Victor Peskin and Mieczyslaw P. Boduszynski state that '[i]t remains uncertain how close the ICTY was to actually indicting Norac, either before or after the Rijeka court issued the warrant for the general's arrest. Nevertheless, ICTY Chief Prosecutor Carla del Ponte's decision to defer to the Croatian judiciary on February 21 clearly bolstered Račan's position vis-à-vis the nationalists and helped defuse the crisis' (Peskin and Boduszynski 2003: 23f.).

33. http://www.stormfront.org/forum/t60750-2/

34. Moreover, the religious rhetoric applied in each of the songs inevitably situates Croatia in civilised Christian Europe, whereas Serbia and Bosnia are associated with the heathen, barbarian Balkans.

35. Mirko Norac is and will remain closely connected to his home town. During one of his paroles he was married by a local Franciscan to his long-term girlfriend in the *Svetište Čudotvorne Gospe Sinjske*, the Sanctuary of Our Miraculous Lady of Sinj. Since his release from prison in November 2011 he has been living in the village of Otok with his family.

36. During the war the label *vještica* [witch] was frequently used to denounce Croatian peace activists and feminists. This condemnation reached its height during a nationwide smear campaign in which the five feminist writers and journalists Rada Iveković, Jelena Lovrić, Dubravka Ugrešić, Vesna

Kesić and Slavenka Drakulić were openly accused of betraying and 'raping' [*sic*] Croatia.

37. For a description of the 2003 trial and evidence against Mirko Norac and others, see http://www.icty.org/x/file/Outreach/view_from_hague/balkan_040602_en.pdf

38. On 16 March 2005 the General Affairs and External Relations Council (GAERC) decided to postpone the opening of accession negotiations with Croatia due to a lack of full cooperation, and agreed that a bilateral intergovernmental conference (IGC) would be convened by common agreement as soon as the Council had established that Croatia was cooperating fully with the International Criminal Tribunal for the former Yugoslavia (ICTY). See http://www.delhrv.ec.europa.eu/uploads/dokumenti/3a87bfc3ab7e5d6740a3a4b1aef3e26a.pdf, last visited 15 Mar 2008.

39. More than in all other regions, people in Dalmatia are extremely fond of the indicted ex-generals. The town council of Zadar declared Gotovina an honorary citizen in November 2001, and a huge placard celebrating Gotovina as *Heroj* [hero] adorns the historic town wall to the present day. In April 2002 Gotovina and Ademi were both declared honorary citizens of Split-Dalmatia County.

40. In the November 2003 elections, Ivica Račan's centre-left coalition lost the parliamentary majority, and HDZ party leader Ivo Sanader replaced him as prime minister.

41. As an example of how bizarre he considered the accusation of Gotovina, an elderly man in Sinj said to me: 'This is so absurd, Michaela. It is as if you were arrested now with the justification "Michaela has arrived in Sinj and five people have died since. She has to be held responsible for that".

42. Gotovina left the French Foreign Legion in 1978 with the rank of Corporal after having participated in operations in Djibouti, Kolwezi (Congo), Zaire and Ivory Coast.

43. For further reference see http://news.bbc.co.uk/2/hi/europe/4514150.stm, last visited 10 Oct 2007.

44. An English version of the book is available online at: http://www.antegotovina.com/doc/ratnik_jan_20.pdf, last accessed 17 Nov 2012.

45. The report is available online at: http://www.tportal.hr/showtime/estrada/226597/Sve-ljubavi-generala-Gotovine.html, last accessed 24 Nov 2012.

46. Stjepan Mesić, 'Hrvatska neće odustati od tuzbe protiv SCG', in *Danas*, 18 February 2005. (See also: Helsinki Committee Report on Human Rights in Serbia 2005: 412).

47. The July 2006 issue of *Nationalities Papers* edited by Aleksandra Sasha Milicević and Elissa Helms focused on 'Masculinities after Yugoslavia'. Several of the contributors state that of late the international community has been associated with femininity and poses a potential threat to traditional concepts of masculinity (cf. Živković 2006; Greenberg 2006; Miličević 2006).

48. Earlier versions of this section have been published in *Anthropology Matters* (Schäuble 2006) and, in German, in *Berliner Debatte Initial* (Schäuble 2007b).

49. In May 1991, President Franjo Tuđman established the *Zbor Narodne Garde* [Croatian National Guard] from the ranks of police reservists as a quasi-independent army. The troops were poorly equipped and badly organised, as Tuđman initially did not aim to defeat the Serbs militarily but calculated on winning international recognition. Nonetheless, he mobilised scores of volunteers who were willing to go to war and defend Croatia against 'Serb aggression'. A year later, in April 1992, the Bosnian Croats in Herzegovina set up their own militia, the *Hrvatsko Vijeće Obrane* [Croatian Defence Council], or HVO.

50. In their 2003 study, *War Stress: Effects of the War in the Area of Former Yugoslavia*, Mirna Flögel and Gordan Lauc mention that there are currently more then 10,500 diagnosed cases of 'post-traumatic stress disorder' (PTSD) patients in Croatia, whereas a multitude of cases are still unregistered. Referring to Bulman and Kang (1994), they report: 'Studies estimated that patients suffering from PTSD have up to a sevenfold increased incidence of suicides, and a fourfold increased risk of death from all external sources' (Bulman and Kang 1994: 604–10, quoted in Flögel and Lauc 2003: 4). Personally, I prefer not to use the diagnostic construct of post-traumatic stress disorder in my study, as PTSD is just one of many clinically recognisable responses to trauma, and the diagnosis of PTSD tends to stigmatise, marginalise and/or victimise sufferers from trauma-related symptoms and, to some degree, also assigns responsibility and blame. Furthermore, according to Laurence J. Kirmayer et al., the medicalisation of trauma through PTSD has the capacity to 'undermine the need to address the social and political injustices that characterize large-scale traumas of war and genocide' (Kirmayer, Lemelson and Barad 2007: 13). Throughout my text I therefore attempt to avoid the ongoing debates over the universality of war trauma, PTSD, and other trauma-related disorders, and prefer to talk about individual and collective experiences of, and responses to, trauma when referring to the narratives and conditions of my Croatian interlocutors (see also Kienzler 2008).

51. Stef Jansen has pointed out that trauma-centred explanations for the appeal of post-Yugoslav nationalisms tend to reproduce nationalist propaganda. According to Jansen, reformulations of these memories of terror also played a central role in the nationalist discourses that were instrumental in the build-up to the war and in its continuation. Furthermore, such explanations prevent contextualisation of the actual importance of those memories with regard to the recent events (Jansen 2002). More recently, '[a] set of alternative explanations for popular support of nationalism [have been] put forward by local and foreign critics [who] favour what we might call a constructivist perspective. They tend to attribute more explanatory power to political propaganda and media manipulation. Memories of WWII suffering, it is argued here, were first and foremost instruments in the hands of

nationalist politicians and, when assessing them, it is hard to draw the line between indoctrination and trauma' (Jansen 2006: 435).

52. It is striking that suicides and attempted suicides in the whole of former Yugoslavia after the war seem to be related to gender. To my knowledge none of the many women soldiers on all sides have committed suicide, whereas suicides of male ex-combatants are still noticeably on the rise. See therefore also Friedlin 2001 and Stanimirović 2002.

53. The Croatian Ministry of the Family, War Veterans' Affairs and Intergenerational Solidarity (MoFVAIS) has recently initiated a programme with the aim of reintegrating unemployed ex-soldiers into the labour market. The training programme intends to reduce unemployment among war veterans, their spouses and children. According to an EFT study, approximately 9% of all unemployed people in Croatia are ex-soldiers and the majority of them have not completed upper secondary education – 27% completed only elementary school (EFT Country Analysis Croatia 2006: 31).

54. Aleida Assmann argues that in the same way that the 'body scriptures' [*Körperschriften*] applied during initiation rites serve to form a neophyte's identity the 'body scripture' of trauma prevents and destroys identity formation processes (cf. Assmann [1999] 2006: 248).

55. Marina Blagojević states that '[m]en have shown a certain lack of adaptability to the socio-economic upheavals and, more often than women, have tended to use self-destructive strategies, such as psychological withdrawal, the abuse of drugs and alcohol' (Blagojević 2004: 76).

56. Enzensberger's generalising and polemic analysis of violence as an end in itself, however, cannot sufficiently explain how and under which circumstances the rancour of individuals turns into a propensity towards violence of entire 'loser-collectives' or of homogenous radical movements – and under which circumstances it does not (Enzensberger 2006: 41, my translation).

57. Fortunately, the assumed redemptive potential of collective violence has not so far culminated in politically motivated terrorist acts in post-war Croatia, as some preconditions recognised by anthropologists are lacking. 'Promoting prerequisites [for terrorism] can be specified: groups excluded from communication, blockade-experience of political actors, a large reservoir of personnel, as well as "markets of violence" operating as retreat and deployment zones', writes Georg Elwert (2001: 6, my translation). The most powerful prerequisite, however, is the conviction that non-violent political actions have no effect. In the case of former Yugoslavia, this awareness is prevalent and deeply rooted in the previously described world view, in which people experience themselves as victims of history and historiography.

58. While in 2009 the average pension in Croatia was HRK 2,166 (approx. 287 euros), the average military pension amounted to HRK 3,525 (approx. 467 euros), and the average Homeland War veteran's pension was HRK 5,861 (approx. 776 euros) (Badun 2009).

59. Wingfield und Bucur note that trauma is an important element in the increasing drifting apart of men and women during the war, as violence is often gendered – and so are the culturally accepted ways of dealing with it. Whilst violated and/or raped women were often additionally stigmatised and publicly condemned, men were often unable to come to terms with experienced violence in any other way than continuing to commit violent acts upon their return. Such trauma-induced (domestic) violence, however, was largely played down and the traumatic experiences themselves degraded (Wingfield and Bucur 2006: 7).

60. For an encompassing analysis of female soldering in the Croatian and Serbian press, see Žarkov 2007: 191–231.

61. The condition Rajka describes for Croatia after the Homeland War resembles Svetlana Slapšak's historical account of post–Second World War Yugoslavia, when 'women were instrumental in the voluntary work of reconstructing a devastated country, in huge education campaigns (literacy courses), in taking care of invalids, victims of war and orphans. They gained an enormous visibility in political and Party bodies, as MPs, mothers and widows in black in the first rows of conferences, congresses, war crime tribunals and cultural events' (Slapšak 2004: 28). It has to be noted that this activism and visibility soon diminished and was brought under 'patriarchal control' in the communist power system (see also, Wingfield and Bucur 2006).

62. I have been told that Otok, the neighbouring village of Sinj and where Mirko Norac was born, has the highest ratio of unmarried men in the whole of Croatia. However, no official verification or statistic to confirm this information could be found.

63. Jessica Greenberg made a similar point about Serbian politics after the 5 October Overthrow in 2000. In her article 'Nationalism, Masculinity and Citizenship', she demonstrates how notions of democratic citizenship call the dominance of masculinist nationalist citizenship into question (Greenberg 2006: 323).

64. Doctoral research on conscientious objectors in the 1990s in the post-war post-Yugoslav republics is to my knowledge currently being conducted by Oliwia Berdak (School of Slavonic and East European Studies, UCL) and Miriam Schroer-Hippel (Freie Universität Berlin).

⊰· Chapter 5 ·⊱

Mobilising Local Reserves

Regional Forces of Regeneration

Skimming my chapter outlines, and reading subheadings such as *Violent and Violated Identities, Celebrating Victory and Victimhood, Violence and Self-Victimisation* and *Reclaiming Innocence,* a colleague smilingly pointed out that the composition of my chapters resembled the outline of a Catholic sermon and mockingly commented on my successful internalisation of Croatian religious-nationalist rhetoric. Reflecting on this ironic comment, I noticed that a large number of the sermons I heard during my fieldwork did indeed have a similar narrative structure, and for the most part contained rhetorical elements related to the God-willed unity of all Croats and the predestined independence of the country. I have shown so far that religious imagery and metaphors feature prominently in Croatian ethno-nationalist discourse, and I have underlined how a coalition between 'Croatdom' and 'the Divine' finds its expression in the well-known idiom of *Bog i Hrvati,* or 'God and the Croats'. This *'idea of election/chosenness* and an associated perception of divinely ordained specialness' (Skrbiš 2005: 445) is built upon and accompanied by the shared suffering of the Croat people. Along with the unifying experience of shared suffering, '[t]he experience of victimisation, in addition to the role of language, culture and common territory, play a central role in the establishment of national identity or unity and a sense of peoplehood' (Mack 1983: 59). These central elements in Croatian self-understanding are recurrently evoked in political speeches and religious sermons, and are firmly established in the public imaginary.

A sermon that I recorded during a commemoration service in Sinj in August 2005 paradigmatically comprises this mythico-historical dimension of Croatian peoplehood, and implicitly exhorts the congregation to dissociate itself from foreign influences and dependencies. Starting with an analysis of this sermon, this final chapter turns to the cultural resources that resist international economic and political intervention

(Horden and Purcell 2000). I examine the various social, historical, political, religious and geographical milieus described in previous chapters in terms of their potential for strategies of resistance to demands imposed by the international community in the run-up to Croatia's EU accession. In present-day Croatia, and particularly in the coastal regions and Dalmatia, local unease about membership of the European Union and, more broadly, about globalisation processes in general, is mainly perceptible in the revival of traditional family, kinship and gender arrangements as well as in the proliferation of alternative economies. Despite a 2007 Croatian Labour Force Survey that states that the share of employment in agriculture is decreasing,[1] many households, especially in rural areas, are continually, if not increasingly, dependent on subsistence and backyard farming as well as small-scale livestock breeding. Apart from concerns of pure material maintenance, many households also thereby seek to gain greater independence from institutionalised and centralised power structures. In this process, patronage and patriarchal kinship systems tend to become reinforced in their support of the social cohesion of local community and extended family networks. However, I do not intend to provide here an encompassing analysis of family structures or of the transition to market economics and ownership in twenty-first-century rural Dalmatia, as these topics have already been comprehensively researched (i.e. Kaser 1995, 2000; Grandits and Gruber 1996; Grandits 2002; Leutloff-Grandits 2006a, 2006b). My concern is rather to call attention to the transformation currently at stake in these areas and to demonstrate that these changes can be understood in terms of the mobilisation of reserves of consciousness of place and locality against mounting processes of deregulation and globalisation since the country's independence in 1991, and particularly since the end of the war in 1995.

The term 'reserves', as I use it here, describes local perceptions of the exploitation of natural, technological and human resources as well as reactive behaviour towards damaged or lost access to these resources (Hauschild 2007, 2008; Gronover 2007). According to Hauschild, the term also accounts for a perception of catastrophes inherent in descriptions of cultural, social and economic situations of the everyday – particularly in regions of the Mediterranean – and refers to landscapes and geo-ecological premises that fail to provide a solid foundation for lasting mass production and complex infrastructures. When attachments to soil and terrain gain momentum, it hampers the development of statehood, family structures and industrial modernity, and these attachments have a potential to obstruct or to restrain the unfolding of processes of globalisation.

Peregrine Horden and Nicholas Purcell – two major authors who have attempted to reconceptualise the economic and social history of the Mediterranean and have thereby 'recreated the Mediterranean for the new millennium' (*Times Higher Education Supplement*) – refer to landscapes similar to the Dalmatinska Zagora as 'territories of grace' and describe them as crossed by local sanctuaries, holy mountains, sacred springs and sacred graves (Horden and Purcell 2000; Hauschild 2011). Such consecrated landscapes are characterised by a complex interplay of topographic conditions, religious and commemorative ascriptions, and an enormous potential for revivable historicity; they often generate pilgrimage sites such as Sinj and Međugorje, or accommodate other sanctuaries of regional as well as supra-regional importance. The consequences of such religious practices and their potential political scope, however, cannot be fully assessed without taking into consideration the material connection in which they are anchored. Living in an unstable, incalculable landscape not only informs people's modes of living but also changes their relationship with their surroundings and demands a constant safeguarding and stabilisation of (literally) shifting grounds – stabilising tactics that usually encompass pragmatic material as well as religious and spiritual measures. The strengthening of small-scale family structures, enforcement of traditional gender roles and work division, an increasing reversion to subsistence farming, the preservation and re-evaluation of a traditionalist festival like the Sinjska Alka, and the ever-growing historicisation of endured atrocities along with intensified religious adherence – these can all be understood as localised 'forces of regeneration' (Kramer 2000). Such regenerative forces are survival strategies that people draw on, especially at times of transition and insecurity, in order to safeguard the cohesion of their local community vis-à-vis a world that is perceived as increasingly threatening, or degenerate and disenchanted.

In the following, my aim is thus to scrutinise the material and ideational grounds drawn on by people at the margins of Europe when faced with massive structural reorganisations of their livelihoods. Arguing that the material conditions for the creation of a common cultural and social space in the economically underprivileged peripheries have hitherto remained under-examined, I focus on people's physical surroundings and their construction of a local ecological niche in the rough karstic terrain of the Dalmatian hinterland. Dalmatia has historically constituted a crossroads between powerful empires, leading most Dalmatians to perceive the area as a pawn in the hands of visible or invisible political forces that have had little concern for local interests in the past and that continue to neglect such interest in the present (see also Green 2005: 123). Typified as inhabitants of a classic marginal place, the people in Dalmatia – although fiercely patriotic and nationalist – simultaneously ridicule and undermine state authority.[2] The state's margins are imagined as 'spaces, forms, and practices through which the state is continually both experienced and undone through the illegibility of its own practices, documents, and words' (Asad 2004: 279). As self-appointed defenders or protectors not only of Croatia but also of the entire south-eastern borders of Europe, many Dalmatians feel entitled to contest state power at the local level, even as they reproduce this power in various ways. This permanent playful negotiation of marginality and citizenship generates an open space in which people creatively interact with the promises and limitations of official state power and ideologies. Such practices are part of what Herzfeld (1997, 2004) has called 'social poetics', which he describes as the ways in which 'members of the social group fashion and refashion their imagined iconicity' (Herzfeld 1997: 154). The mischievous undermining of the Croatian state's official rhetoric, however, is also a consequence of the strong urban–rural divide in contemporary Croatia and mirrors the relations of power between global, national and local agencies. In the same way that rural Dalmatians are commonly ridiculed and devaluated as backward peasants in public discourse, they themselves ridicule and at times drastically challenge officialdom emanating from the capital. I thus argue that one of the major aspects of the current return to local – environmental, geographic, economic, ecological, religious and social – niches in Dalmatia is the search for alternative scopes of action beyond centralised control on the part of the nation-state.

In Dalmatia and along the Adriatic coast of Croatia, this search has recently led to an intensified affinity with the Mediterranean region. In the midst of current geopolitical contests, the Mediterranean re-emerges as a site of policy and scholarly attention and (re-)gains importance as an experimental field for shifting cultural and social formations. The fact that many Dalmatians envision themselves as part of a Mediterranean entity is in my opinion due to a heightened relevance of regional ecological and economic factors. The Mediterranean as a site of convergence and exchanges evokes visions of a centuries-old cosmopolitanism, and suggests a possibility that trade connections and tourism might secure the economic future of the region. Such reorientation strategies also have to be understood as part of a continual self-positioning towards Europe; I take the Dalmatian orientation towards the Mediterranean as a particular form of regionalism that is promoted by a growing sense of rootlessness, alienation and socio-economic instability. At the same time, chances for a better marketing of local resources (e.g. tourism, trade, revival of cherished traditions) and the prospect of a shared community based on regional solidarities provide an alternative to the currently experienced hegemony of the European Union and the marginalisation of Eastern and South Eastern Europe (cf. Mishkova 2004). The main motive of this reorientation along regional rather than national lines is in my view not so much scepticism towards the modern nation-state as such, but the feared dissolution of it in a supra-national confederation of states, as represented by the European Union. The ongoing expansion of the European Union and its centralised political imagination entails new transnational or regional affiliations as well as a (re-)union of subnational entities *of* and *on* its margins.

Victory and Homeland Thanksgiving Day

The anniversary of Operacija Oluja – the military operation that, according to the Croat version, constituted the decisive battle in the liberation and reconquest of Croat territory in the Krajina region and, according to the Serbian version, featured crimes against humanity including large-scale ethnic cleansing of Serbian civilians – is a national holiday in Croatia, called the 'Victory and Homeland Thanksgiving Day and the Day of Croatian Defenders'. In Serbia, on the other hand, it is marked by commemorations for those who were killed and exiled.

The commemoration is annually held on the fifth of August. In 2005 I attended the celebration of the ten-year anniversary of Operacija Oluja in Sinj, which was solemnised with a Mass held in commemoration of the battle. The *gvardijan* of the Franciscan monastery of Sinj delivered the following sermon, linking the recent events to the Croatian mythico-history and its 'eternal longing' for an independent, sovereign state:

> For centuries we have carried within us the longing for the realisation of our sovereign independent Croatian state. Therefore our poet sings *Dok je srca, bit će i Kroacije* [As long as there is heart, there will be Croatia]. For many centuries we did not have a sovereign Croatia ... Finally, in this Homeland War and due to the blood of our *branitelji*, we accomplished this eternal longing: an independent, sovereign Croatia. Their blood has not been spilled in vain. By having Croatia, we have become a subject, we have our own name and without this we would have been erased from these places. The bravery and courage of the Croatian soldier has been renowned throughout history, but hitherto we have always fought under foreign flags. Now, finally united after many centuries, we have fought under our own flag for an independent, free Croatia. We have accomplished this under the

guidance of our first president, Dr Franjo Tuđman. This is a historical fact that nobody can erase ... Therefore, the bells are ringing in the whole of Croatia today, ten years after the liberation, and holy masses of thanksgiving will be held during which we pray particularly for the fallen knights who have sanctified this Croatian soil with their sweat and blood. We are also thankful to those who are still alive and have made such great contributions to the liberation of the homeland.

It hurts us that many have wrongly been sentenced and held in prisons – our general and *Alkarski vojvoda* [Duke of the Alka] Mirko Norac – and that others have been expelled and have no place in the homeland for which they have sacrificed everything. As believers who trust in the victory of the good, we hope that truth and justice will eventually prevail. We must not question the battle for justice and truth. We must not be deceived by the various authorities in this world who at all cost want us to take their lies for the truth. The Christian person, the believer, has to be on the side of truth, just like Christ – on the side of justice and honesty. This is what our Christian faith teaches us. We are a small people, but all people have the right to their freedom, sovereignty and autochthonous culture. History has told us through difficult historical experiences that we cannot trust everybody, because on so many occasions we have been deceived and betrayed. We need to solve our problems solely through our belief in God and in our Croatian people, and must find the way out of the difficult situation in which we find ourselves. It is difficult for the one whose problems are to be solved by a foreigner/stranger.

History is not just an accumulation of economic and political interests. History bears the aspiration for boundlessness and eternity. Just as a river gushes into an infinite ocean, so the river of a people's history gushes into an ocean of the eternal God. It is God who writes the history of a people, and not just the despots of this world. And just as God has written the history of the Jewish people, so he writes the history of our Croatian people.

History is not the outcome of societal principles/laws that necessarily decide our destiny. A people is composed of free individuals, and their free decision for moral values is that on which our future depends. We all carry the responsibility for our future. We accept the pluralism of the opinions of different political parties and seculars, but what we have in common is the love for our homeland and its freedom. We shall never again sell (trade with) our freedom and sovereignty. We can say what our first president has said: '*Sve za Hrvatsku, Hrvatsku nizašto*' [Everything for Croatia, never abandon Croatia for anything]. That is how it shall be! AMEN!

This sermon, which was followed by the singing of the Croatian national anthem, bears the imprint of the master narrative of 'Croatdom'. It conveys the trope of Croats as the chosen people whose centuries-long suffering and subjugation have finally been rewarded. The speaker acknowledges the martyrdom and sacrifice of the *branitelji* who have brought the Croatian nation-state into being, many of whom have 'been wrongly sentenced' while others 'have been expelled and have no place in the homeland for which they have sacrificed everything'. The latter is an uncoded allusion to Ante Gotovina, who, at the time of the sermon, was still on the run to escape extradition to the war crimes tribunal in The Hague. With this comment the *gvardijan* emphasises the legitimacy and dignity of the Homeland War and simultaneously declares his conviction that no indictable war crimes were committed during Operacija Oluja. On the contrary, he proclaims that the 'fallen knights' have 'sanctified th[e] Croatian soil with their sweat and blood'; with this metaphor he reproduces the primary ingredients of (romanticised, fascistic) nationalism, namely rurality, blood and soil, and combines the lived-in world of peasantry and agriculture with the religiously informed notions of self-sacrifice and martyrdom.

Another basic pattern of the sermon is its motif of distrust and treachery. Croatia is depicted not only as the victim of years of foreign occupation but also as a puppet of recent international power politics. With his self-righteous claim on behalf of Croatians to be in possession of sole 'truth', the preacher opposes any form of historiography that holds Croatia responsible for war crimes or that doubts the legitimacy of the Croatian state. The comment that '[i]t is difficult for he, whose problems are to be solved by a foreigner/stranger' is a clear dig at foreign intrusion, at international institutions (the ICTY) and at organisations (NATO and the UN) that interfere with 'Croatian affairs', and the *gvardijan* directly appeals to the public to defy their authority. Consequently, the line '[w]e need to solve our problems solely through our belief in God and in our Croatian people' – which is a reference to the famous dictum *Bog i Hrvati* [God and the Croats] – clarifies that international interference of any kind is undesired in Croatia. The motto *Bog i Hrvati* originates from a speech by the Croatian politician and writer Ante Starčević to the Croatian Parliament in 1861, in which he stated that the future of Croatia should not be decided in Austria, but by 'God and the Croats'. Starčević, who is commonly referred to in Croatia as *Otac domovine*, or 'father of the Homeland', demanded the reintegration of the Croatian lands, the 'large kingdom of Croatia of old [the medieval Kingdom of Croatia], the homeland of one people, with the same blood, language, past and (God willing) future'. By indirectly referring to Starčević and invoking the sacred union between God and the Croats, the *gvardijan* delineates the history of Croatia in terms of a Braudelian *longue durée* that prioritises long-term historical structures over 'an accumulation of economic and political interests'. The underlying understanding of history as a linear development undermines the primacy of events and is described in terms of a geographical metaphor according to which the 'river of a people's history gushes into the ocean of the eternal God'. By constructing history as a God-given purposeful endeavour, the notion of the suffering of the Croatian people is construed as meaningful in relation to an experience of ultimate heavenly redemption.

A subtext that underlies the sermon in Sinj is fear of losing the country's newly gained independence to the various directives of the European Union. Despite resting on joint international jurisdiction, the common trade policy, the agricultural and fishery policies and the common regional development policies of the European Union are seen as threatening to a small country like Croatia, as yet unable to compete in a free international market. Furthermore, the clash of local claims to European identity with European claims about 'Balkan otherness' fuels a widespread apprehension of ranking among the losers of Europeanisation. Also, working on the peripheries of Europe, Tsypylma Darieva and Wolfgang Kaschuba have observed that '[t]he negative mode of "experiencing Europe" is characterized by the well-known threat of the loss of strong national traditions and local morality, and the creation of more "losers" in the process of the neo-liberal transition, comprising a majority of the population in these regions' (Darieva and Kaschuba 2007: 19). In Croatia, neoliberalism is widely experienced as a losing game. The feeling of not having profited from the postsocialist transition and scepticism towards state authority culminated in the following statement uttered by my host in one of countless discussions on politics and the role of the Croatian state: 'Democracy is as much a fiction as communism was. Nothing has changed for us, really'. This disillusionment and feeling of stagnation is often accompanied by distrust towards the state, and engenders various forms of dissent and/or alternative forms of self-definition on cultural, social, economic and political levels.

In previous chapters I have given account of the corroboration of narratives about national heroes and the country's glorious past as it is represented for instance by the Alka tournament. I have also dwelt at length on the resurgence of religious practices and traditions in the postsocialist era. In the following, I now emphasise various social aspects of the reconfiguration of local power relations, such as the maintenance or even growing importance of close family and kinship ties as well as patronage systems. Simultaneously, the breakdown of ties between the state centre and its periphery shows itself in the increasing number of the self-employed and of subsistence farmers in search of greater economic independence. In the following I will expand on these phenomena and describe a growing pattern of Euroscepticism, particularly in the remote areas of the Dalmatinska Zagora.

Rural Economies in Dalmatia

Kinship, Family Structures and Gender Arrangements

Discourses about the role of women, family and reproduction are crucial in the legitimation of politics. Social change after socialism and political-economic processes of postsocialist transformation are shaped by ideas about gender and gender relations. Gal and Kligman have noted that 'ideas about gender difference and sexuality are often recruited to construct continuities with the past, with nature with the general good', and can thus be used to gain authority for postsocialist political institutions, practices and political actors (Gal and Kligman 2000: 12). In the case of present-day Croatia, conservative currents in conjunction with religiously inspired attitudes to morality consider the traditional family as a value per se, and (re-)construct it as the basis of communal as well as individual stability. Within the context of nationalist discourse, families, understood as loci of continuity and markers of a nation's reproductive capacity, corporeally constitute the entities by and within which national selves are produced. In this respect, the family – and with it questions of reproduction, contraception, normative sexuality, and ultimately the division of labour in public and private sectors – is turned into a politicised category within civil society that also takes note of the altered situation of the free market economy.[3]

The traditionalist concept of the 'Balkan family' has mainly been conceptualised and elaborated by the Austrian historian Karl Kaser who defines historical Balkan society as a patriarchal social system (Kaser 1992a, 1992b, 1995, 2000; Kaser and Halpern 1994; Kaser and Katschnig-Fasch 2005). In his monumental work *Familie und Verwandtschaft auf dem Balkan* [Family and Kinship in the Balkans] he suggests a regional differentiation of 'Balkan family types', but mostly claims that the typical patriarchal 'Balkan family' is constituted by patrilineality (inheritance of property, material and symbolic commodities, names, and titles to agnates through the male lineage), by patrilocality (a married couple resides with or near the groom's father's house or compound), and by male-dominated customary law (Kaser 1995; cf. Čapo Žmegač 2001: 271). According to Kaser, this social system also evinces male privilege and authority, a hierarchy among men based on age, as well as the formal submission of females (Kaser and Halpern 1994: 2; Kaser 1995: 677–78; see also Čapo Žmegač 2001: 271). This definition of static 'Balkan family types' – Kaser himself speaks of a 'petrified society' (Kaser 1992a: 2) – was, although in a much more differentiated way, anticipated by Vera Stein Erlich, who described the heightened importance of patriarchal family structures and the incidence of individual (male) heroism as a specific characteristic of the Dinaric mountain region (Stein Erlich 1971: 372f.).[4] Unfortunately, these and similar discussions of different family types and kinship in the area have produced a number of crude geographical determinist characterisations over time that culminated in Kaser's use of such classifications as explanatory models for the escalation of violence during the latest wars and led to his infamous essentialist ascription of a 'deeply rooted tendency towards violence' and 'violent potential' within the Balkans (Kaser 1995: 1, 10, my translation; cf. Kaser and Halpern 1994; Grandits and Halpern 1994: 101).

Ethno-psychological ascriptions of the 'Dinaric character' in particular have become part of wider internal Yugoslav inter-ethnic characterisations that were used in and have fuelled the developments that came to be known as the violent disintegration of Yugoslavia (cf. Živković 1997). Marko Živković has conclusively shown that the distinction between 'violent highlanders and peaceful lowlanders' is particularly charged in this matter. 'The Dinaric mountaineer is a category long used by the Yugoslavs themselves as a tool of self-understanding or self-criticism, and, particularly in times of conflict, as a rhetorical weapon in inter-ethnic conflicts', he writes (ibid.). I am well aware that such crude culture-area stereotypes and anthropo-geographical terms are indefensible and that one has to be careful not to link regional developments such as a particular family structure to essentialist pseudo-psychological ascriptions.[5] The fact that the family structure in the region in which I conducted fieldwork differs considerably from family structures and social arrangements I have encountered in Croatia's urban centres, along its coastlines and on its islands evidently allows no inferences to unchanging regional features such as 'live spirit, sharp intelligence, deep feelings, rich fantasy, impulsiveness provoked by nonmaterial motives, national pride, and the ideas of honor, justice and freedom' – as the Croatian-American sociologist Dinko Tomašić claimed up until the 1940s (Tomašić 1941: 54–55).[6] I am convinced, however, that people in the Dalmatian hinterland creatively and consciously play with these stereotypes down to the present day, and reverse them ad libitum as a strategy of evading claims of the nation-state or whenever they intend to stress their exceptional and noteworthy status within Croatia.[7]

In my view, the geo-ecological niche structure of the Dalmatinska Zagora additionally supports the strengthening of traditional family structures and furthers the revival of small-scale agriculture (Todorova 1993: 151ff.). Not surprisingly, the present arguments of advocates of regional autarchy bear striking similarities with nineteenth-century traditionalist views of the *zadruga* that Todorova describes as follows:

> Traditionalists (or indigenists, authochtonists, protochronists, or simply conservative nationalists) saw in it the unique local institution that would save the peculiarity and cultural identity of the peoples vis-à-vis the disruptive modernizing influence of the West by promoting virtues such as solidarity and mutual aid. (Todorova 1993: 163)

This understanding of independent family units still prevails amongst contemporary traditionalist and conservative nationalists who consider large households and patriarchal, patrilocal families as guarantors of stability and cohesion. Notions of kinship, family and marriage can thus be understood as highly gendered, constituent elements in the formation of personal as well as regionally anchored identities.

'A Woman Holds Three Corners of the House': Gender Relations in the Post-War Era

Hardly anything, however, has changed in the conception of the house as a primarily female domain. The common Croatian saying, '[a] woman holds three corners of a house', not only indicates that the family and the home rely primarily on women but also shows that women's influence continues to be mainly restricted to the domestic sphere. During the election campaign in Croatia in December 1999, women's groups launched a counter-slogan to this saying, which proclaimed: 'I exchange one corner of the house for a seat in parliament' (cf. Kesić 2001: 80). And although as regards gender equality and women's rights, the government has taken measures to raise general awareness as part of the national policy for the promotion of gender equality, the continued separation of private and public spheres facilitates a classic division of labour between men and women, and in the long run helps to entrench gender-specific stereotypes.

I pointed out earlier that of late many Croatian men have been trying to reclaim their traditional roles as breadwinners and heads of the household that they had partly lost, either when away on the front line or as a result of incipient de-professionalisation in the aftermath of war. Such attempts, however, aim at gradually retraditionalising gender roles and strengthening long-established family structures. A stable family – ideally assembled in a multiple-generation household – is increasingly construed as an autonomous entity devoid of corruption and state intervention, and thus widely perceived as a guarantor of stability in the context of a 'weak state'.[8] 'In the communist era the danger was understood to be the intrusiveness of the state; now it is more often the uncertainty and untrustworthiness of state action and the insecurity of markets and employment', write Gal and Kligman, who also maintain that '[t]he image of a stable, autonomous family survives, despite the fact that in East Central Europe too, over the last decades, there have been profound changes' (Gal and Kligman 2000: 69). As a constant in a world of social insecurities and second economy, the nuclear family appears to provide the most efficient framework for dealing with the devastating impact of social and economic change.

Rather ironically, the outstanding significance of the 'Balkan family' had also been encouraged by repressive ideologisation of family life under socialism, when it was claimed that decadent capitalism and feminism would eventually destroy the family and family values – not unlike conservative attitudes today. In disagreement with Verdery, who argues that state socialism emphasised the family as a basic element in the polity, Vesna Kesić holds that the family in Yugoslavia was not sufficiently supported in its role as a mediator between the individual and the state (Verdery 1994: 230; Kesić 2001: 69). Despite many positive family laws, 'the negative side of this "Yugoslav way" of overlooking the family and relinquishing it to the private sphere was that women's status and rights within the family were never adequately protected by law or socially considered'. Kesić thus maintains, that 'although traditional patriarchy was seemingly destroyed through the quick modernization and the socialist equality principle, patriarchal structures and gender relations remained unquestioned' (Kesić 2001: 69f.). This led to a 'hidden patriarchy' (ibid.) in Socialist Yugoslavia that was replaced by a growing and less concealed masculinisation and militarisation of society, with the nationalists' rise to power in the beginning of the 1990s – just at a point when legislation had started to change in a 'woman friendly' direction (Kesić 2001: 72; see also Duhaček 2001).

The role gender issues played in the growing ethnicisation after the decline of state socialism should not be underestimated. The political philosophers Rada Iveković and Julie Mostov state that:

> [i]n the case of the former Yugoslavia, gender hierarchies and deeply
> anchored patriarchies at different levels sustained all of the post-so-
> cialist nationalisms. Gender and patriarchal hierarchies facilitated the
> reshuffling of the social structure, communal order and the state ... The
> collective entity of class was replaced by (ethno)nation and an old/new
> hierarchy of national guardians emerged together with sexually repres-
> sive gender roles, return to 'traditional' values, misogynistic rhetoric,
> and a hyper-virile militarism. (Iveković and Mostov 2002: 17f.)

The increasing militarisation went hand in hand with a (ethno-)nation-
alist demographic rhetoric that constituted an unmistakable prelude to
war. Ethno-nationality based on ancestry and kinship ties provided the
ground upon which the warring parties were configured. The historian
Hannes Grandits observed that '[d]uring wartime, the national group
was propagated as the most important loyalty group and was equalled
to (patriarchal) concepts of kinship' (Grandits 2005: 120). According to
him, marriage is hence no longer perceived as a private affair, but is crucial for the unity of the national community and an important factor in
the context of community stability (ibid.).

In the Croatian post-war scenario, family cohesion seems of utmost
importance. Especially in rural areas such as the Dalmatian hinterland,
family, relatives and godfathers [*kumovi*] are local reference points that
ensure better and quicker access to resources than hard-to-reach state
funding and, in addition, provide more reliable protection against elu-
sive and threatening conditions in a rapidly changing socio-economic
environment. During the presidential elections in Croatia in January
2005 when I lived in Sinj, the local parish gazette, for instance, openly
appealed to the community to 'vote Catholic' (meaning HDZ, I assume),
the main argument being that Croatia had suffered a drop in the birth
rate. The author pointed out that it was the 'responsibility and duty of
every Croat man and woman to ensure that there are more cradles than
graves' in Croatia in the future. Such church-backed demographic appeals to women to reproduce the independent nation in the private
sphere continue to fuel the repressive tendencies in the family that currently prevail in Croatia.

It seems that the encounter with the transnational world that demands new gender codes gradually fosters 'neo-patriarchal role expectations' and brings the post-war Croatian society back to the familiar
dichotomy of independent male and dependent female in need of masculine protection (Grandits 2005: 113; see also Novikova 2001: 186).
This, however, is a tendency on the level of domestic family and gender policies that Croatia shares with other prospective or marginalised

new EU-member states. Writing on the role of the family in postsocialist European public discourse, Gal and Kligman state that '[i]n the face of massive social change, the family is popularly considered the one institution that provides continuity with the past. Both men and women idealize the family in ways similar to the familiar romanticization of the peasantry as "authentic"' (Gal and Kligman 2000: 68). It is this very idealisation of the peasant lifestyle and revaluation of rural simplicity that – in concordance with a tribute to family life – informs the nationalist imaginary and visions of inviolated home rule in the ultraconservative and right-wing circles of present-day Croatia.

'Economy of Jars', Subsistence Farming and Backyard Husbandry

In the peripheries of South Eastern Europe the economic restructuring of national economies has tended to foster small-scale and service sector marketisation. In rural areas in Croatia the emerging market economy has most notably affected cultivators and subsistence farmers.[9] Having suffered from economic hardship throughout the years of the centrally planned economy, the peasantry has increasingly grown in confidence, if not necessarily in importance and income, since the political-economic transformation of the early 1990s; and it now affirms itself as a 'site of resistance' to urban neoliberalism. At every possible opportunity my host in Sinj, for instance, declared, 'I am proud to be a peasant', thus not simply expressing a regional farmer's pride and devotion to nature, but also stating his disapproval of large agribusiness companies, food imports and global markets – and the extreme exposure to price volatility that comes with this.[10] He had in fact worked as a car mechanic all his life but always held a small patch of land in Glavice near Sinj and raised a few animals in his backyard. During the years of the Homeland War, he and his family, like most people in the region, eked out an existence as subsistence cultivators and lived off the reserves (home-made vegetable conserves, gammon, smoked bacon, sausages, etc.) they had accumulated during the previous years – and shared them with numerous refugees from adjacent villages who had been displaced or fled assaults.

Since the end of the war, severe unemployment has accompanied the restructuring of the labour market, and levels of inequality and poverty have increased. The economic divides between the city and the country – a continuation of earlier inequalities under state socialism – have deepened further. Possibilities of alternative occupations have been particularly limited in rural areas such as the Dalmatinska Zagora, where poverty, income inequality and lack of prospects have inevitably given rise to an expansion in informal economies. Individual and household livelihood strategies in a context of neoliberal austerity thus not only involve the mobilisation of 'social assets' in the form of an economy of gifts and favours within networks of relatives and friends to which individuals or households can appeal for help or to which they are obligated (Burawoy, Krotov and Lytkina 2000: 47), but also entail recourse to historically situated practices such as subsistence and backyard farming.

In Dalmatia the population has always been reliant on agricultural activity. The cultivation of allotments and small-scale peasant plots connected to family homes were a common trait of state socialist models of economy and development across South Eastern and Central Europe. The economic geographer Adrian Smith writes that '[d]espite the large-scale industrialisation and urbanisation of these relatively underdeveloped rural economies after the Second World War under a model of "forced industrialisation" for the war economy of the Cold War (Smith 1998; Kaldor 1990), these connections to land and agrarian practices were maintained throughout the post-war period' (Smith 2007: 213).[11] Smith's appraisal coincides with the narratives of my interlocutors in rural Dalmatia and helps to explain why the domestic economy of household food production has become central in response to the economic crisis resulting from implementation of neoliberal market reform policies. 'Rural households', he writes,

> were often better positioned to respond to and survive the collapse of the formal economy, as they often had ready access to land. Yet, complex networks of transactions and exchange are also used to sustain the livelihoods of urban households, many of whom retain close linkages into rural areas through parents and grandparents who did not move to towns and cities during the process of state socialist industrialisation and urbanisation. (Smith 2007: 214)

In the same breath Smith warns against treating such practices simply as forms of resistance to neoliberal-induced hardship, and suggests perceiving them as 'rooted in regional agrarian pasts' (ibid.). In the case of rural Dalmatia, however, the 'agrarian past' is inseparably linked to the history of foreign exploitation and local resistance to various regulatory procedures – and, viewed in this light, the transition to capitalism entails yet another form of resistance to regulations pertaining to property relations, land utilisation and food production.[12]

Jonas Frykman has remarked that the ex-Yugoslav peasantry epitomises an extremely static culture that challenges contemporary images of globalisation, technologisation and exploitation (Frykman and Gilje 2003: 170). This challenge, however, is anchored in romanticising the simplicity of rural lifestyle, hard physical labour and the myth of incorruptibility related to it. In addition it is linked rhetorically to narratives of historical peasant exploitation by foreign rule and feudalism – and to attempts to overcome these forms of oppression. In this sense, the peasantry appeals to ideas of independence and autarchy, and is thus suited to represent the suffering of the Croatian people as well as its industrious and robust spirit. Furthermore, the symbolic and emotional equation of land with 'homeland' and the definition of peasant identity as a sense of being rooted in a particular soil have been used as justification for the pursuit of a deeply territorial and nationalist politics. Ideologies of national belonging to a territory that is exclusively Croat have led to an increasing 'nationalisation of village life'. Today, peasants are an important political force in the redefinition of the Croatian nation, and romanticised peasantry has once again – not unlike conditions towards the end of the nineteenth century – become a major element in the celebration of ethnos and national ideology.[13]

The reassessment of traditional values and romanticisation of rural life also entails a gender aspect and goes hand in hand with a reinforcement of patriarchal and religiously motivated role models. Towards the end of socialism, the notion of women as 'mother, wife [and] nurturer' regained strength and contributed to the preservation of mythic rural life (Kesić 2001: 78). This, among other factors, led to an increasing partitioning of rural areas and also affected the urban–rural divide. It was the rural population that profited the least from the changes in the 1970s and 1980s, and the gap between rural and urban standards of living continually widened. It might have been the disillusioning experiences during this period that helped to bring about not only the election success of the nationalistic HDZ in rural areas but also the current aversion towards further 'Westernisation' or globalising tendencies, particularly in areas most neglected during the later years of Yugoslav state socialism.

In Jadranka Kosor's conservative cabinet, scepticism towards unlimited liberalisation and marketisation of the national economy prevailed, and the hardworking peasantry was extolled as the backbone of Croatia's economy. Accordingly, in 2008, Croatia's previous minister of Agriculture, Fisheries and Rural Development, Božidar Pankretić, addressed the visitors to the ministry's homepage as follows:

> Globalisation knocks at the doors everywhere and consequently it cannot be avoided in Croatia either. Liberalisation in agriculture is the issue often used for intimidation of agricultural producers. In Croa-

tia, as is well known, agricultural producers are quite numerous, but considering the fact that, at the same time, their holdings are on average very small, they certainly have reason for concern ... However, on countless occasions in history Croatia's rural areas have demonstrated an extraordinary tenacity and power of endurance ... The hardworking people, farmers and fishermen are the priceless treasure of Croatia.[14]

This brief passage reflects the ministry's earlier hesitant attitude towards globalisation per se, and acknowledges the dangers that a liberal market economy poses to Croatian small-scale farmers. At the same time, the text invokes the 'tenacity' of the rural population and appeals to their endurance in view of the developments that (may) lie ahead on the path to EU accession. The minister was well aware of the country's problems in the agricultural sector and suspected that Croatia might not be fit for competition in a global market – especially since many issues regarding property relations and rural development policy have remained unresolved or have stagnated after Croatia's secession from Yugoslavia.

Fragmentation of land due to inheritance laws, demographic transition and the monetarisation of the economy was a problem from the nineteenth century onwards when increasing numbers of local peasants lost their land titles (Leutloff-Grandits 2006a: 68). Private property was further parcelled out and, as a consequence, the little land people owned was cultivated for subsistence use – a development which continues to obstruct structural changes and the diversification of farm activities. In 2005 the Republic of Croatia set development objectives to improve rural development, and it started 'The Croatian Plan for Agriculture and Rural Development' (the SAPARD Plan). The aims of the plan include a reduction in regional disparities within the country by creating favourable conditions for social-economic development in the most backward regions, improved competitiveness and efficiency of primary agricultural, forestry and fishery production, and additional employment opportunities and income for farmers and all others living in rural areas.

The main beneficiaries of EU pre-accession support schemes should ideally include remote rural areas like the Sinjska krajina – a region that is still basically bucolic and poor, with most of the population living in hamlets and struggling to make a living from small-scale agriculture. It is also in these regions, however, that implementation of the Common Agricultural Policy is most heavily disputed, due to a general mistrust towards centralised rural development plans. In the Sinj region, most farming continues to be conducted at a subsistence level and relies mainly on 'private property, social networks and a moral economy based on kinship or community relations' (Leutloff-Grandits 2006a: 41). The majority of households in villages and hamlets surrounding Sinj combine animal husbandry with the cultivation of plants. The animals – pigs, turkeys, rabbits and large numbers of chickens – are kept in wooden sheds or stone barns, usually located in the backyard of the household site. Sheep (and more seldom horses) are left in the mountains with the shepherds during the summer months. Furthermore, almost every household cultivates a small field or a garden in which tomatoes, peppers, zucchini, cucumber, onion, carrots, *blitva* [Swiss chard] and potatoes are grown. The growing of vegetables is combined with the tending of grapes and fruit trees, necessary for the production of wine and *rakija* that is distilled from fermented fruit, i.e. plums [*šljivovica*], grapes [*lozovača*] and figs [*smokvovača*]. Occasionally, liqueur is made from rose buds. In terms of meat, vegetables and fruit, most households in the region are virtually self-sufficient.

The production, preparation and consumption of food and drink are highly important features and take up large parts of the daily routine of those people who proudly self-identify as peasants. A Zagreb city-dweller once condescendingly told me that in Sinj people would eat anything that flies, crawls, walks or swims. The Cetina region is indeed known for great crayfish, trout, *Arambaše*,[15] and lamb recipes, and frogs are considered a rare delicacy. The cultivation of small-scale peasant plots connected to family homes in rural areas produces what Cellarius has called an 'economy of jars', as it involves the circulation of both fresh and pickled, preserved and canned products – often through forms of non-commodified exchange and reciprocity (Cellarius 2000; see also Smith 2007: 213). In the context of a wider economy of favours, this 'economy of jars' is an essential element of the cohesion of the local community as well as an important factor in supporting the livelihoods of the households of relatives and friends who live in urban areas.

The quest for self-sufficiency and independence from agricultural policy and state-controlled price monitoring occasionally verges on the absurd. My hosts recently told me over the phone, for example, that they were now sinking a well in their *polje*, their field. The reason, I was told, was not only to have a direct water supply in the field but to be independent of the municipal water supply in case of water shortages or rises in water prices. This search for autonomy might be related to memories of communist times when the region was deliberately devoid of access to centralised facilities such as water supply, electricity, sewage disposal, telephones and central heating. Nowadays, however, as the infrastructure even in the remotest areas of the Dalmatinska Zagora is fairly well engineered, such measures are primarily symbolic.

During the course of my fieldwork it became increasingly clear to me that the cultivation of land shapes people's daily lives and strongly affects their perception not only of their physical surroundings but also of time. The names of the months, for example, derive from the agricultural activities of that time of year, and illustrate how notions of cohabitation and conduct of life are embedded in the agricultural cycle. The Croatian term for 'December', for example, is *prosinac* and derives from the verb *prositi*, meaning 'to beg', but it also describes the notion of donating and giving alms. It was explained to me by an informant that this expression stems from a time prior to industrialisation and 'before people had fridges. That's why people stored supplies for the winter and spring in their houses. That's what I am still doing, as you know. I have plenty of food supplies in reserve'. *Prositi*, denoting 'needy' or 'in need of something', makes *prosinac* the month in which those who have no reserves are particularly needy and those who have stored supplies have full cellars. *Prositi*, I was told, also means that if people in need want to beg for alms they should ask in December when there is actually something to give. The whole notion thus consists of three aspects: firstly, the request for help [*prositi*], the act of giving [*darovati* or *darivati*], and finally the exchange of goods [*razmijeniti* or *razmjenjivati*], through which those who received 'alms' are indebted to those who supported them. They are expected to reciprocate at a later date. My informant also made it clear that 'having a full cellar' is a sign of diligence and sensible economising that is highly regarded, and *darovati*, giving alms, improves one's social status. This example – and the same principle applies to all other months – paradigmatically illustrates the concept of 'reserves' as objects of recourse to reinforce supplies in states of emergency caused by severe socio-economic change, war, or deliberately induced neo-constitutions such as, for instance, entry into the European Union (cf. Hauschild 2007: 4, my translation). Practical-technical exhaustion of the environmental resources in the form of subsistence farming and part-time pastoralism – in conjunction with the circulation through a complex network of transactions and exchange – turns the evaluation of the region's rural backwardness on its head, and constitutes a peasant identity that is diametrically opposed to notions of a 'peasant Other who is constrained by simplicity and social fractiousness' (Herzfeld 1987: 60) that had for a long time dominated academic discourses on peasant societies.

Croatian agriculture has a substantial environmental impact, and the pride of Dalmatian peasants, who to a considerable extent produce their own food supply, often goes hand in hand with their assertions on the wholesomeness of local food, the biological diversity of flora and fauna as well as the cleanliness of the environment. This praise of Dalmatian 'purity' is contrasted with the assumed degeneration of 'Westerners' and 'Western lifestyles' – a degeneration that rural Dalmatians often also extend to Croatian urbanites, state officials and bureaucrats. 'The people in Zagreb lead completely different lives from ours. They don't know our unemployment and they don't know our history. They are arrogant and think that we are backward farmers. But they have no idea how we live here. The biggest problem in Croatia today is that the sacrifices people have made for our country are not equally shared', said a local Franciscan priest, indicating that those who were not directly afflicted by repression and war could not have as loyal a relationship to their home country as, for example, the inhabitants of conflict-torn and disadvantaged areas such as Sinj. In this statement it becomes clear that suffering and self-sacrifice are used as indicators for the affinity to a God-given homeland. The distinction as to whether this affinity is 'deserved' or not is measured according to people's (sacrificial) relationship with their material surrounding, and is employed to affirm and strengthen the gap between rural and urban lifestyles. The deep social and economic disparities between the peripheral region of the Dalmatian hinterland and urban centres (even towns on the Dalmatian coast, like Split, Zadar and Šibenik) continue to gain momentum as rural Dalmatians embellish their exclusion from urbanity and their rejection of Western liberal institutions (Jakir 1999; Clewing 2001; Leutloff-Grandits 2006a, 2006b). Intending to stand out against the standardising policies of the European Union's notions of culture and nature, Dalmatian villagers reinterpret their remoteness and the institutional traditions of patriarchal life as virtue, and intentionally reconstruct the marginality of the region (cf. Lowenhaupt Tsing 1993; Green 2005).

'Is Brussels the new Belgrade?' Euroscepticism and Ethno-Regionalism

On the Way to EU Membership

During my fieldwork (2003–2005) in rural Dalmatia I was recurrently startled by the strong anti-European sentiment that I encountered, although this issue had not been an initial research topic of mine. Yet whenever I talked to people, I was treated like a representative of the European Union and asked whether and how, in my opinion, Croatia would benefit from EU membership. In 2003 Croatia had officially applied for

EU membership and the European Council granted 'candidate country' status a year later. The entry negotiations, however, did not start until October 2005. At that time, the centre-right conservative government under Prime Minister Ivo Sanader (HDZ; in office December 2003–July 2009), together with the pro-European centrist President Stjepan Mesić, ambitiously promoted Croatia's accession to the EU, whereas large numbers of the population still disapproved of this political course.[16] According to a Gallup World Poll conducted in 2007, only one-third of the Croatian population was convinced that Croatian membership of the European Union would be good.[17] However, five years later, on 22 January 2012 when a referendum on the EU accession of the Republic of Croatia was held, 66.27 per cent of the Croatian population voted in favour of the accession, and only 33.13 per cent were against.[18] Despite the low voter turnout of only 43.51 per cent that some right-wing politicians interpreted as distrust of Croatian citizens in the government, the accession treaty was ratified in March 2012. On 1 July 2013 the Republic of Croatia joined the European Union as its twenty-eighth member state.

However, the prearrangements to the referendum did not run as smoothly as looked-for by the pro-membership and informational campaign. Opponents of the 'yes' vote – members of the ultra-right-wing Croatian Party of Rights (HSP), veteran associations, as well as various non-parliamentary nationalist groups – warned of a loss of sovereignty, just two decades after Croatia's independence. In addition, more than a thousand signatories of a petition requested that the referendum be postponed until generals Ante Gotovina and Mladen Markač were released by the ICTY. Ironically, Gotovina himself made an announcement from his holding cell in Scheveningen early in 2012 urging the citizens of Croatia to vote in favour of joining the EU – and less than a year after the referendum, he and Markač were indeed acquitted by the ICTY.

Unsurprisingly, lowest support for the EU accession was recorded in Dalmatia, and of the eighteen (out of 556) cities or municipalities in Croatia that voted against the referendum, most were located in Dalmatia. Considering the growing disenchantment with the EU in the wake of the European sovereign debt crisis, Dalmatian Eurosceptics had tragically anticipated some of the doubts and uncertainties regarding the structure of the Eurozone system, trade imbalances, as well as the economic and monetary union that currently concern all EU member states.[19] For many Eurosceptics, the rediscovery of regionality – and in the particular case of Dalmatia, recourse to a Mediterranean identity – seems a feasible alternative to the advancement of supra-national economic and political blocs. In the ongoing process of socio-economic and political transformation, different understandings of region and regionalism are set to provide an antidote to unrestrained industrialisation, centralisation and homogenisation.

Christian Giordano distinguishes between ethnic regionalism and cosmopolitan regionalism. According to his distinction, the Dalmatian regionalist movement would clearly qualify as ethnic regionalism, defined as 'a socio-political movement striving to build an imagined collectivity whose belief in commonality is based on ethnic criteria regarded as qualities unique to one's group such as origin, ancestry, history, traditions, culture, religion, language, and – not least – territory' (Giordano 2007: 50). And although the Dalmatian case is not nearly as radical as the Padanian or Catalonian examples that Giordano refers to, and has hardly any serious separatist tendencies, it is still an ethno-regionalism that resembles a very specific form of conservative nationalism. In this respect, Dalmatian regionalism is not a *counter-* but a *co-*phenomena concerning Croatian ethno-nationalism, but it is still a dissenting and subversive force when it comes to challenging globalisation and handing over shares of political, economic and social sovereignty to a centralised government and to supra-national organisations such as the European Union.

Looking at the above-mentioned characteristics and conditions concerning the redefinition of Dalmatian identity, it becomes increasingly clear that Dalmatia's (self-)marginalised role within Croatia corresponds with and, in microcosm, mirrors Croatia's role within the association of States of the European Union. Constructed as peripheral, underdeveloped and conflict-laden by the respective superordinate centres, the position of Dalmatia within the Republic of Croatia, like Croatia's position within Europe, is characterised by an ambiguous core–periphery relationship that, from the marginalised's perspective, oscillates between the quest for acceptance and the disaffirmation of hegemonic power.

From a historical point of view, the Mediterranean and the entire Balkan peninsula became a region that was peripheral to the European centres from the sixteenth century onwards, and today this consistent marginalisation is reflected in the fact that virtually all the EU regions with the weakest economies are located in the Mediterranean. Such anamneses do not provide an appealing prospect for South East European countries such as Croatia that, despite the current Eurozone crisis, pin their hopes on economic benefits from EU development plans and programmes. Instead, however, the sense of being cut off from the centre and kept on a short leash is quite widespread in the south-eastern peripheries of Europe. Sarah Green has analysed the dynamics of marginality and ambiguity in the process of the implementation of EU programmes around the Greek–Albanian border area in Epirus, and her observations are chiefly transferable to the Dalmatian case. Green notes, for example, that people in Epirus know that they are considered irrelevant by the state authorities and various supra-national entities, such as the EU, while 'at the same time acknowledging that this ideology that renders them irrelevant ha[s] teeth; they ha[ve] to live with it, whatever they th[ink] about it' (Green 2005: 125). This is to say that no matter whether people believe in the state's/EU's ideology or consider it a false construction, they are eventually forced to recognise the construction's 'teeth' and to reproduce hegemonic authority (cf. Žižek 1989; Navaro-Yashin 2002). In Dalmatia, these feelings of subjection, along with the sense of being at the mercy of unswayable global powers, often lead to passivity and surrender. A young Franciscan from Sinj described the situation to me as follows: 'We have lost all self-initiative during communism. J.F. Kennedy once said, "Don't ask what your country can do for you, but what you can do for your country and yourself" [he quotes in English]. Waiting for a better life is good for nothing. But what are our perspectives? Europe is a one-way street that won't do us any good'. This comment attests to the perception of economic stasis and conveys an impression of the grave disillusionment that prevails regarding the standstill in people's desire for progress. Furthermore, it entails the apprehension that the Croatian people might not be capable of adjusting to neoliberal conditions. Apart from being temporally locked-in between the country's socialist past and its way to EU membership, many Croatians also feel spatially locked-in, in what is perceived as a potentially threatening neighbourhood, with more powerful EU member states on one side and former war enemies on the other. 'Our neighbours in the EU are former occupying powers: Italy, Austria, Hungary ... they all have exploited our small country', another interlocutor said, and with his statement he encapsulated the Croatian wariness towards an integrating multicultural European project. The apparent absence of alternatives to Croatia's EU membership spurs a cynical, if not resigned and apathetic attitude regarding the country's role in a globalised world. And although many Croatian citizens might be sceptical or cynical about the nation-state and/or the EU, they simultaneously acknowledge power of the state and the EU, and still hope for financial support and recognition (Herzfeld 1997; Navaro-Yashin 2002; Green 2005: 161). It is this discrepancy that causes continual disappointment and confusion regarding people's expectations and their strategies of resistance to arbitrariness and uniformity.

At present, many rural Croatians perceive their region's underdevelopment to be a result of the prevalent core–periphery relationship, whereas current EU policies and incentives increasingly focus on supporting local development and generally privilege regionalism over nationalism (Harvie 1994; cf. Green 2005: 219). Considering the 'centrality of the regional framework to the EU architecture', the centralising process of European Unionisation is dissipating in a somewhat ironic twist (Ballinger 2007: 62). Ulf Brunnbauer states that

> [t]he processes of decentralization are also facilitated by the technicalities of European integration: the administration of funds for regional development, from which the new member states benefit significantly, is dependent on the creation and subsequent functioning of regional administrative bodies which, in time, may become loci of political power and identification. (Brunnbauer 2007: 6)

Such capacities concern environmental-geographical features as well as the ecology, political economy and cultural resources of the regions. Yet to realistically evaluate the worth of regional identity as a counterweight to national identity and/or identification with supra-national entities such as the EU, it is crucial to distinguish between etic and emic understandings of the region. On the one hand, a growing number of political activists and scholars – most of them anthropologists – recognise the 'modernity' of the region and its potentially post-national character and emphasise the fact that the region and regional identity 'now often figure as the space of multicultural, even "cosmopolitan", imaginings' (Ballinger 2007: 67). As an emic category, however, I argue that regionalism does not inevitably imply tolerance of diversity and pluralist coexistence. Most notably, Dalmatian ethno-regionalism is marked by an exclusive, provincial character that links notions of belonging to territorial and familial rootedness and tradition – and an assumed superiority to other areas of Croatia. According to this perspective, the regional is primarily located in rural village life, which also explains the resurgent romanticisation and glorification of rurality and anachronistic peasant lifestyles in the Dalmatian hinterland since the mid-1990s.

The Croatian journalist Dragan Antulov attempts to explain the development that Dalmatian self-marginalisation assumes the shape of consistent regionalism by taking Dalmatia's special role within the history of the Croatian nation-state into account. Although Croatia seemed to be the country least suited to a transplant of regionalist ideas from the West, he argues that regionalism in Croatia nevertheless became a far more important political factor than in most post-communist countries in the area, most notably due to geographical (diverse climates, topographies, natural resources) and historical factors (Antulov 2000). Citing the country's heterogeneity and the fact that Croatia was divided into four distinct administrative territories within the Habsburg Empire when other European countries began to form homogeneous nation-states in the nineteenth century, Antulov explains the continuous existence of distinct regional identities, and implicitly acknowledges the practical value of the regionalist idea. Furthermore, he mentions the geographic diversity of the country and points out that the 'cultures' of the various regions – most notably Slavonia, Istria and Dalmatia – differ from that of the Croatian nation-state as a whole. This regionalist tradition, however, clearly obstructed the nation-building processes in the Balkan Peninsula in the nineteenth century, and all young Balkan nations eventually followed the centralist French model – adopted by the Ottoman Empire in the mid-nineteenth century – which granted little power to the traditional provinces and regions. 'As a consequence, all new Southeast European nations divided their territories into politically weak and fully dependent administrative units, similar to the French prefectures, and often disregarded grown historical regions' (Roth 2007: 23).

The fact that it was Tito's communist regime that successfully managed to build the Croatian nation-state (with its own centralised administration) under the federal system of post–Second World War Yugoslavia, made it clear that after independence, decentralisation would pose the greatest threat to the young Republic of Croatia. When the HDZ first came to power in 1990, it recognised the danger entailed in regionalism, and immediately sought to centralise the administration – and thus promoted the fears of regionalists that the freedom and right of the regions to determine their own economic and cultural paths would be narrowed down.[20] Tuđman even attempted to eradicate reminders of the country's heterogeneous past by proposing a number of renamings, including changing the name 'Dalmatia' to 'Southern Croatia' (Antulov 2000). This fear also points towards 'the decreased capacity of national centres to create and extract feelings of attachment in times of economic crisis during the transformation period', as Ulf Brunnbauer pointed out (Brunnbauer 2007: 6).

The regional movement in Dalmatia, however, is by no means anti-nationalist, even if it advocates policies of regional autonomy and self-management. The main regional party, *Dalmatinska Akcija*, DA [Dalmatian Action], thus never endeavoured to resist the HDZ's attempts to dominate the regional political structure, as was the case, for instance, in Istria where the *Istarski Demokratski Sabor*, IDS [Istrian

Democratic Assembly] ran for a more regionalised Istria and rejected all forms of Croatian centralism and nationalism (cf. Ashbrook 2006: 624, 635).[21] In contrast to Istrian regionalism, political regionalism in Dalmatia does not promote demilitarisation or key ideologies associated with Western political systems (such as the promotion of citizen sovereignty, multiethnic toleration, human rights, and free media), but, on the contrary, explicitly excludes ethnic minorities and focuses on threats to local identity from outside powers – even more than the nationalist politics of the HDZ. Whilst the IDS stressed Istria's multiethnic composition and favoured that peninsula becoming part of an Alpine-Adriatic macro-region, and thus included in the Assembly of European Regions, Dalmatian regionalists increasingly locate Dalmatia in the Mediterranean. This step is a strategic attempt to stress the region's historical tie to (ancient) Europe and to secure Western recognition whilst avoiding direct advances towards the European Union. A more pragmatic reason for this association is certainly also the hope for economic recovery of the region and its claim to subsidies as well as a share in the prosperity of the tourist industry.

But even the Regional Policy of the European Union – the stated aims of which are to remove disparities of wealth across the EU, to restructure declining industrial areas and to diversify rural areas suffering from declining agriculture – is widely repudiated in Dalmatia as well as other parts of the country for being exerted 'from above' and for therefore being unauthentic. This repudiation mainly rests on a fear of control by external forces, and culminates in the rhetorical question of one of my interlocutors: 'We have danced to Belgrade's tune long enough now – or should Brussels be our new Belgrade?' Polemical remarks of this kind operate by deliberately blurring the boundaries between two historically incommensurable projects of state affiliation, and are often followed by definite appeals to halt the sale of land, real estate, banks and other state property to foreign investors in what is perceived as a 'sell-out of the homeland' since the end of the war. Elaborating on these apprehensions of 'foreign infiltration', I will now briefly consider some local comments on globalisation processes and analyse the strategies used by Croatian Eurosceptics and Dalmatian ethno-regionalists to oppose Croatia's EU membership.

'We don't need Europe, but Europe needs us'

Many Eurosceptics who endorse ethno-national or ethno-regional attitudes see Croatia's recently gained independence threatened by the EU, and frequently utilise comparisons with former Socialist Yugoslavia to express these fears. Its natural resources and the income of the (mainly Istrian- and Dalmatian-based) tourist industry make Croatia a principally 'rich' country that according to their understanding had previously been economically exploited and had had to help to provide for the other republics within the Yugoslav federation. The same, Eurosceptics argue, would be the case once within Europe, and the equation EU = YU can be regularly heard or seen as a popular graffito.

The most frequently expressed motives of Croatian Eurosceptics are their doubts concerning the EU's hybrid system of inter-governmentalism and supra-nationalism. They contest the raison d'être for supranational bureaucratic and ideological unification, are critical of the European Union's common trade policy, especially for agriculture and fisheries, they frequently ridicule the European Convention on Human Rights (ECHR), and rigorously reject a common legislative procedure. The principal cause underlying all these misgivings is the fear of subjection and the assumption that with accession to the European Union, Croatia would (again) be a pawn in the hands of the Great Powers. To a certain extent, this scepticism and suspicion traces back to Tuđman who was always critical of the European Union and argued that multicultural entities would not be viable in the long term (Razsa and Lindstrom 2004; Jović 2009: 8). The political analyst Dejan Jović notes that

> [f]or Croatian nationalists, it was difficult to accept that one day, in an enlarged European Union, there would be no heavily guarded border with Serbia, or Bosnia-Herzegovina (and in particular with its Republic of Srpska), and that the level of integration with these neighbours would become higher than it had been in the last years of Yugoslavia. (Jović 2009: 8)

In the summer of 2005, one of my informants told me:

> In '91–95 the same happened to us that is now happening in Iraq, we simply did not understand it at the time. Today we know that it was the Serbs who attacked us, but that they were only puppets of the US. For five years no one intervened so we could mutually lacerate ourselves – and then America stepped in and pretended to be the 'liberator' ... and now, the US and the EU have the nerve to blackmail us.

This interpretation of stages of the violent disintegration of Yugoslavia as orchestrated by 'the West' is very widespread throughout all ex-Yugoslav republics, and corroborates notions of the 'guiltless' victim status of the respective local parties – but it also concurs with Perry Anderson's laconic comment '[w]hen actual wars threatened in Yugoslavia, far from preventing their outbreak, the Union if anything helped to trigger them' (Anderson 2007). And albeit coming from the other end of the political spectrum, the majority of my interlocutors would immediately subscribe to Anderson's assessment and argue that, for exactly this reason, EU accession clauses were an impertinence that should have been denied.

When in February 2011 more than ten thousand demonstrators called on the Croatian government to protect war veterans after a Croat was arrested in Bosnia on charges of war crimes, one of the organisers of the protests said: 'We were not dying for our country to be prosecuted now, and [for] our workers, peasants and fishermen to have a life without dignity' (Ilić 2011). This comment and the somewhat abrupt mentioning of veterans' sacrifices in the Homeland War in the same breath as living conditions in post-war Croatia points towards the widely held interleaving of Croatia's struggle for independence and the ensuing economic hardship in the context of having to meet EU requirements. This veteran was upset because he felt that Croatia's autonomy that he had fought for in the 1990s was at stake, and that the conditions for joining the EU were being met at the expense of individual Croatian workers, peasants and fishermen who, in his view, were not being properly protected from the higher productivity of the 'northern economies' within the European Union, and/or were becoming increasingly dependent on transfer payments and losing all autonomy.

I have already mentioned that one of the main arguments of the Eurosceptics is the threat that EU regulations pose to Croatian economic power. This assessment mainly appeals to the Stabilisation and Association Agreements (SAA) that create a free trade area preparing the candidate countries for EU membership. Demanded revisions of *acquis*, especially with regard to agriculture and rural development, food safety, veterinary policies, fisheries and last but not least environmental issues, repeatedly meet with opposition from local actors. Relating to the Common Agricultural Policy (CAP), for instance, many Eurosceptical small farmers fear the intended replacement of subsidy payments linked to specific produce by direct payments based on farm size, instead preferring stronger protectionist measures against imports of foreign agricultural and other products into Croatia. One of my interlocutors, a smallholder from Sinj, was convinced that the CAP would undercut small famers in the peripheries all over Europe. He said: 'The idea of Europe is good, but the practice isn't. Our small enterprises won't stand a chance. Trucks from Europe will arrive here and sell potatoes for 50 cents per kilo, [whereas] our own will cost two euros. What am I supposed to do then?' And another farmer said: 'When the EU comes, I will be a servant (*sluga*) in my own house. I will become a servant, a foreigner (*tuđ*) in my own house and on my own land'. These comments convey local fears of price dumping, foreign regulation and dictation of production that are perceived as highly alienating and existentially threatening. 'I couldn't slaughter my own pigs anymore, couldn't smoke the meat myself any longer and I couldn't distil my schnapps, my wine ... ', an elderly farmer, who vehemently objected to Croatia's EU membership, told me. Knowing that the EU's small farmers only receive 8 per cent of CAP's available subsidies, Croatian subsistence and small-scale farmers are afraid in future of losing even more of what remains of their autarchy (Jeffery 2003). In their view, the trade agreements of the European Union continue the list of foreign forces that exploit Croatia's natural resources and tourist revenues. In this context, the saying

> *Tko je jači taj prednjači* [The one who is stronger will go ahead/lead]

was used to describe the Darwinist 'survival of the fittest' rationale that, in the view of many Croatian Eurosceptics, characterises the neoliberal policy of the EU.

In a recent essay, in which he argues that the future of Europe lies in the regeneration of its southern (i.e. Mediterranean) regions, the German political scientist Claus Leggewie advocates that '[a]n agrarian economy that is ecologically sensitive and much better adapted to local needs and markets needs to be negotiated, as does a more balanced trading system with the North and a sensible migration regime' (Leggewie 2012). Regional development subsidies, structural assistance and eventually EU rescue funds 'only make sense in the mid- to long-term if they are directed at alternative energies, sustainable tourism, fair trade and maritime development (among other things). Only then can vague and ad hoc restructuring lead to sustainable development and the political tutelage of the North turn into cooperation between equals', he argues (Leggewie 2012). But as long as truly sustainable development plans fail and the gap between top and bottom in the EU grows, for new members states such as Croatia the prospect of self-determined economic and social development (and with it the welfare and stability that come from social democracy) seems to further recede into the distance. And it would be naive, not just from the point of view of Croatian Eurosceptics or ethno-regionalists, to turn a blind eye to the fact that with Croatia as a new member state, the EU has acquired a new periphery of cheap labour.

Last but not least remains the topic of effective implementation of judiciary and fundamental rights, including – at least until the recent acquittal of ex-generals Gotovina and Markač – the highly touchy issue of Croatia's collaboration with the International Criminal Tribunal for the former Yugoslavia (ICTY), the protection of minority and human rights (particularly concerning refugee returns), and the strengthening of prevention measures in the fight against corruption and organised crime. Pan-European human rights standards are introduced through the European Convention for the Protection of Human Rights and Fundamental Freedoms (ECHR), but hitherto, Croatian courts have failed to apply the ECHR properly for a number of different reasons, and these legal frameworks meet a lot of resistance on judicial and political levels as well as in public discourse.[22] In my opinion, the major challenges regarding the implementation of the ECHR – that are also the most emotionally charged topics – remain tolerance towards minorities (not only towards Croatian Serbs and the Roma minority, but also the LGTB community), refugee return issues, and the improved handling of domestic war crimes cases, especially as the majority of crimes have yet to be successfully prosecuted.

One way or another, the resistance to EU accession reveals that politicised emotions have become a powerful source of policy making in contemporary Croatia. Analysing the strategies of resistance in the Polish campaign against EU membership, Golanska-Ryan has noted that '[t]he dynamics of political change, in this case EU membership, served as a political tool in the reinforcement of the nationalist sentiments, and emotions, in particular feelings of disillusionment and mistrust, have been deployed by ... opposing global processes' (Golanska-Ryan 2006: 160). The same mechanisms also hold true for recent campaigns against EU membership in Croatia.[23] The disillusionment and mistrust that accompany processes of globalisation in Croatia are also often complemented by fear of victimisation as well as rebellious pride (ibid.: 169). There are various strategies of responding to and coping with scepticism regarding Croatia's future in the EU, and my analysis of anti-European arguments suggests the differentiation of three specific tactics in doing so: self-victimisation, blatant resistance to EU politics – including intermittent oscillation between resistance and resignation – and the formation of a sense of superiority.

Discourses of recurrent victimisation and suffering are the core elements of Croatian self-positioning within Europe, and the stirring up of old fears is a common tactic by which the need for national self-protection is propagated. Reminiscent of the Polish case, this implies the evocation of emotional memories of Croatia's history of foreign exploitation, and subsequently informs fears of loss of the country's recently gained independence and self-determination. The resentment of foreign powers that Stef Jansen – with particular reference to Serbia, but similarly applicable to Croatia – has tellingly described as the protest of 'victims, underdogs and rebels' produces a specific rebellious tactic that rests in (self-)victimisation and categorically anticipated disadvantage (Jansen 2000).

Strategies of resistance to incorporation by global power structures and interrelated worries about growing alienation exist not only in Croatia but prevail to varying degrees throughout all the republics of the former Yugoslavia. Writing on rural Bosnia, Tone Bringa, for instance, notes that '[t]o insist on "our customs" as if they were an unchanging essence of a community's identity, is to express resistance to change, but under specific circumstances it can also express resistance to assimilation pressures from a dominant culture' (Bringa 1995: 82). Respectively, many Croats perceive the 'dominant culture' as an arbitrary, exchangeable 'Americanised' culture that is prone to moral deceit, fraud and greediness. Not unlike the rhetoric applied to connect the indictment of the Croatian ex-generals, the opprobrium cast on the 'dominant culture' is used as a strategy of self-affirmation in which the national, and even more so the regional, are indubitably seen as repositories of 'tradition', 'authenticity' and 'ethics'. According to this world view, the politics of the EU and NATO are equated with a new form of imperialist rule and the requirements are perceived as corruptible stipulations that should best be answered by uncompromised objection. 'If I were the president of Croatia, I would say: "Stop! Enough now!" What is the EU to us? Nothing! If the EU wants something from us, they should treat us with respect. Currently, Croatia acts like a dog whose fur can only be brushed one way. But we have to make sure that we brush it the wrong way, too'. Using the metaphor of Croatia as a submissive dog, my host in his comment insinuated that the Croatian government should show more self-confidence in terms of 'showing teeth' to great power politics and not resign itself to blinkered conformism. According to him, responsible politicians should have the courage to face the uncomfortable consequences that may arise from voicing their country's own concerns and demands within the Union. 'Should there be doubts among other member states about Croatia's admission to the EU – f–k them! You will see what you get: no transit and no visas for EU citizens!' he said on another occasion. This rebellious and rather offensive attitude towards EU member states that objected to Croatia's entry rests on a desperate feeling of subjection. The fear of Croatia being considered a (politically and economically) weak and insignificant country, and of therefore being overruled, is deep-seated and often coupled with a resignation and fatalism about the country's significance on the stage of Great Powers. Obstinacy and the threat of refusal of transit admission and visas are but one way of expressing a severe disenchantment with politics. 'If only we were finally left in peace by international politics' is a pervasive lament with which many disillusioned Croats express their frustration vis-à-vis their country's future prospects, and simultaneously repudiate their own responsibility for Croatia's standing – both, regarding past war guilt and its present and future role in Europe.

Yet another, and probably the most exalted, strategy for expressing Euroscepticism is the emphasis on Croatia's supremacy over other countries that consider themselves 'European'. '*Sta je Evropa? Mi smo Evropa!*' [What is Europe? We are Europe!] and 'We don't need Europe, but Europe needs us!' were proclamations I regularly heard during my fieldwork. Megalomaniac statements like this are used to draw a boundary against exclusivist definitions of Europe and to invert 'Western' self-essentialising tendencies. The conceptualisation and renegotiation of national identity in Croatia thus often results in the blatant statement that Croatia is superior to the rest of Western Europe – a basic yet rather widespread rhetorical trope that Michael Herzfeld has extensively explored for Greek identity, and, more recently, elaborated in his launch of the provisional category of 'crypto-colonialism' (Herzfeld 1987: 20ff.; Herzfeld 2002). He defines crypto-colonialism as

> the curious alchemy whereby certain countries, buffer zones between the colonized lands and those yet untamed, were compelled to acquire their political independence at the expense of massive economic dependence, this relationship being articulated in the iconic guise of aggressively national culture fashioned to suit foreign models. Such countries were and are living paradoxes: they are nominally independent, but that independence comes at the price of a sometimes humiliating form of effective dependence. (Herzfeld 2002: 900f.)

A classic buffer zone – historically set up between the Austro-Hungarian and the Ottoman empires, later conceptualised as a bulwark of Western democracy against communism, and since the 9/11 attacks suggested as a buffer zone against terrorism in Europe – Croatia is simultaneously located *interior* and *exterior* to Europe, which makes it an effectively dependent 'living paradox' indeed. Equally, Herzfeld's assertion that crypto-colonial countries share the 'aggressive promotion of their claims to civilizational superiority or antiquity, claims that almost always appear disproportionate to their political influence' (Herzfeld 2002: 902) pertained to Croatia's position in the run-up to (the heavily contested) EU membership. As a (self-)attributed 'bulwark of Christianity', Croatia's historical role in protecting the borders of Europe stands in stark contrast to the country's current exclusion from European realpolitik, and positions it in a classic crypto-colonial situation, as defined by Herzfeld. In Croatia, the trope of civilisational superiority also results in a dismissal of countries ironically held to be not honestly or authentically European, such as, for instance, the U.K. and France. In an interview with a retired subsistence farmer in Sinj, I was told: 'As long as England and France are members of the EU, we wouldn't even want to enter.' Such resentments are mainly caused by the role these two countries played in the Second World War and in the Homeland War, making them traitors in the eyes of large numbers of the Croatian population. This polemical comment signifies an ostentatious challenge to the supremacy of France and the U.K. in the EU (deliberately leaving Germany aside), based on an assertion of Croatia's pre-existing entitlement to Europeanness. This premeditated dissociation of a hegemonic 'European centre' by way of self-marginalisation – on the basis of an asserted superiority – recurs on the regional level. I argue that Dalmatian ethno-regionalists deploy similar strategies of dissociation from the representational centre of 'the state', the government in Zagreb, as do Croatian Eurosceptics from Brussels as the representational site of the politics of the European Union. Many Dalmatians therefore self-identify not only as marginal, but as 'marginal within the marginal' (Green 2005: 6), and employ the Mediterranean label as a category of identification, both to evade demands by the state as well as the European Union, while at the same time colluding in the reproduction of their own 'othering' (Herzfeld 2005: xi) and thus advancing their affiliation to these very 'institutions'.

Furthermore, claims to Croatian superiority are frequently accompanied by comparisons to Switzerland. In an interview, a young unemployed man from Dalmatia exclaimed: 'I wish Croatia could be a country like Switzerland. Why should that not be possible? We are also small but have it all, too: beautiful mountains, fertile agricultural land, natural resources, mineral oil, the cleanest water ... and what is more, we even have the sea'. When I pointed out that Switzerland's prosperity and sovereignty are not simply tied to the country's natural resources or its scenery but also to its consistent political neutrality – a neutrality that, at least according to my understanding, is diametrically opposed to the political atmosphere in Croatia – my interlocutor agreed. 'Yes,' he said, 'it's politics that has ruined everything for us.' This brief excerpt from my interview not only illustrates the eccentricity of Croatian self-assessment but also shows how strategies of hubris and self-victimisation are closely intertwined in providing a framework for positing the young country within the European association of states. The notion of Switzerland as a promising role model for Croatia, uttered ten years after the end of the war, indicates that abstention from (international) politics and/or political neutrality are envisioned as a potential guarantor for peace and prosperity. 'Peace', however, was never directly mentioned as a specific vision for the future in any of the conversations I had during my fieldwork. Prospects were usually formulated in a negative frame, and whenever I carefully inquired about possible reconciliation processes I was referred to the past, present and anticipated future suffering of the Croatian people that rendered any dialogue with one's 'enemies' impossible. It is this rhetoric of self-victimisation, combined with a sense of superiority and latent resignation, that informs the predominant nationalist discourse and largely excludes any acknowledgment of the suffering of others.

'Cream and Cheese for President'

Anti-EU Campaigns

This last section examines the discursive practices of resistance in recent Croatian campaigns against EU-membership negotiations, before the referendum in 2012. In my analysis I concentrate on the rhetoric of Eurosceptics rather than on actual political programmes, as I am primarily interested in the ways in which people construct locality as an economic, political and cultural site of resistance. Furthermore, I look at the 'authentic' peculiarities anti-EU campaigners refer to, and consider whether or how they are mobilised as local reserves against globalising processes.

In the summer of 2004 the fringe right-wing and explicitly Eurosceptic political party SIN – *Samostalnost i Napredak* [Independence and Progress] – launched a militant political campaign against EU-membership for Croatia.[24] They placed 794 tables and 1,351 billboards with various anti-European and pro-nationalist slogans along the main roads of Zagreb, all of which admonished of the dangers proceeding from the European Union and/or promoted the quality of local – mainly agricultural – products. The slogan that first caught my attention was

> *EU nije cool, sir i vrhnje jesu* [The EU is not cool, (but our) cheese and cream are]

Sir is probably best translated as fresh cream cheese and *vrhnje* as sour cream, and they make up the typical breakfast in rural areas. Apart from its obvious witticism, this catchphrase not only alludes to local eating habits but also offers a hint of the agricultural aspects of the Eurosceptic debate. Natural resources and the high quality of local products are seen as the country's capital and are perceived as superior to EU standards – which in turn are seen as a potential threat to the manufacture and prices of local products. Cool cream cheese also means fresh cream which entails short routes of transport and ultimately implies the avoidance of import and export of agricultural goods. One of the main concerns of Croatian Eurosceptics and Dalmatian ethno-regionalists alike is for a self-sufficient economy. The country's strongest points are seen to lie in its natural resources, its scenic beauty and its various agricultural products. In my opinion, the propagation of economic autonomy through subsistence farming and small-scale agriculture is one of the most vital local reserves currently being mobilised against international companies and against the franchise and sale of property and land rights to foreigners in Croatia. The slogan 'The EU is not cool [but our] cheese and cream are' thus expresses the importance of local agricultural products and food habits for local identity that is constructed in opposition to EU norms (see Buden 2005).

Other slogans of the campaign included:

> *Koga za predsjednika države? Sir i vrhnje – se razme*
> [Who is the president? Cheese and cream, of course]

> *Treba nam Europa, a ne EU*
> [We need Europe, but not the EU]

> *Europska unija – gubitak radnih mjesta i pad standarda. Jasno?!*
> [European Union – decrease of employment and of (living) standard.
> Got it?!]

Yet another poster showed the EU emblem with its gold stars on a blue ground while the letters 'EU' in the middle were replaced by the words *Cista pušiona*, which literally translates as 'totally wrong' or 'false decision'. These slogans are straightforward and can be understood without further explanation. One poster, however, left me puzzled for a while. At a busy crossing in Zagreb I read the following:

> *Ne bojiš se terorizma? Ne želiš kulen i pršut? Onda glasuj za njih!*
> [You aren't afraid of terrorism? You don't like sausage and ham? Then
> vote for them!]

Njih [them] clearly refers to the EU. But why would one only vote in favour of the EU if one were not afraid of terrorism? Talking about this issue with a number of my interlocutors, I came to understand that terrorism is perceived as a threat that primarily endangers North America and Western Europe as a result of their roles in global politics as well as their exploitative economic policies. The slogan therefore indicates: if we join the EU and NATO, Croatia might soon be a target for global terrorists, too. If, however, we stick to ourselves and reject the role as a buffer zone against terrorism in Europe, we will probably be left in peace.[25] With their reference to *kulen* (a particular sort of ham sausage) and *pršut* (ham), the campaigners once more allude to local food habits as powerful tokens of local identity. Assuming that everybody is afraid of global terrorism in the same way that every Croat likes his/her *pršut*, the campaigners thus managed to symbolically associate emotions of anxiety with the EU and contrast them to identity-establishing eating habits associated with home and belonging. In other words, this poster suggests that if people would take their actual fears and preferences seriously, they would never vote in favour of Croatian EU membership.

The last slogan I recorded is the following:

Sanaderu, ne skidaj hlače!
[Sanader, don't let your pants down!]

The former prime minister of Croatia, Ivo Sanader, had initially severely criticised the ICTY indictments against Croatian Army generals, and in 2001 took part in the massive rally against the conviction of the Dalmatian general Mirko Norac in Split, giving a speech in which he revived the ultranationalist rhetoric of the late Franjo Tuđman (Jović 2009: 2). Step by step, however, he distanced himself from the protests, and by 2003 the HDZ had completely abolished its anti-ICTY rhetoric. At the time of the SIN campaign, Sanader's aim was to transform HDZ into a modern pro-European party. His government – whose main foreign goal was Croatia's entry into the European Union and NATO – was challenged by the rising tide of Euroscepticism in the country, and the arrest of Ante Gotovina also had a damaging effect on his popularity. The slogan 'Don't let your pants down!' can thus be understood as an appeal that Sanader should not strip off his initial convictions and expose himself in order to meet or please EU norms. However, because the slogan was also potentially open to crude sexual interpretations, this poster was quickly removed from public display.

Although this campaign and the founder of SIN – Nenad Ivanković, author of Ante Gotovina's 2001 biography – have been subject to frequent ridicule by liberal intellectuals, many people throughout Croatia with various political backgrounds also greet the tenor of the campaign with approval. Anti-globalists and many young people in Zagreb favour the rigid Euroscepticism, and it is rather astonishing how much the arguments of the extreme right and the left resemble each other in this matter. Researching reactions to the SIN campaign on the internet, I encountered the 'weblog' of a Croatian youth, who had written:

> SIN is an organisation that opposes the EU membership. When they put up a stand in the city, they usually hand out *sir* and *vrhnje*, as well as promotion materials. They recently had a stand and everyone who filled in a membership card got some *sir* and *vrhnje* in a plastic cup. But they didn't have spoons. Not even plastic spoons. I also oppose the EU membership, like many others, only we don't talk about it publicly. What could we gain from an EU membership? I think, nothing at all. It is true that we cannot compare ourselves to Switzerland or the Netherlands. But we could deal with that if we were only more reasonable and did not export our common sense. Half the country has been sold already anyway, and if we entered the EU we would sell the other half, too. That's about it.[26]

This attitude is according to my assessment rather widespread amongst Croatian adolescents. On the one hand it reflects a critical attitude towards the comparison of Croatia to other small nation-states that are considered wealthy and independent role models, such as Switzerland and the Netherlands. On the other hand, however, the fear of a sell-out of the country is shared with the Eurosceptics, who base their reasons on an ethno-nationalist (or ethno-regionalist) mind-set.

By referring to local agricultural products, particularly to *sir* and *vrhnje*, the SIN campaign also touches upon heavily charged symbolic motives. The Croatian anthropologist Renata Jambrešić Kirin has closely analysed the semantics of dairy products and the milk cow in Croatian public discourse. Referring to the SIN campaign, she points out that the slogan '*EU nije cool, sir i vrhnje jesu*' alludes to a multimedia documentation project called '*sir i vrhnje*' that had taken place in Zagreb in 2002 (Jambrešić Kirin 2007). The Croatian artist Kristina Leko, in collaboration with the 'Local Basis for the Refreshment of Culture' (BLOK), presented the project 'Milk 2002–2003' through which they aimed to improve the position of the *mljekarice*, the dairy women of Zagreb, and to support their claims for self-organisation. According to Jambrešić Kirin, the SIN slogan '*EU nije cool, sir i vrhnje jesu*' was developed with reference to this project. This additional background information supports my introductory argument that the self-organisation and strengthening of local institutions and products is of major importance for the Eurosceptic's policy of autonomy. Accordingly, the SIN activists were very eager to promote their campaign and appeared on a number of television and radio shows. In some of these media appearances they would also invite the *mljekarice* to enable them to voice their concerns and in turn to publicly support the SIN campaign. Jambrešić Kirin mentions a 2005 television show that included the appearance the founder of SIN, Nenad Ivanković, and that featured a 'tel-evote' after the discussion. The options that the audience could vote for, however, were not the self-government of the dairywomen versus an EU-adjusted agrarian policy, but people had to decide in favour of either Ante Gotovina or EU accession. As one might expect, the results turned out unambiguous, with 91 per cent of callers opting for Gotovina, and only 9 per cent for EU membership (Jambrešić Kirin 2007). This example illustrates that the levels of argument in public EU debate are not only oversimplified and clearly confused but also largely dominated by a fear that Croatia might (again) be at a disadvantage in a confederation of states. It is in this climate of exasperation, distrust and suspicion that the takeover of Croatian companies and real estate by foreign investors can be rhetorically linked to the indictments of Croatian ex-generals, and that global threats like terrorism are mentioned in the same breath as local food and eating habits.

Return to the Mediterranean

Repositionings in the Periphery

In 1909 the Austrian writer Hermann Bahr published an account of his voyage to Dalmatia in which he refers to the Adriatic coast as *Sonnenland, Märchenland, Zauberland* [Land of sun, Land of fairy tales, Land of magic] (Bahr 1909: 2). The mythic character of this description is reminiscent of the romantic tradition in which the yearning for the South, and the Mediterranean in particular – paradigmatically embodied by Goethe's *Mignon*, as a powerful trope of insatiable longing and dislocation – is expressed. Today's recalling of Goethe's musing finds its most apparent equivalent in the tourist industry. Year after year millions of foreign as well as domestic tourists visit the Croatian coast or one of the country's thousand-plus islands to enjoy a 'Mediterranean holiday steeped in history', as a travel agency recently advertised. It is therefore not greatly surprising that the official slogan of the Croatian Tourist Board to promote Croatia as an internationally attractive travel destination is 'Croatia – the Mediterranean as it once was'. This telling slogan not only defies all doubts as to whether or not Croatia is part of the Mediterranean, but, moreover, links the country directly to classical antiquity – this both defines Croatia as the cradle of European civilisation and avoids any connection with the unpredictability and bloodshed commonly associated with the Balkans.

Since Croatia has a coastline on the Adriatic Sea, it is generally not considered a Mediterranean country per se and has hitherto been neglected in discourses on the Mediterranean as a field of research. Mainly due to its previous location on the other side of the Iron Curtain, the Balkan region as a whole has generally been marginalised in Mediterranean studies until now. Recently, however, the question of Croatia's belonging (at least in part) to the Mediterranean has been reassumed as the boundaries of the Mediterranean world are negotiated anew. Particularly in the context of the newly founded 'Union for the Mediterranean,' regional cooperation within the Mediterranean has been endowed with a new meaning. For Croatia, this alliance opens a chance to get access to subsidies and to establish a stable foundation upon which to build a modern (inter-)regional economy – directly and independently of the country's EU membership.[27] According to newspaper records, Gordan Jandroković, who served as Croatian Minister of Foreign Affairs until December 2011, stated that Croatian membership of the Union for the Mediterranean would help the country to affirm its Mediterranean dimension, which, according to him, had been neglected so far. 'Our great interest is to collaborate concretely in the fields of economy, infrastructures, ecology and protection of the Adriatic Sea,' said Jandroković.[28] This statement illustrates that Croatia increasingly envisions itself as embedded in a Mediterranean web of regional cooperations, most of them related to the agricultural and tourism sectors. In its official statement on foreign policy aims, the Ministry of Foreign Affairs and European Integration defines and highlights the geostrategic importance of the region as follows:

> Croatia is located at the heart of Europe as a Mediterranean, Central European and Danube region country, and its geographical location is one of its key strategic advantages. The current European integration processes add a special value to its location, turning it into a potentially key impetus for the country's overall economic development.[29]

This appraisal – that bears a striking resemblance to Dunja Rihtman-Auguštin's 1998 regionalist statement in which she had claimed that Croats and Croatia belong in each of the Mediterranean, Danube and Balkan worlds (Rihtman-Auguštin 1998: 103–20) – clarifies the geopolitical understanding of Croatia as part of a wider, culturally diverse Mediterranean that is not perceived as a contested borderline, but as a site of European connectedness.

The discussion about the positioning of Croatia is centuries old, but gained momentum in opposition to what was perceived as Western attempts to force Croatia into some new Balkan union after the country's independence (Razsa and Lindstrom 2004: 642). Tuđman, who ran his successful 1997 presidential campaign under the slogan '*Tuđman, a ne Balkan*' [Tuđman, not the Balkans], was very anxious in case Croatia was misrecognised as culturally Balkan, and he tirelessly stressed that the country had always belonged to Europe. In January 1997, in a speech at the Southeast European Cooperative Initiative (SECI), he proclaimed: 'By its geopolitical position, by all of its fourteen-century history, by its civilization and culture, Croatia belongs to the central European and Mediterranean circles of Europe. Our political links with the Balkans between 1918 and 1990 were just a short episode in Croatian history, and we are determined not to repeat that episode again' (quoted in Razsa and Lindstrom 2004: 642). And two years later, in March 1999, the Croatian National Parliament passed a declaration opposing the 'regional approach' of the European Union, rebuffing 'all attempts for Croatia to be included in some sort of regional integration of south eastern Europe and the Balkans'.[30] Tuđman's nationalist rhetoric aimed at reassuring the Croatian people that he and his HDZ government would stand up against the 'Great Powers', reckoning that their fight against Balkan integration would generate an alternative, regionally anchored affiliation. Croatian journalist Dalibor Foretić, for example, seconded Tuđman's paradoxical position by declaring 'we want to be everything – Central European, Mediterranean, Transcarpathian – and not just a Balkan country' that was being 'pushed into some kind of Balkan hole' (Rihtman-Auguštin 1997: 46). When HDZ lost the parliamentary elections in 2000, Croatia's relationship with the EU improved almost instantly. However, the question of where Croatia located itself – and was being located by 'the West' – remained vital. In an interview, the new Social Democrat prime minister, Ivica Račan, in a far less megalomaniac manner than Tuđman, but nonetheless self-confident, reiterated Croatia's partial Mediterranean identity by saying:

> I think that the geopolitical and geostrategic position of Croatia is an outstanding value and virtue. We are a central European state, also a Mediterranean state, and at least in a small part, a Balkan state. This shows the complexity of our identity, and also the importance of our

position in this part of Europe. (Quoted and translated in Žanić 2005: 72)[31]

By highlighting the complexity of Croatian identity – and, at least in part, acknowledging the country's Balkan belongings again – Račan explicitly redefined the symbolic geography and reappraised the country's multiple positions as a fundamentally positive feature. According to this perspective, the location at the crossroads of Europe is not a facet that separates, but rather connects Croatia to its neighbours – and can thus be understood as a reference to the genuinely Mediterranean topos of connectivity and mobility across borders. This abridged outline of Croatia's geopolitical and geostrategic self-positioning since the mid-1990s illustrates how the Mediterranean (re-)emerged as a site for an alternative situatedness: not just to distinguish Croatia from its Balkan-ness, as ultra-nationalists did after the war, but also as a framework that embraces diversity as a unifying principle.

The concept of the Mediterranean itself has been profoundly challenged in academic discourse, and heated debate among anthropologists working in the Mediterranean has raged for more than five decades (cf. Pitt-Rivers 1963, 1971 and 1977; Boissevain 1965, 2013; Peristiany 1966, 1976; Braudel 1972; Blok 1974, 2001; Gellner and Waterbury 1977; Davis 1977; Wolf and Lehmann 1984; Herzfeld 1984, 1987; Peristiany and Pitt-Rivers 1999; Albera 1999; Albera, Blok and Bromberger 2001; Harris 2005; Hauschild, Kottmann and Zillinger 2007; Hauschild 2008). From the 1950s through to the 1970s, classical topoi such as hospitality, patronage, kinship, (amoral) familism, poverty, corruption and political instability, as well as the notorious 'honour and shame' complex, characterised the respective small-scale community studies and added to the repertoire of unitary Mediterranean stereotypes. The various paradigm shifts that followed in the 1970s, 1980s and 1990s, however, gradually overruled these topoi, and deconstructive critiques eventually created so many uncertainties regarding the concept of 'the Mediterranean' that anthropological research in the area was almost brought to a halt.

Formerly often perceived as 'a liminal zone between the situated ethics of exotic peoples and the ordered morality of European culture' (Herzfeld 1987: 130), the Mediterranean is no longer understood as a 'cultural area unified by a shared social ethos' (Greverus, Römhild and Welz 2001: 1). And although – or rather, because – essentialism continues to lurk in Mediterranean studies, circum-Mediterranean areas are now consequently considered as transitional zones that consist of shifting micro-regions and polities. Further, since the turn of the millennium, the Mediterranean has increasingly been rediscovered as a paradigmatic laboratory for interplay between the local and the global (cf. Albera 1999; Driessen 2001). Recent works by historians such as Peregrine Horden and Nicholas Purcell (Horden and Purcell 2000), as well as cultural anthropologists like Dionigi Albera, Christian Bromberger, Anton Blok and Thomas Hauschild (Albera, Blok and Bromberger 2001; Hauschild, Kottmann and Zillinger 2007; Hauschild 2008), however, are based on the assumption that the 'aspect of "unity in diversity" (Horden and Purcell 2000: 9–26) is more densely present, and historically more deeply documented [in the Mediterranean] than in any other region in the world' (Hauschild et al. 2007: 4). Therewith these scholars critically seize and further develop Pitt-Rivers' comparative circum-Mediterranean, or rather pan-Mediterranean, perspective, in which he had stated that

> [t]he communities of the Mediterranean possess both more similarities between different countries and more diversities within their national frontiers than the tenets of modern nationalism would have us believe ... A social anthropology of the Mediterranean must start with these diversities rather than with the stereotypes of national 'culture'. For behind the diversities there is room to discover continuities which run counter to the varying political hegemonies, observing the exigencies of the ecology or the entrenched conservatism of the local settlement. (Pitt-Rivers 1963: 10)

Transferring these re-readings to the current Mediterranean condition, the fragile entity of niches and connectivities can be seen as generating a revaluation of local and small-scale political and cultural phenomena that are revived and/or constructed in direct contrast to national demarcations and corporate globalisation. In Dalmatia, the recently observable trend to retreat to the Mediterranean as a geographical niche is characterised by a strong resistance to international economic and political intervention in the region, and is accompanied by a redefinition of regional versus national identities.

As if he had anticipated the slogan 'Croatia – the Mediterranean as it once was', Michael Herzfeld wrote in his essay 'Hospitality, Ethnography and the Stereotype of the Mediterranean Society':

> Certainly those who sell the images of this Mediterranean quintessence to West European and North American tourists have rarely hesitated to exploit the image of a uniformly romanticized 'Mediterranean culture'. Ethnographers might have unwittingly contributed to

the creation of this stereotype ... which also served the interest of the
industrialized nations who patronize the Mediterranean lands. (Herzfeld 1987: 76)

Herzfeld's paradigmatic critique of so-called 'Mediterraneanism' implies
that the region is extrinsically constructed as a negative (or romanticised) image that aims to strengthen West European identity. This, however, equally works the other way round. Herzfeld himself has argued for
the Greek case, and Pina-Cabral for the Portuguese, that in the context
of the reification of the Mediterranean the ambiguous 'Europeanness'
of Southern Europe's countries has to be taken into account. 'Their mis-
giving about their European identity both permitted the Mediterranean
labelling and meant that they did not oppose it', writes Pina-Cabral
(Pina-Cabral 1989: 400). I argue that it is this very 'ambiguous Europeanness' that generates the reference to the Mediterranean in present-day
Croatia, and in Dalmatia in particular.

The term 'Mediterranean' as an emic category of self-reference is
at present – apart from its operationalisation in the tourist industry – mainly used by Dalmatians who thereby identify themselves in
opposition to 'the politics of the North', namely the decisions made
in the capital Zagreb, or 'the state'. References to the Mediterranean
are therefore an expression of regionalism that challenges the North–
South divide within the country. This gulf between Zagreb and the
historical regions which compose present-day Croatia (Istria, Slavonia, the city-state of Dubrovnik, and Dalmatia) has its origin in the
long-lasting traditions of local autonomy, be it in the Ottoman or the
Habsburg empires, as well as in the frequent changes of governmental and administrative systems, treaties and alliances in the respective
provinces. And particularly in Dalmatia – which in the eighteenth century had been conceived of as part of the 'Adriatic Empire' of Venice
and subsequently came to be absorbed by different offshore empires
– the continuous changeover of foreign rule has obstructed the formation of a uniform identity linked to a specific national entity. The
heterogeneous and shifting quality of Dalmatian self-understanding
grounds in the capacity to occasionally obstruct modern nationalism
and to claim a right to cultural hegemony emanating from regional centres. One characteristic that seems to have been consistent throughout
the last centuries, however, is Dalmatian self-marginalisation. Many
Dalmatians position themselves as a distinct geographical unit within
an independent Croatian nation-state, and deliberately peripheralise
themselves from the projects of governance. I argue, however, that
centre–periphery political distinctions are presently characterised by

a combination of imposed as well as self-ascribed marginality that is largely in dialogue with state policies and regional politics.

Henk Driessen has noted that of late the geopolitical implications of Dalmatia's marginal position within Croatia have led to a renewed negotiation of the relations between the capital and the coastal area, particularly in view of the economic reallocation of Dalmatia's natural resources (Driessen 2001:16). This process, however, is taking the shape of a top-down development policy that causes an atmosphere in which state power is conceived as both shaping and threatening Dalmatia; as external yet hegemonic. As a consequence, along with historical, political and geographical divergence, cultural difference is stressed at the margins as a sign of distinction from the centre. Implied in this conception might also be the search for an alternative discourse on modernity as a homogenous entity and the respective models of (state) power related to it. But instead of insisting on the experience of modernity as multiple in character, the articulation of regional self-awareness and/or redefinition of a geopolitical setting all too often go hand in hand with consistent auto-stereotyping.[32]

Underlying this Mediterranean re-identification is the realisation that Dalmatian marginality has certain advantages over the capital and over the rest of the country. And this recently revaluated discovery brings with it the promotion of environmental sustainability and the cultural specialities mentioned above – mainly bearing on the Adriatic Sea, on fishing, agriculture and 'cultural heritage'. A very important factor in the recent infrastructural changes and the realisation of transnational cooperations such as Euroregions is the fact that they are not associated with 'Balkan backwardness' or located outside of the European Union's institutional framework.[33] 'In such turbulent political arenas there is a need for new identifications which not only have roots in ancient history, but are also flexible and intermediate, and thus serve as alternatives ... for the nation-state ... . The "Mediterranean" label seems to meet this need', writes Driessen (Driessen 2001: 14). For Dalmatian regionalists, the Mediterranean label seems indeed to provide a feasible redefinition of locally embedded identity. It serves as a counter-hegemonic space that entails the possibility of building new alliances and (partly) escaping state control without directly aiming at destabilising central authority.

On a national level, the renaissance of the Euro-Mediterranean identity suggests a rediscovery of its potential as a bridge between a variety of diverse ethnic, religious and cultural traditions that goes far beyond the geographical dimension. Claus Leggewie has recently proposed that it 'is legitimate in the current crisis to search in [the] history [of the Mediterranean world] for the basis for a polymorphic structure of contemporary Europe' (Leggewie 2012). He pleads for a regeneration of the Mediterranean region that draws on its legacy of cosmopolitan democracy. On a policy level, the vision of Europe as a polymorphic structure that borrows from the image of the Mediterranean as a crossroads defined by multiple belongings, might help to mitigate national, ethnic and religious antagonisms without invoking an oversimplified, romanticised multiculturalism that is not applicable in inherently multicultural places such as the former Yugoslavia. After all, the Mediterranean has always been 'the place where, in spite of Catholic and Islamic holy wars, crusades, the Reconquista, the two Ottoman sieges of Vienna, the sad history of colonialism and the bloody wars of colonial liberation, no universalism or fundamentalism was ever permanently established' (Zolo 2005). On a more abstract, theoretical level, the 'Mediterraneanisation' – as an analysis of relations, interactions and overlapping structures of the Mediterranean region – might in the long run contribute to a decentring of Europe.

Notes

1. The 2007 European Commission Progress Report for Croatia states that agriculture's share of output declined to 7.4% in 2006 (from 7.6% in 2005) and agriculture's share of employment showed a marked fall to 14% (2005: 17%), while industry rose slightly to 29% (2005: 28%) and the services sector posted a more pronounced rise to 57% (2005: 55%). Given the already large service sector, there were only marginal shifts in the sector structure of the economy. See http://ec.europa.eu/enlargement/pdf/key_documents/2007/nov/croatia_progress_reports_en.pdf, last visited 15 Aug 2008.
2. In *Cultural Intimacy*, Michael Herzfeld (1997) has given an in-depth account of these mechanisms in Greece and cogently conceptualised the interplay between official and unofficial accounts of Greekness. Sarah Green seizes on these notions of mockery, subversion and assertion of power of the nation-state, and in *Notes from the Balkans* illuminates the relationship between marginality and citizenship, using the example of Epirus in Greece (Green 2005: 123ff.).
3. Gal and Kligman have pointed out that, despite a number of adverse regulations, the division of labour in the household was never fundamentally transformed by state socialism, and women retained almost sole responsibility for household work and childbearing (Gal and Kligman 2000: 48). Despite actively participating in the paid labour force and becoming a numerically important presence in the public sphere, women during state socialism were by tendency more dependent on the state and exposed to an increased 'intrusion of state institutions into what was formerly a private sphere of family' (ibid.).

4. In her study on the transformation of the Yugoslav family, Vera Stein Erlich distinguishes between two phases of patriarchy in Yugoslavia. According to her, the earlier phase prevailed until the 1930s and was widespread in Macedonia and Muslim Bosnia. The second, more recent phase that was accompanied by 'turbulent transformations' is located in the Christian parts of Bosnia, Serbia and the southern and central parts of Croatia (Stein Erlich 1971: 30f.; see also Čapo Žmegač 2001: 275). Geographically she distinguishes between 'oriental' (Bosnia and Macedonia), 'tribal' (Dinaric mountains and foothills, i.e. Montenegro, Herzegovina, Dalmatian hinterland, Serbia, etc.) and 'Austrian' (mainly Slavonia) variants of the patriarchal system (Stein Erlich 1971: 366). For a detailed analysis of the uses and abuses of ethno-geography in the Balkans, see Živković 1997.

5. The stereotypical notion of a specific 'Dinaric character' that is particularly prone to violence prevails to the present day. In a 1994 *New York Times* article, John Kifner drew the reader's attention to 'the rocky spine of the Dinaric Alps, for it is these mountains that have nurtured and shaped the most extreme, combative elements of each community: the western Herzegovinian Croats, the Sandzak Muslims, and, above all, the secessionist Serbs ... Like mountaineer communities around the world, these were wild, warlike, frequently lawless societies whose feuds and folklore have been passed on to the present day like the potent home-brewed plum brandy that the mountain men begin knocking back in the morning' (Kifner 1994, quoted in Živković 1997).

6. A more recent variant of this reasoning can be found in Stjepan Meštrović's *Habits of the Balkan Heart: Social Character and the Fall of Communism* and *The Barbarian Temperament: Towards a Post-Modern Critical Theory*, both published in 1993.

7. Živković somewhat cynically points out that '[d]ormant at times of relative stability, the Dinaric Highlander seems to pop up at the times of crisis and turmoil as a notion that natives and outsiders alike use to gain understanding, criticize or extol, or further their political agendas' (Živković 1997).

8. For a more detailed analysis of the 'weak state phenomenon' and its implications for the post-Yugoslav Balkan states, see http://www.ndc.nato.int/download/publications/rakipi.pdf, accessed 08 Jul 2008.

9. According to OECD criteria, in 2001, of the total area of Croatia 91.6% was classified as rural and 8.4% as urban. As regards the population, approximately 47.6% of Croats lived in rural areas and 52.4% in urban.

10. Unlike Pitt-Rivers' (1954) and Redfield's (1956) assessments of the mid-1950s conveying that the dignity of agricultural work was lacking on the shores of the Mediterranean, the previous marginalisation of peasantry is converted into its opposite in contemporary rural Croatia where people proudly refer to themselves as peasants.

11. In her study on the dynamics of property relations and ethnic conflict in the Knin region, Carolin Leutloff-Grandits states that under socialism, land as property 'lost some of its importance but remained an economic asset as well as a source of social identity. The economic significance of private

agriculture was strengthened by a successful partnership between the agricultural cooperative and private farmers' (Leutloff-Grandits 2006a: 40).

12. In the 1940s, two million peasants were forced into collective farms in Yugoslavia, but the programme was cancelled soon after because of low output. In the 1980s, 82% of farmland was still owned by 2.6 million peasant families on farms averaging about nine acres. For a more detailed description of peasant lifestyle in Dalmatia in the nineteenth and twentieth centuries, as well as on changes in the agrarian sector under state socialism, see Leutloff-Grandits 2006a: 51–59, 76–86.

13. The same rhetoric is applied by nationalist Serbs; and Vojislav Šešelj, the Serb ultranationalist leader of the Nationalist Party, has allegedly been celebrating the country's isolation by remarking: 'We don't need anyone's help; we have mushrooms and raspberries for everyone in this country' (quoted in Seierstad 2005: 294).

14. http://www.mps.hr/eng/ministarstvo/, accessed 15 Mar 2008 (no longer available).

15. *Arambaše* are cabbage rolls stuffed with mincemeat and rice that are named after the leaders of the special military-territorial units set up by the Venetian authorities, who collected the taxes, kept law and order and led their troops into battle. I have been told that the name of the dish (which elsewhere in the former Yugoslavia is called *šarma*) refers to the fact that in the Cetina region only rich local elites could afford to eat meat and that the denomination can thus be understood as a reminder of the region's poor and underprivileged past.

16. For an excellent analysis of the repositioning of the HDZ from extreme right to moderate conservative pro-EU centre-right party and its radical change regarding cooperation with the ICTY, see Jović 2009.

17. Results from a Gallup World Poll, conducted in February 2007, show Croatians were mixed on the issue of their country's plan to join the EU. When asked for their opinions on Croatia's potential membership, 34% thought it would be good and 29% said it would be bad. A further 28% thought it would be neither good nor bad, while 9% offered no opinion. For further reference, see http://www.gallup.com/poll/27901/Croatians-Mixed-Benefits-Membership.aspx, accessed 14 Aug 2008.

18. The Croatian constitution requires that a binding referendum be held on any political union that would reduce national sovereignty. The 2012 accession referendum was the first referendum held in Croatia in more than twenty years, the prior occasion being the momentous Croatian independence referendum in 1991.

19. A public opinion survey in the European Union, conducted by TNS in 2012, showed that, for the European Union overall, those with a positive image of the EU are down from a high of 52% in 2007 to a low of 31% in May 2012. About 60% of EU citizens do not tend to trust the European Union as an institution, and those who think that their country's interests are looked after well in the EU are now in a minority (42%). Accessible

at http://ec.europa.eu/public_opinion/archives/eb/eb77/eb77_anx_en.pdf, accessed 13 Nov 2012.

20. Antulov gives an account of legal implementations against regionalists by Tuđman's regime, and states that 'the most obvious measure directed against regionalists, and the one that had the most lasting effects, [was] the new administrative organisation of Croatia ... Regions were divided among various counties, and territorial divisions were intended to guarantee quarrels and political divisions between regionalist forces' (Antulov 2000).

21. In contrast to Dalmatian regionalism, Istrian regionalism seems to reflect a multiculturalist, multilingual model of diversity and inter-ethnic coexistence. According to Pamela Ballinger, however, even 'cosmopolitan' Istrian regionalism is based on a territorialised understanding of identity. For a more detailed analysis of Istrian regionalism and the dilemmas of territoriality, see Ballinger 2007: 68–72. For a detailed analysis of the unique case of Istrian regionalism, see also Ashbrook 2006, 622–58. In the case of the Dalmatian Action party, it failed to withstand the pressure of the various intimidations by the HDZ regime, and by 1995 had already receded to the margins of national, regional and even local politics (Antulov 2000).

22. A monitoring report on Croatia's accession preparations issued by the European Commission in April 2012 is accessible online at: http://ec.europa.eu/commission_2010-2014/fule/docs/news/20120424_report_final.pdf, last accessed 1 Dec 2012.

23. The EU referendum in Poland was held on the 7 and 8 June 2003. Despite a strong non-EU campaign, an overwhelming majority (78%) of the Polish population voted in favour of the country's EU accession.

24. The party was established in 2004 by Nenad Ivanković, a Croatian journalist who has also written a hagiographic biography of Ante Gotovina entitled *Ratnik pustolov i general* [Adventurous Warrior and General]. SIN gained some popularity with its aggressive marketing of Eurosceptic ideas. Unfortunately, the the party's political programme, which was at http://www.hrvatsko-zvono.hr/PDF-ovi/HZ%20PROGRAM%20-%20k%5B1%5D.pdf (last accessed 15 Sep 2008), is no longer available online.

25. The accession of Croatia to NATO took place in 2009. After initial plans to hold a referendum on NATO membership, in 2007 the then Croatian president Stjepan Mesić, then prime minister Ivo Sanader and the president of parliament somewhat unexpectedly declared that the Croatian constitution does not require a referendum on this issue. A poll conducted in the same year and commissioned by the government showed that NATO membership was backed by 52% of the population. See http://www.seeurope.net/?q=node/9134, last accessed 15 Nov 2012.

26. Unfortunately, this entry can no longer be accessed.

27. The predecessor to the Union for the Mediterranean, the Euro-Mediterranean Partnership, exclusively admitted EU member states, and was thus considered by many to have failed in focusing on purely Mediterranean issues. The Adriatic Charter, on the other hand, has proved an effective

instrument in demonstrating to NATO the acceptability of (inter-)regional cooperation (Tarifa 2005: 8–19; Seroka 2008: 20).

28. Accessible at http://www.javno.com/en/croatia/clanak.php?id=163988, accessed 13 Nov 2012.

29. Accessible at http://www.mfa.hr/MVP.asp?pcpid=30, accessed 13 Nov 2012.

30. Croatian Foreign Press Bureau's *Daily Bulletin* 36/99, 8 March 1999; see also Razsa and Lindstrom 2004: 642.

31. This is an excerpt from an interview that Račan gave to the editor-in-chief of the Catholic weekly *Glas Koncila*, Ivan Miklenić, and that was published on 9 April 2000 as 'Izaći ćemo iz krize ...' [We Shall Overcome the Crisis ...] in *Glas Koncila* 15: 6.

32. In contrast to a homogenising tendency, the 'unity in diversity' paradigm that dominates the recent recurrence of area studies in the historical geography of the Mediterranean stresses the multiplicity of movement and communication across and around the sea (Horden and Purcell 2000: 9–26). 'It is not the particular physical characteristics of Mediterranean microregions that make them distinctively Mediterranean, but the extent to which they share a common mutability and diversity: the differences that resemble each other' (ibid.: 305). The new regional vision in Dalmatia, however, rather refers to the 'original' Mediterranean – as the centre of European civilisation since the classical antiquity – and thus constructs a fairly distinctive and homogeneous region or culture.

33. The 'Adriatic Euroregion' or 'Jadranska euro-regija' was founded in Pula in Istria in 2006, and countries as diverse as Bosnia-Herzegovina, Albania, Slovenia, Italy, Montenegro and Croatia participate in it. As part of the Splitsko-Dalmatinska County, the town of Sinj is directly involved in this Euroregion. For further information, see http://www.adriaticeuroregion.info/index.php?option=com_content&view=category&layout=blog&id=56&Itemid=93&lang=en, accessed 13 Nov 2012.

Concluding Remarks

'Good Patriots' or 'Rebellious Citizens'?

To get a break from fieldwork I once visited my friend Tatjana and her mother Rajka in Bjelovar, a small town in Western Slavonia. We were sitting together in the evening watching the Croatian version of the popular television show 'Who Wants to Be a Millionaire?' When the 8,000 kunas (approx. 1,100 euros) question 'Where was the first pharmacy in Europe located?' came up, I cried out 'Trogir!' even before the four option answers were given. Tatjana and Rajka looked at each other and burst out laughing. 'They really did a good job down in Sinj teaching you all the nationalist basics', Rajka said. 'Did they also tell you that Adam and Eve were actually born in Dalmatia?'

With her sarcastic remark, Rajka ridiculed the legendary national pride of my Dalmatian hosts as well as my occupational eagerness to absorb their narratives. Hinting at the assumption that Dalmatia is considered the 'cradle of humanity', she confirmed the established stereotype of Dalmatians as retrogressive nationalists – and simultaneously distanced herself from this form of national consciousness. Mention of Dalmatinska Zagora in general and of Sinj in particular still elicits suspicion and ridicule from urban middle-class Croats. To them, rural Dalmatians remain backward and fearsome mountain dwellers – mocked, distrustfully eyed, and maybe secretly admired for their supposed chauvinist patriotism and their lawlessness. And in this attributed capacity they seem to shift back and forth in public perception, from 'good patriots', fierce in their struggle for independence, to 'rebellious citizens', categorically rejecting centralised authority and bureaucratic domination (Herzfeld 1985: 26ff).

This study has focused on the (self-)marginalisation of a community in the Dalmatinska Zagora and may seem to confirm the renowned fascination of anthropologists with remote, out-of-the-way places (cf. Herzfeld 1985: 8f.). However, my interest in Sinj and its environs has not rested simply on an assumption that this community might somehow eccentrically exemplify the national entity. Rather, my concern has been with a possibility that the sustained resistance of the inhabitants to various forms of foreign domination, due to its location in a repeatedly contested border area, and resultant attempts to maintain and/or remake borders and to seal off the community, might shed light on the ambiguity of belonging to and evading the nation-sate – and thus with the possibility that a focus on this ambiguity might enable a novel perspective for studying current transformation processes in the south-eastern periphery of Europe. This approach also accounts for the contradictions and inconsistencies of local attempts to mark clearly bounded entities and to revert to 'authentic traditions and values' – particularly at times when talk of Europeanisation and globalisation is on everyone's lips. In this respect, my study illustrates that '[i]n the border areas, national identity confronts regional difference' (Herzfeld 1985: 9) – and, as in the case of my rural Dalmatian informants, to such an extent that even the distinction between good patriots and rebellious citizens is made ambiguous.

Drawing on an ethnographically grounded analysis of local narratives and socio-political and religious practices in the current postsocialist, post-war scenario, I have addressed the historical inequities my interlocutors claim to be repetitively confronted with, and have interpreted these inequities within the framework of (self-)victimisation as local strategies of empowerment and as expressions of an attempt to have a say in the determination of official historiography. Showing how rural Dalmatians 'cast their own agendas as historic, and those of others as in need of correction' (Brown 2003: 249), this work has focused on the weight of the past in the present, and on its significance for political visions (or premonitions) of the future. Along with the continuous recapitulation of the region's violent history, discourses of locality and cultural authenticity are brought to bear on the contemporary experience of the people of the Dalmatinska Zagora.

The tension between national identity and regional difference seems to have increased in the years following the war of the 1990s, and in the preceding sections I have shown the connection between this tension and growing Eurosceptic, anti-Europeanist and anti-globalist sentiments. In a political context that remains insecure, transnational processes such as the approaching EU membership of Croatia generate scepticism within the local population and stimulate fears of being annexed by supra-national powers and international organisations. The resultant resurgence of ethnonationalism and ethno-regionalism – both articulated as forms of resistance to global processes – follow a specific argumentative and rhetorical pattern. On one occasion, after listening to the 2005 opening speech of the Alka tournament, a 22-year-old student from Zagreb, who helped me with the translation, laughingly called out, 'This is so fascinating! You get all the "political" key words, but the speaker does not even bother to construct full and consistent sentences around them. It is totally void of content and coherent meaning. You could use the transcript, put your name under it and sell it as a post-modern novel. I bet you'd be quite successful with it.' This comparison to postmodernity, or rather to the postmodern credo of 'anything goes', is quite interesting and revealing in this context. The seemingly arbitrary combination of historical information, polemical catchphrases and nationalist imagery applied in many of the speeches and sermons I listened to points towards the narrative construction of a uniform reasoning that can easily be invoked by certain key terms. On a related note, Stef Jansen argues that '[p]eople's narratives constructed around a set of catchwords and phrases can ... be seen as mechanisms by which they position themselves, consciously and unconsciously, in relation to dominant discourses in confusing times' (Jansen 2006: 437). This observation strongly corresponds with my impression that specific nationalist rhetoric serves as a bracket or parenthesis by means of which rather arbitrary narratives of Croat disadvantage are framed and consolidated. By quoting certain catchwords, phrases or story lines, people position themselves in relation to (or in dissociation of) official historiography and thus confirm prevalent narratives of (self-)victimisation.

Rural Dalmatians' construction and performance of selfhood rests heavily on recourse to a set of 'authentic' social values and the creation of a moral community that is based on an assumed moral superiority and the exclusion of non-Dalmatians, including the inhabitants of the major coastal towns. Drawing on their isolation and hardships of life in the physical environment, the inhabitants of Sinj and adjacent villages consciously distance themselves from the 'corrupted and degenerate' world that surrounds them. The mainstays of their views of life are religious practices and beliefs, attitudes to morality and a particular understanding of history. But folkloristic elements, such as festivals, costumes, music (*klapske pjesme*), myths and legends, specific local foods and linguistic idiosyncrasies are also important aspects of their collective self-image. In addition, references to the natural beauty and 'purity' of the region round off the celebrations of a distinct 'culture, nature and heritage' (cf. Green 2005: 39). I have subsumed and interpreted these elements as 'local reserves' that people – often with recourse to 'old', rejected or long-lost habits, practices and beliefs – resort to or mobilise for regeneration when facing deprivation, insecurity and powerlessness.

In '*We, the people of Europe?*', the French philosopher Étienne Balibar holds that 'in reality the Yugoslavian situation is not atypical but rather constitutes a *local projection* of forms of confrontation and conflict characteristic of all Europe' (Balibar 2004: 5) and continues to argue that 'the fate of European identity as a whole has been played out in Yugoslavia and more generally in the Balkans' (ibid.: 6). According to his understanding, the ambiguity of European notions of 'interior' and 'exterior' contribute to the possibility or impossibility of European unification. Especially in the context of the wars in the former Yugoslavia, it became apparent that, on the one hand, the Balkans were considered to be within the borders of Europe and that a military intervention was occurring on European soil and justifiable as the defence of principles of Western civilisation; on the other hand, Europe located the Balkans in an 'exterior' space to guard its own unifying principles against the danger of Balkan fragmentation. In view of this inherent contradiction, Balibar pleads that the Balkans should not be pushed to the geographical margins and played out on behalf of the centre. Rather, instead of labelling the 'Balkan situation' as an outcome of Balkan monstrosity, Europe should recognise and embrace it as an image and effect of its own history; a position, he claims, that would assist Europe to transform itself from within (ibid.). This perspective, however, can also be reversed. Viewed from the margins, the Balkans, and more specifically the Croats, should not consider their 'border identity as an obstacle to achieving their own autonomous nation-state and privileged place in Europe' (Razsa and Lindstrom 2004: 649). Rather, the potential for an unquestioned position within Europe lies in embracing this radically ambivalent (geographic) location at the border and reframing it as a powerful 'ex-centric' site that is not marginal, but constitutes the centre of the fundamental contradictions plaguing European unification.

I want to end this study with a plea for a revised self-orientation instead of a Croatian self-orientalisation and self-victimisation, and rather optimistically argue that the region ought be re-imagined as a site of political engagement and critique. The Balkans' apparently postmodern character, showing itself in the continual deconstruction of borders and continual conflicts over the truth of history, threatens clearly resolved modernist separations and rather calls into question oppositions between 'West' and 'East', 'Orient' and 'Occident' (Green 2005). Previous and most recent attempts to resolve these ambiguities by imposing fixed borders and classifying the Balkans into clearly separated-out entities have not only proved unsuccessful but have displayed an inherently violent structure (Green 2005: 129; Todorova 1997: 59). I have argued that this understanding is of central importance regarding the (im)balances of power and the place of Croatia – and other republics of the former Yugoslavia and Mediterranean borderlands of the EU – within Europe. The region continues to be characterised as a zone that has the potential to perpetuate and proliferate insecurity by imposing set borders and spreading conflicts elsewhere. At the same time, Europe's emphasis on multiculturalism, transnationalism and transmigration is of limited use and applicability to places where local actors assert essentialist notions of culture and identity in an attempt to guarantee lasting stability.

Glossary and Abbreviations

Alka or **Sinjska Alka** ('Alka of Sinj') – (a) the 'Alka of Sinj' is a knight tournament that has been held in the Dalmatian town of Sinj since 1715 in commemoration of the victory over attacking Ottoman troops. Drawing upon the medieval tradition of tournaments and horsemanship competitions (carousels), the 'Alka of Sinj' is held in historic costumes and has been declared a historical monument of the highest order and has been inscribed in UNESCO Intangible Heritage lists in 2010. Only men born in the Sinjska Krajina can take part in this game of skill on horseback, and it is considered a great honour to win the Alka tournament. (b) *alka* is also the name of the ring target used in the tournament. It is made of two concentric rings linked with three bars and hung on a rope above the racetrack. The tilter (*alkar*) rides his horse down the racetrack and tries to hit the central ring of the *alka* with his spear at full gallop.

alkar (Sg.), **alkari** (Pl.) – The Alka horsemen; tilters.

alkarski vojvoda – *voivod* or *vojvoda* is a Slavic title that originally denoted the principal commander of a military force. During military actions the *voivod* was in charge of a conscripted army that consisted of local populations. The term gradually came to designate the governor of a province and corresponds to a 'duke'. In the context of the Sinjska Alka, *vojvoda* is a ceremonial title, representing the commander of the *alkari*.

Arambaša (Sg.), **Arambaše** (Pl.) – (a) leader of the special military-territorial units set up by the Venetians in their lands (*acquisto nuovo*) that they had newly acquired from the Turks after the Treaty of Karlowitz was signed in 1699. The Venetians imposed taxations, military service and various forms of forced labour on the settlers in these new acquisitions. The *Arambaša* was set up as the representative of his men before the Venetian authorities; he collected the taxes, kept law and order, and led the troops into battle. (b) leader of the squires (*momci*) during the Alka. (c) stuffed cabbage rolls, named after the representatives in the 'new Venetian acquisitions'. The name of the dish indicates that it is served on special occasions and is considered to be a meal for the privileged.

Bela Garda – white guard, part of the Slovene Homeguard (Slovensko Domobranstvo, SD) and Axis collaborators in Slovenia during the Second World War.

Bleiburg (Slovene: *Pliberk*) – a small town in Carinthia near the Slovenian border. In Croatia, the town's name is in general used synonymously for the Bleiburg massacre in the course of which Yugoslav Partisans killed thousands of Ustaše, Domobrani, Četniks, and Slovenian white guards, along with a large number of civilians who had fled ahead of the advance of the Partisans in May 1945. Hoping to surrender to and gain the protection of the Allies they tried to cross the border into Austria where the 38th British Infantry Brigade was stationed. The British troops, however, forcibly returned the fleeing militia and refugees back into Yugoslavia, where the Partisans executed most of them. The question of how many people were actually killed at Bleiburg remains highly controversial. While some Croatian nationalists insist that up to two hundred thousand were killed, others have put the final death toll at thirty thousand. The Bleiburg massacre has become paradigmatic for the betrayal of the Croatians by the Allied (and more precisely, the British) troops and is commonly used as *the* trope of Croatian victimisation.

Bljesak or **Operacija Bljesak** – Operation Flash; a brief offensive conducted in the beginning of May 1995 by the Croatian Army (HV) in the course of which forces the Republic of Serbian Krajina (RSK) were expelled from the small pocket in Western Slavonia.

Bošnjak (Sg.); **Bošnjaci** (Pl.) – Bosniak; Bosnian Muslim.

branitelj (Sg.); **branitelji** (Pl.) – lit. translation 'defender'; the term is used for Croatian war veterans who fought in the Homeland War (Domovinski rat) 1991–1995.

Bog i Hrvati – 'God and the Croats' is a well-known Croatian dictum that originates from a speech by the Croatian politician and writer Ante Starčević to the Croatian Parliament (*Sabor*) in 1861, in which he stated that the future of Croatia should not be decided in Austria, but by 'God and the Croats'.

bratstvo i jedinstvo – 'Brotherhood and Unity' was a popular slogan of the Communist party of Yugoslavia which evolved into both a guiding principle of Yugoslavia's post-war inter-ethnic policy and a national motto of the country.

bura – chilly winter north wind.

Cetina – a river in Dalmatia that has its source on the north-western slopes of the Dinara mountains. It passes through the town of Sinj and empties into the Adriatic Sea at Omiš.

Cetinska krajina – a region in Central Dalmatia that stretches along the valley of the River Cetina and whose historical centre is the town of Sinj. Cetinska krajina encompasses Sinjsko polje, and spans between the Dinara and Kamešnica mountain ranges East of Herzegovina.

Četnik (Sg.); **Četnici**, (Pl.) – a Serbian nationalist/royalist paramilitary organisation operating before and during both World Wars.

Država – the state.

Domobran (Sg.); **Domobrani** (Pl.) – Croatian Home Guard; the regular armed forces of the Independent State of Croatia (NDH).

domovina – home, homeland.

Domovinski rat – 'Homeland War', also frequently referred to as 'Croatian War of Independence' (1991–1995).

Gospić massacre – During the Homeland War, Gospić was a front-line town embattled by the Croatian government forces and rebel Serb forces of the self-proclaimed Republic of Serb Krajina (RSK). Between 16–18 October 1991, 100–120 mostly Serb civilians were killed by members of the Croatian military unit. The commander of the unit, Mirko Norac, was later convicted for his involvement in the massacre. With the military Operation Oluja in August 1995, control of the area finally devolved to the Croatian government.

Gospa – The Virgin Mary.

Gospa Sinjska – The Virgin Mary of Sinj; the painting of Gospa Sinjska (Our Blessed Virgin Mary of Mercy) that originates from an unknown sixteenth-century Venetian artist is said to have miraculous powers. It constitutes the centrepiece of the sanctuary Svetište Gospe Sinjske, one of the major pilgrimage shrines in Dalmatia and, according to the legend, protected the people of the town Sinj and the Cetinska Krajina during wars, against the plague, droughts and earthquakes.

grad – town, city.

HDZ (Hrvatska Demokratska Zajednica) – Croatian Democratic Union; the main centre-right political party in Croatia. Founded in June 1989 by Croatian nationalist dissidents under the leadership of Franjo Tuđman, the HDZ ruled Croatia from 1990 to 1999 and, in partial coalition, from 2003 to 2011.

Hrvat (Sg.); **Hrvati** (Pl.) – Croat, Croats; there are around five million Croats living in south-eastern Europe. Republika Hrvatska is the nation state of the Croats, while in the adjacent Bosnia and Herzegovina (BiH) they are one of the three 'constitutive nations'. The Croat diaspora comprises an estimated additional four million Croats (mainly living in the United States, Australia and Germany).

Hrvatska, or **Republika Hrvatska** – Republic of Croatia. Croatia borders with Slovenia and Hungary to the north, Serbia to the north-east, Bosnia and Herzegovina (BiH) to the east, and Montenegro to the far south-east. Its southern and western flanks border the Adriatic Sea, and it also shares a sea border with Italy in the Gulf of Trieste.

Hrvatska Republika Herceg-Bosna – Croatian Republic of Herzeg-Bosnia; an unrecognised entity in Bosnia and Herzegovina that existed between 1991 and 1994 as a result of secessionist politics during the war in Bosnia. The capital city of Herceg-Bosna was Western Mostar. Herceg-Bosna ceased to exist in 1994 when it was joined to the Federation of Bosnia and Herzegovina.

HSP (Hrvatska Stranka Prava) – Croatian Party of Rights; a right-wing political party with an ethnocentric platform in Croatia. The 'Rights' in the party's name refer to the idea of Croatian national and ethnic rights that the party has vowed to protect since its founding in the nineteenth century.

HSS (Hrvatska Seljačka Stranka) – Croatian Peasant Party; a conservative political party in Croatia that was founded in 1904 by the brothers Stjepan and Ante Radić.

ICTY (International Criminal Tribunal for the former Yugoslavia) – a body of the United Nations (UN) established to prosecute serious crimes committed during the wars in the former Yugoslavia. The tribunal is an ad-hoc court located in The Hague in the Netherlands. In 1999 Carla del Ponte was appointed Chief Prosecutor of the ICTY, and he was succeeded by Serge Brammertz in January 2008. In Croatia, however, it is Carla del

Ponte's name that is synonymously linked to the investigation – as well as to the fervent rejection – of the ICTY.

HOS (Hrvatske Obrambene Snage) – Croatian Defence Forces; the military arm of the Croatian Party of Rights (HSP) from 1991 to 1992 during the first stages of the Homeland War. In 1992 HOS dissolved and was allocated to the Croatian Army (in Croatia) and the Croatian Defence Council (HVO) in Bosnia and Herzegovina. The Croatian abbreviation of the organisation, HOS, is identical to the abbreviation for the military of the fascist Independent State of Croatia (NDH).

HV (Hrvatska Vojska) – the 'Croatian Army' (Ground Force) is a branch of the Armed Forces of the Republic of Croatia (Oružane Snage Republike Hrvatske) that further consists of the Croatian Navy (Hrvatska Ratna Mornarica) as well as the Croatian Air and Defense Force (Hrvatsko Ratno Zrakoplovstvo i Protuzračna Obrana).

HVIDRA (Udruga hrvatskih vojnik invalida Domovinskog rata) – Croatian Disabled Homeland War Veterans Association; an association of disabled war veterans who fought in the Homeland War. The association that was founded in many Croatian towns during or immediately after the war has currently about thirty-three thousand members. HVIDRA is one of the most vocal veteran associations in Croatia, frequently weighing in on national politics. At the turn of the century, in the year 2000, members of HVIDRA started to criticise the political course of HDZ for not sufficiently representing the interests of former soldiers.

HVO (Hrvatsko Vijeće Obrane) – Croatian Defence Council; the main military formation of the Hrvatska Republika Herceg-Bosna during the war in Bosnia. It was the first organised military force with the aim of controlling the Croat populated areas.

Jasenovac Concentration Camp – the largest concentration and extermination camp in Independent State of Croatia (NDH) during the Second World War. It was established by the Ustaša regime in August 1941. The largest number of victims were from amongst the Serbs, Jews, Roma as well as Croatian resistance members, most notably Partisans.

JNA (Jugoslovenska Narodna Armija) – Yugoslav People's Army; the military of the Socialist Federal Republic of Yugoslavia.

kafana – coffee house.

kafić – coffee bar.

kamičak – a clock tower in the centre of the town Sinj. The remains of a small fortress held in the eighteenth century by the sentinel of the crew of the main fortress. Today, the building still sports a turret with a clock.

Krajina – the term *Krajina* refers primarily to the border/borderland of a country or its military frontier. The word also refers to a region, area, or landscape surrounding a smaller town. In colloquial use, the term *Krajina* often refers to the region surrounding Knin, that has previously been declared Republic of Serbian Krajina (RSK).

Kukuriku koalicija – The Kukuriku coalition was formed in 2010 and is a political alliance that consists of four centre-left and centrist parties in the Croatian parliament: Social Democratic Party of Croatia (SDP), Croatian People's Party – Liberal Democrats (HNS), Istrian Democratic Assembly (IDS – DDI), and Croatian Party of Pensioners (HSU). In December 2011 the Kukuriku coalition won an absolute majority in the country's parliamentary election. Their election manifesto is called 'Plan 21'.

kulturno – cultivated, educated.

kum; kuma – godfather; godmother.

kumstvo – godparenthood.

kuna – the currency of Croatian. 1 Kuna = 0.14 Euro. The word *kuna* literally translates as 'marten' and refers to the use of marten pelts as units of value in medieval trading.

Maslenica or **Operacija Maslenica** – Operation Maslenica; a Croatian Army offensive launched in January 1993 to retake territory in northern Dalmatia and Lika from separatist Krajina Serb forces, with the stated military objective of pushing the Serbs back from approaches to Zadar and Maslenica Bay, allowing a secure land route between Dalmatia and northern Croatia to be opened.

Matica hrvatska – one of the oldest Croatian cultural institutions (founded in 1842), Matica Hrvatska is currently the largest publisher of Croatian language books. The organisation has 130 local branches throughout Croatia and Bosnia-Herzegovina that entertain cultural–political circles and organise various cultural events.

mačkula – a special type of small cannon, fired from the old fortress in Sinj to mark the beginning of the Alka festivities. The cannon shots from the *mačkula* also indicate that an *alkar* has hit the centre (*srida*) of the *alka* ring during the tournament.

momak (Sg.); **momci** (Pl.) – squire; accompanies and carries the weapons of the *alkari* during the Alka tournament.

narod – nation.

narodni – national.

NDH (Nezavisna Država Hrvatska) – Independent State of Croatia; a puppet state of Nazi Germany that was established in 1941 after the Kingdom of Yugoslavia had been attacked by the Axis forces. The NDH was controlled by the governing fascist Ustaše movement, and the absolute leader of the state was Ante Pavelić, who was referred to as 'poglavnik' (headman).

Operacija Oluja, or **Oluja** – Operation Storm; the code name for a military operation carried out by the Croatian Armed Forces between 4–7 August 2005 to retake the Krajina region into Croatia, which had been controlled by separatist Serbs since 1991. Operation Storm lasted only eighty-four hours during which forces under the command of Lieutenant General Ante Gotovina captured Knin, the capital of the self-proclaimed 'Republika Srpska'. The battle was documented as the largest European land offensive since the Second World War, and ended with a complete victory for the Croatian forces. In Croatia, the commemoration of the military operation is celebrated as a national holiday, the 'Dan pobjede i domovinske zahvalnosti i dan hrvatskih branitelja' (Victory and Homeland Thanksgiving Day and the Day of Croatian Defenders). On the Serbian side, however, Operation Oluja is not only perceived as a major site of military defeat but also synonymously associated with devastation and war crimes against Serb civilians.

općina – county, district, municipality.

planin – mountain.

polje – plain, field.

pršut – smoked ham, prosciutto.

raki(ja*)* – brandy; schnapps.

Republika Srpska (Cyrillic: Република Српска) – one of the two political entities that represent a lower level of governance in the present-day country of Bosnia and Herzegovina (BiH). The other entity is the Federation of Bosnia and Herzegovina.

RSK (Cyrillic: Република Српска Крајина, РСК) – Republic of Serbian Krajina; a self-proclaimed Serbian entity within Croatia during the 1990s. Established in 1991, it was only recognised by the FR Yugoslavia and the Republika Srpska. Its main portion was overrun by Croatian forces in the military operation 'Oluja' in 1995. A rump remained in existence in Eastern Slavonia under UN administration until its peaceful reincorporation into Croatia in 1998.

Sabor – Croatian Parliament.

SDP (Socijaldemokratska Partija Hrvatske) – Social Democratic Party of Croatia; the party evolved from the League of Communists of Croatia when a delegation left the 14th Congress of the Communist Parties of Yugoslavia due to their refusal to cooperate with the Serbian Communist Party led by Slobodan Milošević. Later, after the dissolution of the socialist state of Yugoslavia, the party added Party of Democratic Changes (Stranka demokratskih promjena, SDP) to its name. In 1994 they merged with the Social Democrats of Croatia (SDH) to form the Social Democratic Party of Croatia (SDP).

selo – village.

Sinjsko polje – the fertile karstic field that Sinj and adjacent settlements are situated on.

Sinjska krajina – area in Dalmatinksa *Zagora* around the town of Sinj; sometimes considered as a part of Cetinska krajina.

sir – cheese.

SVK (Srpska Vojska Krajine) – Serbian Army of the Krajina; formed in 1992 as military force of the RSK. The SVK occupied an area of some 17,028 km^2 within Croatian territory at its greatest extent, and had fifty-five thousand soldiers to cover this front. During the military operations Bljesak and Oluja, the SVK was resoundingly defeated in 1995.

trg – square.

turci – Turks; colloquially used as pejorative term for Bosnian Muslims (*Bošnjaks*).

tvrđava – fortress.

UHBDDR (Udruga Hrvatskih Branitelja Dragovoljaca Domovinskog Rata) – Croatian Homeland War Volunteer Veterans Association. According to its statute, the aims of this association are the assembly of all volunteer veterans in a single collective, the maintenance and conservation of traditions that emerged during the Homeland War, as well as the affirmation and vindication of the status as volunteer veteran of the Homeland War.

ulica – street.

Ustaša (Sg.); Ustaše (Pl.) – a far-right, ultra-nationalist, and fascist movement in Croatia, led by Ante Pavelić. Founded in 1929, it engaged in terrorist activity before the Second World War and came to power, under protection from Fascist Italy and Nazi Germany, in the Independent State of Croatia (NDH). After German forces withdrew from Yugoslavia in 1945, the Ustaše were defeated and expelled by the Yugoslav Partisans, an anti-fascist resistance movement organised by Josip Broz Tito. Today, Croatian law officially forbids Ustaše symbols and associated references, but they are still widespread in certain contexts.

Viteško Alkarsko Društvo – Chivalric Association of Alkars in Sinj; appoints the statute of the Alka and also carefully monitors each contestant's compliance with the rules.

vrhnje – cream, sour cream.

Vukovar – a Croatian town in Eastern Croatia that was completely devastated during the Homeland War (1991–1995). Sieged by JNA-supported Serbian troops, Vukovar was fortified by approximately two thousand self-organised defenders before it was eventually overrun and completely demolished. It is estimated that two thousand civilians and defenders of Vukovar were killed, eight hundred went missing and twenty-two thousand were forced into exile. Vukovar is notorious for the devastation it suffered, and in present-day discourse the town's name is often used synonymously with the disastrous war damage and violence that Croatia suffered during the Homeland War.

zadruga – older ethnographic term for large family households, cooperatives, or family enclaves.

Zagora or Dalmatinska Zagora – Dalmatian hinterland; an area in the southern inland region of Croatia. The term *zagora* translates as 'behind the hills', which is a reference to the fact that it denominates the non-coastal part of Dalmatia. The Dalmatinska Zagora spans from the hinterland of Šibenik to the east, where it borders with Herzegovina.

zajednica – togetherness, community; local term for large family households.

ZNG (Zbor Narodne Garde) – The Croatian National Guard; a guard composed of 'special police' forces the Croatian Ministry of the Interior recruited from the ranks of police reservists and established as a quasi-independent Croatian Army (that later came to constitute the Hrvatska Vojska, HV) in response to the Serb uprisings in the Knin region in May 1991. The troops were poorly equipped and badly organised, as Tuđman initially did not aim to defeat the Serbs militarily, but calculated on winning international recognition.

župa – **parish**

županija – county, district.

župnik (Sg.); **župnici** (Pl.) – parish priest; pastor.

Bibliography

Aguilar, P. 2002. *Memory and Amnesia: The Role of the Spanish Civil War in the Transition to Democracy*. New York: Berghahn Books.

Alaupović-Gjeldum, D. and S. Batarelo. 1987. 'Tournament Horses and Harness', *The Alka Tournament of Sinj*. Belgrade: Jugoslovenska Revija.

Albera, D. 1999. 'The Mediterranean as an Anthropological Laboratory', *Anales de la Fundacion Joaquin Costa* 16: 215–32.

Albera, D. , A. Blok and C. Bromberger (eds). 2001. *L'anthropologie de la Méditerranée / Anthropology of the Mediterranean*. Paris: Maisonneuve et Larose, Maison méditerranéenne des sciences de l'homme.

Aleksov, B. 2004. 'Marian Apparitions and the Yugoslav Crisis', *Southeast European Politics* 5(1): 1–23.

Alexander, J.C. 2004. 'Toward a Theory of Cultural Trauma', in J.C. Alexander, R. Eyerman, B. Giesen, N.J. Smelser and P. Sztompka (eds), *Cultural Trauma and Collective Identity*. Berkeley: University of California Press, pp. 1–30.

Allcock, J.B. 2000. 'Constructing "the Balkans"', in J.B. Allcock and A. Young (eds), *Black Lambs and Grey Falcons: Women Travellers in the Balkans*. New York and Oxford: Berghahn Books, pp. 217–40.

Anderson, B. 1983. *Imagined Communities: Reflections on the Origin and Spread of Nationalism*. London: Verso.

Anderson, P. 2007. 'Depicting Europe', *London Review of Books* 29(18): 13–21. Retrieved 18 Nov 2012 from http://www.lrb.co.uk/v29/n18/perry-anderson/depicting-europe

Andrić, I. 1990. *The Development of Spiritual Life in Bosnia under the Influence of Turkish Rule*, ed. and trans. Zelimir Juričić and Hohn F. Loud. Durham, NC: Duke University Press.

Antulov, D. 2000. 'Regionalism in Croatia: Between Tradition and Reality', *Central Europe Review* 2(19). Retrieved 18 Nov 2012 from http://www.pecina.cz/files/www.ce-review.org/00/19/antulov19.html

Antze, P. and M. Lambek. 1996. 'Introduction: Forecasting Memory', in P. Antze and M. Lambek (eds), *Tense Past: Cultural Essays in Trauma and Memory*. New York and London: Routledge, pp. xi–xxxviii.

Asad, T. 1993. *Genealogies of Religion: Discipline and Reasons of Power in Christianity and Islam*. Baltimore, MD: Johns Hopkins University Press.

——— . 2004. 'Where are the Margins of the State?', in V. Das and D. Poole (eds), *Anthropology in the Margins of the State*. Santa Fe, NM: School of American Research Press, pp. 279–88.

Ashbrook, J. 2006. 'Locking Horns in the Istrian Political Arena: Politicized Identity, the Istrian Democratic Assembly, and the Croatian Democratic Alliance', *East European Politics & Societies* 20(4): 622–58.

Ashplant, T.G., G. Dawson and M. Roper. 2000. 'The Politics of War Memory and Commemoration: Contexts, Structures, Dynamics', in T.G. Ashplant, G. Dawson and M. Roper (eds), *The Politics of War Memory and Commemoration*. London and New York: Routledge, pp. 3–86.

Assmann, A. 1999. 'Das Gedächtnis der Orte', in U. Borsdorf and H.T. Grütter (eds), *Orte der Erinnerung: Denkmal, Gedenkstätte, Museum*. Frankfurt/M.: Campus, pp. 59–77.

―――. (1999) 2006. *Erinnerungsräume. Formen und Wandlungen des kulturellen Gedächtnisses* 3. Auflage. Munich: C.H. Beck.

Assmann, J. 1988. 'Kollektives Gedächtnis und kulturelle Identität' in J. Assmann and T. Hölscher (eds), *Kultur und Gedächtnis*. Frankfurt/M.: Suhrkamp, pp. 9–19.

―――. 1997. *Moses the Egyptian: The Memory of Egypt in Western Monotheism*. Harvard and London: Harvard University Press.

Auerbach, E. 1967. *Mimesis: Dargestellte Wirklichkeit in der Abendländischen Literatur* 4. Auflage. Bern: Francke.

Bađun, M. 2009. 'Pension Beneficiaries who have been Granted Pensions under More Favourable Conditions', Institute of Public Finance, Newsletter No. 44. Retrieved 10 Nov 2012 from http://www.ijf.hr/eng/newsletter/44.pdf

Badurina, A. 1982. 'Der Einfluss von Byzanz auf die Kunst der Franziskaner in Kroatien', *800 Jahre Franz von Assisi. Franziskanische Kunst und Kultur des Mittelalters*. Krems-Stein: Niederösterreichische Landesausstellung, pp. 399–403.

Bahr, H. 1909. *Dalmatinische Reise*. Berlin: Fischer Verlag.

Baker, A.R.H. 1992. 'Introduction: On Ideology and Landscape', in A.R.H. Baker and G. Biger (eds), *Ideology and Landscape in Historical Perspective: Essays on the Meanings of Some Places in the Past*. Cambridge: Cambridge University Press, pp. 1–15.

Baker, C. 2006. 'Once Upon a Time in Croatia: Popular Music amd Myths of Croatian Nationhood'. Paper presented 22 March 2006. London: UCL School of Slavonic and East European Studies.

―――. 2010. *Sounds of the Borderland: Popular Music, War and Nationalism in Croatia since 1991*. Aldershot: Ashgate.

Bakić-Hayden, M. 1995. 'Nesting Orientalisms: The Case of Former Yugoslavia', *Slavic Review* 54(4): 917–31.

Balibar, É. 2004. *We, the People of Europe? Reflections on Transnational Citizenship*, trans. James Swenson. Princeton: Princeton University Press.

Ballinger, P. 2003. *History in Exile: Memory and Identity at the Borders of the Balkans*. Princeton: Princeton University Press.

―――. 2004a. '"Authentic Hybrids" in the Balkan Borderlands', *Current Anthropology* 45(1): 31–60.

―――. 2004b. 'Exhumed Histories: Trieste and the Politics of (Exclusive) Victimhood', *The Journal of Southern Europe and the Balkans* 6(2).

——. 2007. 'Beyond the "New" Regional Question? Regions, Territoriality, and the Space of Anthropology in Southeastern Europe', in U. Brunnbauer and K. Roth (eds), *Region, Regional Identity and Regionalism in Southeastern Europe. Special Issue of Ethnologia Balkanica* 11. Münster: LIT-Verlag, pp. 59–78.

Bašić, N. 2004a. 'Kampfsoldaten im ehemaligen Jugoslawien: Legitimationen des Kämpfens und des Tötens', in R. Seifert (ed.), *Gender, Identität und kriegerischer Konflikt. Das Beispiel des ehemaligen Jugoslawien.* Münster: LIT-Verlag, pp. 89–111.

——. 2004b. *Krieg als Abenteuer. Feindbilder und Gewalt aus der Perspective ex-jugoslawischer Soldaten 1991–1995.* Gießen: Psychosozial-Verlag.

Becker, A. 1994. *La Guerre et la Foi. De la Mort à la mémoire. 1914–1930.* Paris: Armand Colin.

Bell, B. 2012. 'Hague War Court Acquits Croat Generals Gotovina and Markac', in *BBC News Europe*, 17 November 2012. Retrieved 17 Nov 2012 from http://www.bbc.co.uk/news/world-europe-20352187

Belting, H. 1993. *Giovanni Bellini: Pietà.* Frankfurt/M.: Fischer.

Belting, H. 2004 [1990]. *Bild und Kult. Eine Geschichte des Bildes vor dem zeitalter der Kunst.* Munich: C.H. Beck.

Bennett, J.S. 2012. *When the Sun Danced: Myth, Miracles, and Modernity in Early Twentieth-Century Portugal.* Charlottesville: University of Virginia Press.

Bjelić, Dušan I. 2006. 'The Balkans: Europe's Cesspool', *Cultural Critique* 62: 33–66.

Bjelić, Dušan I. and O. Savić (eds.). 2005. *Balkan as a Metaphor. Between Globalization and Fragmentation.* Cambridge & London: The MIT Press.

Bjelić, Dušan. 2005. 'Introduction: Blowing Up the "Bridge"', in D.I. Bjelić and O. Savić (eds), *Balkan as a Metaphor: Between Globalization and Fragmentation.* Cambridge and London: The MIT Press, pp. 1–22.

Bjelić, Dušan I. and Lucinda Cole. 2005. 'Sexualizing the Serb', in D.I. Bjelić and O. Savić (eds), *Balkan as a Metaphor: Between Globalization and Fragmentation.* Cambridge and London: The MIT Press, pp. 279–310.

Blagojević, M. 2004. 'Ethnic Conflict and Misogyny: Continuity of Oppositions. Why Misogyny?', in R. Seifert (ed.), *Identität und Kriegerischer Konflikt: Das Beispiel des Ehemaligen Jugoslawien.* Münster: LIT-Verlag, pp. 68–88.

Blaskovich, J. 1997. *Anatomy of Deceit: An American Physician's First-hand Encounter with the Realities of the War in Croatia.* New York: Dunhill Publishing.

Blažević, Z. 2007. 'Rethinking Balkanism – From Orientalism to the Postcolonial Theory', *Balkan Studies (Études balkaniques)* 1: 87–106.

Blok, A. 1974. *The Mafia of a Sicilian Village, 1860–1960: A Study of Violent Peasant Entrepreneurs.* Prospect Heights, IL: Waveland Press.

——. 2000. 'The Enigma of Senseless Violence', in G. Aijmer and J. Abbink (eds), *Meanings of Violence: A Cross-Cultural Perspective.* Oxford and New York: Berg Publishers, pp. 23–38.

——— . 2001. *Honour and Violence*. Cambridge: Polity Press.

Boddy, J. 1989. *Wombs and Alien Spirits: Women, Men, and the Zar Cult in Northern Sudan*. Madison: University of Wisconsin Press.

Boissevain, J. 1965. *Saints and Fireworks: Religion and Politics in Rural Malta*. LSE Monographs in Social Anthropology, No. 30. London: Berg Publishers.

——— . 2013. *Factions, Friends, and Feasts: Anthropological Perspectives on the Mediterranean*. Oxford and New York: Berghahn Books.

Bonifačić Rožin, N. 1967–68. 'Narodna Drama i Igre u Sinjskoj Krajini,' in *Narodna Umjetnost. Studije I Grada O Sinjskoj Krajini*. Knjiga 5–6, pp. 517–578.

Borger, J. 2012. 'War crimes convictions of two Croatian generals overturned', *The Guardian*, 16 Nov 2012. Retrieved 16 Nov 2012 from http://www.guardian.co.uk/world/2012/nov/16/war-crimes-convictions-croat-generals-overturned

Borić, R. 1997. 'Against the War: Women Organizing across the National Divide in the Countries of the Former Yugoslavia', in R. Lentin (ed.), *Gender and Catastrophe*. London and New York: Zed Books, pp. 36–49.

Bošković-Stulli, M. 1968. 'Narodne Pripovijetke i Predaja Sinjske Krajine', *Narodna Umjetnost* (5–6): 303–432.

Bougarel, X. 2007. 'Death and the Nationalist: Martyrdom, War Memory and Veteran Identity among Bosnian Muslims', in X. Bougarel, E. Helms and G. Duijzings (eds), *The New Bosnian Mosaic: Identities, Memories and Moral Claims in Post-War Societies*. Aldershot: Ashgate, pp. 167–91.

Bourdieu, P. 1999. 'The Abdication of the State', in P. Bourdieu et al. (eds), *The Weight of the World: Social Suffering in Contemporary Society*. Cambridge: Polity Press, pp. 181–88.

Bowman, G. 1994. 'Xenophobia, Fantasy and the Nation: The Logic of Ethnic Violence in Former Yugoslavia', in V. Goddard, J. Llobera and C. Shore (eds), *Anthropology of Europe: Identity and Boundaries in Conflict*. London: Berg Publishers, pp. 143–71.

——— . 2003. 'Constitutive Violence and the Nationalist Imaginary: Antagonism and Defensive Solidarity in "Palestine" and "Former Yugoslavia"', *Social Anthropology* 11(3): 37–58.

Bracewell, W. 2000. 'Rape in Kosovo: Masculinity and Serbian Nationalism', *Nations and Nationalism* 6(4): 563–90.

Bracewell, W. and A. Drace-Francis. 1999. 'South-Eastern Europe: History, Concepts, Boundaries', *Balkanologie* 3(2): 47–66.

Braš, M., V. Milunović, M. Boban, L. Brajković, V. Benković, V. Đorđević and O. Polašek. 2011. 'Quality of Life in Croatian Homeland War (1991–1995) Veterans who Suffer from Post-Traumatic Stress Disorder and Chronic Pain', *Health and Quality of Life Outcomes* 9(56): 1–8. Retrieved 10 Nov 2012 from http://www.hqlo.com/content/pdf/1477-7525-9-56.pdf

Braudel, F. 1972. *The Mediterranean and the Mediterranean World in the Age of Philip II*. Trans. Sián Reynolds. London: Collins.

Bridger, S. and F. Pine. 1998. 'Introduction: Transitions to Post-Socialism and Cultures of Survival', in S. Bridger and F. Pine (eds), *Surviving Post-Socialism: Local Strategies and Regional Responses in Eastern Europe and the Former Soviet Union*. London: Routledge, pp. 1–15.

Bringa, T. 1995. *Being Muslim the Bosnian Way: Identity and Community in a Central Bosnian Village*. Princeton: Princeton University Press.

Brown, K. 2003. *The Past in Question: Modern Macedonia and the Uncertainties of Nation*. Princeton: Princeton University Press.

Brunnbauer, U. 2007. 'Editorial', in *Region, Regional Identity and Regionalism in Southeastern Europe*. Special Issue of *Ethnologia Balkanica* 11. Münster: LIT-Verlag, pp. 5–15.

Buden, B. 2000. 'Europe is a Whore', in N. Skopljanac Brunner, S. Gredelj, A. Hodžić and B. Krištofić (eds), *Media and War*. Zagreb: Centre for Transition and Civil Society Research.

———. 2005. 'Hrvatstvo i nije ništa drugo nego sirek i dve-tri mjerice vrhnja'. Intervju vodio Rade Dragojević, *Zarez* 30. lipnja, VII/158, pp. 24–25.

Bulman, T.A. and H.K. Kang. 1994. 'Post-Traumatic Stress Disorder among Vietnam Veterans', *Journal of Nervous and Mental Disorder* 182: 604–10.

Burawoy, M., P. Krotov and T. Lytkina. 2000. 'Involution and Destitution in Capitalist Russia', *Ethnography* 1(1): 43–65.

Caillois, R. (1961) 1979. *Man, Play, and Games*. New York: Schocken Books.

Campbell, J. K. 1966. 'Honour and the Devil', in J. G. Peristiany (ed.), *Honour and Shame: The Values of Mediterranean Society*. London: Weidenfeld and Nicolson, pp. 112–175.

Čapo Žmegač, J. 2001. 'Der Blick von außen: Kroatien und das Modell der Balkanfamilie', in J. Čapo Žmegač, R. Johler, S. Kalapoš and H. Nikitsch (eds), *Kroatische Volkskunde/Ethnologie in den Neunzigern*. Vienna: Verlag des Instituts für europäische Ethnologie, pp. 269–87.

Carroll, M.P. 1986. *The Cult of the Virgin Mary: Psychological Origins*. Princeton, NJ: Princeton University Press.

Cartier, C. 2008. 'Croatian Wives Contend with War's After Shocks', *Women's E-news*, 14 September 2008. Retrieved 10 Nov 2012 from http://womense-news.org/story/war/080914/croatian-wives-contend-wars-after-shocks

Cellarius, B.A. 2000. '"You can buy almost anything with potatoes": An Examination of Barter During Economic Crisis in Bulgaria', *Ethnology* 39(1): 73–92.

Ceribašić, N. 1995. 'Gender Roles during the War: Representations in Croatian and Serbian Popular Music 1991–1992', *Collegium Anthropologicum* 19(1): 91–101.

Certeau, M. de. 1984. *The Practice of Everyday Life*. Berkeley: University of California Press.

Christian, W. Jr. 1972. *Person and God in a Spanish Valley*. London and New York: Seminar Press.

———. 1984. 'Religious Apparitions and the Cold War in Southern Europe', in E.R. Wolf and H.H. Lehmann (eds), *Religion, Power and Protest in Local*

Communities: The Northern Shore of the Mediterranean. Amsterdam and Berlin: Mouton, pp. 239–65.

Clark, J.N. 2013a. 'Reconciliation through Remembrance? War Memorials and the Victims of Vukovar', *International Journal of Transitional Justice* 7: 116–35.

———. 2013b. 'Giving Peace a Chance: Croatia's *Branitelji* and the Imperative of Reintegration', *Europe–Asia Studies* 65(10): 1931–53.

Claverie, É. 2003. *Les guerres de la Vierge: Une anthropologie des apparitions.* Paris: Gallimard.

Clewing, K. 2001. *Staatlichkeit und nationale Identitätsbildung: Dalmatien in Vormärz und Revolution.* Munich: R. Oldenbourg Verlag.

Čolović, I. 1993. *Bordel Ratnika: Folklor, Politika i Rat.* Belgrade: Biblioteka XX Vek.

———. 2002. *The Politics of Symbol in Serbia: Essays in Political Anthropology.* London: Hurst and Company.

———. 2004. 'A Criminal-National Hero? But Who Else?', in M. Todorova (ed.), *Balkan Identities: Nation and Memory.* New York: New York University Press, pp. 253–68.

Comaroff, J. 1985. *Body of Power, Spirit of Resistance: The Culture and History of a South African People.* Chicago: University of Chicago Press.

Connerton, P. 1989. *How Societies Remember.* Cambridge: Cambridge University Press.

Coomaraswamy, R. 2003. *Integration of the Human Rights of Women and the Gender Perspective/Violence against Women.* The Commission on Human Rights, United Nations Report E/CN.4/2003/75/Add.1.

Corder, M. 2012. 'Tribunal Overturns Convictions of Croat Generals', *Associated Press*, 16 November 2012. Retrieved 16 Nov 2012 from http://news.yahoo.com/tribunal-overturns-convictions-croat-generals-085736798.html

Cosgrove, D. 1984. *Social Formation and Symbolic Landscape.* London: Croon Helm.

Crane, S.A. 1997. 'Writing the Individual Back into Collective Memory', *American Historical Review* 102: 1372–85.

Crapanzano, V. 2004. *Imaginative Horizons: An Essay in Literary-Philosophical Anthropology.* Chicago and London: University of Chicago Press.

Crčić, E. 2001. 'Former Croatian General Surrenders', *Associated Press*, 22 February.

Creed, G.W. 1995. 'The Politics of Agriculture: Identity and Socialist Sentiment in Bulgaria', *Slavic Review* 54(4): 843–68.

———. 1999. 'Deconstructing Socialism in Bulgaria', in M. Burawoy and K. Verdery (eds), *Uncertain Transition: Ethnographies of Change in the Postsocialist World.* Lanham, MD, and Oxford: Roman & Littlefield, pp. 223–43.

Croitoru, J. 2003. *Der Märtyrer als Waffe: Die historischen Wurzeln des Selbstmordattentats.* Munich: Deutscher Taschebuch Verlag.

Csordas, T.J. 1994. 'Introduction: The Body as Representation and Being-in-the-World' in T.J. Csordas (ed.), *Embodiment and Experience: The Existential Ground of Culture and Self*. Cambridge: Cambridge University Press, pp. 1–24.

Cutileiro, J. 1971. *A Portuguese Rural Society*. Oxford: Clarendon Press.

Cviić, C. 1982. 'A Fatima in a Communist Land?', *Religion in Communist Lands* 10(1): 4–9.

CWWPP. 2004. Coalition for Work with Psychotrauma and Peace: Annual Report. Vukovar. Retrieved 15 Apr 2008 from http://www.cwwpp.org/

Dalbelo, I. 2001. 'Comments on Costumes', in B. Ljubičić (ed.), *Alka*. Sinj: Viteško alkarsko društvo.

DaMatta, R. 1991. *Carnivals, Rogues, and Heroes: An Interpretation of the Brazilian Dilemma*. Trans. John Drury. Notre Dame and London: University of Notre Dame.

Darieva, T. and W. Kaschuba. 2007. 'Introduction: Politics and Identities on the "Margins" of New Europe', in T. Darieva and W. Kaschuba (eds), *Representations on the Margins of Europe: Politics and Identities in the Baltic and South Caucasian States*. Frankfurt/M.: Campus, pp. 11–27.

Davis, D.L. 1988. 'The Variable Character of Nerves in a Newfoundland Fishing Village', *Medical Anthropology* 11: 63–78.

Davis, J. 1977. *People of the Mediterranean: An Essay in Comparative Social Anthropology*. London: Routledge and Kegan Paul.

——— . 1984. 'The Sexual Division of Labour in the Mediterranean', in E.R. Wolf and H.H. Lehmann (eds), *Religion, Power and Protest in Local Communities: The Northern Shore of the Mediterranean*. Amsterdam and Berlin: Mouton, pp. 17–50.

Dawson, G. 1994. *Soldier Heroes: British Adventure, Empire and the Imagining of Masculinities*. London and New York: Routledge.

Denich, B. 1991. 'Unbury the Victims: Rival Exhumations and Nationalist Revivals in Yugoslavia', *American Anthropological Association Annual Meeting*. Chicago: American Anthropological Association.

——— . 1994. 'Dismembering Yugoslavia: Nationalist Ideologies and the Symbolic Revival of Genocide', *American Ethnologist* 21.

Devisch, R. and A. Gailly (eds). 1995. 'Symbol and Symptom in Bodily Space-Time', Special Issue of the *International Journal of Psychology* 20: 389–663.

Ditchev, I. 2005. 'The Eros of Identity', in D.I. Bjelić and O. Savić (eds), *Balkan as Metaphor: Between Globalization and Fragmentation*. Cambridge and London: MIT Press, pp. 235–50.

Drakulić, S. 1996. *Café Europa – Life after Communism*. London: Abacus.

——— . 2004. *They Would Never Hurt a Fly*. London: Abacus.

Driessen, H. 2001. 'People, Boundaries and the Anthropologist's Mediterranean', in I.-M. Greverus, R. Römhild and G. Welz (eds), *The Mediterraneans: Reworking the Past, Shaping the Present, Considering the Future*. Special Issue of *Anthropological Journal on European Cultures* 10: 11–23.

Dubisch, J. 1995. *In a Different Place: Pilgrimage, Gender, and Politics at a Greek Island Shrine*. Princeton: Princeton University Press.

Dubisch, J., and M. Winkelmann (eds), 2005. *Pilgrimage and Healing*. Tucson: The University of Arizona Press.

Duhaček, D. 2001. 'Gender Perspectives on Political Identities in Yugoslavia', in R. Iveković and J. Mostov (eds), *From Gender to Nation*. Europe and the Balkans International Network. Ravenna: Longo Editore, pp. 113–29.

Eade, J. and M.J. Sallnow (eds). 2000. *Contesting the Sacred: The Anthropology of Pilgrimage*. Urbana and Chicago: University of Illinois Press.

Egger, H. 1982. 'Franziskanischer Geist in mittelalterlichen Bildvorstellungen', in *800 Jahre Franz von Assisi. Franziskanische Kunst und Kultur des Mittelalters*. Niederösterreichische Landesausstellung. Minoritenkirche Krems-Stein, pp. 471–505.

Elshtain, J.B. 1995. *Women and War*. Chicago: University of Chicago Press.

Elwert, G. 2001. 'Terroristen: rational und lernfähig. Wer die Terroristen des 11. September bekämpfen will, muss zuerst ihre Logik begreifen', *Der Überblick* 3: 1–8.

Enloe, C. 1988. *Does Khaki Become You? The Militarization of Women's Lives*. London: Pandora Press.

———. 1989. *Bananas, Beaches and Bases: Making Feminist Sense of International Politics*. London: Pandora.

———. 1993. *The Morning After: Sexual Politics at the End of the Cold War*. Berkeley and London: University of California Press.

———. 2000. *Maneuvers: The International Politics of Militarizing Women's Lives*. Berkeley: University of California Press.

Enzensberger, H.M. 2006. *SchreckensMänner: Versuch über den radikalen Verlierer*. Frankfurt/M.: Suhrkamp.

Eriksen, T.H. 1993. *Ethnicity and Nationalism: Anthropological Perspectives*. London: Pluto Press.

Esherick, J.W. and J.N. Wasserstrom,. 1990. 'Acting Out Democracy: Political Theater in Modern China', *The Journal of Asian Studies*, 49(4): 835–65.

ETF – European Training Foundation, Country Analysis Croatia 2006, Working Paper. Retrieved 15 Apr 2008 from http://www.etf.europa.eu/web.nsf/pages/newsarchive_EN?Opendocument

Feuchtwang, S. 2007. 'On Religious Ritual as Deference and Communicative Excess', *The Journal of the Royal Anthropological Institute*, 13(1): 57–72.

Filippucci, P. 2010. 'In a Ruined Country: Place and the Memory of War Destruction in Argonne (France)', in N. Argenti and K. Schramm (eds), *Remembering Violence: Anthropological Perspectives on Intergenerational Transmission*. Oxford and New York: Berghahn Books.

Flögel, M. and G. Lauc. 2003. 'War Stress: Effects of the War in the Area of Former Yugoslavia'. University of Zagreb: Faculty of Pharmacy and Biochemistry. Retrieved 15 Apr 2008 from http://www.nato.int/du/docu/d010306c.pdf

Fortis, A. 1778. *Travels Into Dalmatia: Containing General Observations on the Natural History of that Country and the Neighbouring Islands; the Natural Productions, Arts, Manners and Customs of the Inhabitants* (Iter Buda Hadrianopolin anno MDLIII. exaratum ab A. Verantio), London.

Frančišković, T., A. Stevanović, I. Jelušić, B. Roganović, M. Klarić and J. Grković. 2007. 'Secondary Traumatization of Wives of War Veterans with Post-traumatic Stress Disorder', *Croat Medical Journal* 48(2): 177–84.

Friedlin, J. 2001. 'Bosnia: Suicide on the Rise'. Institute for War and Peace Reporting. BCR 303, 12 December 2001. Retrieved 22 Dec 2012 from http://iwpr.net/report-news/bosnia-suicides-rise

Friedman, J. 1992. 'Narcissicism, Roots and Postmodernity: The Constitution of Selfhhood in the Global Crisis', in S. Lash and J. Friedman (eds), *Modernity and Identity*. Oxford: Blackwell, pp. 331–66.

Frykman, J. *When the Dead Come Alive* (unpublished manuscript), 18 pages.

Frykman, J., and N. Gilje (eds). 2003. *Being There: New Perspectives on Phenomenology and the Analysis of Culture*. Lund: Nordic Academic Press.

Gal, S., and G. Kligman. 2000. *The Politics of Gender after Socialism: A Comparative-Historical Essay*. Princeton: Princeton University Press.

Gamulin, J. 1987. 'Alka Tournament Arms', *The Alka Tournament of Sinj*. Belgrade: Jugoslovenska Revija, pp. 92–98.

Gellner, E. and J. Waterbury (eds). 1977. *Patrons and Clients in Mediterranean Societies*. London: Duckworth.

Gilbert, A., J. Greenberg, E. Helms and S. Jansen. 2008a. 'Reconsidering Postsocialism from the Margins of Europe: Hope, Time and Normalcy in Post-Yugoslav Societies', *Anthropology News* 49(8): 10–11.

——— . 2008b. 'Organizers' Summary of Manchester Workshop "Towards an Anthropology of Hope? Comparative Post-Yugoslav Ethnographies"'. Workshop held at the University of Manchester, 9–11 November 2007 (unpublished document).

Gillis, J.R. 1994. 'Memory and Identity: The History of a Relationship', in J.R. Gillis (ed.), *Commemorations: The Politics of National Identity*. Princeton: Princeton University Press, pp. 3–24.

Giordano, C. 1996. 'Just Society and Cultural Norms', *Etnološka Tribina* 19: 15–20.

——— . 2007. 'Ethnic versus Cosmopolitan Regionalism? For a Political Anthropology of Local Identity Constructions in a Globalized World System', in U. Brunnbauer and K. Roth (eds), *Region, Regional Identity and Regionalism in Southeastern Europe. Special Issue of Ethnologia Balkanica* 11. Münster: LIT-Verlag, pp. 43–58.

Glenny, M. 1992. *The Fall of Yugoslavia*. London: Penguin Books.

——— . 1999. *The Balkans: Nationalism, War and the Great Powers, 1804–1999*. New York: Penguin Books.

Goffman, E. (1961) 1968. *Asylums: Essays on the Social Situation of Mental Patients and Other Inmates*. Harmondsworth: Penguin.

——— . 1971. *Relations in Public: Microstudies of the Public Order*. New York: Basic Books.

Golanska-Ryan, J. 2006, 'Strategies of Resistance in the Polish Campaign against EU Membership', in M. Svašek (ed.), *Postsocialism: Politics and Emotions in Central and Eastern Europe*. New York and Oxford: Berghahn Books, pp. 159–77.

Gordy, E. 2012. 'Today is a Good Day to be a Criminal', in *East Ethnia: Balkan Politics and Academics*. Retrieved 18 Nov 2012 from https://eastethnia.wordpress.com/2012/11/16/today-is-a-good-day-to-be-a-criminal/

Grandits, H. 2002. *Familie und sozialer Wandel im ländlichen Kroatien (18.–20. Jahrhundert)*. Vienna: Böhlau.

———. 2005. 'Gender Relations in Post-War Social Life: The Example of Multinational Herzegovina', *Anthropological Journal of European Cultures* 14: 113–42.

Grandits, H. and S. Gruber. 1996. 'The Dissolution of the Large Complex Households in the Balkans: Was the Ultimate Reason Structural or Cultural?', *History of the Family* 1(4): 477–96.

Grandits, H. and J.M. Halpern. 1994. 'Traditionelle Wertemuster und der Krieg in Ex-Jugoslawien', *Beiträge zur Historischen Sozialkunde* 24(3): 91–102.

Grčić, M. 1987. 'A Legend Lives On', in *The Alka Tournament of Sinj*. Belgrade: Jugoslovenska Revija, pp. 15–18.

Green, S.F. 2005. *Notes from the Balkans: Locating Marginality and Ambiguity on the Greek-Albanian Border*. Princeton and Oxford: Princeton University Press.

Greenberg, J. 2006. 'Nationalism, Masculinity and Multicultural Citizenship in Serbia', *Nationalities Papers* 34(3): 321–42.

Grimshaw, A. 2001. *The Ethnographer's Eye: Ways of Seeing in Modern Anthropology*. Cambridge: Cambridge University Press.

Gronover, A. 2007. *Religiöse Reserven: Eine Ethnographie des Überlebens in Palermo*. Forum europäische Ethnologie. Münster: LIT-Verlag.

Grünfelder, A.M. 1999. 'Marija – kraljica hrvata: Kritički ženski osvrt na oblike štovanja marijina u crkvenoj i pučkoj pobožnosti', *Treća* 2(1): 17–25.

Guarnaccia, P.J., V. De La Cancela and E. Carrillo. 1988. 'The Multiple Meanings of "Atagues de Nervios" in a Latino Community', *Medical Anthropology* 11: 47–62.

Gulin, V. 1997. 'Morlacchism between Enlightenment and Romanticism', *Narodna Umjetnost* 34(1): 77–100.

Gupta, A., and J. Ferguson. 1997. *Culture, Power, Place: Explorations in Critical Anthropology*. Durham, NC: Duke University Press.

Gurung, G.S., and M. Kollmair. 2005. 'Marginality: Concepts and their Limitations', *NCCR North-South-Dialogue*. IP6 Working Paper No. 4, Berne. Retrieved 19 May 2007 from http://www.nccr-pakistan.org/publications_pdf/General/Marginality.pdf

Haberlandt, M. 1911. 'Die Volkskunst in Istrien und Dalmatien', in E. Brückner (ed.), *Dalmatien und das österreichische Küstenland*. Vienna and Leipzig: Franz Deuticke, pp. 189–200.

Halbwachs, M. (1941) 1971. *La Topographie légendaire des Evangiles en Tierre sainte: Etude de mémoire collective*. Paris: Presses Universitaires de France.

———. (1950) 1980. *The Collective Memory*. New York: Harper & Row Colophon Books.

Halpern, J.M. and D. Kideckel (eds). 2000. *Neighbors at War: Anthropological Perspectives on Yugoslav Ethnicity, Culture and History*. University Park: Pennsylvania State University Press.

Hann, C. (ed.). 2002. *Postsocialism: Ideas, Ideologies and Practices in Eurasia*. London and New York: Routledge.

Haraway, D. 1988. 'Situated Knowledges: The Science Question in Feminism and the Privilege of Partial Perspective', *Feminist Studies* 15(3): 575–99.

Harris, W.V. (ed.). 2005. *Rethinking the Mediterranean*. Oxford: Oxford University Press.

Harrison, S. 2004. 'Forgetful and Memorious Landscapes', *Social Anthropology* 12(2): 135–51.

Hartinger, W. 1985. *Mariahilf ob Passau. Volkskundliche Untersuchung der Passauer Wallfahrt und der Mariahilf-Verehrung im deutschsprachigen Raum*. Passau: Verlag des Vereins für Ostbairische Heimatforschung Passau.

Harvie, C. 1994. *The Rise of Regional Europe*. London: Routledge.

Hasan-Rokem, G. 2003. 'Martyr vs. Martyr: The Sacred Language of Violence', in J. Bendix (ed.), *Sleepers, Moles and Martyrs: Secret Identifications, Societal Integration and the Differing Meanings of Freedom. Special Issue Ethnologia Europea* 33(2): 99–104.

Hauschild, T. 2002. *Magie und Macht in Italien. Über Frauenzauber, Kirche und Politik*. Gifkendorf: Merlin Verlag.

——— . 2003. 'Erdbeben und das Ewige in Süditalien – Zur Geophysik der Macht', in D. Groh, M. Kempe and F. Mauelshagen (eds), *Naturkatastrophen. Beiträge zu ihrer Deutung, Wahrnehmung und Darstellung in Text und Bild von der Antike bis ins 20. Jahrhundert*, Tübingen: Gunter Narr, pp. 395–415.

——— . 2007. 'Reserven gegen die Globalisierung in mediterranen Gesellschaften', Rahmenpapier zu Anträgen auf Sachbeihilfe für ethnologische Feldforschungen, u.a. [unpublished manuscript].

——— . 2008. *Ritual und Gewalt: Ethnologische Studien an europäischen und mediterranen Gesellschaften*. Frankfurt/M.: Suhrkamp.

——— . 2011. *Power and Magic in Italy*. New York and Oxford: Berghahn Books [Revised translation of *Magie und Macht in Italien*].

Hauschild, T., S.L. Kottmann and M. Zillinger. 2007. 'Syncretism in the Mediterranean: Universalism, Cultural Relativism and the Issue of the Mediterranean as a Cultural Area', *History and Anthropology* 18(3): 309–32.

Hayden, R.M. 1994. 'Recounting the Dead: The Rediscovery and Redefinition of Wartime Massacres in Late- and Post-Communist Yugoslavia', in R.S. Watson (ed.), *Memory, History, and Opposition under State Socialism*. Santa Fe, NM: School of American Research Press, pp. 167–84.

——— . 1996. 'Imagined Communities and Real Victims: Self-Determination and Ethnic Cleansing in Yugoslavia', *American Ethnologist* 23(4).

——— . 2007. 'Moral Vision and Impaired Sight: The Imagining of Other People's Communities In Bosnia', *Current Anthropology* 48(1): 105–17.

Heady, P., and L.L. Gambold Miller. 2006. 'Nostalgia and the Emotional Economy: A Comparative Look at Rural Russia', in M. Svašek (ed.), *Postsocialism: Politics and Emotions in Central and Eastern Europe*. New York and Oxford: Berghahn Books, pp. 34–52.

Hedl, D. 2000. 'Living in the Past: Franjo Tudjman's Croatia', *Current History*. Retrieved 10 Nov 2012 from http://www.currenthistory.com/org_pdf_files/99/635/99_635_104.pdf

——. 2002. 'Croatia: Storm over War Pensions', Institute for War and Peace Reporting, 10 September 2002. Retrieved 10 Nov 2012 from http://iwpr.net/print/report-news/croatia-storm-over-war-pensions

——. 2012. 'Generals' Release Poses Dilemma for Croatian Courts', *Balkan Insight*, 19 November 2012. Retrieved 19 Nov 2012 from http://www.balkaninsight.com/en/article/generals-release-poses-dilemma-for-croatian-courts

Heimo, A. and U.-M. Peltonen. 2003. 'Memories and Histories, Public and Private: After the Finnish Civil War', in K. Hodgkin and S. Radstone (eds), *Contested Pasts: The Politics of Memory*. London and New York: Routledge, pp. 42–56.

Helms, E. 2006. 'Gendered Transformations of State Power: Masculinity, International Intervention, and the Bosnian Police', *Nationalities Papers* 34(3).

Helsinki Committee Report on Human Rights in Serbia. 2006. 'Human Security in an Unfinished State: Serbia 2005'. Retrieved 18 Sep 2007 from www.helsinki.org.yu/doc/reports/eng/Report2005.pdf

Herzfeld, M. 1984. 'The Horns of the Mediterraneanist Dilemma', *American Ethnologist* 11(3): 439–54.

——. 1985. *Poetics of Manhood: Contest and Identity in a Cretan Mountain Village*. Princeton: Princeton University Press.

——. 1987. *Anthropology through the Looking Glass: Critical Ethnography in the Margins of Europe*. Cambridge: Cambridge University Press.

——. 1991. *A Place in History: Social and Monumental Time in a Cretan Town*. Princeton: Princeton University Press.

——. 1997. *Cultural Intimacy: Social Poetics in the Nation-State*. London: Routledge.

——. 2002. 'The Absent Presence: Discourses of Crypto-Colonialism', *South Atlantic Quarterly* 101(4): 899–926.

——. 2004. *The Body Impolitic: Artisans and Artifice in the Global Hierarchy of Value*. Chicago: Chicago University Press.

——. 2005. 'Foreword', in D.I. Bjelić and O. Savić (eds), *Balkan as Metaphor: Between Globalization and Fragmentation*. Cambridge and London: MIT Press, pp. ix–xii.

Hirsch, E. and M. O'Hanlon. 1995. *The Anthroplogy of Landscape: Perspectives on Place and Space*. Oxford: Oxford University Press.

Hodgkin, K. and S. Radstone (eds). 2003a. *Memory, History, Nation: Contested Pasts*. New Brunswick and London: Transaction Publishers.

———. (eds). 2003b. *Memory Cultures: Memory, Subjectivity and Recognition*. New Brunswick and London: Transaction Publishers.

Holbach, M. 1908. *Dalmatia: The Land where East meets West*. London and New York: John Lane.

Höpken, W. 2001. 'Kriegserinnerung und Kriegsverarbeitung auf dem Balkan', *Südosteuropa-Mitteilungen* 41(4): 371–89.

Horden, P. and N. Purcell. 2000. *The Corrupting Sea: A Study of Mediterranean History*. Oxford: Blackwell.

Horvat, R. (1942) 1992. *Hrvatska na mučilištu*. Zagreb: Školska knjiga.

Humphrey, C. 2002. *The Unmaking of Soviet Life: Everyday Economies After Socialism*. Ithaca, NY: Cornell University Press.

Ilić, I. 2011. 'Clashes Erupt after Croatian War Veterans' Rally', *TrustLaw*, 26 February 2011. Retrived 10 Nov 2012 from http://www.trust.org/trustlaw/news/croatian-war-veterans-protest-against-arrest-govt

Ingold, T. 2000. *The Perception of the Environment: Essays in Livelihood, Dwelling and Skill*. London and New York: Routledge.

Ivanišević, B. 2012. 'Hague Failed to Justify Gotovina Acquittal', *Balkan Insights*, 19 November 2012. Retrieved 19 Nov 2012 from http://www.balkaninsight.com/en/article/hague-failed-to-justify-gotovina-acquittal

Ivanković, N. 2001. *Ratnik: pustolov i general: jedna biografija*. Zagreb: Honos. English translation: *The Warrior – and adventurer and general*. Retrieved 10 Nov 2012 http://www.antegotovina.com/doc/ratnik_jan_20.pdf

Iveković, R. 2001. *Autopsie des Balkans: Ein psychopolitischer Essay*. Graz and Vienna: Droschl.

Iveković, R. and J. Mostov. 2002. 'Introduction', in Rada Iveković and Julie Mostov (eds), *From Gender to Nation*. Ravenna: Longo Editore, pp. 9–25.

Jackson, M. 1996. *Things As They Are: New Directions in Phenomenological Anthropology*. Bloomington: Indiana University Press.

———. 1998. *Minima Ethnographica: Intersubjectivity and the Anthropological Project*. Chicago: University of Chicago Press.

Jackson, T.G. 1887. *Dalmatia, the Quarnero, and Istria*. Oxford: The Clarendon Press.

Jakir, A. 1999. *Dalmatien zwischen den Weltkriegen: Agrarische und urbane Lebenswelt und das Scheitern der jugoslawischen Integration*. Munich: R. Oldenbourg Verlag.

Jalušić, V. 2004. 'Gender and Victimisation of the Nation as Pre- and Post-War Discourse', in R. Seifert (ed.), *Gender, Identität und kriegerischer Konflikt. Das Beispiel des ehemaligen Jugoslawien*. Münster: LIT-Verlag.

Jambrešić Kirin, R. 2004. 'The Politics of Memory in Croatian Socialist Culture: Some Remarks', *Narodna Umjetnost* 41(1): 125–43.

———. 2007. '"EU nije cool, sir i vrhnje jesu": figura krave u dvjema umjetničkim praksama' ['The EU is not cool, cheese and cream are': The Figure of the Cow in Artistic Practices], in S. Marjanić and A. Zaradija Kiš (eds), *Kulturni Bestijari*. Zagreb: Institut za etnologiju i folkloristiku – Hrvatska sveučilišna naklada, pp. 645–70.

Jambrešić Kirin, R. and T. Škokić (eds). 2004. *Između roda i naroda: etnološke i folklorističke studije*. Centar za ženske studije i Institut za etnologiju i folkloristiku. Zagreb: Biblioteka Nova etnografija.

Jansen, S. 1999. 'Identities, Memories and Ideologies', *Social Anthropology* 7: 327–32.

———. 2000. 'Victims, Underdogs and Rebels: Discursive Practices of Resistance in Serbian Protest', *Critique of Anthropology* 20(4): 393–420.

———. 2002. 'The Violence of Memories: Local Narratives of the Past after Ethnic Cleansing in Croatia', *Rethinking History* 6(1): 77–94.

———. 2006. 'The (Dis)Comfort of Conformism: Post-War Nationalism and Coping with Powerlessness in Croatian Villages', in T. Otto, H. Thrane and H. Vandkilde (eds), *Warfare and Society: Archaeological and Social Anthropological Perspectives*. Aarhus: Aarhus University Press, pp. 433–46.

———. 2007. 'The Frajer and the Father: Cross-National Recognitions of Masculinity after the Bosnian War'. Croatian version published 2008 as 'Frajer i otac: međunacionalna prepoznavanja muškosti poslije rata u Bosni i Hercegovini', in R. Jambrešić-Kirin and S. Prlenda (eds.), *Promišljanje sjevera i juga u postkolonijalnosti*. Zagreb: Institut za etnologiju i folkloristiku / Centar za ženske studije, pp. 42–62.

Jansen, S., and Staffan Löfving. 2007. 'Introduction: Movement, Violence, and the Making of Home', *Focaal. European Journal of Anthropology* 49: 3–14.

Jeffery, S. 2003. 'The EU Common Agricultural Policy', *The Guardian*, 26 June 2003. Retrieved 20 Aug 2008 from http://www.guardian.co.uk/world/2003/jun/26/eu.politics1

Jenkins, J.H. and M. Valiente. 1994. 'Bodily Transactions of the Passions: el calor among Salvadorian Women Refugees', in T.J. Csordas (ed.), *Embodiment and Experience: The Existential Ground of Culture and Self*. Cambridge: Cambridge University Press, pp. 163–82.

Jesus, L. de. 1995. *Fatima in Lucia's Own Words*. Still River, MA: The Ravengate Press.

Jones, A. 1994. 'Gender and Ethnic Conflict in Ex-Yugoslavia', *Ethnic and Racial Studies* 17(1): 115–34.

Jonjić, T. 2007. 'Organised Resistance to the Yugoslav Communist Regime in Croatia in 1945–1953', *Review of Croatian History* 3(1): 109–45.

Jović, D. 2009. 'Croatia after Tudjman: The ICTY and Issues of Transitional Justice', *Chaillot Paper* 116. Retrieved 10 Nov 2012 from https://dspace.stir.ac.uk/bitstream/1893/1993/2/Jović%2c%20Chaillot%20Paper%20116%2c%20June%202009%2c%20as%20published%5b1%5d.pdf

———. 2012. 'The War that is Not Allowed to be Forgotten: Nationalist Discourse on the "Homeland War" (1991–1995) in Contemporary Croatia', *Südosteuropa Mitteilungen* 52(3): 52–69.

Jurić, D. 1987a. 'The Alka Knightly Tournament Society', *The Alka Tournament of Sinj*. Belgrade: Jugoslovenska Revija, pp. 73–75.

———. 1987b. 'The Tournament Field', *The Alka Tournament of Sinj*. Belgrade: Jugoslovenska Revija, pp. 76–77.

Jurić, Šime. 1965. *Sinjska Alka: Informativni vodič po Cetinskoj krajini*. Zagreb: Odbor za proslavu 250. godišnjice Sinjske alke.

———. 1987a. 'History of Sinj and the Cetina March', *The Alka Tournament of Sinj*. Belgrade: Jugoslovenska Revija, pp. 19–57.

———. 1987b. 'History of the Alka Tournament', *The Alka Tournament of Sinj*. Belgrade: Jugoslovenska Revija, pp. 58–69.

———. 1987c. 'What Happens on Tournament Day', *The Alka Tournament of Sinj*. Belgrade: Jugoslovenska Revija, pp. 110–52.

Kalb, D. 2005. 'From Flows to Violence: Politics and Knowledge in the Debates on Globalization and Empire', *Anthropological Theory* 5(2): 176–204.

Kalb, D., M. Svašek and H. Tak. 1999. 'Approaching the "New" Past in East-Central Europe', *Focaal. European Journal of Anthropology* 33: 9–23.

Kalb, D., and H. Tak. 2006. 'The Dynamics of Trust and Mistrust in Poland: Floods, Emotions, Citizenship and the State', in M. Svašek (ed.), *Postsocialism: Politics and Emotions in Central and Eastern Europe*. New York and Oxford: Berghahn Books, pp. 196–213.

Kaldor, M. 1990. *The Imaginary War: Understanding the East–West Conflict*. Oxford: Blackwell.

Kaser, K. 1992a. 'Hirten, Helden und Hajduken: zum Männlichkeitskult im jugoslawischen Krieg', *L'Homme: Zeitschrift für feministische Geschichtswissenschaft* 3(1): 155–62.

———. 1992b. *Hirten, Kämpfer, Stammeshelden: Ursprünge und Gegenwart des balkanischen Partriarchats*. Vienna: Böhlau.

———. 1995. *Familie und Verwandtschaft auf dem Balkan: Analyse einer untergehenden Kultur*. Vienna: Böhlau.

———. 2000. *Macht und Erbe, Männerherrschaft, Besitz und Familie*. Vienna: Böhlau.

Kaser, K. and J.M. Halpern. 1994. 'Contemporary Research on the Balkan Family: Anthropological and Historical Approaches', *Septieme Congres International d'Etudes du Sud-Est Europeen (Thessalonique, 29 aout – 4 septembre)*. Athens: Rapports, pp. 103–32.

Kaser, K. and E. Katschnig-Fasch (eds). 2005. *Gender and Nation in South Eastern Europe*. Münster: LIT-Verlag.

Kašić, B. 2001. 'The Dynamic of Identifications within Nationalistic Discourse: From Archetypes to Promising Female Roles', in R. Iveković and J. Mostov (eds), *From Gender to Nation*. Europe and the Balkans International Network. Ravenna: Longo Editore, pp. 189–200.

Kesić, Vesna. 2001. 'Gender and Ethnic Identities in Transition: The Former Yugoslavia – Croatia', in R. Iveković and J. Mostov (eds), *From Gender to Nation*. Europe and the Balkans International Network. Ravenna: Longo Editore, pp. 63–80.

Kideckel, D. (ed.). 1995. *East European Communities: The Struggle for Balance in Turbulent Times*. Boulder, CO: Westview Press.

Kienzler, H. 2008. 'Debating War-trauma and PTSD in an Interdisciplinary Arena', *Social Science & Medicine* 67(2): 218–27.

Kifner, J. 1994. 'Through the Serbian Mind's Eye', *New York Times*, 10 April 1994.

Kimmel, Michael S. 2000. *The Gendered Society*. New York and Oxford: Oxford University Press.

———. 2002. 'Global Masculinities: Restoration and Resistance', in B. Pease and K. Pringle (eds), *A Man's World? Changing Man's Practices in a Globalized World*. London and New York: Zed Books, pp. 21–37. See also: http://www.ucm.es/info/rqtr/biblioteca/masculinidad/Global%20 Masculinities.pdf

Kirmayer, L.J. 1989. 'Mind and Body as Metaphors', in M. Lock and D. Gordon (eds), *Biomedicine Examined*. Dordrecht: Kluwer Academic Publishers, pp. 57–94.

———. 1992. 'The Body's Insistence on Meaning: Metaphor as Presentation and Representation in Illness Experience', *Medical Anthropology Quarterly* 6: 323–46.

Kirmayer, L.J., R. Lemelson and M. Barad (eds). 2007. *Understanding Trauma: Integrating Biological, Clinical, and Cultural Perspectives*. Cambridge: Cambridge University Press.

Kiš, D. 1990. *Čas Anatomije*. Sarajevo: Svetlost.

Kleinman, A. 1988. *The Illness Narratives: Sufferings, Healing, and the Human Condition*. New York: Basic Books.

Kleinman, A., V. Das and M. Lock. 1997. 'Introduction', in A. Kleinman, V. Das and M. Lock. (eds), *Social Suffering*. Berkeley: University of California Press, pp. ix–xxvii.

Kleinman, A. and J. Kleinman. 1991. 'Suffering and its Professional Transformation: Towards an Ethnography of Experience', *Culture, Medicine, and Psychiatry* 15: 275–302.

Kozole, L. 2003. 'The War over War Crimes', *Transitions Online*, 1 April 2003. Retrieved 10 Nov 2012 from http://www.tol.org/client/article/9155-the-war-over-war-crimes.html?print

Krajina, M. 1994. *Vukovare, Hrvatski Viteže* [Vukovar, you Croatian Knight]. Cakovez.

Kramer, F. 2000. 'Praktiken der Regeneration. Baumgärten und agrarische Riten in Afrika', *Historische Anthropologie* 8: 410–22.

Kramer, F. 2005. *Schriften zur Ethnologie*. Frankfurt/M: Suhrkamp.

Kretzenbacher, L. 1963. *Ritterspiel und Ringreiten im europäischen Südosten. Südost-Forschungen*. München Band XII.

Kржelj, Z. 2002. 'Norac i Gotovina nisu došli, ali svi ostali jesu!', *Novi list*, 17 September.

Kukuriku. 2011. Plan 21. Retrieved 10 Nov 2012 from http://www.kukuriku. org/files/plan21.pdf

Lambek, M. 1996. 'The Past Imperfect: Remembering as Moral Practice', in P. Antze and M. Lambek (eds), *Tense Past: Cultural Essays in Trauma and Memory*. New York: Routledge, pp. 235–54.

Leach, E. 1977. *Custom, Law and Terrorist Violence*. Edinburgh: Edinburgh University Press.

Leder, D. 1990. *The Absent Body*. Chicago: Chicago University Press.

Leggewie, C. 2012. 'Decadence or Renewal? Deciding the Future of the Mediterranean', Eurozine, 10 September 2012. Retrieved 12 Nov 2012 from http://www.eurozine.com/articles/2012-09-10-leggewie-en.html

Leutloff, C. 2000. 'Politics, Religion and Remembering the Past: The Case of Croatian Serbs in the 1990s', *Max Planck Institute for Social Anthropology Working Papers* No. 17.

Leutloff-Grandits, C. 2006a. *Claiming Ownership in Post-War Croatia: The Dynamics of Property Relations and Ethnic Conflict in the Knin Region*. Münster and London: LIT Verlag.

———. 2006b. 'Claiming Ownership in Post-war Croatia: The Emotional Dynamics of Possession and Repossession in Knin', in M. Svašek (ed.), *Postsocialism: Politics and Emotions in Central and Eastern Europe*. New York and Oxford: Berghahn Books, pp. 115–37.

Lewis, I.M. 1988. *Ecstatic Religion: A Study of Shamanism and Spirit Possession*. London: Routledge.

Lien, M.E. and M. Melhuus. 2007. 'Introduction', in M.E. Lien and M. Melhuus (eds), *Holding Worlds Together: Ethnographies of Knowing and Belonging*. New York and Oxford: Berghahn Books, pp. ix–xxiii.

Lilly, C.S. and J.A. Irvine. 2002. 'Negotiating Interests: Women and Nationalism in Serbia and Croatia 1990–1997', *East European Politics and Societies* 16(1): 109–44.

Lisón-Tolosana, C. 1966. *Belmonte de Los Caballeros: A Sociological Study of a Spanish Town*. Oxford: Clarendon Press.

Lock, M. 1991.'Nerves and Nostalgia: Greek-Canadian Immigrants and Medical Care in Quebec', in B. Pfleiderer and G. Bibeau (eds), *Anthropology of Medicine: A Colloquium on West European and North American Perspectives. Special Issue of Curare*. Braunschweig: Vieweg, pp. 87–104.

Lock, M. and P. Dunk. 1987. 'My Nerves are Broken: The Communication of Suffering in a Greek-Canadian Community', in D. Coburn, C. D'Arcy, P. New and G. Torrence (eds), *Health in Canadian Society: Sociological Perspectives*. Toronto: Fitzhenry and Whiteside, pp. 295–313.

Longinović, T.Z. 2005. 'Vampires Like Us: Gothic Imaginary and "the Serbs"', in D.I. Bjelić and O. Savić (eds), *Balkan as Metaphor: Between Globalization and Fragmentation*. Cambridge and London: MIT Press, pp. 39–59.

Lovrić, I. (1776) 1948. *Bilješke o putu po Dalmaciji opata Alberta Fortisa*. Zagreb: Izdavački Zavod Jugoslavanske Akademije.

Lowenhaupt Tsing, A. 1993. *In the Realm of the Diamond Queen*. Princeton: Princeton University Press.

Lowenhaupt Tsing, A. 2004. *Friction: An Ethnography of Global Connection*. Princeton: Princeton University Press.

Lutz, C. and L. Abu-Lughod (eds). 1990. *Language and the Politics of Emotion*. Cambridge: Cambridge University Press.

Lutz, C. and G. White. 1986. 'The Anthropology of Emotion', *Annual Review of Anthropology* 15: 405–36.

McClintock, A. 1996. "'No Longer in a Future Heaven'": Nationalism, Gender, and Race', in G. Eley and R. Grigor (eds), *Becoming National: A Reader*. Oxford and New York: Oxford University Press, pp. 260–84.

McLaughlin, E. 1974. 'Equality of Souls, Inequality of Sexes: Woman in Medieval Theology', in R. Radford Ruether (ed.), *Religion and Sexism: Images of Woman in the Jewish and Christian Traditions*. New York: Simon and Schuster, pp. 213–66.

Mack, J. 1983. 'Nationalism and the Self', *The Psychohistory Review* 11: 47–69.

Mappes-Niediek, N. 2005a. 'Krawalle an der kroatischen Adria', *Frankfurter Rundschau*, 12 December 2005.

———. 2005b. 'Ein General vor Gericht. Der Fall Ante Gotovina: Ganz Kroatien sieht sich in Den Haag angeklagt', *Die Zeit*, 15 December 2005.

Masturzo, P. and R. Colognola. 2005. *Between the Cross and the Crescent: Printed Books on Croatia and Dalmatia from the Fifteenth to the Twentieth Centuries. A Selection from the Dubravčić Collection*. Catalogue of an exhibition in Leiden University Library, 20 Jan – 20 Feb 2005.

Mayerfeld Bell, M. 1997. 'The Ghosts of Place', *Theory and Society* 26: 813–36.

Merleau-Ponty, M. (1942) 1962. *The Phenomenology of Perception*. London: Routledge and Kegan Paul.

Meštrović, S.G. 1993a. *The Barbarian Temperament: Towards a Post-Modern Critical Theory*. London and New York: Routledge.

———. 1993b. *Habits of the Balkan Heart: Social Character and the Fall of Communism*. Texas A&M University Press,

———. 1996. 'Introduction', in Stjepan G. Meštrović, *Genocide after Emotion: The Postemotional Balkan War*. London and New York: Routledge, pp. 1–30.

Meštrović, S.G., S. Letica and M. Goreta (eds). 1993. *Habits of the Balkan Heart: Social Character and the Fall of Communism*. College Station: Texas A&M University Press.

Mihaylova, D. 2006. 'Social Suffering and Political Protest: Mapping Emotions and Power among Pomaks in Postsocialist Bulgaria', in M. Svašek (ed.), *Postsocialism: Politics and Emotions in Central and Eastern Europe*. New York and Oxford: Berghahn Books, pp. 53–73.

Milić, A. 1993. 'Women and Nationalism in the Former Yugoslavia', in N. Funk and M. Mueller (eds), *Gender Politics and Post-Communism: Reflections from Eastern Europe and the Former Soviet Union*. New York and London: Routledge, pp. 109–22.

Miličević, A.S. 2006. 'Joining the War: Masculinity, Nationalism and War Participation in the Balkan War of Succession, 1991–1995', *Nationalities Papers* 34(3): 265–87.

Miličević, J. 1967. 'Narodni Običaji I Vjerovanja u Sinjskoj Krajini', in *Umjetnost. Studije I Grada O Sinjskoj Krajini*. Knjiga 5–6, pp. 433–515.

Mishkova, D. 2004. 'The Uses of Tradition and National Identity in the Balkans', in M. Todorova (ed.), *Balkan Identities: Nation and Memory*. New York: New York University Press, pp. 269–93.

Močnik, R. 2005. 'The Balkans as an Element in Ideological Mechanisms', in D.I. Bjelić and O. Savić (eds), *Balkan as Metaphor: Between Globalisation and Fragmentation*. Cambridge and London: MIT Press, pp. 79–115.

Moqué, A.L. 1914. *Delightful Dalmatia*. New York: Funk and Wagnalls.

Mosse, G.L. 1996. *The Image of Man: The Creation of Modern Masculinity*. New York and Oxford: Oxford University Press.

Mühlfried, F. 2007. 'Von versteckten Schätzen in den Bergen und einem Staat, der kommt und geht – Siedlungspolitik "von unten" im georgischen Hochland', *Max Planck Institute for Social Anthropology Working Papers*, No. 92.

Müller, B. 2006. 'The Misgivings of Democracy: Personal Resentment and Alternating Power in a Czech Village', in M. Svašek (ed.), *Postsocialism: Politics and Emotions in Central and Eastern Europe*. New York and Oxford: Berghahn Books, pp. 178–95.

Müller, J.-W. (ed.). 2002. *Memory and Power in Post-War Europe*. Cambridge: Cambridge University Press.

Munn, J. 2006. 'Gendered Realities of Life in Post-Conflict Kosovo: Addressing the Hegemonic Man', *Nationalities Papers* 34(3): 265–88.

Nagel, J. 1998. 'Masculinity and Nationalism: Gender and Sexuality in the Making of Nations', *Ethnic and Racial Studies* 21(2): 242–69.

Narotzky, S. and P. Moreno. 2004. 'Fighters, Martyrs, Victims: Political Conflict, Ambivalent Moralities and the Production of Terror and Modes of Governance in Contemporary Spain', in F. Pine, D. Kaneff and H. Haukanes (eds), *Memory, Politics and Religion: The Past Meets the Present in Europe*. Münster: LIT.

Navaro-Yashin, Y. 2002. *Faces of the State: Secularism and Public Life in Turkey*. Princeton: Princeton University Press.

Nixon, R. 1997. 'Of Balkans and Bantustans: Ethnic Cleansing and the Crisis in National Legitimation', in A. McClintock, A. Mufti and E. Shohat (eds), *Dangerous Liasons: Gender, Nation, and Postcolonial Perspectives*. Minneapolis and London: University of Minnesota Press, pp. 69–88.

Nora, P. 1989. 'Between Memory and History: Les Lieux de Memoire', *Representations* 26: 7–25.

——— . 1997. *Les lieux de mémoire*. Gallimard: Paris.

Novak, G. 1971. 'Morlaci (Vlasi) gledani s mletacke strane', *Zbornik za narodni život i običaje* 45: 579–603.

Novikova, I. 2001. 'Gender, Ethnicity and Identity Politics in Latvia', in R. Iveković and J. Mostov (eds), *From Gender to Nation*. Europe and the Balkans International Network. Ravenna: Longo Editore, pp. 171–87.

Øien, Cecilie. 2007. *Pathways of Migration: Perceptions of Home and Belonging Among Angolan Women in Portugal*. Manchester University: Unpublished Ph.D. dissertation.

Olujić, M.B. 1998. 'Embodiment of Terror: Gendered Violence in Peacetime and Wartime in Croatia and Bosnia-Hercegovina', *Medical Anthropology Quarterly* 12(1): 31–50.

Ots, T. 1991. 'Phenomenology of the Body: The Subject–Object Problem in Psychosomatic Medicine and Role of Traditional Medical Systems', in B. Pfleiderer and G. Bibeau (eds), *Anthropology of Medicine: A Colloquium on West European and North American Perspectives. Special Issue of Curare.* Braunschweig: Vieweg, pp. 43–58.

Owen, D. 1995. *Balkan Odyssey.* San Diego, CA: Harvest Books.

Pandolfi, M. 1991. 'Memory within the Body: Women's Narrative and Identity in a Southern Italian Village', in B. Pfleiderer and G. Bibeau (eds), *Anthropology of Medicine: A Colloquium on West European and North American Perspectives. Special Issue of Curare.* Braunschweig: Vieweg, pp. 59–65.

Papić, Ž. 1994. 'From State Socialism to State Nationalism: The Case of Serbia in Gender Perspective', *Refuge* 14(3): 10–15.

——— . 2003. 'Europe after 1989: Ethnic Wars, the Fascistization of Civil Society and Body Politics in Serbia', in G. Griffin and R. Braidotti (eds), *Thinking Differently: A Reader in European Women's Studies.* London: Zed Books, pp. 127–44.

Paštar, T. 2001. 'Mirko, ne damo te, čekamo te na Alci', *Slobodna Dalmacija,* 10 February 2001. Retrieved 10 Nov 2012 from http://arhiv.slobodnadalmacija.hr/20010210/novosti.htm

Pavlaković, V. 2004 'Matija Gubec Goes to Spain: Symbols and Ideology in Croatia, 1936–1939', *Journal of Slavic Military Studies* 17(4): 727–55.

Pavlović, T. 1999. 'Women in Croatia: Feminists, Nationalists and Homosexuals', in S.P. Ramet (ed.), *Gender Politics in the Western Balkans: Women and Society in Yugoslavia and the Yugoslav Successor States.* University Park: Pennsylvania State University Press, pp. 131–52.

——— . 2001. 'Remembering/Dismembering the Nation: The Archaeology of Lost Knowledge', in R. Iveković and J. Mostov (eds), *From Gender to Nation.* Europe and the Balkans International Network. Ravenna: Longo Editore, pp. 131–52.

Perica, V. 2002. *Balkan Idols: Religion and Nationalism in Yugoslav States.* New York: Oxford University Press.

Peristiany, J.G. 1966. *Honor and Shame: The Values of Mediterranean Society.* Chicago: University of Chicago Press.

——— (ed.). 1976. *Mediterranean Family Structures.* Cambridge and New York: Cambridge University Press.

Peristiany, J.G. and J. Pitt-Rivers (eds). 1999. *Honor and Grace in Anthropology.* Cambridge: Cambridge University Press.

Peskin, V. and M.P. Boduszynski. 2003. 'International Justice and Domestic Politics: Post-Tuđman Croatia and the International Criminal Tribunal for the Former Yugoslavia', *Europe–Asia Studies* 55(7): 1117–42.

Pina-Cabral, J. 1986. *Sons of Adam, Daughters of Eve: The Peasant Worldview of the Alto Minho.* Oxford: Clarendon Press.

Pina-Cabral, J. 1989. 'The Mediterranean as a Category of Regional Comparison: A Critical View', *Current Anthropology* 30(3): 399–406.

Pine, F., D. Kaneff and H. Haukanes (eds). 2004. *Memory, Politics and Religion: The Past Meets the Present in Europe.* Münster: LIT-Verlag.

Pitt-Rivers, J.A. (ed.). 1963. *Mediterranean Countrymen: Essays in the Social Anthropology of the Mediterranean*. Westport, CT: Greenwood.

———. (1954) 1971. *The People of the Sierra*. Chicago: Chicago University Press.

———. 1977. *The Fate of Shechem or The Politics of Sex: Essays in the Anthropology of the Mediterranean*. Cambridge: Cambridge University Press.

Povrzanović, M. 2000. 'The Imposed and the Imagined as Encountered by Croatian War Ethnographers', *Current Anthropology* 41(2): 151–62.

Pulić, N. 1994. *Sinjska Alka*. Ilustracije Miljenko Romić. Zagreb: Alfa.

Raivo, P.J. 1999. 'In this Very Place: War Memorials and Landscapes as an Experienced Heritage', *The Thingmount Working Papers Series on the Philosophy of Conservation*. TWP 99–07, Lancaster University. Retrieved 10 Nov 2012 from http://www.lancs.ac.uk/depts/philosophy/awaymave/onlineresources/in%20this%20very%20place%20(raivo).pdf

Rakowski, T. 2006. 'Gatherers of Central Poland: A Field Study', in M. Schäuble (ed.), *Doing Fieldwork in Eastern Europe. Special Issue Anthropology Matters* 8(1). Retrived 10 Nov 2012 from http://www.anthropologymatters.com/journal/2006-1/rakowski_2006_gatherers.pdf

———. 2007. 'The Voices of Collapse: Destructive and Self-Destructive Expressions among the Former Miners in Wałbrzych (Southwest Poland)', in A. Lüse and I. Lázár (eds), *Cosmologies of Suffering Post-communist Transformation, Sacral Communication, and Healing*, Newcastle upon Tyne: Cambridge Scholars Publishing, pp. 182–205.

Ramet, P. 1982. 'Catholicism and Politics in Socialist Yugoslavia', *Religion in Communist Lands* 10(3): 256–74.

———. 1985a. 'The Miracle at Medjugorje: A Functional Perspective', *The South Slav Journal* 8(1): 12–20.

———. 1985b. 'Factionalism in Church–State Interaction: The Croatian Catholic Church in the 1980s', *Slavic Review* 44(2): 298–315.

———. 1989. 'Religion and Nationalism in Yugoslavia', in P. Ramet (ed.), *Religion and Nationalism in Soviet and East European Politics*. Durham & London: Duke University Press, pp. 299–327.

Razsa, M. and N. Lindstrom. 2004. 'Balkan is Beautiful: Balkanism in the Political Discourse of Tuđman's Croatia', *East European Politics and Societies* 18(4): 628–50.

Redfield, R. 1956. *Peasant Society and Culture: An Anthropological Approach to Civilization*. Chicago: University of Chicago Press.

Ries, N. 1991. 'The Power of Negative Thinking: Russian Talk and the Reproduction of Mindset, Worldviews, and Society', *Anthropology of Eastern Europe Review* 10(2): 38–53.

Rihtman-Auguštin, D. 1997. 'Zašto i otkad se grozimo Balkana', *Erasmus* 19: 27–35.

———. 1998. 'A Croatian Controversy: Mediterranean, Danube, Balkans', in *Narodna Umjetnost* 36(1).

Ristić, K. 2012. 'Silencing Justice: War Crime Trials and the Society in Former Yugoslavia' *Südosteuropa Mitteilungen* 52(3): 32–42.

Rosaldo, R. 1987. 'Politics, Patriarchs and Laughter', *Cultural Critique* 6: 65–86.

Roth, K. 2007. 'What's in a Region? Southeast European Regions Between Globalization, EU-INtegration, and Marginalization', in U. Brunnbauer and K. Roth (eds), *Region, Regional Identity and Regionalism in Southeastern Europe*, Special Issue of *Ethnologia Balkanica* 11: 17–42.

Rubin, E. 1995. 'Souvenir Miracles: Going to See the Virgin in Western Herzegovina', *Harper's Magazine*, February, pp. 63–71.

Schaeffer-Duffy, S. 1994. 'Mary, Queen of Peace, Missing amid Medjugorje Nationalism', *National Catholic Reporter* 30(15): 18.

Schaik, E. van. 1988. 'Paradigms Underlying the Study of Nerves as a Popular Illness Term in Eastern Kentucky', *Medical Anthropology* 11: 15–28.

Schäuble, M. 2006. '"Imagined Suicide": Self-Sacrifice and the Making of Heroes in Post-War Croatia', in M. Schäuble (ed.), *Doing Fieldwork in Eastern Europe. Special issue of Anthropology Matters* 8(1). Retrieved 13 Aug 2007 from http://www.anthropologymatters.com/journal/2006-1/schauble_2006_imagined.pdf

———. 2007a. 'The Body of the Saint: Iconographies of Suffering in a Catholic Commemoration Ceremony in Vukovar, Croatia', in A. Lūse and I. Lázár (eds), *Cosmologies of Suffering Post-communist Transformation, Sacral Communication, and Healing*. Newcastle upon Tyne: Cambridge Scholars Publishing, pp. 159–81.

———. 2007b. 'Spiel mit dem Terror? Reflexionen über die Gewaltinszenierung eines traumatisierten Soldaten im Nachkriegskroatien', *Berliner Debatte Initial: Zeitschrift für sozialwissenschaftlichen Diskurs* 3: 24–35.

———. 2009. 'Contested Masculinities: Discourses on the Role of Croatian Combatants during the "Homeland War" (1991–1995)', in R. Seifert and C. Eifler (eds), *The Relevance of Gender in Violent Conflict*. Bern: Peter Lang Verlag, pp. 169–97.

———. 2011. 'How History takes Place: Geographical and Sacralised Landscapes in the Croatian–Bosnian Border Region', *History and Memory* 23(1): 23–61.

———. 2014. '"Friedenskönigin", "Apokalyptische Frau" oder Handlangerin nationalistischer Demagogen? Der Kult der Gospa Sinjska als visuelle Manifestation lokaler Erinnerung an Krieg und Gewalt', in S. Troebst and A. Gąsior (eds), *Zwischen religiöser Tradition, kommunistischer Prägung und kultureller Umwertung. Die Erinnerungskulturen Ostmitteleuropas vor und nach 1989*. Vienna: Böhlau Verlag (forthcoming).

Scheer, M. 2006. *Rosenkranz und Kriegsvisison. Marienerscheinungskulte im 20. Jahrhundert*. Tübingen: Tübinger Vereinigung für Volkskunde.

Scheper-Hughes, N. 1992. *Death without Weeping: The Violence of Everyday Life in Brazil*. Berkeley and Los Angeles: University of California Press.

Scheper-Hughes, N. and P. Bourgois. 2004. 'Introduction: Making Sense of Violence', in N. Scheper-Hughes and P. Bourgois (eds), *Violence in War and Peace: An Anthology*. Malden, MA: Blackwell Publishing, pp. 1–32.

Schreiner, K. 1994. *Maria, Jungfrau, Herrscherin*. Munich and Vienna: Carl Hanser Verlag.

——. 2002. 'Maria Victrix: Siegbringende Hilfen marianischer Zeichen in der Schlacht auf dem Weißen Berg (1620)', in J. Altenberend (ed.), *Kloster – Stadt – Region: Festschrift für Heinrich Rüthing*. Bielefeld: Verlag für Regionalgeschichte, pp. 87–144.

Schroer-Hippel, M. 2011. 'Kriegsveteranen in der Friedensarbeit – militarisierte Männlichkeit als Friedenspotenzial?', in B. Engels and C. Gayer (eds), *Geschlechterverhältnisse, Frieden und Konflikt: Feministische Denkanstöße für die Friedens und Konfliktforschung*. Baden-Baden: Nomos, pp. 95–112.

Schwandner-Sievers, S. 2004. 'Times Past: References for the Construction of Local Order in Present-day Albania', in M. Todorova (ed.), *Balkan Identities: Nation and Memory*. New York: New York University Press, pp. 103–28.

Seierstad, Å. 2005. *With Their Backs to the World: Portraits from Serbia*. London: Virago.

Seifert, R. 2001. 'Genderdynamiken bei der Entstehung, dem Austrag und der Bearbeitung von kriegerischen Konflikten', *Peripherie. Zeitschrift für Politik und Ökonomie der Dritten Welt* 84(21).

——. 2004. 'Einleitung: Identität, Gender und kriegerische Konflikte', in R. Seifert (ed.), *Gender, Identität und kriegerischer Konflikt. Das Beispiel des ehemaligen Jugoslawien*. Münster: LIT-Verlag, pp. 9–25.

——. 2007. 'The Female Body as Political Body: Rape, War and the Nation', *Difesa Sociale* (2): 241–254.

Senjković, R. 1995. 'Ideologies and Iconographies' – Croatia in the Second Half of the 20th Century, *Collegium Antropologicum* 19(1): 53–64.

——. 1996. 'Image of the Warrior', *Narodna Umjetnost* 33(1): 41–57.

——. 2002. 'Motherland Is Female Gender', *Narodna Umjetnost* 39(1): 133–50.

——. 2004. 'Romaticising Rambo: Masculinity and Perceptions of War in Croatia 1991–1995', in S. Naumović and M. Jovanović (eds), *Gender Relations in South Eastern Europe: Historical Perspectives on Womenhood and Manhood in 19th and 20th Century*. Münster: LIT-Verlag, pp. 287–304.

Seroka, J. 2008. 'Issues with Regional Integration of the Western Balkans', *Journal of Southern Europe and the Balkans* 10(1): 15–29.

Seymour, S. 2000. 'Historical Geographies of Landscape', in B. Graham and C. Nash, *Modern Historical Geographies*. Harlow: Pearson Education Limited, pp. 193–217.

Silber, L., and A. Little. 1995. *Death of Yugoslavia*. London: Penguin Books.

Šimunović, D. (1922) 1948. *Alkar*. Zagreb: Mala Biblioteka No. 14.

Skokić, T. 2001. 'Must We Know Who We Are?', in R. Iveković and J. Mostov (eds), *From Gender to Nation*. Europe and the Balkans International Network. Ravenna: Longo Editore, pp. 201–12.

Skrbiš, Z. 2003. 'The Emotional Histriography of Venetologists: Slovene Diaspora, Memory, and Nationalism', *Focaal. European Journal of Anthropology* 39: 41–56.

———. 2005. 'The Apparitions of the Virgin Mary of Medjugorje: The Convergence of Croatian Nationalism and her Apparitions', *Nations and Nationalism* 11(3): 443–61.

———. 2006. 'The First Europeans' Fantasy of Slovenian Venetologists: Emotions and Nationalist Imaginings', in M. Svašek (ed.), *Postsocialism: Politics and Emotions in Central and Eastern Europe*. New York and Oxford: Berghahn Books, pp. 138–58.

Skultans, V. 1998. *The Testimony of Lives: Narrative and Memory in Post Soviet Latvia*. London: Routledge.

Slapšak, S. 2004. 'Gender and War in the Post-Socialist World', in R. Seifert (ed.), *Gender, Identität und kriegerischer Konflikt: Das Beispiel des ehemaligen Jugoslawien*. Münster: LIT-Verlag, pp. 26–39.

Slotkin, R. 1992. *Gunfighter Nation: The Myth of the Frontier in Twentieth-Century America*. New York: Atheneum.

Smith, A. 1998. *Reconstructing the Regional Economy: Industrial Restructuring and Regional Development in Slovakia*. Cheltenham: Edward Elgar.

———. 2007. 'Articulating Neo-Liberalism: Diverse Economies and Everyday Life in "Post-Socialist" Cities', in H. Leitner, J. Peck and E.S. Sheppard (eds), *Contesting Neoliberalism: Urban Frontiers*. New York and London: Guilford Press, pp. 204–22.

Soja, E. 1989. *Postmodern Geographies: The Reassertion of Space in Critical Social Theory*. London: Verso Press.

Stanimirović, S. 2002. 'Serbia: Suicide on the Rise'. Institute for War and Peace Reporting. BCR 344, 20 June 2002. Retrieved 10 Nov 2010 from http://www.iwpr.net

Stanley, J. 2000. 'Involuntary Commemorations: Post-Traumatic Stress Disorder and its Relationship to War Commemoration', in T.G. Ashplant, G. Dawson, M. Roper (eds), *The Politics of War Memory and Commemoration*. London and New York: Routledge, pp. 240–59.

Steindorff, L. 2003. 'Schichten der Erinnerung. Zur Klassifizierung von Gedächtnisorten in Kroatien', in R. Jaworski, J. Kusber and L. Steindorff (eds), *Gedächtnisorte in Osteuropa: Vergangenheiten auf dem Prüfstand*. Frankfurt/M.: Peter Lang, pp. 157–82.

Stein Erlich, V. 1971. *Jugostanvenska porodica u tranformaciji*. Zagreb: Liber.

Stojanović, D. 2004. 'Construction of Historical Consciousness: The Case of Serbian History Textbooks', in M. Todorova (ed.), *Balkan Identities: Nation and Memory*. New York: New York University Press, pp. 327–38.

Stulli, B. 1967/1968. 'Kroz Historiju Sinjske Krajine', *Narodna Umjetnost, Studije i Grada o Sinjskoj Krajini* 5–6: 5–93.

Šuber, D. 2004. 'Kollektive Erinnerung und nationale Identität in Serbien. Zu einer kulturalistischen Interpretation des Anfangs vom Ende Jugoslawiens', in B. Giesen and C. Schneider (eds), *Tätertrauma. Nationale Erinnerungen im öffentlichen Diskurs*. Konstanz: UVK, pp. 347–79.

———. 2006. 'Myth, Collective Trauma and War in Serbia: A Cultural-Hermeneutical Appraisal', in M. Schäuble (ed.), *Doing Fieldwork in Eastern Europe*.

Special Issue of *Anthropology Matters* 8(1). Retrieved 10 Nov 2010 from http://www.anthropologymatters.com/journal/2006-1/suber_2006_myth. pdf

Svašek, M. 2002. 'The Politics of Emotions: Emotional Discourses and Displays in Post–Cold War Contexts', *Focaal, European Journal of Anthropology* 39(1): 9–28.

———— (ed.). 2006. *Postsocialism: Politics and Emotions in Central and Eastern Europe*. New York and Oxford: Berghahn Books.

Sztompka, P. 2004. 'The Trauma of Social Change: A Case of Post-Communist Societies', in J.C. Alexander, R. Eyerman, B. Giesen, N.J. Smelser and P. Sztompka (eds), *Cultural Trauma and Collective Identity*. Berkeley: University of California Press, pp. 155–96.

Tanner, M. 2001. *Croatia: A Nation Forged in War*. New Haven and London: Yale Nota Bene.

Tarifa, F. 2005. 'The Adriatic Europe: Albania, Croatia, Macedonia', *Macedonian Quarterly* 16(4): 8–19.

Theweleit, K. 1977/1978. *Männerphantasien*, Bd. 1: 'Frauen, Fluten, Körper, Geschichte'. Bd. 2: 'Männerkörper – zur Psychoanalyse des weißen Terrors'. Frankfurt/M.: Roter Stern.

Tilley, C. 1994. *A Phenomenology of Landscape: Places, Paths and Monuments*. Oxford: Berg Publishers.

Todorova, M.N. 1993. *Balkan Family Structure and the European Pattern: Demographic Developments in Ottoman Bulgaria*. Lanham, MD: American University Press.

————. 1997. *Imagining the Balkans*. New York: Oxford University Press.

Tomašić, D. 1941. 'Sociology in Yugoslavia', *The American Journal of Sociology* 47: 53–69.

Turner, V. 1969. *The Ritual Process: Structure and Anti-Structure*. Chicago: Aldin.

————. 1973. 'The Center Out There: Pilgrim's Goal', *History of Religions* 12(3).

————. 1987. *The Anthropology of Performance*. New York: PAJ Publications.

———— and Edith Turner 1978. *Images and Pilgrimage in Christian Culture*. New York: Columbia University Press.

Ugrešić, D. 1998. *The Culture of Lies: Antipolitical Essays*. London: Phoenix House.

Verdery, K. 1991. *National Ideology Under Socialism: Identity and Cultural Politics in Ceausescu's Romania*. Berkeley: University of California Press.

————. 1994. 'From Parent-State to Family Patriarchs: Gender and Nation in Contemporary Eastern Europe', *East European Politics and Societies* 8(2): 230–38.

————. 1996. *What Was Socialism, And What Comes Next?* Princeton: Princeton University Press.

————. 1999. *The Political Lives of Dead Bodies: Reburial and Postsocialist Change*. New York: Columbia University Press.

Volkan, V.D. 1988. *The Need to Have Enemies and Allies: From Clinical Practice to International Relationships*. Northvale, NJ: Aronson.

Vukušić, A.-M. 2002. 'Transformacija pojma vitestva u Sinjskoj alki', *Etnološka tribina* 32(25): 9–26.

Vuletić, B. 1987. 'Tito and the Alka Tournament', *The Alka Tournament of Sinj.* Belgrade: Jugoslovenska Revija, pp. 70–72.

Waterfield, B. 2012. 'Croatian Hero Ante Gotovina Acquitted of War Crimes', *The Telegraph*, 16 November 2012. Retrieved 16 Nov 2012 from http://www.telegraph.co.uk/news/worldnews/europe/croatia/9682855/Croatian-hero-Ante-Gotovina-acquitted-of-war-crimes.html

Weigel, S. 1996. 'Pathologie und Normalisierung im deutsche Gedächtnisdiskurs. Zur Dialektik von Erinnern und Vergessen', in G. Smith und H.M. Emrich (eds), *Vom Nutzen des Vergessens*. Berlin: Akademie Verlag, pp. 241–63.

Wenk, S. and I. Eschebach. 2002. 'Soziales Gedächtnis und Geschlechterdifferenz. Eine Einführung', in I. Eschebach, S. Jacobeit and S. Wenk (eds), *Gedächtnis und Geschlecht. Deutungsmuster in Darstellungen des nationalsozialistischen Genozids*. Frankfurt/M. and New York: Campus, pp. 13–38.

Widmer, P. 2004. *Kroatien im Umbruch. Ein Land zwischen Balkan und Europa*. Zürich: Verlag neue Züricher Zeitung.

Wilkes, J.J. 1969. *Dalmatia*. London: Routledge and Kegan Paul.

Wilkinson, J.G. 1848. *Dalmatia and Montenegro with A Journey to Mostar in Hercegovina and Remarks on the Slavonic Nations; the History of Dalmatia and Ragusa; the Uscocs; &c. &cc*, 2. Vols. London: Murray.

Willerslev, R. 2007. '"To have the World at a Distance": Reconsidering the Significance of Vision for Social Anthropology', in C. Grassini (ed.), *Skilled Visions: Between Apprenticeship and Standards*. New York and Oxford: Berghahn Books, pp. 23–46.

Winchester, S. 1999. *The Fracture Zone: My Return to the Balkans*. New York: Perennial.

Wingfield, N.M. and M. Bucur. 2006. 'Introduction: Gender and War in Twentieth-Century Eastern Europe', in N.M. Wingfield and M. Bucur (eds) *Gender and War in Twentieth-Century Eastern Europe*. Bloomington: Indiana University Press.

Wolf, E.R. and H.H. Lehmann (eds). 1984. *Religion, Power and Protest in Local Communities: The Northern Shore of the Mediterranean*. Amsterdam and Berlin: Mouton.

Wolff, L. 2001. *Venice and the Slavs: The Discovery of Dalmatia in the Age of Enlightenment*. Stanford: Stanford University Press.

World Bank. 2011. 'Croatia: Policy Options for Further Pension System Reform', July 2011, Retrived 12 Nov 2012 from http://siteresources.worldbank.org/INTCROATIA/Resources/Croatia_Policy_Notes-Pension.pdf

Yuval-Davis, N. 1997. *Gender and Nation*. Sage: London.

Yuval-Davis, N. and F. Anthias (eds). 1989. *Woman-Nation-State*. Macmillan: London.

Žanić, I. 2005. 'The Symbolic Identity of Croatia in the Triangle *Crossroads–Bulwark–Bridge*', in P. Kolstø (ed.), *Myths and Boundaries in South-Eastern Europe*. London: Hurst & Co., pp. 36–76.

Žarkov, D. 1995. 'Gender, Orientalism and the History of Ethnic Hatred in the Former Yugoslavia', in H. Lutz and N. Yuval-Davis (eds), *Crossfires: Nationalism, Racism, and Gender in Europe*. London: Pluto Press.

——. 2000. 'Feminist Self/Ethnic Self: Theory and Politics of Women's Activism', in S. Slapšak (ed.), *War Discourse, Women's Discourse: Essays and Case Studies from Yugoslavia and Russia*. Ljubljana: Topos, pp. 167–94.

——. 2001.'The Body of the Other Man: Sexual Violence and the Construction of Masculinity, Sexuality and Ethnicity in Croatian Media', in C.O.N. Moser and F.C. Clark (eds), *Victims, Perpetrators or Actors? Gender, Armed Conflict and Political Violence*. London: Zed Books, pp. 69–83.

——. 2007. *The Body of War: Media, Ethnicity and Gender in the Break-up of Yugoslavia*. Durham, NC: Duke University Press.

Zerilli, F.M. 2006. 'Sentiments and/as Property Rights: Restitution and Conflict in Postsocialist Romania', in M. Svašek (ed.), *Postsocialism: Politics and Emotions in Central and Eastern Europe*. New York and Oxford: Berghahn Books, pp. 74–94.

Ziegler, J.E. 1992. *Sculpture of Compassion: The Pietà and the Beguines in the Southern Low Countries, c.1300 – c.1600*. Brussels and Rome: The Belgian Historical Institute of Rome.

Zimdars-Swartz, S. 1991. *Encountering Mary*. Princeton, NJ: Princeton University Press.

Živković, M. 1997. 'Violent Highlanders and Peaceful Lowlanders: Uses and Abuses of Ethno-Geography in the Balkans from Versailles to Dayton', in *Replika. Special issue on Ambiguous Identities in the New Europe*. Retrieved 10 Nov 2005 from http://www.c3.hu/scripta/scripta0/replika/honlap/english/02/08zivk.htm

——. 2000. 'The Wish to be a Jew: The Power of the Jewish Trope in the Yugoslav Conflict', *Cahiers de L'URMIS* 6: 69–84.

——. 2006. 'Introduction. Ex-Yugoslav Masculinities under Female Gaze, or Why Men Skin Cats, Beat Up Gays and Go to War', *Nationalities Papers* 34(3): 256–63.

Žižek, S. 1989. *The Sublime Object of Ideology*. London: Verso.

——. 1995. 'Multiculturalism, or the Cultural Logic of Multinational Capitalism', *New Left Review* 225: 28–52.

——. 1997. *The Plague of Fantasies*. London and New York: Verso Books.

——. 1999. 'You May!', *London Review of Books* 21(6), 18 March.

Zolo, D. 2005. 'Towards a Dialogue Between the Mediterranean Cultures', *Jura Gentium* 1(1). Retrieved 20 Nov 2012 from: http://www.juragentium.org/topics/med/tunis/en/zolo.htm

Index

Space and Place

CPSIA information can be obtained
at www.ICGtesting.com
Printed in the USA
LVOW05s0504230817
546049LV00001B/10/P